TESTING CHRISTIANITY'S TRUTH CLAIMS

TESTING CHRISTIANITY'S TRUTH CLAIMS

Approaches to Christian Apologetics

Gordon R. Lewis

UNIVERSITY
PRESS OF
AMERICA

Lanham • New York • London

Copyright © 1990 by
University Press of America®, Inc.
4720 Boston Way
Lanham, Maryland 20706

3 Henrietta Street
London WC2E 8LU England

Copyright © 1976 by The Moody Bible
Institute of Chicago

All Scripture quotations, except those identified
otherwise, are from the New American Standard
Bible, © 1960, 1962, 1963, 1968, 1971, 1972, 1973,
1975, and 1977 by the Lockman Foundation, and are
used by permission.

Library of Congress Cataloging-in-Publication Data

Lewis, Gordon Russell, 1926-
Testing Christianity's truth claims : approaches to Christian
apologetics / Gordon R. Lewis.
p.   cm.
Reprint.   Originally published: Chicago : Moody Press, 1976.
Includes bibliographical references and index.
1. Apologetics—History—20th century.   I. Title.
BT1117.L48   1990   239—dc20   90–42226 CIP

ISBN 0–8191–7838–1 (alk. paper)

To
VERNON C. GROUNDS
whose exemplary life and ministry
have immeasurably challenged, encouraged,
and helped me for more than
thirty years

CONTENTS

PREFACE

A BUSINESSMAN from Karachi, West Pakistan, acquainted with Hinduism, Buddhism, and Islam, heard Christian preaching for two months. Arriving for an appointment with the Christian missionary, he asked, "Should we accept religion without reasoning or should we use some sense, reason, and judgment?"

Then he said, "Kindly enlighten me as to how we can avoid confusion and arrive at the right conclusions in choosing among religions."

Similar queries arise among thinking people everywhere in the face of conflicting religious claims. This book seeks to answer the first question in chapter 1, and the second question (with reference to Christianity) in the subsequent chapters.

It is not the purpose of this book to survey the similarities between the religions and philosophies of the world. Similar ethical teachings, such as the golden rule, fail as a basis for pronouncing all religions the same. Neither does this book advocate a magnification of differences among religions where these are compatible, that is, not contradictory. However, where the same thing is affirmed and denied at the same time and in the same respect, choices must be made. Standards are discovered for testing contradictory truth-claims in the religions and Christianity. A person who applies these criteria will know why he accepts or rejects any religious claim.[1]

The present volume is primarily concerned with the basic claims of historic Christianity which are denied by non-Christian thinkers. Classical Christianity has affirmed (1) that a triune Lord of history lives eternally, (2) that God became incarnate to reconcile fallen men only in the Person of Jesus Christ, and (3) that the truth con-

---

1. For a survey and criticism of recent non-Christian claims see Os Guinness, *The Dust of Death* (Downers Grove, Ill.: Inter-Varsity, 1972).

cerning God's loving provision for a lost world is revealed with supreme authority in the Bible.

The reader is not asked arbitrarily to assume the truth of these claims, but to be open-minded enough to consider the case for their truth by men who have spent their lives examining them. The interested reader may be one who is himself struggling with these amazing affirmations, or who talks with those who are.

The choice of writers who evaluate basic Christian truth-claims was guided by several considerations. First, the writers selected are *contemporary* in that they have produced their major works since 1945.[2] From that time there has been a resurgence of literature in apologetics (defense of one's faith). The contributions of these recent scholars merit a comparative study.

Second, the writers chosen are *orthodox* and *evangelical* Christians. Treatises defending non-evangelical versions of Christianity are numerous. One of the best of these, John B. Cobb's *Living Options in Protestant Theology,* does not even pretend to give a fair presentation to conservative and orthodox theologians. The task there left undone is here undertaken. And the great variety of approaches to the defense of Christianity's basic claims by the conservatives surveyed in this book should dispel the notion that orthodox writers simply mouth pat answers to difficult questions.

Third, the book gives priority to *systems* of thought developed in favor of historic Christianity's truth-claims. When one thinks for any length of time in a field his ideas either contradict each other or fit consistently into a system. The writers selected have developed a consistent approach to five controversial issues: the logical starting point, common ground or points of contact with non-Christians, the test of truth, the role of reason, and the resultant basis of faith in God as revealed in Christ and the Bible. Chapter 12 surveys several writers who are developing systems in defense of Christian faith. A popular communicator of the faith to non-Christians, C. S. Lewis, did not publish systematic works on these issues, but his contribution is treated in the Appendix.

Fourth, the book features *distinctive* systems in defense of Christian truth-claims. Six such systems are expounded: the pure empiricism of J. Oliver Buswell, Jr. (chap. 2), the rational empiricism of Stuart

2. A valuable survey of types of apologetics systems from before 1945 can be found in Bernard Ramm, *Varieties of Christian Apologetics* (Grand Rapids: Baker, 1965).

C. Hackett (chap. 3), the rationalism of Gordon H. Clark (chap. 4), the biblical authoritarianism of Cornelius Van Til (chap. 5), the mysticism of Earl E. Barrett (chap. 6), and the verificational approaches of Edward John Carnell from facts, values, psychology, and ethics (chaps. 7-10). While most of these writers articulate a single system in their numerous books and articles, Edward John Carnell's approach incorporates four distinctive and harmonious approaches. Four chapters were required to present these to the student in a useful way.[3]

The varied approaches are expounded as objectively as space and ability in research from the original sources permits. Comparisons and contrasts are introduced to stimulate the reader's thought. Sections evaluating the positions may be supplemented and altered according to the reader's (or teacher's) point of view. A large class may profitably be divided into small "buzz" groups to assess strengths and weaknesses of each approach. Leaders then share these with the whole class. One may choose to study the chapters in a different order. For example, if interest is high in immediate experience, Chapter 6, "The Test of Personal Experience," might be studied prior to Chapter 2.

This work is intended primarily for people who are not philosophy majors, but may have some acquaintance with philosophical problems formally or informally. As far as possible, philosophical terminology has been defined for those without a formal introduction to philosophy. The glossary which appears at the end of the book indicates the present usage of several key terms.

Those who wish to pursue the various approaches further will find an annotated bibliography of books and articles at the end of each chapter headed, "Resources for Research."

My sincere appreciation is expressed to all of the apologists studied, for each has made valuable contributions to my own life and thought. But special gratitude is due those under whom I have been priviledged to study personally: Vernon C. Grounds, who stimulated keen interest in my first course in apologetics; the late Edward John

---

3. Edward John Carnell's approach seems the most explicit answer to Colin Brown's call for an apologetic which considers Christianity as a good hypothesis because it makes sense of the maximum number of observed facts. See Brown's introduction to the main thinkers and schools of thought from the middle ages to the present day, *Philosophy and the Christian Faith* (Downers Grove, Ill.: Inter-Varsity, n.d.), pp. 265, 273.

12   *Testing Christianity's Truth-Claims*

Carnell, whose teaching was the highlight of my college experience; and J. Oliver Buswell, Jr., whose courses in seminary developed a deep respect for evidence and inductive study.

Without a sabbatical leave of eight months from teaching duties at the Conservative Baptist Theological Seminary (Denver) this book would not have been written. The suggestions of my students through the years have been valuable, and particularly those of Mr. Andrew Dhuse who read a previous draft of the manuscript. Stimulating dialogue with my colleagues at the seminary has also been influential. In matters of style particularly, I am grateful to Dr. Ralph Keiper. For an accurate typescript I am indebted to the efficiency and dedication of Miss Elaine Potter.

1

THE PROBLEM OF TESTING CHRISTIANITY'S TRUTH-CLAIMS

FORTY PERCENT of the collegians responding to a recent poll said, "Science deals with truth, while religion is what you believe." Similarly, forty-four percent replied, "When we say a religion is true, we mean that it gives those who believe in it a feeling of security."[1] Responses like this reflect the increasing tendency to consider religious assertions noncognitive. That is, religious statements are thought to tell us nothing either true or false about actual states of affairs.

Of course some religious language may reflect nothing more than the subjective feelings of the speaker. Integral to the Judeo-Christian tradition, however, are some assertions about a God who is with us here and now, a revelation of His purposes, and a report of His acts making an observable difference in history. Christianity claims, furthermore, that Jesus of Nazareth is both Lord and Christ. Such propositions cannot be reduced to security feelings of some religious people. What these statements assert is either true or false. Christians claim it is true.

Examination of Christianity's truth-claims (proposals for acceptance and action) is inescapable. Sooner or later both insiders and outsiders put them to the test. Often inquiry takes place during college days. One campus minister found three questions most frequent: Does a loving Lord of history live today? Was Jesus what He claimed to be? Is the Bible God's Word to man? Billy Graham has found

1. Dirk W. Jellema, "Faith and Madness: The Post Modern Mind," *Christianity Today*, May 8, 1961, pp. 3-4.

that students want to know, "not so much about institutionalized religion as about Christ and faith in God."[2] Such questions will not be suppressed; they relate to the living of life. Do we have to do with the living God, the risen Christ, and Holy Scripture or not?

The sheltered may find these inescapable issues painful. A twenty-one-year-old coed from the University of Alabama exclaimed, "When I start to think about it (religion), I get all in a tizzy. I know I believe in God, and that is as far as it goes. I think it is a form of security." And a Roman Catholic head of the student senate at the University of Rhode Island confessed, "One reason I'm afraid to question too much, is because I'm really afraid if I do that I'll lose my faith. I desperately do not want to do that."[3] Uncomfortable as it may be, the most sheltered Christians inevitably meet persuasive non-Christians or confront their ideas through the communications media in this shrinking world.

CONFLICTING TRUTH-CLAIMS

Several influential non-Christian trends intensify the issue of Christianity's truth. If these non-Christian proposals are true, then Christian proposals must be false. For example, Professor William Hamilton alleges that God has died in our generation. He thinks he can no longer believe that an active God distinct from the world guides history to commendable ends. During the infancy of civilization, he claims, God was believed to be the solver of our problems. Now that we have grown up, Hamilton thinks, we can solve them ourselves. He claims that man has no God-shaped vacuum within and is not restless until he finds rest in God. Furthermore, Hamilton argues, if a good God ruled history, never would He have allowed the death of six million Jews in Nazi concentration camps. So Hamilton says, "The confidence with which we thought we could speak of God is gone, and our faith, belief, experience of him are very poor things indeed."[4] Obviously if Hamilton's proposal is true, the Christian claim is false that an eternal, wise, and good God governs history.

Similarly, if Marxist materialism is true, Christianity is false. Communists see no need for a Lord of nature since traditionally they sup-

---

2. Billy Graham, "My Word to Students Today," *Collegiate Challenge*, 5 (Fall 1966): 3.
3. "Campus '65," *Newsweek*, March 22, 1965, p. 57.
4. William Hamilton and Thomas J. J. Altizer, *Radical Theology and the Death of God* (Indianapolis: Bobbs-Merrill, 1966), pp. 40-41.

posed that matter was eternal and had power to produce whatever is. They explained everything that happened, not by an all-wise providence, but by an inexorable law of dialectic. That law produces inevitable tension between economic classes until a classless utopia will arrive. Meanwhile, religious beliefs act as an opiate to dull the senses of the expropriated masses while promising them "pie in the sky bye and bye."[5] Jesus was not God or even a good man. Like the founder of every religion he was a peddler of the "dope" of a burgeois plot to defraud the laboring masses. Communist truth-claims and Christian truth-claims cannot both be true.

Logical Positivists said that Christian claims were neither true nor false, but meaningless. Oriented toward science, this philosophy maintained that any assertion not verifiable by sense data was factually meaningless. To be verifiable a statement had to be confirmable, at least in principle, by sight, hearing, taste, touch, or smell. But no man has ever seen God, nor can see Him (1 Ti 6:16). So a verificationist has set up rules of meaning in such a way as to make statements about God's loving purposes and redemptive acts meaningless. With all the modifications of positivism by more recent philosophical analysts, the principle of verifiability remains for many the standard of truth about factual existences. This arbitrary limitation of what exists to physical things is far from open and cautious science. It is dogmatic scientism or secularism. Paul Van Buren in *The Secular Meaning of the Gospel* expresses it this way, "Unless or until a theological statement can be submitted in some way to verification, it cannot be said to have meaning."[6] If such pronouncements (themselves unverifiable) are true, the central message of Christianity is meaningless.

Nontheistic existentialists also think Christianity meaningless, but on quite different considerations. Existentialists start their thinking with individual persons, not intellectual principles or methods of verification. People, they insist, are not doctrinal propositions or chemical elements. If we are to know human persons we do not simply observe passive objects. People actively reveal themselves. They become the subjects, not merely the objects of our knowledge. In communicating, each person contributes something of his own inter-

5. See Karl Marx, *The Communist Manifesto* and *Capital*.
6. Paul M. Van Buren, *The Secular Meaning of the Gospel* (New York: Macmillan, 1966), p. 105.

ests. Each human being is distinct from every other. Christianity,
existentialists allege, does not take sufficient account of individual
uniqueness in making assertions about all men as sinners and the
means by which all must be recovered. Furthermore, Christianity
is said to destroy a person's freedom. If God had an intelligent concept of man in mind before creating man, the true essence of humanness was logically prior to the first existing person. For Jean-Paul
Sartre, however, the existence of an individual is prior to the essence
of humanness.[7] Human existence, Sartre thinks, has no fixed nature.
We are free to choose our own being. There is no reality except in
action.[8] Why we are flung into the world we do not know. A person
is completely free to make of himself what he wills without reference
to God or His will. Quite to the contrary, Christians think themselves
most fully free when filled by the Holy Spirit to do God's will. Clearly
the claims of nontheistic existentialists and of Christians cannot both
be true.

We live in a world bombarded with claims mutually exclusive of
orthodox Christianity: the death of God, Marxism, scientism and
existentialism. A thinking person must consider which, if any, are
true. It has become popular, however, to say that the more important
issue is not truth, but relevance. The need to show the relevance
of one's philosophy is crucial indeed. The crying needs of people
in all levels of society call for action. But the committed in any of
these religious and philosophical perspectives defend the relevance
of their teaching. Nevertheless their respective truth-claims remain
mutually exclusive. No one can commit himself to all, even for the
sake of meeting desperate human need. Responsible people must determine whether a personal Lord of all is dead, a capitalistic hoax,
logically meaningless, personally meaningless, or with us here and
now.

Often it is thought that we can escape the responsibility of judgment by being tolerant. Tolerance, however, does not scuttle intelligence and require the absurdity that every theory is as true as another. No amount of tolerance permits belief in contradictory statements. The tolerant person, while firmly committed to one point
of view as true, respects the right of others to hold contradictory views

7. Jean Wahl, *A Short History of Existentialism* (New York: Philosophical Libr.,
1949), p. 19.
8. Jean-Paul Sartre, *Existentialism* (New York: Philosophical Libr., 1947), p. 27.

without threat of violence. The great value of tolerance in no way exempts us from seeking to resolve the issue of conflicting truth-claims.

The fundamental necessity of resolving issues of truth became clear when leading philosophers and theologians met at New York University's fourth annual Institute of Philosophy (1960) to discuss religious symbols, faith, and meaning. Among the conclusions of abiding import noted by Professor Sidney Hook was this, "The question of truth once more becomes of paramount importance."[9] Of course ultimacy of truth does not rule out the necessity of treating relevance at the same time. Truth and relevance are not mutually exclusive. Nothing is more relevant to human need than truth spoken in love.

Is Truth in Religion Possible?

Although face to face with conflicting religious truth-claims, agnostics say we lack the resources to discover if any are in fact true. It is more fitting, they insist, to admit that no one knows whether there is a God or not. We can then supposedly simply enjoy studying the contradictory positions. But to remain unbelieving before Christianity's truth-claims is tantamount to rejecting them. The passing of life requires decisions, however difficult. Our style of life and language discloses either our acceptance or rejection of Christianity's basic tenets. For temporary evaluation we withhold commitment, but in the long run we live as if Christian claims are either true or false.

Is it not presumptuous even to think that we can settle the question of truth in religion? It may be. Admittedly the temptation to premature finality is as great for philosophers of religion as for others. All too easily people of various persuasions overlook the limitations of their finiteness and perversity. In shying away from arrogant dogmatism, however, we become unrealistic if we shun responsible investigation, decision, and action. Commitment to Christianity need not be haughty. "The moment of truth is always a moment of acceptance, never a moment of mastery."[10] That statement by English scholar Harry Blamires expresses an attitude of humility before the

---

9. Sidney Hook, ed., *Religious Experience and Truth* (New York U., 1961), p. xiii.
10. Harry Blamires, *A Defense of Dogmatism* (London: SPCK, 1965), p. 101.

evidence of revelation. Is the convinced Christian more self-assuming than one who places unbounded confidence in the unaided human intellect to yield endless progress? Blamires adds, "The theology of indefinitely extended progress towards truth is itself presumptuous because it is based on the assumption that men are going to learn more about God in this life than in fact they are capable of learning."[11]

Granting that the claim to religious truth may be made without arrogance, is it justifiable? In many details it is not. In numerous respects Christians remain skeptics. The claim to some religious truth is not a claim to all religious truth. Now Christians claim to know only in part. Even that part may be seen indirectly and dimly. They do not claim fully to comprehend everything regarding that which has been disclosed. On matters not made clear in nature or Scripture Christians are not dogmatic. They make a crucial distinction between their word and the word they think is from God. They invite consideration of that which they have reason to think comes from God.

Theists are sometimes thought to be guilty of wishful thinking. But those who do not believe in God are no less subject to Freudian projections of their desires. Unbelief as well as belief has been shown to be the result of unhappy childhood experiences, ignorant fear, or social pressures.[12] Rationalization of nonrational drives is not the exclusive property of the religious. Often people reject childish notions of Christianity rather than Christianity itself. Mature investigators will not be turned away by emotive reactions to unfortunate Sunday school experiences. The open-minded will carefully examine the evidence of Christianity's best apologists and follow the evidence where it leads. Wishful thinking will not change the case in either direction.

Because all knowledge is relative to individual knowers, some think we can never tell which religious claims are true. They think we can only tell which are true *for us*. If that were the case then the statement, "All religious knowledge is relative," would be true only for the one who made it. Then it need not be considered true for all men everywhere. Relativism simply cannot be *the truth*. But the element of truth in relativism is that many factors from our cultural

11. Ibid., p. 18.
12. Vernon C. Grounds, "Study for Skeptics," *His*, 18 (April 1958): 8-14.

backgrounds condition our knowing processes. Observation of these factors is a sound descriptive procedure when referring to the origins of ideas. Whoever reduces all knowledge to these factors, however, commits the genetic fallacy. He thinks that a description of the circumstances of an idea's origin determines the truth or falsity of its content. While all ideas are influenced by the knower's background, not all are equally valid or invalid. All knowledge is interpretative, but some interpretations are better informed than others.[13] Although all statements in religion are influenced by the individual's environment, some are better informed than others.

Informed interpretations can be shared in spite of different cultural backgrounds. Linguist Eugene Nida has explained that although absolute communication is not possible, effective communication is possible, even between persons of different cultures. He offers three reasons for this fact: " (1) the processes of human reasoning are essentially the same, irrespective of cultural diversity; (2) all people have a common range of experience, and (3) all peoples possess the capacity for at least some adjustment to the symbolic 'grids' of others."[14] While Christians differ culturally with many non-Christians both in the west and the east, an apologetic can be presented. Of course there are different perspectives, but with a common range of experience and reasoning ability coupled with a mutual desire to seek understanding, some truth is not only attainable, but also communicable.

WHAT IS TRUTH?

The long history of religious and philosophical thinking contains an "apparently unanimous agreement on the nature of truth," according to Mortimer J. Adler, editor of the *Great Books of the Western World*. He explains, "Just as everyone knows what a liar is, but not as readily whether someone is telling a lie, so the philosophers seem able to agree on what truth is, but not as readily on what is true." Whether the idea is thought to correspond to reality, cohere with reality, or to participate in reality, Adler finds all the thinkers concurring that the truth of ideas "depends on their conformity to reality."[15] So when we ask about the truth of religious assertions, we ask

13. See Ben F. Kimpel, *Language and Religion* (New York: Philosophical Libr., 1957), p. 45.
14. Eugene A. Nida, *Message and Mission* (New York: Harper, 1960), p. 90.
15. Mortimer J. Adler, ed., *The Great Ideas: A Syntopicon of Great Books of the Western World*, vol. 2 (Chicago: William Benton, 1952), p. 916.

whether or not they conform to reality. True assertions about Christianity are those which conform to what actually is the case.

Truth is not only a quality of propositions expressed in sentences, but also of persons who live up to a standard. A true friend embodies the standards of lasting friendship. A true Christian personally exists in accord with the standards of Christianity. Truth in this sense, philosopher Samuel M. Thompson has observed, is "the realization in being of what ought to be."[16] In the Old Testament truth (*emeth*) frequently indicated the *faithfulness* of people to the divine Covenant.[17] The New Testament term for truth (*aletheia*) often designated a person's integrity in speech, action, and thought.[18] Christians are exhorted not only to know the truth, but to walk in the truth. Jesus, who perfectly embodied authentic human life, was called the truth.

In seeking truth we seek ideas which conform to reality and a life which conforms to those ideas. Christianity, as J. Gresham Machen said, "is life based on doctrine."[19] Doctrine is not an end in itself, but a guide to authentic living. So Christianity purports to be a way of responsible thinking and of personal existence. Rationalists distort the Christian claim if they simply contemplate it. Existentialists distort the Christian claim if they try to live it without guidelines. To examine the truth of Christianity is to examine its claims upon both thought and life. Truth-claims are assertions proposed for acceptance and action.

Christianity's primary proposals for acceptance and action may be more precisely delineated. Christianity claims: (1) that an all-wise, all-good, all-powerful God who is distinct from the world actively sustains and rules the world, (2) that the eternal Word (*logos*) of God became flesh in Jesus of Nazareth, died for our sins, and rose again from the grave, (3) that God expressed His redemptive purposes through prophetic and apostolic spokesmen in Scripture, and (4) that people who are not what they ought to be may be forgiven

16. Samuel M. Thompson, *A Modern Philosophy of Religion* (Chicago: Henry Regnery, 1955), p. 399.
17. Francis Brown, S. R. Driver, and Charles A. Briggs, *A Hebrew and English Lexicon of the Old Testament* (Oxford: Clarendon, 1907).
18. Rudolph Bultmann, *"aletheia,"* in *Theological Dictionary of the New Testament*, ed. Gerhard Kittel, trans. Geoffrey W. Bromily, vol. 1 (Grand Rapids: Eerdmans, 1964).
19. J. Gresham Machen, *What Is Christianity? and Other Addresses* (Grand Rapids: Eerdmans, 1951), p. 22.

and regenerated by repenting of their sin and trusting Christ's redemption.

For any truth-claims to be taken seriously, they must meet certain criteria. William A. Christian has suggested four such standards for distinguishing bona fide truth-claims from counterfeits.[20] First, they must be logically consistent. Christian claims do not violate the logician's law of non-contradiction. Second, genuine truth-claims must be meaningful to others than the proposer. Christian claims can be regarded meaningless only by arbitrarily reducing meaning to sense data, a self-defeating effort. Third, something must conceivably count for or against the proposal's truth. We shall be noting data such as history's tragic evils, which are often alleged to count against Christian claims. Fourth, some support must be presented for the truth of particular proposals. Each succeeding chapter presents a different way of supporting Christian claims. Before we can survey these varied forms of support, however, we must pause to consider objections to attempting any such defense of Christian faith—and they are many.

DOES CHRISTIANITY NEED DEFENSE?

Statements supporting the truthfulness of basic Christian claims have traditionally been called apologetics. That term comes from a Greek word (*apologia*) meaning defense. It was the ordinary word for a lawyer's defense of a client in court. When early Christians were attacked for their faith, those who rose to defend their beliefs came to be called apologists. In this volume apologetics designates the science and art of defending Christianity's basic truth-claims. Apologetics is not theology. Theology presupposes the primary tenets of Christianity and sets forth their implications in systematic detail. Apologetics, on the other hand, examines Christianity's most basic presuppositions. It considers *why* we should start with Christian presuppositions rather than others.

Objections to defending Christianity's basic truth-claims come from many different vantage points. Philosophers like Samuel M. Thompson have called apologetics "an illegitimate discipline." Thompson reasoned, "If it assumes its premises it is special pleading or else a mere restatement of the theology it purports to defend, while if it

20. William A. Christian, *Meaning and Truth in Religion* (Princeton, N.J.: Princeton U., 1964), p. 24.

examines its premises it is philosophy and so can plead no case but
that of truth itself."[21] Apologetics, as we have defined it, does examine its premises and pleads no cause but truth. It need not be called
a bad name, but classified as a department of philosophy. The fact
that apologists defend convictions does not detract from genuine
philosophical enterprise. No one expresses this better than Professor
Thompson in the preface to *A Modern Philosophy of Religion.* "I
make no apology for my support of a definite point of view in this
book. No book of philosophy can avoid commitment; only a book
about philosophy which is not itself a search for true answers to
philosophy's questions, can be neutral." Since philosophers can legitimately defend various positions, apologists can legitimately defend
Christianity.

Why should we philosophize, it may be asked, when countless people stand in desperate psychological need? Surely those who suffer
debilitating neuroses should seek the help of counsellors to alleviate
avoidable tensions. But what of the ever present anxieties that accompany the very fact of human existence? Paul Tillich has summed up
the thought of many contemporaries by showing how life is filled
with a deep-seated anxiety resulting from the fear of death, a sense
of guilt, and a threat of meaninglessness. The way to prevent despair,
he argues, is to structure a sound view of ontology (what actually
is).[22] Whatever we may think of Tillich's theology otherwise, we
must agree that healthy living requires openness to truth about existence, guilt, and the grave. The apologist, for one, seeks that truth.
In the final analysis, then, by constructing a sound defense of his
view of reality he is really making a necessary contribution to people's
most basic psychological needs.

A psychologically mature person, among other things, develops a
consciously chosen criterion for distinguishing existential reality from
unreality and an openness to reality. The mature person also reflects
upon his own position in contrast to the stance of others. Intelligent
consideration of comparisons and contrasts with other perspectives
relieves unnecessary anxiety and helps one's position stand out to
him with vividness and meaning. As its significance is realized it
evokes appropriate emotional and volitional responses. Apologetics

21. Thompson, pp. 30, vii.
22. Paul Tillich, *The Courage to Be* (New Haven, Conn.: Yale U., 1952), pp. 32-85.

helps to meet the psychological needs of people by encouraging an attitude of openness to all reality, establishing a criterion of truth which will not exclude anything that in fact exists, and comparing other world-views. Apologetics thus contributes to a mature realization of one's Christian commitments and so to the meaningful experience of the whole man.

Just as psychologists explain much present behavior in terms of past experiences, some may think that a person's Christian beliefs are completely explained by events in his past. No reasoned defense is thought to be relevant since the faith is biographically explained. Biographical accounts of a person's faith, however, do not justify that faith in contrast to others which conflict. Interesting biographies can be produced "explaining" the beliefs of people in all the leading philosophies and religions of the world. Are none of these mutually exclusive commitments more worthy than others? Surely some can be discredited. Can nothing be said in favor of any? If Christianity is held to be true, some considerations should be offered to justify this particular claim. The question of Christianity's truth is not a psychological question calling for a biographical description of believers, but a philosophical question calling for a meaningful justification of beliefs.

Is rational argument so seldom the cause of conviction that apologists are "wasting their shot?" Writing on apologist C. S. Lewis, Austin Farrer answered,

> The premise is true, but the conclusion does not follow. For though argument does not create conviction, the lack of it destroys belief. What seems to be proved may not be embraced; but what no one shows the ability to defend is quickly abandoned.[23]

Apologetic argument may not create belief, but it creates the atmosphere in which belief can come to life. Because the atmosphere does not create life, is it therefore useless? Because apologetics does not create convictions, is it therefore without point? Admittedly other factors are important in persuasion. But these do not displace the necessity of sound reasoning. Professors Brembeck and Howell in their volume *Persuasion: A Means of Social Control* conclude that a persuader cannot overlook either the logical or psychological factors.

23. Jocelyn Gibb, ed., *Light on C. S. Lewis* (London: Geoffrey Bles, 1965), p. 26.

All his utterances, they find, should have both psychological and logical aspects.[24] As long as logical considerations have a place in persuasion, apologetics has a place.

A social ethics professor once asked whether Christians ought to
spend time on apologetic theory or do something for the tragic social
needs of the world. Surely the apologist's concerns are no substitute
for other Christian responsibilities. Suffering individuals find it difficult to follow lengthy arguments! By all means feed the starving,
clothe the destitute, and offer a cup of cold water to the thirsty. But
in whose name? And why in Christ's name and not another? Apologetic answers help give direction and meaning to social activism.
Without that guide to truth, attempts to serve men may fall short
of their greatest value. Jesus did not say, "If any man will deny himself, take up his cross and follow any good cause he will be my disciple." Rather, to be His disciple, we must follow Him. His way
includes both life and truth. And the truth the apologist seeks is not
mere theory. He defends convictions to live by. He supports the
basis on which activists may appeal to Christ and Scripture to enhance
their causes.

Some devout people feel that religion is too complex, too personal,
and too mysterious to allow for reasoned defense. Indeed talk about
God is far from experience of God. And investigation of conversion
is not conversion. But we do not remain silent on such matters. When
we speak, if we expect others to understand, we must utilize the basic
laws of logic (the principles of identity, contradiction, and excluded
middle). The penalty if we do not is failure to communicate with
any precision. And even in our own thinking about religion we must
employ the laws of logic. The penalty, if we do not, is ambiguity in
interpretation and fallacious implications in drawing inferences from
it. Amplifying this point, Professor Charles Frankel of Columbia
University adds that

> this is not to deny the right of any individual to live by incommuni-
> cable mysteries. It is certainly not to say that his deepest feelings
> have no value, or that his intuitions are any less rich or compelling
> to him than they are. It is merely to say that his feelings and intu-

24. Brembeck and Howell, *Persuasion: A Means of Social Control* (Englewood Cliffs,
N.J.: Prentice-Hall, 1952), p. 126.

itions, and his mysteries, can make no claim on the assent of others. It is to say that he cannot say that he *knows*. He does not, it should always be remembered, have to say this; he can enjoy his soliloquies in solitude. But if he does ask that others credit them as clues to the truth, he enters a domain in which rules of social communication take over.[25]

Is not religious commitment so passionate as to render objective reasoning impossible? Are not genuine believers so involved that they cannot reason in a detached manner? Analyzing this consideration in *The Religious Revolt Against Reason*, L. Harold De Wolf suggests that the detachment which reason requires is not indifference. Even a mathematician is rarely indifferent to the results of his inquiry. Furthermore,

> The more firmly one is convinced that the Christian faith is true, the more eager one should be to provide himself and others with proof of the fact by disinterested examination of the evidences for his faith in hours of disciplined detachment. What is needed would seem to be not a life of passionate disregard of truth on the one hand and a passionless indifference on the other, but a passionate search for the truth in which emotional experience will provide its full share of the evidence.[26]

But the anti-apologists reply that the Bible needs no defense. "The Bible, like a lion, is quite capable of defending itself. Just loose it and let it go." The king of the jungle may need no defense in his proper habitat, but it would stand little chance on a busy superhighway or in the face of modern weapons. The question is not the inherent power of the lion or the Bible. If the Bible expresses God's eternal truth, of course that needs no support from men. The question has to do with the image of the Bible in the minds of young people who for twelve to sixteen years of public school education have heard the Bible's authority questioned and its teachings challenged. To defend is to act, speak, or write in favor of something. Shall these people hear nothing in favor of the Bible's truth? *As far as they are concerned* does the Bible need no defense? Is it sufficient simply to repeat what they consider to be outdated advice and pre-

25. Charles Frankel, *The Love of Anxiety and Other Essays* (New York: Harper and Row, 1965), p. 28.
26. L. Harold DeWolf, *The Religious Revolt Against Reason* (New York: Harper, 1949), p. 113.

scientific fable? Do they not have a right to hear the case, if there is one, in support of the Bible's truth? A Christianity which can be joyfully propagated without defense, J. Gresham Machen noted, must be so diluted as to be completely in accord with the age. True Christianity, on the other hand, "now, as always, is radically contrary to the natural man, and it cannot possibly be maintained without a constant struggle." And Machen added, "Certainly a Christianity that avoids argument is not the Christianity of the New Testament."[27]

But you cannot reason anyone into the kingdom of heaven. Of course not! No apologist purports to do that. Because reasoning is insufficient, however, it is not therefore unnecessary. The simplest announcement of the gospel must present it as true. No amount of emotional appeal can stimulate people to accept a message they consider to be false. Speech in favor of the Bible's truth is one of many means the Holy Spirit employs in bringing men to full commitment. The Holy Spirit alone regenerates; but the Holy Spirit has chosen not to regenerate alone. He has chosen to utilize human instruments. Any argument against the use of argument applies with equal force against the use of preaching, teaching, personal witnessing, mass evangelism, and any other form of missionary outreach. As Benjamin B. Warfield said, "The action of the Holy Spirit in giving faith is not apart from evidence, but along with evidence; and in the first instance consists in preparing the soul for the reception of evidence.[28]

The case against apologetics is not yet finished. Christianity, we are told, is a matter of faith, not reason. So apologetics is unnecessary. Is it? What is faith? How is faith different from wishful thinking, gullibility, and mere opinion? Is it possible to have Christian faith without Christian knowledge? Do Christians worship an unknown God? Is it sufficient to have zeal without knowledge? Faith is an act of the will directed by truth to an object which is real. As Aurelius Augustine put it, "What is believing but consenting to the truth of what is said? and this consent is certainly voluntary."[29] Even when voluntary trust is placed in persons, knowledge is necessary. We trust those who have given signs in word or deed of being trustworthy. So traditional analyses of faith have included in them the elements of

27. Machen, pp. 126-30.
28. B. B. Warfield, *Studies in Theology* (New York: Oxford U., 1932), p. 15.
29. Aurelius Augustine, "On the Spirit and the Letter," in *Nicene and Post-Nicene Fathers*, ed. Philip Schaff, vol. 5 (Grand Rapids: Eerdmans, 1956), p. 107.

knowledge, assent, and commitment (*notitia, assensus,* and *fiducia*). The Sunday school boy was mistaken in defining faith as "believing what you know ain't true." Rather, as David Elton Trueblood has said, "Faith is not belief without proof, but trust without reservation."

If knowledge is necessary to faith, the question inevitably arises, how much knowledge? An examination of the New Testament indicates that faith is conditioned upon assent to just a few explicit propositions. These include: (1) that God exists as an active rewarder of those who seek Him (Heb 11:6), (2) that the Christ who was God (Jn 1:1) became flesh (Jn 1:14, 18; 1 Jn 4:1-3), (3) that Christ's death was an expiation for our sins (Ro 3:25), and that God raised Him from the dead (Ro 10:9-10). Each of these assertions is made an explicit item of knowledge and assent for saving faith in the New Testament. They sum up the heart of the kerygma or gospel (1 Co 15:3-4). As long as assent to the truth of such propositions is essential to Christian faith, defense of their truth will be indispensable to Christian outreach.

IS APOLOGETIC REASONING BIBLICAL?

Although numerous considerations make a defense of Christianity's truth-claims seem necessary, some think the Bible disparages apologetics. For example, from people of varied theological persuasions we hear that while the Bible everywhere assumes the existence of God, it never seeks to support that assertion. Before such shibboleths are repeated to infinity they ought to be checked. Of course, when addressing believers in God the Bible writers do not reason as with unbelievers. And much of the Bible is addressed to the committed. But when their confidence is shaken, or when unbelievers are addressed, God's existence is not assumed, but supported. Consider several instances.

In response to Moses' plea to release the Jews from Egyptian slavery, Pharaoh said, "I do not know the LORD" (Ex 5:2). The ruler was not asked to assume God's existence, but was given the "signs" of the plagues. Their intensity increased until the oldest son in each family died. After letting the Israelites go, Pharaoh changed his mind and pursued them. Fleeing in the wilderness the Israelites complained against Moses in unbelief. Then God promised deliverance through the Red Sea. The purpose of that additional sign was that "the Egyptians shall know that I am the Lord, when I am honored through Pharaoh, through his chariots and his horsemen" (Ex 14:18). After that remarkable deliverance, not only the surviving Egyptians were convinced, but so were the Israelites. When they "saw the great power which the LORD had used against the Egyptians, the people feared the LORD; and they believed in the LORD and in His servant Moses" (Ex 14:31).

During the crisis in which Baal worship threatened to wipe out worship of the Lord, His existence was again supported by observable evidence. Elijah did not say to the fifty prophets of Baal, "I assume the existence of the Lord and you assume the existence of Baal. No one can argue about basic assumptions. I have nothing more to say." Quite the contrary, Elijah proposed to put the conflicting religious truth-claims to the test. "You call on the name of your god, and I will call on the name of the LORD, and the God who answers by fire, He is God" (1 Ki 18:24). Hours of sincere prayer to Baal made no observable difference. But in response to Elijah's request that the people might know that the Lord was God, fire fell upon a drenched altar and consumed the sacrifice. "And when all the people saw it, they fell on their faces; and they said, 'The LORD, He is God; the LORD, He is God'" (1 Ki 18:39). Again the Bible did not presuppose the Lord's existence, but reported signs indicating it.

When idol worshipers later threatened to attract the unfaithful Israelites, Isaiah did not hide behind unchallengeable axioms. By skillful argument he reduced idol worship to absurdity and presented a case for trust in the Lord. The idols, he said, were made by men in their likeness out of trees they selected. And with all that they were profitable for nothing, they could not see or know or answer prayer. In contrast, the prophet reasoned, the Lord created and chose Israel, redeemed Israel from Egypt, was tireless, and knew the end from the beginning so that He predicted the future inerrantly (Is 40:12—48:5).

When the existence of God was at issue in New Testament times, the conclusion was not merely assumed. At Athens, the university center of the ancient world replete with an estimated 30,000 gods and goddesses, the apostle Paul presented meaningful proposals. In several negative and affirmative propositions expressed in communicative ways he set forth truth-claims concerning the Lord of all. Before this God, he warned, every one of them would be judged. Was this his own private presupposition? Hardly. The great Christian missionary appealed to evidence. He said that God "furnished proof to all men by raising Him from the dead" (Ac 17:31). Paul referred to an event attested by hundreds of competent witnesses, many of whom were still alive. When God's existence is at stake the Bible defends the truth of assertions proposed for belief in Him. Apologetic reasoning is not minimized in Scripture; it is vividly exemplified by prophets and apostles.

The use of apologetic is equally clear when Christian claims concerning Christ are under investigation. The imprisoned John the Baptist sent a follower to Jesus asking, "Are you he who is to come, or shall we look for another?" Jesus did not reply that His Messiahship was to be accepted by an irrational leap of blind faith. Jesus said, "Go and tell John what you hear and see: the blind receive their sight and the lame walk, lepers are cleansed and the deaf hear, and the dead are raised up, and the poor have good news preached to them" (Mt 11:2-5, RSV). When Jesus' own word was questioned, He said, "though you do not believe Me, believe the works; that you may know and understand that the Father is in Me, and I in the Father" (Jn 10:38). Greater than the significance of others' testimony was the evidence of His miracles, said Jesus, "the very works that I do, bear witness of Me, that the Father has sent me" (Jn 5:36). Of course people could make idols out of the signs and follow in the hope that He would again feed the thousands a free lunch. Any good thing can become an idol—an apologetic system or a clever attack on apologetic systems. "Sophomoric" enthusiasm for apologetics, as for any other new field of study, frequently needs to be checked. But that can hardly be an excuse for taking a view of evidence that would make Jesus an idolatrous worshiper at the shrine of reason.

Regardless of scriptural instances of apologetic reasoning, opponents of the discipline frequently appeal to passages thought to forbid it. For example, they quote Colossians 2:8, "See to it that no one takes you captive through philosophy and empty deception, according to the tradition of men, according to the elementary principles of the world, rather than according to Christ." This passage warns against philosophies drawn from sources merely human and natural to the exclusion of Christ. In no way does it warn against philosophy in defense of Christ. And how can Christians best avoid deception by humanism and naturalism? By knowing nothing about these philosophies or by knowing them well, in their strengths and limitations? Paul presupposed a knowledge of the gnostic philosophy by the Colossian Christians. In formulating his own position in Christ he utilized the familiar gnostic terms: "wisdom," "knowledge," "fullness," "mystery," and "philosophy." Professor Arthur Holmes explained Paul's usage:

> Did he use such terminology with none of its original meaning, he would merely equivocate; the Gnostics would use a given term in sense A and he would use it in sense B; the two senses would have nothing in common; the word itself would convey nothing. Did he use their terminology uncritically and make predications akin to their own, then he and they would differ not at all. But by the skillful use of words in new contexts, he successfully modified their meanings while drawing sufficiently close analogies to make the necessary contact with cultural thought-patterns.[30]

Far from being opposed to apologetics, then, Colossians 2:8 in its context exemplifies apologetics par excellence.

It has often been alleged that 1 Corinthians is anti-apologetic. On the contrary, it only opposes naturalistic philosophies. A divisive party spirit had developed at Corinth as some followed Peter, some Apollos, and some Paul. So Paul distinguished the wisdom of all men from the wisdom of God. He said, "yet we do speak wisdom among those who are mature; a wisdom, however, not of this age, nor of the rulers of this age, who are passing away" (1 Co 2:6). If Paul's wisdom is not drawn from the elements of nature by men, what is its source? It is the wisdom of God (1 Co 2:7) which God revealed through the Holy Spirit's inspiration and illumination (1 Co 2:10-14). Although to the unbeliever the divinely revealed message may *appear* to be foolishness, it is not foolishness. It is the wisdom of God. The cause of offense is the content of the message, not its illogical presentation. So the apologist for divinely revealed wisdom hardly merits identification with those who disclaim such revelation.

30. Arthur Holmes, *Christianity and Philosophy* (Chicago: Inter-Varsity, 1960), p. 28.

In no way does 1 Corinthians oppose speaking in favor of the wisdom of God. Paul does not contradict his own ministry, "I am appointed for the defense of the gospel" (Phil 1:16). And all members of the church share "in the defense and confirmation of the gospel" (Phil 1:7).

Another passage often employed against the use of apologetic records Paul's address before the Areopagus (court) in Athens (Ac 17:16-34). Sir William Ramsey and others consider this defense of Christianity a tragic mistake because of: (1) negligible results, (2) Paul's hasty departure from Athens, (3) contradiction of 1 Corinthians 1-2 and Romans 1-3, (4) Paul's later emphasis on the Word, and (5) his refusal ever again to speak in philosophic style.[31] Upon examination, however, none of these arguments hold.

The results of Paul's address were not negligible. Several people believed, including two known widely enough to be named (Dionysius and Damaris). In the heart of the university center of the ancient world before an audience of philosophers and lawyers this is remarkable success. It is not clear that Paul left Athens in haste. Haste is no necessary part of the connotation of "depart" (18:1). If it were, it would not necessarily demonstrate dissatisfaction with the address. No contradiction between the content of Acts 17 and Romans 1 exists, any more than between Acts 17 and 1 Corinthians. Paul's references to the Stoic belief in a God of providence, the creative Fatherhood of God, and brotherhood of man, are simply illustrations of his view in Romans 1 that the invisible things of God are clearly seen in the things that are made. Just as Paul found the unevangelized to be without excuse for failing to live up to the light they had (Ro 1:20), he summoned the cultural Athenians to repentance before God. Paul used Stoic terminology of Athens as he had Gnostic terminology with the Colossians, but he did not compromise any Old Testament doctrine. For six verses of his sermon (17:24-29) Nestle's Greek New Testament lists some twenty-two Old Testament quotations and allusions. Hebrew thought was not totally different from that of the Greek philosophers. Quite the contrary. These two perspectives were in agreement at certain key points and appeal could be made to that common ground. And Paul could hardly have been more preoccupied with the Word later at Corinth than he was

31. W. M. Ramsay, *St. Paul the Traveller and the Roman Citizen* (New York: Putnam, 1896), p. 252.

at Athens (18:5). The inference that he was not engrossed in the
Word at Athens flies in the face of abundant evidence of reference
to Scriptural teachings.

And Paul never abandoned philosophical reasoning! That is a
theory which simply ignores extensive data to the contrary. Every
Sabbath at Corinth he reasoned (*dialegomai*) in the synagogue
(18:4) and won both Jews and Greeks. In Ephesus he reasoned
(*dialegomai*) with the Jews for three months. When opposition
arose, did he give up his approach? Far from it. Rather, he moved
to the school of Tyrannus where for two years he engaged in daily
dialogues (19:8-9). At Troas on communion Sunday Paul "talked
with them" (*dialegomai*) until midnight (20:7). Long after his
experience at Athens, Paul reasoned seven days a week in market
places, synagogues, and churches with Jews and Gentiles.

The case against following Paul's example at Athens collapses before biblical data. But the case for following his philosophical approach is strong. After his dramatic conversion, Paul was called to
be an apostle to the Gentiles (Ro 11:13). Luke, the author of Acts,
included the report of Paul's message at Athens to show how the gospel went beyond Jerusalem, Judea, and Samaria to the uttermost
parts of the earth (Ac 1:8). Paul had been personally called and
uniquely prepared for this dramatic moment of history. At last Jew
met Gentile, Jerusalem confronted Athens, Christianity faced philosophy, and faith engaged reason. Who can believe that this moment
for which Paul was called and gifted should be uninstructive for
other ministries in similar contexts? If we reject Paul's approach to
cultured Gentiles, whose shall we prefer? Here we have the Bible's
chief paradigm for presenting the truth of Christianity to educated
outsiders. It is increasingly relevant to our burgeoning population
today.[32]

Biblical teaching does not oppose the use of apologetic, it commands it. No amount of objection to apologetic can exempt a Christian from obedience to a passage like 1 Peter 3:15. To believers whose
faith is being challenged by opponents, Peter writes, "Have no fear
of them, nor be troubled, but in your hearts reverence Christ as Lord.
Always be prepared to make a defense (*apologian*) to anyone who

32. For an extensive discussion of the apologetic significance of Paul's Areopagus
address see my four-part series, "Gospel On Campus," *His* 27 (October 1966-January
1967).

calls you to account for the hope that is in you, yet do it with gentleness and reverence." The clear exhortation is to give an account or reason (*logon*) in defense of one's faith. That reasoned defense is not to be motivated by self-glory, but a heart committed to Christ's glory. Such a dedicated use of reason is no more unspiritual than a dedicated use of music. The apologist's attitude is not boastful, but kind and respectful. Peter's exhortation does not stand alone in Scripture. It is similar to Paul's in 2 Timothy 2:24-26:

> And the Lord's bond-servant must not be quarrelsome, but be kind to all, able to teach, patient when wronged, with gentleness correcting those who are in opposition; if perhaps God may grant them repentance leading to the knowledge of the truth, and they may come to their senses and escape from the snare of the devil, having been held captive by him to do his will.

Anyone who aspires to Christian service must be a defender of the Christian faith, or he fails to meet a fundamental scriptural condition for the ministry. Among the traits necessary, Titus 1:9 demands that the prospective bishop or elder "holding fast the faithful word which is in accordance with the teaching, that he may be able both to exhort in sound doctrine and to refute (confute, expose, rebuke) those who contradict." Like Paul, a candidate for the ministry should be able to reason with Jews out of the Old Testament (Ac 17:2), and to Gentiles "as one outside the law" becoming all things to all men in order to save some (1 Co 9:21-22).

No one can do justice to these and similar passages by saying that the Christian's sole responsibility in witnessing is to quote John 3:16 or simply tell what has happened to him. Each of these approaches may be necessary, but others may also help. For example, many factors contributed to the conversion of Augustine. The corrective for his materialistic and skeptical notions was the philosophical reasoning of Plotinus. Augustine's confidence in astrology was removed by the argument of Nebridius. Erroneous impressions of biblical and Christian teachings were clarified by the expository preaching of Ambrose. And that pastor demonstrated Christian compassion for this troubled young man. With the evidences for the truth of Christianity which Ambrose added, Augustine's intellectual problems with the faith evaporated. But his moral struggle continued. Assistance came in the form of the counsel of older Christians and the testimonies of committed men of similar age and gifts. Still he said, "not yet." Finally his mother's prayers were answered as he read a verse of Scripture (Rom.13:13-14) and received Christ as his Lord.[33] Reasoning was but one of the preparatory steps to Augustine's conversion; but it was a most necessary step. Without minimizing the other contributing factors, Christians have a biblical mandate to reason as effectively as possible in defense of their faith. Christians who find a place for defense of Christianity's truth are by no means agreed on the form that reasoning should take. To those differences we now turn.

PROBLEMS IN STRUCTURING A REASONED DEFENSE

If reason may play some part in supporting Christianity's truth-claims, we ask, how? Are Christianity's truth-claims conclusively established by witnessing to a very personal experience of conversion? Some will interpret that testimony as a case study in abnormal psychology. Transforming conversions occur in philosophies, religions, and cults with contradictory claims. If the testimony of Christians establishes Christianity's claims, why does the testimony of others not establish the truth of theirs?

Is Christianity more firmly supported by appeal to the Bible's claims for itself? It purports to have originated with God and to have come to us through prophetic and apostolic spokesmen. If that claim settles the question for Christians without further consideration, then it must serve as well for other sacred writings which make equivalent claims. Mohammed claims a divine origin for the *Koran,* Joseph Smith for the Mormon revelations, and Mary Baker Eddy for *Science and Health with Key to the Scriptures.* If the Bible's claims are self-authenticating, why aren't these?

Can the issue be solved by appeals to objective, scientific evidence? Does archaeology, for instance, support the validity of the Bible and not other revered books? Is it possible for anyone to be completely objective in such an investigation? If so, or relatively so, does the evidence support Christian claims to a high degree of probability? Is probability sufficient for commitment?

33. For an account of Augustine's conversion read the author's "See Yourself in Augustine," *The Collegiate Challenge* 1 (May-June 1962): 8-9.

Is the answer a simple witness to the Lordship of Christ? Then which Christ? The Jehovah's Witness's highest created angel? The Muslim's prophet? The modernist's marvelously good man? The communist's "dope" peddler? The Christian Scientist's practitioner? The Spiritualist's medium? Or the Christian's eternal Word who was God and became flesh? A simple witness is given to all these claims concerning Christ. But all cannot be established as true, for some are mutually exclusive.

Shall the devoted of each religion and philosophy then withdraw behind their respective authorities? But dogma cannot be accepted as true simply because pronounced for centuries by leaders in an impressive church. If it were, the conflicting claims of all religions would be established. Dogma is accepted from authorities because it is believed to be true. Authorities are respected because they are thought best qualified to determine truth. How then do we know when people are qualified? Until that question can be answered, the truth-claims of Christianity are not confirmed.

John Wisdom's Invisible Gardener

The complexity of Christianity's truth-claims and the questions they raise necessarily require an investigation into many fields. The problem of God's existence and possible ways of seeking an answer are further focused by John Wisdom of Cambridge University in a now famous illustration.[34] Two people return to a long neglected garden and find among the weeds a few surprisingly vigorous plants. To account for the plants one believes in an invisible gardener; the other does not. What makes the difference between belief and unbelief in the invisible gardener? That is the challenging question.

Is it the case that one has overlooked evidence the other sees? Or is the observable evidence the same for both? Does one reason logically, the other illogically? Or is it more a matter of attitudes than evidence or logic? Possibly the difference lies in varied feelings toward the same state of affairs. Have we something like an aesthetic question? One looks at the garden "picture" with reverent awe and relish; the other has no taste for it. Is one "blind" to what the other "sees?" Is it that one accepts reasons of the heart, but the other

34. John Wisdom, *Philosophy and Psychoanalysis* (New York: Philosophical Libr., 1953), pp. 154-55.

passes them off with a knowing smile? On the other hand, are religious differences analogous to problems of guilt or innocence in a
court of law? If so, we could only expect circumstantial evidence and
the credible testimony of eyewitnesses to events we ourselves have
not seen. Differences like these will be at issue among the apologists
to be studied. They are not mere academic debates. They bear significantly upon the entire mission of the Christian church to outsiders
and many insiders as well.

John Wisdom's illustration of belief and unbelief in the invisible
gardener points up the major problem with which each apologist is
concerned. So it will be alluded to at the end of each succeeding
chapter to provide the occasion for summing up the respective apologetic thrusts.

A PREVIEW OF THE APOLOGETIC SYSTEMS

How then do the writers to be studied arrive at the conclusion that
Christianity is true? A glimpse of their procedures will provide a
map for the road ahead.

1. J. Oliver Buswell, Jr. finds Christianity's claims true by examination of observable evidence. On this approach inquirers do not
start the investigation with any particular principles of reasoning,
faith, presuppositions, or hypotheses. The mind as a blank tablet
receives impressions from the observed data, traces their implications,
and draws the most probable conclusions. The inductive method and
principles of inference are themselves derived from experience. A
conclusion is held to be true when it corresponds to or integrates
with, the relevant facts. No claim can be shown to be true beyond a
high degree of probability. In view of the evidence he presents from
the existence and order of the world, Buswell concludes that it is
overwhelmingly probable that God exists.

2. Stuart C. Hackett thinks that Christianity's truth can be conclusively proved since the human mind brings with it to the investigation of evidence some "built-in" principles which make valid conclusions certain. Inherent in the minds of all men are the principles
of logic (e.g., contradictories cannot both be true), and of causality
(i.e., every effect must have an adequate cause). With the help of
principles like these the mind systematizes its experience and draws
necessary conclusions. A true conclusion coheres with the mind's

categories and the facts of experience. From objective evidence similar to Buswell's (the existence and order of the world) Hackett "demonstrates" that God exists.

3. Gordon H. Clark agrees with Hackett that the human mind has principles of reasoning "programmed in." But he does not agree that the starting point of thought is objective experience. Any attempt to discover objective facts without an interpretative principle is pressed to the logical extreme of skepticism. Clark says that no such thing as scientific knowledge about reality is possible. Science merely gives us useful operational procedures for improving our temporal facilities. If evidence cannot tell us whether Christianity is true or not, what can? He answers, the interpretative principle that gives the most consistent system. Since everyone comes to evidence with presuppositions, Christians should admit that they do. Frankly Clark starts his thinking by assuming the existence of God and the truth of the Bible. He considers these to be fundamental axioms (analogous to mathematical reasoning) necessary to all thought about Christianity. Starting with the God of the Bible he deduces a consistent system of philosophy with the certainty of logical syllogisms. Christian truth-claims are accepted, then, because they enable him to devise the most consistent system of thought with the fewest difficulties.

4. Cornelius Van Til also begins his apologetic with the presuppositions of the triune God of Christianity and the truth of Scripture. But he does not justify them by their consistency or their confirmation by facts. Only one who starts with these presuppositions, he argues, can interpret facts according to their true meaning. There can be no common ground epistemologically in principle with those who start thinking from non-Christian assumptions. From the beginning apologists must challenge non-Christians to turn from their "facts" or principles of reasoning supposed to be meaningful whether God exists or not. Only from the Bible can logicians and scientists find their proper role. But why start with the Protestant Bible? Simply because it says it is God's Word. It is self-authenticating. If it violates the law of non-contradiction, then that law of logic can be broken on divine authority. If biblical history seems difficult to reconcile with certain facts, Van Til declares that the "facts" under discussion must be what Scripture says they are if they are to be intelligible at all. All truth is a single whole. A piecemeal approach can

only lead to irrationalism and skepticism. Unless we start with Christian presuppositions, no fact or argument stands still long enough to hold meaning. Unless we believe in God, Van Til reasons, we can logically believe in nothing else. All would then be chaos and old night. By giving meaning to everything that is, Christianity authenticates itself.

5. Earl E. Barrett sees serious limitations in Van Til's authoritarian approach as well as the empirical and rational systems. The case for Christianity, he declares, is more significant from internal and immediate experience of God Himself. Although this Christian mysticism incorporates several emphases from the other systems, no argument is considered convincing until a person has a unique, personal encounter with God. Then the best procedure is not to construct logical or empirical proofs, but to witness to one's experience of God. Christian mystical experiences of God are self-authenticating. One who through reading Scripture has confronted God needs no further evidence. He has an immediate psychological certitude of God's existence and the truth of His Word. Then he will see the coherence of Christian teaching, and not before. So Barrett confirms Christianity's truth-claims primarily by his direct experience of God.

6. Edward John Carnell treats Christianity's truth-claims as scientific hypotheses to be verified by man's total experience. The hypothesis that can consistently account for both internal and external data with the fewest difficulties is true. The starting point is not the mind as a blank tablet, general principles of reasoning, or unsupported Christian presuppositions, but a hypothesis to be tested. The proposed explanation of the world is the existence of the triune God of the Bible. An inquirer is asked simply to consider whether this hypothesis, among many others, may be true. The test of verification is twofold, involving logical consistency and factual adequacy. Carnell finds the biblical revelation of Deity to be consistent and to fit the facts. It fits the facts of the external world: the data of history, science, fulfilled prophecy, and miracles. It also fits the facts of the internal world; the data of conversion experience, values, ethics, and psychology. With overwhelming intellectual probability Christianity is thus shown to be true and so Christianity may be embraced with moral certainty.

7. Carnell builds not only upon man's quest for consistency and

adequacy, but also upon the quest for satisfying values. Non-Christian religions and philosophies fail to satisfy the whole man, he points out. Many of the things people consider vitally important are frustrated by living for "wine, women, and song," communism, scientism, rationalism, humanism, mere theism, universalism, Romanism, and existentialism. On the other hand, in evangelical Christianity Carnell finds all the values that make life worth living. Freed from lesser masters, the Bible believer is motivated to serve God and man. He knows why he should preserve human values, and where to turn when he fails to love as he ought. In addition he is renewed to utilize the best fruits of his earnings, science, and logic for the glory of God and the good of men everywhere. No more rewarding fulfillment can be provided by any other philosophy or religion. Christianity is true because it alone satisfies the values of the complete person.

8. Another apologetic devised by Dr. Carnell displays the relevance of Christianity to man's deepest psychological needs. Psychologists have discovered the importance of humility and honesty in acknowledging the past sources of alienation. The Bible summons us to enter the kingdom of God in the humility and honesty of a little child. Pride must be displaced by self-giving love. The love exemplified supremely by Jesus Christ then supplies resources for psychological health. In the midst of rejection by society, friends, and even family, a person who trusts Christ can be assured of acceptance with God. Overwhelmed by undeserved kindness and truth, he need not seek to prove himself, but contentedly leave the work of salvation to God. Then he finds potential for self-understanding, self-identity, self-acceptance, self-release, and self-investment. Christianity uniquely integrates anxious and estranged lives. For that reason Carnell justifies his acceptance of Christianity's truth-claims.

9. A further defense of Christianity explicated by Dr. Carnell is oriented toward ethics. The argument is that Christianity alone resolves man's moral predicament. The simplest activity discloses our obligation to respect other people. Our responsibility to them means that we are liable to give account of our action in relation to them. Account can be given only to a personal Administrator of justice, i.e., God Himself. Before Him, however, we stand guilty of injustice, inconsideration, and lack of love. But the Bible informs us of Christ's sacrifice, made to justify sinners. God turned away His holy wrath

by this overwhelming act of His love. The repentant sinner is not perfect in action, but by faith stands in a right relation to God through the cross. So the Christian gospel alone shows how a sinful person can be just before God. The biblical message not only has the answer to our individual ethical need, but also to society's urgent social needs. The gospel does more than reeducate, it renews the whole man, vitalizing his awareness of God and neighbor, his sense of morality and duty, and his concerns of love and sanctified compassion.

As each apologist is studied the reader is urged to follow the counsel of the noted English philosopher Bertrand Russell, although he is by no means a Christian apologist. Russell said, "In studying a philosopher, the right attitude is neither reverence nor contempt, but first a kind of hypothetical sympathy, until it is possible to know what it feels like to believe in his theories."[35] Only after such a serious attempt to understand these men has one earned the right to assess the significance of their contributions.

RESOURCES FOR RESEARCH

Blamires, Harry. *A Defense of Dogmatism*. London: SPCK, 1965. Christianity is more than fellowship with a Person, Blamire argues, it is a systematic formulation of truths in propositional form. "Dogmatism" acknowledges biblical revelation by admitting it does have some answers; holds a relation to eternity, not just to a naturalistic "future"; creates no antithesis between faith and reason, scientific investigation, emotion, or religious experience. Because Christianity contains intellectual answers it can be defended by its internal and external consonance with experience.

Boillat, Maurice. "Evangelism and Proselytism." *Christian Heritage* 27 (January 1966) : 12-13, 32.· Although there are certain similarities between the two, evangelism (apologetics) is not proselytism because it is grounded in Scripture, motivated by the glory of God rather than a party, based on personal experience of Jesus Christ, lovingly concerned for the individual and deeply grounded in theology.

Bruce, F. F. *The Defense of the Gospel in the New Testament*. Grand Rapids: Eerdmans, 1959. A New Testament scholar finds that the kerygma must in some degree be apologia. Apologetic is not an in-

---

35. Bertrand Russell, *Dictionary of Mind, Matter and Morals* (New York: Philosophical Libr., 1952), p. 179.

vention of the apostles; they had received it from the Lord. So Christians must refute error and prepare the way for acceptance of truth by removing obstacles, seizing every appropriate point of contact, and showing the richness of truth in Christ.

Christiani, Leon. *Why We Believe.* Trans. by Dom Mark Pontifex. New York: Hawthorne, 1959. An analysis of the history of apologetics from the second century featuring Roman Catholics. Pontiflex concludes, "We do not prove Christianity but we prove its right to our adherence through faith and love."

Clark, Gordon H. "Apologetics." In *Contemporary Evangelical Thought.* Ed. by Carl F. H. Henry. Great Neck, N.Y.: Channel, 1957, pp. 137-61. An evaluative survey of recent evangelical apologetics by an evangelical philosopher.

———. "Apologetics." In *The Encyclopedia of Christianity.* Ed. by Edwin H. Palmer. Vol. 1. Wilmington, Del.: National Foundation for Christian Education, 1964. Two basic types of apologetic systems are found, Thomistic and Augustinian. The only "choice-worthy" philosophy, Clark concludes, is the Augustinian.

DeWolf, L. Harold. *The Religious Revolt Against Reason.* New York: Harper, 1949. A survey of Barthian and existentialist attacks upon a reasoned defense of Christianity, with an answer to them by the author of *The Case for Theology in the Liberal Perspective.*

Frankel, Charles. "The Anti-Intellectualism of the Intellectuals." In *The Love of Anxiety: and other Essays.* New York: Harper and Row, 1965, pp. 12-39. A brilliant answer to arguments of anti-intellectualism, such as: "Reason is an enemy of insight and originality, a method of sub-subduing the individual to the dictatorship of the collective." "The belief in reason is a form of hubris (pride). It encourages a belief in human infallibility and in the infinitude of man's powers." "Reason is analytic, dissective, and discursive. It cuts up the living reality, and puts into words what eludes words," and abstract thought is cold to significant human values.

Gilmore, R. Eugene. "A Reappraisal of Liberal Apologetics." *Religion in Life* 23 (Winter 1962-63) : 369-79. An analysis of liberal apologists from Kant and Schleiermacher to John Baillie with the prediction that the approach will continue beyond the Barthian challenge.

Hazelton, Roger. *New Accents in Contemporary Theology.* New York: Harper, 1960, pp. 115-40. The most noteworthy feature of ancient and modern apologetics is its invitation to non-believers to share the good news as not only good, but true.

Holmes, Arthur. *Christianity and Philosophy*. Chicago: Inter-Varsity,
  1960. A valuable introduction to the relation of Christianity with its
  truth-claims and philosophy to its quest for a comprehensive, clear
  world view.

——. "Philosophy and Religious Beliefs." *Pacific Philosophy Forum* 5,
  (May 1967) : 4-51. Between skepticism and rationalism, Holmes seeks
  a defense of the truth of Christianity on a middle ground. "Christian
  apologetics should be, and in measure has always been, an attempt to
  show the personal disclosure-value of what is believed, but this still
  involves showing how well the hypothesis 'fits' relevant facts, and how
  coherent is the scheme which results."

——. "The Nature of Theistic Apologetics." *Bulletin of the Evangelical
  Theological Society* 2 (Spring 1959) : 1-5. Classifies three types of
  apologetic approaches: (1) dogmatism, (2) scepticism, and (3) criticism (including elements of both previous types).

Lewis, Gordon. "Gospel on Campus." *His* 27 (October-January, 1966-67).
  An exposition of the most extensive biblical example of apologetics to
  Gentiles without common ground in the Old Testament (Ac 17). Implications for contemporary apologetics are drawn from Paul's Athenian
  address.

Machen, J. Gresham. "Christian Scholarship and Defense of the Faith."
  In *What is Christianity? And Other Addresses*. Grand Rapids: Eerdmans, 1951, pp. 126-37. An effective answer to such popular arguments
  against defending the Bible and Christianity as: "The Bible needs no
  defense." "All our differences will disappear if we just pray together."
  "Instead of polemics we need evangelism." "In place of doctrinal controversy we ought to seek the power of the Holy Spirit." "Our preaching should be positive rather than negative."

——. *What is Faith?* Grand Rapids: Eerdmans, 1946. Effectively accomplishes its purpose of showing the indispensability of intellectual truth
  to a genuinely Christian faith. Written prior to the prominence of
  existentialist denials of propositional truth, but still very relevant.

Mavrodes, George, and Hackett, Stuart, eds. *Problems and Perspectives in
  the Philosophy of Religion*. Boston: Allyn and Bacon, 1967, pp. 8-91.
  Part 1, "Reason, Faith and Philosophy," contains important selections
  on the nature of faith and its relation to reason and revelation by
  Aquinas, Clifford, James, Royce, Campbell, Brunner, and Tillich.

Parker, Francis H. "Traditional Reason and Modern Reason." In *Faith
  and Philosophy*. Ed. by Alvin Plantinga. Grand Rapids: Eerdmans,
  1964, pp. 37-50. A philosophical, technical defense of the possibility of
  a proposition being both necessarily true and about real existence. The

inescapable case in point is the law of non-contradiction. "To say that 'the law of non-contradiction does not hold true of objective reality' is to allow that the contradictory of this very proposition itself may also be true." Then it may also be true that the law of non-contradiction does hold true of objective reality.

Pike, Kenneth L. *With Heart and Mind*. Grand Rapids: Eerdmans, 1962. While pointing up the limitations and relativities of a person's logical processes, the professor of linguistics nevertheless maintains "fruitful discourse in science or theology requires us to believe that *within* the contexts of normal discourse *there are some true statements*. Man *must*, sometimes, act as if he believed it—or die."

Ramm, Bernard. *Protestant Christian Evidences*. Chicago: Moody, 1954, pp. 13-44. Defines and relates theology, apologetics, and evidences. Ramm compares his perspective with some other writers in the field.

——. "The Evidence of Prophecy and Miracle." In *Revelation and the Bible*. Ed. by Carl F. H. Henry. Grand Rapids: Baker, 1958, pp. 251-63. One of the clearest statements of the need for evidences and their relation to the witness of the Holy Spirit. "It is the Scripture itself which sets up the structure of Christian evidences, and not, to the contrary, the work of apologists who have imposed a structure upon Scripture." Furthermore, "the prophetic word and the accomplished miracle are part of the Word of God in which the Spirit witnesses."

——. *Varieties of Christian Apologetics*. Rev. ed. Grand Rapids: Baker, 1965, pp. 11-27. Defines apologetics and points up some of the key problems in the field: the relationship between philosophy and Christianity, the question of theistic proofs, the particular theory of truth, the effects of sin upon man's ability to attain religious truth, the character of revelation, the type of certainty possible, common ground between believers and unbelievers, the nature of faith, and the place of Christian evidences.

Rule, Andrew K. "Apologetics." In *Twentieth Century Encyclopedia of Religious Knowledge*. Ed. by Leffoerts A. Loetscher. Grand Rapids: Baker, 1955. A brief account of problems faced by apologists during the first half of the twentieth century.

Rust, Eric. "The Apologetic Task in the Modern Scene." *Review and Expositor* 61 (April 1959) : 178-200. On a point of contact with contemporary men we are challenged by a spectrum of positions from Barth's denial of common ground to Bultmann's capitulation to non-Christian existentialism. In his inaugural address at Southern Baptist Theological Seminary, Rust favors contact at the point of man's poignant sense of alienation.

Trueblood, David Elton. *Philosophy of Religion.* New York: Harper, 1957, pp. 3-76. A valuable discussion of the necessity of reason in religion, its relation to faith, the possibility of truth, the mystery of knowledge, and the nature of evidence.

Warfield, Benjamin Breckinridge. "Apologetics." In *The New Schaff-Herzog Encyclopedia of Religious Knowledge.* Vol. 1, pp. 232-38, or in *Studies in Theology.* New York: Oxford U., 1932, pp. 3-21. Against the "wide-spread inclination" in his day to set aside apologetics in favor of the witness of the Spirit, Warfield says, "Though faith is the gift of God, it does not in the least follow that the faith which God gives is an irrational faith. . . . The action of the Holy Spirit in giving faith is not apart from evidence, but along with evidence; and in the first instance consists in preparing the soul for the reception of the evidence."

Wisdom, John. "Gods." In *Philosophy and Psychoanalysis.* New York: Philosophical Libr., 1953, pp. 149-68. As people consider a garden where among the weeds there are some healthy plants, some believe in an invisible gardener and some do not. This analogy effectively focuses attention on the basic issue of apologetics. What makes the difference tween believers in God and unbelievers?

Wolsterstorff, Nicholas P. "Faith and Philosophy." In *Faith and Philosophy.* Ed. by Alvin Plantinga. Grand Rapids: Eerdmans, 1964. Contemporary philosophy, while less systematic and speculative than traditional philosophy, is no less synoptic. In seeking the meaning and "hang" of things the philosopher gets a "vision" of the whole structure of men's thoughts. Such perspectives are held to be less a matter of argument than of truth-claims as to what can be or cannot be. The role of apologetics is minimized in the adoption of world views.

2

THE PURE EMPIRICISM OF
J. OLIVER BUSWELL, JR.

The Test of Objective Evidence

The best known and most readily understood reply to questions about Christianity's truth is, "Look at the evidence!" The source of truth, not only in science, but also in religion, is experience. No true ideas are innately present in the mind from birth. And truth cannot be invented by the mind without the data of experience. This theory of knowledge opposes any rationalism which thinks the mind can derive truth independently of experience. Since "experience" comes from the Latin *experientia,* and that in turn from the Greek *empeiria,* this view is called empiricism.

Empirical theories of knowledge follow the distinguished tradition of the Greek philosopher, Aristotle. In that tradition Thomas Aquinas, the thirteenth century Roman Catholic thinker, proposed five experientially based arguments for the existence of God. And ever since, empirical apologies have had competent spokesmen and critics. Among the capable evangelicals setting forth an empirical apologetic is J. Oliver Buswell, Jr., Dean Emeritus of Covenant Theological Seminary, St. Louis, Missouri. With earned degrees from McCormick Theological Seminary and the Universities of Minnesota, Chicago, and New York, Buswell has taught philosophy and theology since 1926 and has been president of Wheaton College (Illinois) and Shelton College. A chaplain during the Meuse-Argonne drive in World War I, Buswell saw his regiment reduced in four days from 3200 men to 623 not killed or wounded. Ministering to the casualties with shell holes in his canteen and the canister of his gas mask, Buswell prayed, "Lord, if you want me to go home and be a gospel preacher, you'll have to look after those bullets." He was convinced that "God answered a young chaplain's prayer that day." This, and similar personal experiences related in a *His* magazine article, "Why I Believe in God," undoubtedly contributed to his empirical perspective.[1]

No Unexamined Presuppositions

Not even the most ardent contemporary empiricist can be unaware of the fact that men do not think in a vacuum; all thought begins with presuppositions. Dr. Buswell, as an empiricist, however, is not willing even to exempt presuppositions from experiential confirmation. As he puts it, "There is nothing in our assumptions as Christian students of theology, which we are not willing to examine and for which we are not ready to state our reasons." The presupposition of one argument may be the conclusion of another. So he says, "Our presuppositions are not dogmatically stated in a 'take it or leave it' attitude. They are convictions, conclusions, at which we have arrived, conclusions of the utmost importance."[2]

To avoid ambiguity, the Christian's presupposition is not just "Jesus Christ," but "Jesus Christ as the Second Person of the sovereign Triune Godhead, as presented in the Bible, His infallible Word."[3] In support of this presupposition, however, Dr. Buswell appeals to evidence considered as cogent for unbelievers as for believers. In contrast, others (Clark and Van Til) claim that Christian presuppositions can be supported by no evidence whatsoever since they are the beginning of every meaningful appeal to truth. Still others (Hackett and Hamilton) hold that the basic principles of reasoning are inherent to the mind and not the probable conclusion of observation. For Dr. Buswell, however, no logical or Christian presuppositions are innate or self-attesting. Like the noted empiricist John Locke, Dr. Buswell holds that the mind prior to impressions made upon it by sense perception is a blank tablet (*tabula rasa*). All ideas arise by reflection upon experience. We do not reason from

1. J. Oliver Buswell, Jr., "Why I Believe in God" *His* 18 (October 1957): 3-5.
2. J. Oliver Buswell, Jr., *A Systematic Theology of the Christian Religion*, vol. 1 (Grand Rapids: Zondervan, 1962), p. 19.
3. Ibid., p. 15.

innate generalities to particulars (deductively), but from particulars experienced toward general conclusions (inductively).[4] And "learning as such is not merely a matter of educational psychology. The content of learning is objective. It lies in the world of material and spiritual substantive entities and relationships."[5] Summing up Buswell's position so far, all knowledge is objective, all knowledge begins with sensory experience, the mind has no innate principles of reasoning, and Christianity has no presuppositions which can be called self-authenticating. So Buswell is a pure empiricist. For him *all* knowledge is rooted in experience *alone*. His apologetic for Christianity, therefore, is derived from experience.

TESTING TRUTH-CLAIMS

All knowledge of truth is inferred from experiential facts. No extended definition of fact is found in Buswell's works, but as synonyms he utilizes such terms as data, evidence, and reasonable evidence open to public investigation. Further explication of Buswell's concept of facts may be seen from the examples to which he appeals in his evidences for the existence of God and the validity of the laws of logic. Factual data is not only reported by the five senses. Buswell's "experience" includes as well, personality, morality, and an idea of God. It is sufficient here to note that his view of fact includes all that is given in human experience whether through sense data or not.

Knowledge on our part requires the drawing of inferences from that which experience presents to us. Contrary to existentialist theories, the mere presentation experientially is not knowledge. That is only the raw material of knowledge. Truth is obtained only as we infer from experienced effects to their causes. By reasoning to causes of our experience, our knowledge is not limited to mere descriptions of happenings. Buswell is not a phenomenalist satisfied only to describe the way things appear to the involved. He is a realist, claiming to know what actually lies behind these experiences. All his knowledge of these underlying realities, however, is inferential. In this life we have no direct encounters with things in themselves, not even with God in the sense of the beatific vision (unmediated, "face-to-face" meeting, as in heaven). We know all things by inference: material

4. J. Oliver Buswell, Jr., *A Christian View of Being and Knowing* (Grand Rapids: Zondervan, 1960), p. 168.
5. Ibid., p. 166.

things-in-themselves by inference from their effects, and minds-in-themselves by inference from their effects. Buswell even denies any direct intuition of his own mind-as-such. He argues for the existence of his own mind as the cause of his experienced purposive activity.[6] Similarly, he knows God by inference from his effects as experienced by men in the world.

Reasoning inductively, as Buswell views it, we take three steps. First, we observe the facts. Second, we reason from these facts as effects to their causes. Third, we draw our conclusions concerning the causes with more or less probability.[7] Basic, then, to all reasoning is an accurate interpretation of the facts given in experience, and the validity of the causal principle. If causality became vulnerable, the whole Buswellian form of reasoning would collapse. And with that would go his defense of Christianity's truth. Disturbing to many as well is the impossibility of certainty. At best, he can only determine the truth of proposed propositions to a degree of probability.

TRUE CONCLUSIONS NOT CERTAIN, BUT HIGHLY PROBABLE

"There is no argument known to us which, as an argument, leads to more than a probable (highly probable) conclusion."[8] Even such an assured conclusion that the sun will rise tomorrow, when examined, turns out to be merely probable. Buswell seeks to show that the five "demonstrations" of God's existence formulated by Thomas Aquinas, contrary to frequent misinterpretation, were not intended to be logically necessary, but empirically probable.[9] That being so, Kant's case against apodictic certainty in Aquinas falls short of the mark. And Soren Kierkegaard's repudiation of mere probability as a guide to faith, Buswell dismisses as unworthy of an answer. "The theistic arguments are no exception to the rule that *all* inductive arguments about what exists are probability arguments. This is as far as arguments, *qua* arguments, claim to go."[10]

How, then, does Buswell correlate the probability of his defense of Christianity with the certainty disclosed in affirmations of Christian faith? As a Calvinist he teaches that the Holy Spirit convicts of sin

---

6. Ibid., pp. 145-46.
7. Buswell, *Systematic Theology*, p. 72.
8. Ibid.
9. Ibid., pp. 75-77.
10. Ibid., p. 72.

and gives faith as a gift, effectually bringing sin-blinded men to Christ. What, then, is the value of probable arguments? He answers, "According to the Bible, and according to Christian experience, we know that the Holy Spirit is pleased to use the arguments in the process of producing conviction and conversion. The arguments in themselves never regenerated anyone but they have been instrumental in the process of evangelism, and this is all that is rightfully claimed for them."[11]

THE LAWS OF LOGIC

The priority given to inductive reasoning in Buswell's thought does not exclude a place for deducing truth by logical inferences as well. The laws of logic, he claims, are not a priori assumptions, but, like all other knowledge, inferred from experience. Before considering the alleged inductive source of the three traditional laws, however, they need to be stated. (1) In a given context a proposition has a single meaning (the law of identity). (2) That meaning is either true or false (the law of opposites). (3) And two such propositions cannot both be true if they affirm and deny the same thing at the same time and in the same respect (the law of non-contradiction).

Although many others claim these laws of thought are necessary and therefore a priori, or innate, Buswell regards them as inductions from experience. Why? The evidence open to public observation from which he infers them is threefold. First, he argues, without them all discourse is at an end. Second, the ensuing confusion would make it impossible for a person to live long on the earth. Third, for those who think Christianity is true, the Bible "explicitly conveys and verifies the laws of reason."[12] From observations such as these Buswell infers the high probability of the three laws of thought. But they are merely empty possibilities of meaningful prediction until filled with the content of specific experiences. Armed with three laws of logic and an empirical method, Dr. Buswell begins his defense of Christianity.

THE APOLOGIST'S STARTING POINT

Since a defense of Christianity need not begin with a particular

11. Ibid., pp. 73-74.
12. Ibid., pp. 20-22.

presupposition, it can begin anywhere. All truth being consistent, a denial of one Christian teaching leads to the denial of others. "Conversely, the establishment of any major part of the Christian system of doctrine leads logically to the establishment of every other part." So the question is not, "where must we necessarily begin by force of logic," but, "where is it practical to begin?"[13] We could begin by supporting the truth-claims regarding Christ, the Bible, conversion, or God. But wherever we begin, we must look at the relevant evidence.

And when subsequent truth-claims are considered, we cannot infer an answer logically from the earlier conclusions, but must look at the evidence again. The system of Buswell's systematic theology is not derived deductively, but inductively. It is not the logically necessary system of a rationalist, independent of experience. One element of the Christian system, although consistent with other elements as an end result, is not necessarily deduced from the others. Reality, as the Christian sees it, is the product of God's acts, not out of rational necessity, but out of free grace. If gracious acts are necessitated, they are no longer gratuitous. "Although the truth never contradicts itself, and never is *ir*rational, there are many truths about existing things which are *non*-rational, that is, not caused by reason."[14] It seemed fitting to Dr. Buswell, apparently for practical reasons, to start with the question of God's existence.

EVIDENCE FOR GOD'S EXISTENCE FROM THE WORLD'S EXISTENCE

Dr. Buswell begins his version of the cosmological argument with three succinct statements:

1. If something exists,
2. something must be eternal, unless
3. something comes from nothing.[15]

That something exists is so obvious to the realist that Buswell does not stop to defend it. But he takes seriously hypothesis (3) that something can come from nothing because of emergent evolutionary theories. His answer points up the total lack of evidence for the supposition that something can come from nothing. "We observe personal

13. Ibid., p. 26.
14. Buswell, *Being and Knowing*, p. 23.
15. Buswell, *Systematic Theology*, p. 82.

causation every day of our lives," he notes, "but the uncaused emergence of any substantive entity has never yet been observed. All the data of experience run to the contrary."[16] So he holds that nothing is uncaused by something else.

If no evidence justifies thinking that something comes from nothing (3), then something must be eternal (2). Is it the world? Evidence, Buswell finds, does not support the eternal existence of the universe, but its beginning in the finite past. The greater probability of the universe having a beginning is supported by the observed rate of disintegration of radioactive minerals, the consumption of hydrogen in the sun (the major source of the world's energy), and the second law of thermodynamics. "It is characteristic of all observable physical processes," as Buswell explains the second law of thermodynamics, "that some energy becomes less available than it was before the particular process began." These considerations, accepted by many scientific authorities, make it more probable than not that the universe had a beginning.

Since the physical universe began in the finite past, it must have come from something eternal. But what? Not physical processes. They are not eternal; they fizzle out. The only other causal agency we know is a will. Was it then a blind will (Schopenhauer) or an unconscious intelligence? In view of our experience this seems inconceivable. "Whenever we observe an unconscious action which is nevertheless intelligent, we postulate a previous intelligence as the cause of it." The conclusion then follows:

> Blind or unconscious intelligence is a far less reasonable postulate than conscious personal intelligence. We know from daily experience what personal intelligence is and does. It is simple and reasonable to believe that eternal personal intelligence is the explanation of the universe. It is unreasonable to believe in any other theory.[17]

Evaluation will be reserved until all the arguments are set forth.

EVIDENCE FOR GOD'S WISDOM FROM THE WORLD'S ORDER

The universe does not simply exist without form and void. It is not a chaos, but a cosmos. The observed purposive order of the uni-

16. Ibid.
17. Ibid., p. 85.

verse is an effect requiring a cause. The most probable cause of
teleology is an intelligent Purposer.

Is it the case that the universe is ordered? Traditionally, instances
of teleology have been cited from details of the eye, and the snow-
flake. Preoccupation with such detailed instances in Buswell's judgment is awkward. With F. R. Tennant, Buswell prefers to rest the
experiential case on the adaptation of the entire universe to the purpose of life. In his book on *The Philosophies of F. R. Tennant and
John Dewey*, Buswell illustrates the difference of emphasis from the
child's view of a kaleidoscope and a mature person's. "Oldsters do not
see the wonder in the individual symmetrical patterns as children do,
although the patterns are indeed beautiful. What they admire is the
cleverness which designed the arrangement of the three mirrors, each
one facing the other two, so that whatever the shapes and arrange-
ments of the odd bits of brightly colored glass, a perfect hexagonal
pattern results."[18] Similarly we admire the beauty of snow crystals,
not so much for their unlimited individual patterns, but for the entire process by which the deeply aerated blanket of snow preserves
life by covering the land and lakes of the temperate zone.

The most important reason for stressing cosmic teleology is its answer to non-theistic evolutionary theories of adaptation. The reason
animals had such intricate eyes was not divine design, but biological
adaptation of the organism to its environment. Only those organisms
which naturalistically developed sight survived. So the organic illustrations of teleology seemed to become evidences of naturalistic evolution. Tennant significantly showed that the inorganic environment is
as plainly adapted to life as living creatures are to their environment.
If indeed there are such inorganic evidences of teleology, no un-
planned evolutionary adaptation is as probable an explanation as
Mind.

The earth's fitness for life does depend upon numerous conditions,
astronomical, thermal, and chemical. A popular presentation of the
case by A. Cressy Morrison may be found in his book entitled *Man
Does Not Stand Alone*.[19] The scientist specifies the speed of the
earth's rotation, the amount of heat received from the sun, the speed
of the earth in travelling around the sun, the size of the sun, the

18. J. Oliver Buswell, Jr., *The Philosophies of F. R. Tennant and John Dewey* (New
York: Philosophical Libr., 1950), pp. 205-6.
19. See A. Cressy Morrison, *Man Does Not Stand Alone* (New York: Revell, 1944).

degree of tilt of the earth's axis, the size of the moon, its distance from the earth, the density of the atmosphere, proper amounts of atmospheric pressure, proper percentages of nitrogen (78%) and oxygen (21%) in the atmosphere, the balance of oxygen and carbon dioxide sustained by the functions of plant and animal life, the amount of water on the earth's surface, its evaporation rate, weight frozen, etc. These are but a few of the many intricate conditions necessary for life on our planet. The probability of all happening on the same planet by irrational chance is infinitesimally small. It is not that we can toss out universes like dice to determine mathematical probability. Tennant explains that the kind of probability the teleologist has in mind is not a mathematical or logical relation, but "the alogical probability which is the guide of life and which has been found to be the ultimate basis of all scientific induction."[20] Dr. Buswell adds that "it is reasonable to conclude from the nature of the Parthenon that it was constructed by rather clever architects!

The greatest problem for teleology is the presence on earth of extensive evil. Both moral evil (responsible sin of creatures) and natural evil (natural events such as floods, hurricanes, and earthquakes) may be traced ultimately to the creature's sin. God is not the author of evil. Sin came about through the voluntary self-corruption of the creature. God endures it in order to bring to actuality His power of judgment and redemption. Realization of these divine values makes the present world immeasurably richer than one in which the abstract possibility of evil had not been allowed to become an actuality. Natural evils may not contribute to our comfort, but are morally good for our souls.[21]

In addition to encompassing evil in a cosmic teleology, Buswell adduces the broad pattern of historical purposiveness related to Jesus Christ. One or two remarkable events might be coincidences. But the centuries of anticipation and preparation for Christ's coming and the establishment of the church which continues to this day indicate an overarching purpose achieving certain ends. Combining the observable effects of Jesus in history with cosmic teleology, Buswell thinks, produces a high degree of probability for the existence of the God of the Bible.

20. Buswell, *Tennant and Dewey*, pp. 201-2.
21. Buswell, *Systematic Theology*, pp. 62, 89.

EVIDENCE FOR PERSONAL QUALITIES IN GOD
FROM PERSONAL QUALITIES IN MAN

Separated from the animals by a bio-cultural gap, man has a unique kind of existence. Granting that animals have a kind of intelligence, man has powers of discursive reasoning, of adapting means to ends, and of moral and spiritual consciousness. Man's unique consciousness is an effect which requires an adequate cause. The cause of man's existence in a purposive cosmos is not likely unconscious, unintelligent, impersonal, and incapable of purposive action. Far more probably, the cause of human existence is a conscious, intelligent, purposeful, personal Being.[22]

EVIDENCE FOR GOD'S MORALITY FROM MAN'S MORALITY

From the cosmos and its order we have moved to man and his experience of moral obligation. The ethical ought is a datum of experience. What is its basis? Highly improbable is the supposition that it may be caused by a non-moral source. All explanations leaving out Christian theism, Buswell says, are contradictory. The only non-contradictory and highly probable cause of an incurably moral creature is a moral Creator.

EVIDENCE FOR GOD'S EXISTENCE AS THE CAUSE OF MAN'S
IDEA OF GOD

In typical empirical style, Buswell denies the validity of the ontological argument for God's existence. No sound argument can proceed from an idea to an existing thing independent of experience. Abstract reason cannot establish the existence of God even by defining God as a necessarily existing Being. "To say that God does not exist is a falsehood, but it is not a self-contradiction. The existence of God is a fact of which we have good and sufficient evidence in His works, but to base His existence upon the abstract laws of logic is an error."[23]

Nevertheless, Buswell finds in the writings of René Descartes a neglected inductive argument for the existence of God. The argument moves from our idea of God to its cause. The datum of experience with which the argument begins is the presence in man's mind of the idea of God. What is its most probable cause? The Greek gods

22. Ibid., p. 91.
23. Ibid., p. 40.

and goddesses were made up from human experiences and characteristics. Dragons had parts of the lion, the serpent, and the eagle. A centaur was a flying horse. But no combination of contingent beings could produce the idea of a necessarily existing Being, incorporeal, omnipresent, omniscient, and omnipotent. Such characteristics are inconceivable as a composite of human experiences.[24] Literary criticism recognizes that all ideas have sources. The most probable source of the biblical idea of God is God Himself. No other cause adequately accounts for the idea of God which men possess.

Combining the evidence of the universe and its order with man's consciousness, morality, and idea of God, Buswell considers his case "as good as inductive arguments can be." They are not mathematical propositions and therefore are not demonstrations. But as existential propositions they hold a high degree of probability. Buswell says, "I must give my testimony that, considering these arguments with all the available evidence, I am more sure of the existence of God, the God of the Bible, than I am of tomorrow morning's sunrise."[25] The sufficiency of this evidence places upon us a moral responsibility.[26] Those who turn away from the evidence do so willfully and culpably. Before God, Buswell holds, they are morally reprehensible and without excuse.

IS THIS THE GOD OF THE BIBLE?

Criticisms of the theistic arguments have been many. One of the most frequent from recent theologians charges that if valid, the arguments support an abstract philosophical notion of Being, rather than the living God of Abraham, Isaac, and Jacob. Buswell explains that as he speaks of the category of being, it is essentially a category of other categories. To assert that something is, is to assert being of some other category. There is no such thing as a category of pure being without any attributes. Whether the verb "to be" is used as a copula or a predicate, it connects the subject with some category other than being.[27] So to conclude that God is, is not merely to conclude that there is being as such, or a ground of being. Buswell has shown that the Being which exists eternally as the cause of the universe is

24. Ibid., p. 99.
25. Ibid., p. 81.
26. Ibid., p. 100.
27. Buswell, *Being and Knowing*, pp. 63-64.

intelligent, purposive, conscious, and moral. In Buswell's judgment, such a Being is clearly the same as the Creator of the Bible. The theistic arguments are not intended to tell everything about God, but what they show, if valid, is not inconsistent with the God of Christianity. Buswell adequately defends himself at this point.

INTERPRETATION OF THEOLOGICAL LANGUAGE

Of course the identification of the God of inductive reasoning and the God of scriptural revelation depends on the interpretation of language attributing characteristics to God. We may understand statements such as "God is moral" and "man is moral" to be: (1) equivocal, (2) analogical, or (3) univocal. If equivocal, "moral" means one thing for man and something totally other than that for God. There is no meaning in common; the similarity of wording actually is deceptive. According to equivocal interpretation, to claim that "God is moral" is to claim nothing. We have no idea what "moral" could mean for God. God is totally unknown. In complete contrast, if "God is moral" is understood univocally, "moral" means the same thing for God as for man. To speak univocally is to speak with "one voice" (meaning) of both God and man. The third interpretation takes "God is moral" to be neither totally different, nor totally the same, but analogical, or proportional.

Buswell, who is Thomistic in many respects, rejects Aquinas' exclusively analogical use of religious language. Admittedly analogies may be used of God and are employed in Scripture. Even then, however, they have a univocal point, or else communication fails. Buswell says, "the univocal meaning of our analogies is transparent, or else we ought to express ourselves differently."[28] When the Bible reports that God is a consuming fire, the analogy is chosen because of a common factor. Metals are purified by fire; men are purified by divine judgment. Removal of impurities is the analogy's univocal point.

Not all the Bible's references to God are figurative. Some are literal. For example, Buswell says, "For God to *be* is, to be what He is, and the word 'to be' has precisely the same univocal meaning in reference to the creature, namely, to be whatever it is." When we say that God may be called good, "the word 'good' is then univocally used, if we but recognize that the word applied to any person or object means

28. Buswell, *Systematic Theology*, p. 29, note.

'good' as being what he or it is."[29] What do we mean by asserting that man is a personal being and that God is a personal being? "From the biblical point of view, a personal being is one who is capable of self-consciousness and self-determination."[30] That is true of both God and man. What is univocal for man is univocal for God as well. "Otherwise to claim that we accept the Bible as the Word of God for us is a mere mockery."[31]

CRITICISM OF CAUSALITY

Objections arise not only to the interpretation of the theistic arguments, but to their validity. Many criticisms are of little significance. However, we must examine one of the most devastating. All the inductive arguments for God's existence depend upon the validity of reasoning from effects to their causes. If causal inferences should be found invalid, Buswell's apologetic would completely collapse. And a major segment of thought since Immanuel Kant has questioned the possibility of reasoning from phenomenal "effects" to metaphysically real things-in-themselves as causes. In the realm of human experience every effect may require an adequate cause. But we have no way of knowing whether that is the case in reality itself, independent of human experience. So many would doubt the validity of causal arguments for underlying, metaphysical causes. And many others under the influence of David Hume deny any necessary connection between alleged causes and effects. So we can never reason apart from observation of conjoined events. Certain events may succeed others in time and be contiguous in space, but no sense impression reports a necessary connection between them. So Hume thought the law of causality a fabrication read into nature. If that is the case, Buswell's apologetic collapses. Has he an answer?

Following John Locke, Charles Hodge, and F. R. Tennant, Buswell regards the law of cause and effect a product of experience. Experience attests a psychological causation. It is an immediate datum that "we have effective ability to form purposes and effective ability, at least in our minds, to carry them out."[32] Experience requires us to

29. Ibid.
30. Ibid., p. 33.
31. Ibid., p. 39.
32. Buswell, *Being and Knowing*, p. 149.

admit a psychological causation because we are immediately conscious of selecting goals and putting them into action.

Experience also supports a mechanical causation. Matter and force are in a constant interplay of causal relationships. Heisenberg's principle of indeterminacy indicates only that we cannot predict detailed behavior of the electron in its orbit with our present instruments. That may be corrected in the future. Even now, however, we can predict with a remarkable degree of accuracy the behavior of atoms in the macroscopic aggregate.[33]

Furthermore, we experience the interplay of personal and mechanistic causes. The interaction may be of either upon the other. When someone chooses to accelerate his automobile, he does not add to its power, but simply releases its power. The interaction is simply a kind of trigger action. Pressing a gun's trigger in no way interrupts the system of natural causation, it simply engages it. "It is a fact, one of the commonest of elementary immediate intuitive experiences, that conscious purpose releases mechanical energy stored up in the muscles and produces changes in the material world."[34] On the other hand physical conditions cause certain psychological effects. All the evidence for psychosomatic illness supports this point. So the body causes effects on the mind, and the mind upon the body. The law of causality is a highly probable induction from experience mentally and physically.

At best Buswell has shown that effects probably have causes. So his theistic arguments ought not to include a premise implying that effects *must* of necessity have adequate causes. The most he can say is that experience to this point has shown that events of all types have had causes, so it is probable that these do. Although his premises are not always so qualified, Buswell claims no more than probability for his conclusions. In that respect he is consistent.

Summing up, if Buswell's observations of experience are sound, and if causality is probable, the theistic cause is probable. Christianity's truth-claim concerning God is most probably true in view of the objective evidence. Is not one to accept Christianity by faith, rather than by painstaking empirical investigation? What places does Buswell give to faith?

33. Ibid., pp. 147-48.
34. Ibid., p. 159.

TRUTH AND FAITH

Dr. Buswell distinguishes an objective and a subjective side to faith. Faith includes what we believe and the act of believing. The two aspects are indispensable. So faith is defined as "the wholehearted acceptance of conclusions for which there is good and sufficient evidence."[35] Because evidence must be respected, "the first step (logical) in any knowledge process must be *faith in reason.*"[36] Faith is indispensable to intuitive experiences for we select what we see and what we hear. We choose what we experience. The selectivity of attention, however habitual and unconscious, shows the place of volitional factors in intuitive experiences. And these in turn determine to a great extent the entire learning process.

Just as fully, volition depends upon the intellect. If we were free to accept or reject as we wished, we might as well believe anything. But with everyone creating his own universe to his own liking, no study of any field would matter. For Buswell subjectivism is impossible. "Ontological truth is there to be discovered whether we discover it or not. . . . If the world is real, and if the so-called laws of reason are true, it would follow that experience of reality would lead to larger and larger integration as experience increases."[37] Erroneous opinions, on the other hand, would not correspond with reality and so would frustrate because providing less integration.

The test of truth, as Buswell sees it, is just such an integration of consistent, verified ideas with life. The acid test of truth is not the mere coherence or consistency of ideas which seem to Buswell synonymous, and reliable as criteria only if taken in a purely negative sense. Taken positively coherence and consistency may characterize theories which later prove to be absurdities. And the correspondence of ideas with the ontological situation as evidenced through an experimental process is also of merely negative value when properly employed. For these reasons Buswell prefers a test of truth which he calls integration. By integration he means that

> the truth will not only be consistent and coherent, and propositions will not only correspond to the results of verification, but truths

35. Ibid., p. 194.
36. Ibid., p. 198.
37. Ibid., p. 197.

when ascertained will be found to work together and supplement one
another in an integrated system as a whole.[38]

Does Christianity's truth-claim concerning God meet Buswell's test
of integration? Christianity claims that the God of the Bible exists.
That claim is not inconsistent or incoherent, it is not rendered untrue by any lack of correspondence with observed data. It corresponds
with verified data in the ordered cosmos and man's moral and intellectual life, and the principle that all such effects most probably have
adequate causes. Acceptance of that theistic claim supplemented with
other Christian claims leads to an integrated view of the world which
works out in an integrated life.

While many say it takes a special kind of faith to accept the Christian theistic truth-claim, Buswell says acceptance of this religious
truth-claim is no different from acceptance of scientific truth-claims.

> Religious cognitive belief requires neither a greater degree nor a
> different kind of faith. Perhaps the reason religious cognition seems
> to have these greater and different requirements of faith, is that a
> change of religious belief, *aside from the cognitive element,* also
> requires a renovation and reorientation of personal nature and
> ethical alignments and loyalties, familiarly called "the new birth."[39]

The Credibility of the Bible as History

Christianity makes truth-claims not only about God, but also about
Christ and the Bible. Dr. Buswell's works defending Christ's deity
and the Bible's truth are out of print. So a more recent work stressing
empirical evidence may be employed. Dr. John H. Gerstner of Pitts-
burgh Theological Seminary, in his *Reasons for Faith,* defends the
existence of God in much the same way as Buswell. His evidences for
the deity of Christ and the truth of the Bible round out the empirical
approach for purposes of this chapter.

In working with a non-Christian who accepts the existence of God,
should we first seek to establish the truth of the Bible or to defend
Christ's deity? Gerstner's approach first defends the Bible's truth as
nothing more than a good history book. From the historical data
about Christ he defends the Lord's supernaturalness. Then on Christ's
authority he establishes the claim that the Bible is God's inspired

38. Ibid., p. 193.
39. Buswell, *Tennant and Dewey,* p. 118.

word. Space will not allow detailing all his evidence; we can only indicate its nature and the structure of his argument.

Gerstner's case does not begin with a defense of the Bible's divine origin. "Rather, we begin with the Bible without assuming its inspiration. This is the very point in question, and we do not beg it at the outset. We begin with the Bible, not as inspired, but merely as a trustworthy document historically speaking."[40] The Bible's historical credibility is supported by archeological discovery and historical criticism. The Bible purports to give historical accounts of events taking place during many centuries in the ancient world. Some of this history can be put to the acid test by scientific study of ancient ruins and writings. Archeology cannot support the Bible's claim to be *redemptive* history, but it can support its claim to be accurate *history*. If it could be determined that Jesus never lived, Christian claims would be discredited. Furthermore, if His resurrection could be shown not to have taken place, then the salvation based on it would be dismissed.

Gerstner relies heavily upon the work of distinguished archeologist William Foxwell Albright in documenting confirmation of names and customs from the patriarchal age, the conquest of Canaan, Solomon's seaport at Ezion-geber, the highly developed copper mines near Ezion-geber, fourteenth century Canaanite poetic forms and stylistic devices in the Psalms, conclusive proof that the Chaldean conquest was accompanied by a thorough devastation of the country, and other facts. Gerstner concludes, "The Bible has not only 'come alive,' but it has come with a new ring of historical authenticity." And that conclusion is supported by Yale University's archeologist, Millar Burrows. He is quoted as saying, "On the whole . . . archeological work has unquestionably strengthened confidence in the reliability of the Scriptural record. More than one archeologist has found his respect for the Bible increased by the experience of excavation in Palestine."[41]

Historical and literary criticism has also tested the accuracy of biblical narratives. The Bible has been the most studied book in the world, the New Testament more than the Old, and the synoptic gospels most of all. "So we may say that the historical life of Jesus has been the most studied single topic in the history of research." And

---

40. John H. Gerstner, *Reasons for Faith* (New York: Harper, 1960), pp. 85-86.
41. Ibid., pp. 116-24.

what has been the result? "Out of the mass of critical studies by conservative, liberal, and radical scholars, there has come an overwhelming consensus that the Synoptic records give us the most authentic ancient history in the world. . . . They leave no doubt that we have an essentially accurate account of His (Christ's) life on earth." In examining the evidence, then, "we know there was such a person as Jesus and that He said and did essentially the things attributed to Him."[42]

THE DEITY OF CHRIST

Having supported the historical credibility of the Bible, Dr. Gerstner attempts to put himself in the position of one who first learned about Jesus of Nazareth. His response is like that of the majority. Christ was "the ideal, the perfect man, the moral paragon of the race." Aware of varied judgments like George Bernard Shaw's statement that there was a time when Christ was not a Christian, Gerstner insists, "the overwhelming testimony of the world is to the perfection, the incomparable perfection, of Jesus of Nazareth."[43]

The exemplar of integrity, however, claimed to be God! If we admit His honesty, we must admit His deity! If we do not worship Him as God, we must despise or pity Him as a man. Imagine any other noble individual making the claims Jesus did! Exactly what did Jesus say of Himself? He said, "I and the Father are one"; "no man cometh unto the Father but by me"; "he that hath seen me hath seen the Father"; "before Abraham was I am"; "all authority is given unto me in heaven and earth"; "lo, I am with you alway." While the world was moved by Christ's claims, few have done more than smile at such statements from the lips of Father Divine. These are by no means characteristic claims for great religious leaders. No such claims were made by Moses, Paul, Muhammad, Buddha, Confucius, or Zoroaster. Jesus of Nazareth alone claimed to be God.

Christ's amazing claims were not made only upon rare occasions; He constantly assumed them. From the Sermon on the Mount Gerstner shows six indications of Christ's underlying claims. In the Beatitudes Jesus declared authoritatively who would and who would not inherit the kingdom of heaven. The prophets were persecuted, He

42. Ibid., p. 86.
43. Ibid., p. 81.

said, "for my sake." Over against Pharisaic interpretation and addition to the law, He declared, "but I say unto you." In the last judgment some will hear Him say, "depart from me; I never knew you."
To build, not on sand, but on solid rock, He claimed, was to build on
His teaching. Add the people's response, "He spoke as one having
authority, and not as the scribes."[44]

Christ's countemporaries included some who scoffed, but remarkably, some who believed. A monotheistic Israelite like Peter said,
"Thou art the Christ, the son of the living God." And cautious
Thomas finally confronted by the risen Christ cried out, "My Lord
and my God." Christ's claims were supported convincingly not only
by His unassailable character, but by the miracles He performed.

Exactly what do the miracles show? Gerstner's specific thesis is that
"miracles as such do not prove Jesus to be the Son of God; this power
could have been given to Him as a mere man. But indirectly they
prove Him to be the Son of God because they prove Him to be a
truthful messenger, and this truthful messenger says that He is
God."[45] Hume's objections to the occurrence of miracles because of
greater testimony to nature's regularity are answered. The regularity
of natural laws is presumed as a backdrop against which to perceive
the extraordinary. The credibility of miracles, it is argued, is neither
improved nor worsened by the unpredictability of events in nature.

The case for miracles rests squarely on the testimony of early Christians. Unquestionably the early church believed in miracles. The
issue focuses upon the validity of this belief. Could the apostles'
character be trusted? Was their intelligence such that it could be
deluded? Neither their character nor intelligence were corrupted,
Gerstner finds, by other-worldly interests, sentimentalism, or fraud,
however pious. The apostles were honest, their claims unchallenged
by their contemporaries, and they themselves were converts from
Judaism. The miracles, furthermore, are of a piece with the character
of Christ Himself—"benign, instructive, redemptive."[46] Christ Himself invited examination of them. And they coincide with Old Testament prophecies of the Messiah and belief in God's reality. As such
the miracles are a divine "sign" confirming Christ's claims and so His
deity.

44. Ibid., p. 83.
45. Ibid., p. 104.
46. Ibid., p. 99.

THE BIBLE AS THE INSPIRED WORD OF GOD

Two major elements of Gerstner's apologetic have been established to a conclusive degree of probability: the historicity of the Bible and the deity of Christ. His third step then appeals to Christ's authority in establishing the Bible's truth as God's inspired Word. Granting Christ's unique knowledge and authority as God manifest in human flesh, what did He teach about the Bible? He said He did not destroy the Old Testament but fulfilled it and that it could not be destroyed until all was fulfilled (Mt 5:17-18). He said the Scripture could not be broken (Jn 10:35). And repeatedly He claimed that all that was written must be fulfilled (e.g., Mt 26:24). "The evidence that Christ did regard the Old Testament Scripture as inspired is so pervasive that it is seldom contested today even by those who themselves do not accept this inspiration but think that Jesus was mistaken, a victim of the 'errors' of his day."[47]

Did Jesus in any way endorse the New Testament which was not yet written? He prepared the disciples for further revelation which they could not receive at the time (Jn 14:26; 15:26; 16:12-13). The apostles, like the prophets, were accredited spokesmen for God. Miracle-working apostles wrote or attested the entire New Testament. "We may say, therefore, that the New Testament was written by the authorized and supernaturally endowed representatives of Christ or their appointees. And consequently it carries the same imprimatur as the Old Testament: Jesus Christ."[48] So the whole Bible has the imprimatur of the living Word, who has infallible authority.

The Bible's truth is confirmed further by the fulfillment of its predictions. Scriptural predictions differ from ordinary sensitivity to the future and Sibylline oracles in that they were not tentative or vague. They had a high degree of specificity, and the prophets themselves claimed divine enlightenment. In parallel columns Gerstner lists predictions and fulfillments. Tyre would be destroyed and never rebuilt. Sidon would be devastated by the Persians, but continue as a city. Egypt would be debased as a weak kingdom, the Jews dispersed throughout the world, and persecuted, yet preserved. Prophecies about the Messiah included His coming as the seed of Eve, Abraham, and David, His birth in Bethlehem, His ministry to others, His ride

47. Ibid., p. 87.
48. Ibid., p. 88.

into Jerusalem as King, His death, burial, and resurrection. The probability that all these predictions came to pass by chance is infinitesimal. Far more probable is the conclusion that omniscience was the cause.

The basic truth-claims of Christianity are established in the opinion of Buswell and Gerstner: the existence of the God of the Bible, the essential truth of the Bible's history, the Deity of Jesus, and the truth of the Bible as God's inspired Word. All of these conclusions are far more probable than their contradictories, in terms of the observable evidence. These conclusions, Gerstner argues, integrate with human life individually and socially. Consider the influence of Christianity upon the world. Christ's disciples have contributed to the eradication of infanticide, murder for pleasure, cannibalism, amelioration if not abolition of slavery, the raising of standards for barbaric peoples, the building of hospitals, the encouragement of charity for the poor, and even the prevention of cruelty to animals. Furthermore, where the church has gone, the school has followed. Christians view nature as the book of God and its study is encouraged for His glory. Most American universities were started by the church. Many of the greatest scholars, scientists, and philosophers have been members of the church. In teaching the illiterate to read, the church has taken the initiative through its active missionary program, which long antedated the Peace Corps.

Individuals have felt the influence of Christianity in vital experiences which also indicate the truth of Christian teaching. To begin with, Christianity produces an experience suited to the state of sinful man—an experience of fear. When man is exposed to such danger as the judgment of a holy God, fear is a feeling he most desperately needs. Since it leads to a beneficial end it need not be paralyzing. Having acknowledged man's doom as a point of contact, Christianity goes on to announce the gospel, the good news. To the repentant man, in contrast, Christianity produces experiences of peace. Love is evoked by divine love. Security is not superficial nor deluded, but genuine. "Christianity gives the most exacting moral imperative, produces the deepest humility, and at the same time provides the greatest possible assurance."[49] It is the assurance of the indwelling of the Lord of Life Himself. To the Christian to live is Christ. The life

49. Ibid., p. 49.

of faith in the son of God is not a mere dream of pie in the sky by and by. Christians have all this and hope of heaven too.

The authenticity of Christian experience is attested by the martyrdom of great multitudes. Unlike other martyrs, Christian martyrs were often not exceptional, but ordinary people. Although they suffered excruciating pain for long periods, they died for their faith in a marvelous spirit and showed amazing strength.

Gerstner's conclusion recognizes the need for "laboratory" work in the field. Faith involves intellectual assent to the evidences, but it also involves emotional and volitional elements. If the argument is valid, the individual who sees it must submit his own life to it, or condemn himself by his own understanding. An apologetics book, Gerstner says, can reason for you, but it cannot believe for you. You alone can do the believing.

EMPIRICISTS AND THE INVISIBLE GARDENER

Why, then, do empirical apologists accept Christianity's claim that an invisible gardener cares for life on this planet? They examine the "garden" in detail and remind us of its existence, order, human life, morality, and concept of God. For each of these items of experience there is most probably a cause. And it is highly probable that the cause exists, is intelligent, personal, moral, and infinite. So they accept Christianity's truth-claim concerning the Creator's existence. From the science of archeology and historical criticism, furthermore, they accept the Bible as a good history book. Historically, then, Jesus lived, made astounding claims, backed up those claims with exceptional moral integrity and remarkable miracles. So these empiricists accept as true Christianity's claims concerning Jesus as God incarnate. And on His authority with the confirmation of fulfilled prophecy they accept the Bible as God's inspired Word to man. The truth of Christian claims is further attested by Christianity's beneficial influence in the world and in the experience of individuals. On these considerations it is held far more probable that Christian claims are true than false. All who live in the "garden" are responsible to examine the evidence and come to the most reasonable conclusion. The evidence is there and it is conclusive. The real difference between believers and unbelievers lies in their response to the data. Those who disregard it are morally without excuse.

EVALUATION

The assessment of a purely empirical defense of Christianity at this point will limit itself to very basic issues. Most of the subsequent writers treated present their positions in contrast to this approach. Their detailed criticisms are found toward the beginning of their respective chapters.

Recent thought has seriously questioned the possibility of complete objectivity in the investigation of evidence. Karl Marx observed that the social and economic status of a person influences his interpretation of facts. So a person's conclusions to empirical investigations, Marx noted, suffer from his particular ideological taint. Sigmund Freud showed that an investigator's past experiences may also seriously affect his observation of "facts" and the drawing of inferences from them. In short, it is generally recognized that people bring with them to investigation of evidence, not a mind similar to a blank tablet, but a mind strongly influenced by certain prior factors. If the mind is like a blank tablet by nature, it becomes slanted by its nurture. That being the case, a mature person always interprets the data from his particular viewpoint. The "facts" from the beginning appear very different to different investigators. What appear to Christians to be evidences of Christianity's truth, may not appear significant to people with naturalistic presuppositions. A pure empiricism does not sufficiently account for this rather obvious datum of experience in the structure of its thought. Other apologetic systems openly admit that the human mind brings with it to the evidence general logical principles, specific, unprovable (Christian or non-Christian) presuppositions, a Christian experience of conversion, or a hypothesis of Christianity's truth to be consciously investigated.

Those who grant the possibility of knowing facts to a high degree of objectivity may nevertheless question whether sheer inductive reasoning leads to a non-observable Divine Cause. The entire case for the existence of God rests upon the validity of the causal law and its applicability beyond the physical realm to the realm of Spirit. Although the causal principle has been under fire since the work of David Hume, John Stuart Mill's revision of it has permeated scientific methods. Admitting the applicability of the law that every observable consequent must have an adequate observable antecedent, it does not follow that every observable consequent in the universe must have an invisible antecedent. Causality in physics is one thing; in metaphysics it is quite another thing. On strict empirical bases the causal principle cannot be applied beyond the observable realm. No verifiable evidence could possibly be produced to support that application of the law. If causality is extended beyond the observable world (as in the theistic arguments) it is not on the grounds of pure empiricism. We must seek an apologetic system which does justice to other elements, then, without dismissing the values of the empirical approach to knowledge.

John Gerstner's case from historical facts about Jesus to the deity of Jesus illustrates one way by which it is possible to move from visible evidence to conclusions about invisible realities apart from the causal principle. That is the authority of a person who gives evidence of being honest and competent. The argument from Jesus' claims to deity is an instance of one person believing another. Although some knowledge of persons may be inferred from observation of their footprints and creative achievements, the primary way to knowledge of persons is through their words. In personal relationships testimony is a major source of truth. Of course persons can deceive or be mistaken. To avoid credulity we must assess a person's character and competence. In the case of Jesus of Nazareth both are confirmed by a critical evaluation of the records. However improbable the claim may seem, we must accept it, or trust no one. When we cannot believe the words of good and competent people, society is jeopardized. We have adequate reason to believe such a man as Jesus. He said that God the Father existed and was revealed in Himself. On the authority of testimony from the invisible God Himself those who believe Jesus can assert information about the metaphysical deity of Jesus Christ and about God's redemptive purposes.[50] This argument follows the Augustinian order of reasoning from observable evidence (*scientia*) to faith in the person of Christ (or prophetic and apostolic spokesmen for God), and then to the invisible, eternal truths they revealed (*sapientia*). *Scientia* is prior to faith in alleged spokesmen for God, but faith in the Christ to whom they testify is

---

50. For other expositions of the argument from Christ's claims for Himself see Jean Danielou, *The Scandal of Truth* (London: Burns and Oates, 1962), pp. 75-96; Vernon Grounds, *The Reason for Our Hope* (Chicago: Moody, 1945), pp. 21-26; Edward John Carnell, *The Case for Orthodox Theology* (Philadelphia: Westminster, 1959), pp. 82-83.

prior to reception of God's redemptive plans and purposes (*sapientia*). Pure empiricism, without faith in the authority of Christ's person, does not establish His deity.[51]

Similarly, pure empiricism does not establish the truth of the whole Bible. Strict empirical investigation must begin with observable evidence, but some of the physical traces of biblical persons, places, and events have been forever wiped out. However, from extant remains many aspects of the biblical record have been confirmed. But archeology in the Near East is young and no lifetime is long enough to canvass all the data relevant to the Bible's vast history. Furthermore, problems are not all solved. Taking an inductive approach to the inspiration of Scripture, Dewey M. Beegle could not conclude that the Bible is true in all that it teaches. In a chapter on the problem phenomena of Scripture he discusses ten passages which seem irresolvable in terms of evidence available to him. So he concludes that "the totality of Biblical evidence does not prove the doctrine of inerrancy to be a fact."[52]

At best a pure empiricism could conclude that the Bible was most probably true in nearly everything investigated to that time and that the number of passages difficult to harmonize with other historical data were being reduced. Dr. Frank E. Gaebelein illustrated the situation in an oral lecture with a solid line representing the biblical data confirmed by investigation and a continuing dotted line representing what remained unconfirmed. Since 1900 the length of the dotted line has been reduced by many discoveries.

    1900 _____ . . . .
    1968 _____ . . . .

Surely the empiricist can say that his conclusion about the truth of the Bible is in the direction the evidence overwhelmingly supports. But the solid line will never be complete even in relation to the Bible's historical content, so the truth of the whole of biblical history cannot be supported by sheer evidence. The valid conclusion of strict inductive inference cannot go beyond the evidence investigated.

The Bible, furthermore, contains much material that is not even observable in principle. Gaebelein's diagram helpfully illustrates the

51. See the author's "Faith and Reason in the Thought of St. Augustine" (Ph.D. diss., Syracuse University, 1959).

52. Dewey M. Beegle, *The Inspiration of Scripture* (Philadelphia: Westminster, 1963), p. 69.

picture relating to the Bible's historical setting. But vast portions of
the Bible had to do with unempirical ethical principles and divine
plans and purposes for time and eternity. It is one thing to confirm
that Jesus died, quite another to confirm that He died *for our sins.*
To complete the diagram of biblical content, then, we must add another dotted line representing empirically unverifiable redemptive
truths disclosing history's meaning.

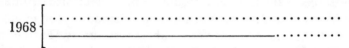

1968

Because Christ and the Bible participated in the world of blood,
sweat, and tears, Christians can expect and employ empirical confirmation. But because much of the Bible communicates ethical
values and redemptive purposes, a purely empirical method provides
only a partial defense.

Do the empiricists go part of the way by inference from evidence
and the rest of the way to Christian conclusions by faith? Because
we have a good history book, shall we believe it is necessarily a good
theology book? Is that the case for conflicting sacred writings? Faith
which goes into a realm without guidance of evidence can easily be
mere wishful thinking or presumption. That is why genuine faith
needs a word from someone who knows God's mind. Those who
claim to speak for God, of course, must authenticate their stupendous
claims by observable "signs." These indications of their competence
and integrity form the bridge between the physical and the spiritual
worlds. Though the bridge is built with the help of empirical data,
it requires faith in personal testimony. To the extent that it rests
on a person's authority, it is no longer strict empiricism. We have
an empiricism wedded to a form of personal trust. Since Christianity
relates to events and persons, no apologist ought to put evidence and
testimony asunder. The question remains whether more can be
joined to this happy union.

In sum, the application of causality to invisible realms is too tenu-
ous a foundation upon which to rest the case for the existence of God.
Observation of data alone can no more successfully lead to Christ's
deity or the Bible's complete truth. But objective evidence may
accredit personal messengers of God. Upon belief in their integrity

it is possible to accept Christ's claims for Himself and the truth of Scripture.

RESOURCES FOR RESEARCH

Aquinas, Thomas. *Summa Theologica.* New York: Benziger, 1947. See Part 1, questions 2-3, article 4. The classic statement of five ways to prove the existence of God by the great Roman Catholic thinker.

Aristotle. *Metaphysics.* 2.2; 9.8; 12.6-7.

———. *Physics.* 7.1; 8.1-6, 10. The argument from the changing world to an unmoved Mover by the Greek philosopher (384-322 B.C.).

Bertocci, Peter Anthony. *Introduction to the Philosophy of Religion.* Englewood Cliffs, N. J.: Prentice-Hall, 1951. An able case for the "wider" teleological argument intended to overcome evolutionary objection to the older form of the argument from design. The professor of philosophy from Boston University writes for beginners in philosophy.

Buswell, J. Oliver, Jr. *A Christian View of Being and Knowing.* Grand Rapids: Zondervan, 1960. An evangelical Presbyterian philosopher-theologian employs an empirical epistemology to establish a dualistic realism in metaphysics.

———. *A Systematic Theology of the Christian Religion.* Vol. 1. Grand Rapids: Zondervan, 1962. Buswell's restatement of the arguments for God's existence defends them against several standard objections.

———. *The Philosophies of F. R. Tennant and John Dewey.* New York: Philosophical Libr., 1950. An extended comparison of a theist and nontheist in the empirical tradition.

Butler, Joseph. *Analogy of Religion Natural and Revealed, to the Constitution and Course of Nature.* New York: Harper, 1875. A case for the probability of Christianity's truth by an Anglican bishop.

Carnell, Edward John. *Introduction to Christian Apologetics.* Grand Rapids: Eerdmans, 1948. An evangelical's critique of arguments from nature to God (chap. 7-8).

Casserley, J. V. L. *Graceful Reason: The Contribution of Reason to Theology.* Greenwich, Conn.: Seabury, 1954. A significant attempt to combine the cosmological argument with recent existentialist approaches.

Cobb, John B. *A Christian Natural Theology: Based on the Thought of Alfred North Whitehead.* Philadelphia: Westminster, 1965. While human experience is held to be a clue to the nature of things, emphasis is placed on God as the principle of changing process.

————. *Living Options in Protestant Theology: A Survey of Methods.* Philadelphia: Westminster, 1962. A survey of the history of natural theology and an examination of E. L. Mascall's recent Thomistic approach, the case of the Boston personalists (of whom Bertocci is the successor), and the apologetic of the liberal, Henry Nelson Wieman.

Flew, A., and MacIntyre, A., eds. *New Essays in Philosophical Theology.* New York: Macmillan, 1955. Criticisms of empirical arguments for the existence of God from the standpoint of philosophical analysis.

Freeman, David Hugh. *Recent Studies in Philosophy and Theology.* Grand Rapids: Baker, 1962. Part 1 contains the Reformed philosopher's evaluation of Neo-Thomism as represented by Etienne Gilson and Jacques Maritain.

Gerstner, John H. *Reasons for Faith.* New York: Harper, 1960. A popular presentation of the evidence for theism and Christianity.

Gilson, Etienne. *Elements of Christian Philosophy.* New York: Doubleday, 1960. An evaluation of Aquinas' arguments by the noted Neo-Thomist.

Grounds, Vernon C. *The Reason For Our Hope.* Chicago: Moody, 1945. Popular radio addresses employing the evidential approach to the faith.

Hick, John, ed. *The Existence of God.* New York: Macmillan, 1964. Readings from important contributions for and against the theistic arguments.

Hume, David. An Enquiry Concerning Human Understanding. Harvard Classics. Vol. 37. New York: Collier, 1910. See sections 6, 7, 10, and 11. One of the most influential and devastating of attacks on the theistic arguments.

————. Dialogues Concerning Natural Religion. Text and Critical Essays Series. Ed. by Nelson Pike. New York: Bobbs-Merrill, 1971.

Hurlburtt, Robert H. *Hume, Newton, and the Design Argument.* Lincoln, Nebr.: U. of Nebr., 1965. Studies in the history of natural theology and its present status by a professor of philosophy.

Kant, Immanuel. *The Critique of Pure Reason.* Argues influentially that the case for God's existence is no stronger than the case against it, and concludes that pure reason can neither prove nor disprove anything about God in Himself.

Keyser, Leander S. *A System of Natural Theism.* Burlington, Iowa: Lutheran Literary Board, 1945. Outline studies of the traditional approach.

————. *A System of Christian Evidences.* Burlington, Iowa: Lutheran Literary Board, 1945. Brief outlines of the traditional indications supporting the deity of Christ and the truth of Scripture.

Lewis, Clives Staples. *Mere Christianity*. New York: Macmillan, 1952. Popular radio broadcasts based on the moral argument for God's existence.

———. *The Problem of Pain*. New York: Macmillan, 1948. An answer to one of the most difficult problems with the theistic arguments.

Little, Paul E. *Know Why You Believe*. Wheaton, Ill.: Scripture Press, 1967. The Director of Evangelism for Inter-Varsity Christian Fellowship gives primarily evidential answers to questions about God, Christ, and the Bible.

Lord, Daniel J. *The Brief Case for the Existence of God*. New York: Queen's Work, 1930. A workbook with simple illustrations for use in lay study groups.

Mascall, E. L. *He Who Is: A Study in Traditional Theism*. New York: Longmans, Green, 1948. One of the most effective recent restatements of the inductive arguments.

Mill, John Stuart. *The Nature and Utility of Religion: Two Essays*. Trans. by George Nakhnikian. New York: Bobbs-Merrill, n.d.

Monsma, John Clover. *The Evidence of God in an Expanding Universe: Forty American Scientists Declare Their Affirmative Views on Religion*. New York: Putnam, 1958. Bypasses the philosophical problems to amass evidence from various scientific fields.

Montgomery, John Warwick. "The Apologetic Approach of Muhammad Ali and Its Implications for Christian Apologetics." *The Muslim World* 51 (April 1961) : 11-22. "Objective empirical evidence for Jesus Christ and his message is the only truly valid Christian apologetic possible, for it alone is subject to the canons of evidence employed in other fields of endeavor." The objective event attested by empirical evidence is the resurrection of Jesus Christ.

———. "History and Christianity: I. Four Common Errors." *His* 25 (December 1964) : 16-23. Four fallacies commonly found in the arguments of those who say we can know almost nothing of the real Jesus of history are pointed out.

———. "History and Christianity: II. The New Testament Documents." *His* 25 (January 1965) : 15-23. Here Montgomery seeks to give positive evidence for the historical validity of the New Testament documents without assuming the thing to be proved.

———. "History and Christianity: III. God Closes In." *His* 25 (February 1965) : 13-21. The documents say unequivocally that Jesus regarded Himself as no less than God in the flesh.

———. "History and Christianity: IV. Historian's Appeal." *His* 25 (March 1965) : 33-39. Supposing that the New Testament documents portray

Christ as divine, was He in fact? Evidence does not support the other alternatives that He was a charlatan, a lunatic, or that the disciples were charlatans, lunatics, or naive exaggerators. Evidence for the resurrection does support His claims.

———. "The Place of Reason." *His* 26 (February 1966) : 9-12. Modernists and others avoid apologetics because they regard religion as a way of life focusing on subjective feeling and moral action, not objective facts. A non-factual religion is of course not capable of factual defense, but Christianity, grounded in the fact of God's entrance into human history in the person of Christ, is the factual and defensible religion par excellence.

———. "The Place of Reason." *His* 26 (March 1966) : 13-16, 31. Since Christ really became flesh, his entrance into the human sphere is open to investigation by non-Christian and Christian alike. "Absolute proof of the truth of Christ's claims is available only in personal relationship with Him; but contemporary man has every right to expect us to offer solid reasons for making such a total commitment" (p. 16).

———. *The Shape of the Past: An Introduction to Philosophical Historiography.* Ann Arbor, Mich.: Edwards, 1962. After evaluating past and present interpretations of history, Montgomery presents "The Validation of the Christian World View." The critical and epistemological essays in Part 2 also have direct relevance to apologetics.

Montgomery, John Warwick, and others. "Faith, History, and the Resurrection." *Christianity Today* 9 (March 26, 1965) : 655-59. The event nature of the resurrection does not depend wholly upon faith. It is the other way around. The faith has its starting point in the event, the objective event, and only by appropriation of this objective event do we discover the final validity of it. The appropriation is the subjective element and this must not enter into the investigation of the event.

Morrison, A. Cressy. *Man Does Not Stand Alone.* New York: Revell, 1944. A scientist's popular case for theism.

Paley, William. *Natural Theology.* Ed. by Frederick Ferre. New York: Library of Liberal Arts, 1964. A classic statement of theism.

Sheen, Fulton J. *Philosophy of Religion.* New York: Appleton-Century-Crofts, 1948. A restatement and defense of the Thomistic arguments.

Taylor, A. E. "Theism." In *Encyclopedia of Religion and Ethics.* Ed. by James Hastings. Scribner's, 1928. Answers Kantian criticisms.

Temple, William. *Nature, Man and God.* London: Macmillan, 1949. A creative case for theism incorporating recent emphases on personal relations.

Tennant, F. R. *Philosophical Theology*. Vols. 1-2. Cambridge: Cambridge U., 1930. The originator of the wider teleological argument and one of the most capable recent defenders of theistic arguments.

Thompson, Samuel M. *A Modern Philosophy of Religion*. Chicago: Henry Regnery, 1955. The philosophy professor at Monmouth College (Presbyterian) presents a thorough restatement and defense of the cosmological argument primarily.

3

THE RATIONAL EMPIRICISM OF STUART C. HACKETT

THE TEST OF OBJECTIVE EVIDENCE AND LOGICAL THOUGHT-FORMS

IS THE CASE IN SUPPORT of Christianity's truth-claims merely probable? Christianity can be defended more conclusively than that, according to Stuart C. Hackett, professor of philosophy at Wheaton College. Hackett, a Phi Beta Kappa graduate of Cornell University, earned an M.A. from Wheaton College and a Ph.D. from Syracuse University. He has also taught at the Conservative Baptist theological seminaries in Portland and Denver and at Louisiana College. Professor Hackett's major work, published in 1957, was entitled *The Resurrection of Theism: Prolegomena to Christian Apologetics*. This introduction to knowledge of God was to be followed by two other volumes. Unfortunately, these two works have not appeared.

Hackett's type of apologetic is applied to the Bible by Floyd E. Hamilton's *The Basis of Christian Faith: A Modern Defense of the Christian Religion* (rev. ed., 1964). The author of several other books, Hamilton pastored the First Reformed Church in Indianapolis, Indiana. For twenty years he served as a missionary to Korea and for fifteen years taught in the Union Christian College of Pyongyang.

The apologetic expressed by Hackett and Hamilton is similar in several respects to Buswell's system of pure empiricism. Both Buswell and Hackett think that all knowledge begins with experience. Both reason inductively from publicly observable data. Both deny that any knowledge, including knowledge of God, can be obtained by deduction from axioms or presuppositions. Both reject any innate ideas of existing things. Furthermore, conflicting truth-claims cannot be settled simply by a testimony to mystical experiences. Truth is derived via inductive inference from experience. In all these ways Hackett's apologetic is similar to Buswell's empiricism.

THE THOUGHT-FORMS OF THE HUMAN MIND

In contrast to Buswell, however, Hackett does not think the laws of reasoning are inductive probabilities based on limited human experience. Rather, these laws apply to reality universally without exception. The law of non-contradiction asserts that *not one* proposition can be affirmed and denied at the same time and in the same respect. Because laws of logic are universal and necessary they cannot be derived from experience. Inductive conclusions are limited to the evidence examined and are only probable. What, then, is the source of the mind's knowledge of universal and necessary principles? Hackett thinks they have been "programmed in" the human mind. The mind brings to its observation of experience a proclivity to think consistently. Because of this emphasis on the mind's rational structure, Hackett's system is not like Buswell's pure empiricism, but a rational empiricism.

The mind, as Hackett sees it, is not a blank tablet; its original equipment includes the laws of logic. He explains:

> I could not be aware of sensing any particular object at all without first being able to distinguish it as this and not that, as one thing rather than another. But I must already be employing the law of contradiction in order to do this, since it is that law whereby I know that a thing cannot be two different objects simultaneously and in the same sense: thus I employ the law at the very beginning of the experience with objects.[1]

Inherent in the mind is not only the law of contradiction, but also the law of causality. Every effect must have an adequate cause. The necessary connection of effect and cause was rejected by David Hume, and by positivists, pragmatists, existentialists, and many evangelicals. But Hamilton and Hackett defend it. Hamilton says:

> Hume was quite right in pointing out that uniform sequence does

1. Stuart C. Hackett, *The Resurrection of Theism* (Chicago: Moody, 1957), p. 64.

not always mean that the two events are causally connected. What we think is the cause of the thing or event invariably following the first may not be the cause at all. But the fact that we can be mistaken in determining the *real* cause does not mean we are at liberty to assume that there is no real cause at all.[2]

As Hamilton insists, "The necessary part of the causal judgment is that *activity by someone or something produces the observed effect.* Every effect must have some cause adequate to produce it." The causal principle is "self-evidently true" because implanted in all men at creation as a bridge to the external world.[3]

In addition to principles of causality and logic, other thought-forms enable us to make sense of our experience. We organize every bit of experience in terms of quantity (unity or plurality), quality (reality or negation), relation (existence, causation, and reciprocity), and modality (possibility or necessity).[4] So every judgment we make must be universal or particular in quantity, affirmative or negative in quality, assertive, hypothetical or disjunctive in relation, and problematical or apodictical in modality. The details of each are not crucial for our purposes. Students of philosophy recognize Hackett's dependence upon Immanuel Kant with slight modification.

This structure of the mind is like the design of a jello mold. Immanuel Kant had held that data of experience are an unformed mass, like the jello before it is poured into a mold. When poured into a beautifully shaped cup the jello takes its form. Similarly when experiential data are received into the mind they are organized by its forms of quantity, quality, relation, and modality. These forms enable us to draw from adequate data conclusions which are not merely probable, but logically certain. A jello desert requires jello plus the cup; truth requires experiential data plus the mind's thought-forms. The sense-data without the mental categories would be without form and meaningless; the forms of thought without the data are empty.

Hackett differs from Kant in not limiting the "jello" of knowledge to sense data. Kant said we could obtain no knowledge of an invisible, spiritual world. Stuart Hackett, in contrast, argues that a statement limiting all knowledge to sense data is itself not drawn from sense

2. Floyd E. Hamilton, *The Basis of Christian Faith*, 4th ed. rev. and enl. (New York: Harper adn Row, 1964), p. 8.
3. Ibid., p. 34.
4. Hackett, pp. 51-52.

data. It contradicts itself and is therefore meaningless. Since Kant showed that knowledge involves non-empirical elements, we cannot limit all knowledge to sense data alone. That being the case, we cannot say a priori that knowledge of God is impossible. Truth about an invisible metaphysical ultimate remains an open possibility.

Hackett also disagrees with Kant's assumption that the "jello" of knowledge is formless before it is "poured" into our minds. Kant had no way of knowing what the real world is like apart from our mental structuring of it. He thought we could never perceive unstructured reality, for the moment we perceive it our categories structure it. So according to Kant, we cannot know that things-in-themselves (*noumena*) are structured. Neither could we know them to be formless, however, as Kant assumed. Professor Hackett contends that the forms of thought are forms of real things-in-themselves.[5] He argues that Kant must have some knowledge of things-in-themselves in order to know that they exist. His view that they exist as totally unknown is self-contradictory, or else leads to skepticism. So Hackett concludes that "the categories do not give us a knowledge of things-in-themselves."[6] Things-in-themselves must be structured in the same way as our minds. Hackett is a realist. Dr. Buswell remains unconvinced and writes, "With all sympathy for Dr. Hackett's Christian devotion and scholarly ability, the prevailing opinion of Christian teachers of philosophy and theology seems to be that Professor Hackett has still left us in the *a priori*."[7]

Hackett's defense of his a priori categories of reason (Kant's synthetic a priori) consists of one basic argument: "positively, that intelligible experience is possible only in terms of such a factor; and negatively, that the denial of the synthetic a priori is either self-contradictory or meaningless."[8] That charge is directed at such alternative theories of knowledge as pure rationalism, empiricism, pragmatism, and intuitionism. All are found self-contradictory or meaningless by a rigorous use of the laws of logic.

The positive argument goes like this. "Every intelligent action presupposes the mind's power of judging with respect to the presented

5. Ibid., p. 53.
6. Ibid., p. 55.
7. J. Oliver Buswell, Jr., *A Systematic Theology of the Christian Religion*, vol. 1 (Grand Rapids: Zondervan, 1962), p. 18.
8. Hackett, p. 56.

data of experience." Similarly, "the power of judging presupposes the mind's initial possession, as tools, or forms of thought, or the basic relations which make intelligent judgment possible."[9] The very first time we say, "this is true" or "this is false" we presuppose a structure of thought in terms of which subject and predicate may be united according to certain relations. So, "either all thought starts with some general principles with which the mind is equipped, or it cannot start at all."[10] They are not derived from experience. "Every attempt to derive the categories from the data of experience presupposes their use in the attempted derivation."[11]

But a child cannot state the law of contradiction or the law of causality! That objection to innate forms of thought, however, misses the point. Awareness of the categories does not temporally precede our experience. We become conscious of the categories, Hackett explains, only when we reflect upon the knowledge process. Although unaware of the logical structure of his mind, a child who begins to think, thinks in accord with its categories. The categories are innate, not as concrete ideas in the consciousness, but as forms by which thought operates.[12]

COMMON GROUND

According to Hackett and Hamilton, believers and unbelievers share not only all publicly observable data of experience, but in addition, all the categories of the human mind. It follows that "there is a common basis or ground in terms of which rational and universally acceptable propositions about reality—whether ultimate or subordinate—may be reached."[13] So metaphysical assertions should commend themselves to all people insofar as they determine their beliefs rationally. On this basis a natural theology can be constructed. And these rational arguments for God's existence should carry a conclusiveness impossible in a pure empiricism. As Hamilton puts it, judgments based on the categories are always true in form for all men. "It is in this formal truth, the same for believers and unbelievers, that there is a point of contact for rational discussion."[14]

9. Ibid., p. 59.
10. Ibid., p. 57.
11. Ibid., p. 62.
12. Ibid., p. 58.
13. Ibid., p. 113.
14. Hamilton, p. 17.

Truth Tested by Coherence

A purely formal consistency, however, is as insufficient a test for truth as a purely factual correspondence. With Buswell, Hackett says a proposal to be considered true must integrate with the data of experience. At the same time the proposal must also cohere with the mind's rational principles. So the truth or falsity of a proposition is determined by: (1) "whether or not the proposition results from a self-consistent application of the categorical structure to experiential data," and (2) "whether or not such a proposition is systematically correlated both with the data in question and with the whole body of previously established propositions."[15] How does Hackett defend the coherence test for truth over against the correspondence theory? The case reduces to one major consideration: "the only way of testing correspondence is by coherence, so that the former is not an adequate theory of truth."[16] So the test of religious truth-claims is their coherence with all relevant experience and the rational categories.

God's Existence

Two major arguments for the existence of God appear in Hackett's work. The first seeks the cause of the categorical structure of things. The second seeks the cause of the existence of things.

Hackett's first argument for the existence of God is not to be confused with the traditional ontological argument. It reasoned from the concept of God's existence to the fact of God's existence. In Hackett's mind the alleged movement from thought to existence is an a priori tautology or a begging of the real question. But he is willing to call his argument from the categories a revision of the ontological argument. By an analysis of experience he discovers the categories structuring all finite minds and all existence. He then reasons to an adequate cause of this fact. The only adequate explanation of the rational structure of thought and things is an existing rational Mind. The architect of the rational categories and the knowable world is God. As Hackett puts it:

> Since the categories are, in our experience, connected with a rational self, we may infer that their presence in the world and in other finite selves is to be similarly explained by reference to a Reason from

15. Hackett, p. 101.
16. Ibid., p. 106.

which both finite selves and their world of experience are derived. In brief, the categorical structure of rationality and existence is grounded in the being of an eternal Reason or God.[17]

Unlike the ontological argument, Hackett's argument starts with an experienced structure and seeks its cause. A non-rational, instructured thing could not cause a rational self and an intelligible world. So the Cause of existence and rational selves must be an existing rational Self.

Hackett's second argument also begins with experience, but this time of particular existing things. No finite thing has within itself all the conditions necessary for its own existence. No finite thing is the cause of its own existence. For its very existence a finite thing is totally dependent upon things other than itself. After it comes to be it faces many limitations not self-imposed. Since each individual thing in the universe is dependent, the universe as a whole must be dependent. The dependent universe then must be caused by something distinct from itself and not dependent on anything in it. So the universe must depend upon an eternal Being transcendent to the world. This "timeless necessity of existence" Hackett calls God. As the argument appears in *The Resurrection of Theism*, it goes like this:

> Any given existing thing is either an effect or not, an effect being defined as an existence whose character and being are determined by antecedent and contemporaneous existences external to itself. Now if such an entity is not an effect, its character and being must be determined by factors within itself: and thus we conclude at once an absolutely necessary being, since such a being is precisely one whose determinate character is completely self-contained.[18]

God exists, then, as the necessary existence upon which the totality of finite existences depends.

It may be objected that an infinite series of finite things is possible. Hackett answers that no series of determinate parts could add up to an actually infinite series. If it did, an actually infinite series could not admit of increase or decrease, the progression of events would be an illusion. That is manifestly false. Since new animals are born daily, the series cannot have been infinite before their birth. Is the

17. Ibid., p. 192.
18. Ibid., pp. 194-95.

infinite series purely mathematical and not of actual things? Then Hackett argues that one could never come to the infinite number. It is not simply that the scribe tires of counting, but that no such enumeration could conceivably add up to infinity. Counting to an infinity of finite causes is not hampered by fatigue, but by futility.[19] So Hackett thinks he has demonstrated the existence of God as the cause of the general categories and of all particular existences.

THE CHARACTER OF THE ETERNAL CAUSE

The next step is to examine the nature of the universe further to see if it reveals more about its Cause. The cosmological argument was drawn from the existence of things, the teleological argument is based upon their arrangement to produce certain results. The adapting of means to ends requires a personal will to consciously select among possible goals and to guide conditions to achieve them.[20]

Evidence of the world's order is found in the infinitesimal world of the microscope and the vast world of the telescope. From the larger perspective Hackett discovers purpose in the fitness of innumerable inorganic conditions necessary to the production and maintenance of life and the world's amazing adaptability to human ends and values.

Man himself is regarded the most amazing indication of a purpose transcending physical forces. In all the vast universe nothing discovered is capable of developing human mentality or morality. Man, "the highest realized level of contingent reality itself possesses a nature that utterly transcends the potentialities and possibilities of the lower levels of life and matter: transcends them in such a way that mind is inexplicable as purely a development from such levels."[21] Behavioristic theories of the human mind do not account for the mind's self-transcendence. The mind cannot be identified with the brain because it transcends time in memory, space in communication, sense-data in the perception of color and bodily movement in experiencing conscious states. Furthermore the human mind attains truth in logical sequence, and purposefully selects ends. So the eternal cause of man's existence must be a transcendent Mind and Will.

Man's choice of ends is not a mere haphazard series of immediate

19. Ibid., pp. 294-95.
20. Ibid., p. 204.
21. Ibid., p. 220.

adaptations. At the summit of rational vision is a supreme end to
which the whole series of subordinate ends is related as a system of
means. A supreme end is considered probable by analogy to the
cosmic process which was found to be directed to the production of
minds. Without such a final goal the achieving of lesser ends would
be pointless. The supreme end is not instrumental to any other; it
is the final intrinsic good which all else serves. And that highest good
imposes an absolute moral imperative upon human activity. So the
meaningfulness of our moral experience requires that the Cause of
man be morally good.

Now we do in fact find men everywhere confronted with righteous
demands. All men know that some things are right and wrong. What
ought to be done is not in the final analysis determined by their tastes
or cultures, for they are accountable for both. And they are accountable to God. This moral argument may be put in syllogistic form
(two premises from which a conclusion logically follows) :

> Rational selves are confronted with a transsubjective and trans-
> temporal supreme end to the realization of which they are uncondi-
> tionally obligated.
>
> Such an eternally valid end cannot subsist alone but must be
> existentially based in an eternal mind whose nature both recognizes
> and embodies the absolute good.
>
> There exists, consequently, just such an eternal mind whose nature
> is absolute goodness.[22]

With such syllogistic certainty Professor Hackett pursues his case
for theism. His observations establishing the first premise of his arguments are, he thinks, more than highly probable. Experience discloses dependent existing things, a natural order, and a sense of
oughtness. Unquestionably man is dependent, intelligent, purposive,
and moral. The causal principle forming the second premise of the
theistic arguments is universal and necessary, so each of these observed
existences and characteristics requires an adequate cause. With the
force of logical demonstration, then, he concludes that a necessary
Being who is intelligent, purposive, and moral exists.

LANGUAGE ABOUT GOD

How does Hackett interpret statements about God's existence, in-

22. Ibid., p. 232.

telligence and morality? Do these terms attribute to God merely human characteristics? Their meaning for God is not totally different or they would be meaningless. Neither are statements about God merely analogical. If "all knowledge of God is analogical," Hackett reasons, "what about that assertion itself?" If "all knowledge of God is analogical," that statement is also analogical, and so on to an infinite regress. Again, if all knowledge of God is analogical, *cause* is also predicated analogically. But then no essential knowledge of God is communicated by the statement that God is the first cause. Those who defend a merely analogical knowledge of God deny that we know anything of God as He is essentially. If, however, the asserted analogy does not hold essentially of God, it tells us nothing of God and is false, or equivocal. "The only thing that makes any analogy meaningful is a univocal element or point of likeness which can be clearly specified."[23] So Hackett, like Buswell, defends some univocal meaning in human assertions about God. God's intelligence is not totally different from man's—God also thinks in accord with the categories of rationality and reality. God's purpose is not totally different from man's—God also chooses worthy objectives and moves toward achieving them.

GOD'S RELATION TO THE WORLD

How then is God related to the cosmos He produced? This question is answered by Floyd E. Hamilton in *The Basis of Christian Faith*. God is not matter. A materialism is discredited, Hamilton asserts, by the discovery that atoms are not solid but composed of electrical energy. Matter is not a solid unchanging substance. Radioactive elements are constantly decomposing and losing weight. Formerly held to be indestructible, matter is now known to be interchangeable with energy, the usefulness of which is "running down." Also pointing to the origin of the universe in the finite past is the fact that it is expanding and scattering its radiant energy. So the universe is not eternal and self-explained as materialists supposed.

Pantheists think of the world's order or unity as divine. But God cannot be identified with a totality inclusive of the changing, the finite, and the evil. God has been found to be independent, transcendent, and good. If God is not identifiable with the world, how is He related to it?

23. Ibid., p. 129.

Two varieties of Christian theism may be held. Christian realism considers God transcendent to the world, but not in the sense of deism. God not only created the world, He sustains it. But Hamilton says the Christian realists do agree with the deists in asserting the reality of both spirit and matter. These two realities continue after creation on their own providentially sustained momentum. God achieves His purposes through regularly guided and controlled second causes, physical and mental. But God may for reasons He deems sufficient achieve His purposes in unusual ways (miracles).

A second variety of theism, Hamilton thinks, does more justice to the discovery that matter is not a hard substance. What is commonly called matter, he says, "is a manifestation of the energy of God's nature."[24] Energy in creatures is not identified with God, but it cannot exist apart from the power of God. No second causes exist on this view for nature is simply the uniform way in which God normally manifests His energy. A miracle is "a change in the uniform way in which God habitually acts."[25] Hamilton's view sometimes sounds like a form of pantheism. He says, "God is the *immediate* cause of . . . sensations in our brains for the sensations are the manifestation of His energy in matter."[26] What he seeks to emphasize in statements like this, however, is his opposition to materialism and support of a form of idealism.

The charge of pantheism is denied by Hamilton on the ground of his distinction between finite persons or spirits and God who is infinite (unlimited). Finite spirits are not a part of God, yet they are spirits just as He is a Spirit. They are separate from God in personality, but not independent of His control. Because reality is composed of energy and persons, Hamilton calls his view "personal idealism." And since there are many persons, not just the one Person, it is a personal, pluralistic idealism. The components of reality on this metaphysical view are a personal God, many finite persons, and their energy.

Hamilton's subsequent case for theism applies to either form—his personal pluralistic idealism or a dualistic realism. On either version of theism, he argues, the universe did not originate out of nothing by some evolutionary means. An extensive review of the authorities

24. Hamilton, p. 30.
25. Ibid., p. 31.
26. Ibid., p. 33.

in biology and genetics leads to the conclusion that no satisfactory explanation of organic evolution is known. And a survey of geology and anthropology shows that evidence from the fossils alleged to support evolution is "at the least very highly questionable."[27] So it remains more reasonable to account for the origin of the universe and life by divine creation.

Since God is, and God created the world, God's miraculous acts in history are *possible*. No alleged uniformity of "natural" law could pose any barrier. God who ordinarily acts in one way can freely choose to act in unusual ways for reasons sufficient unto Himself. And the reconciliation of estranged people is reason enough! Unusual divine action is not only possible, therefore, but highly *probable*. A personal God, who created men with whom to fellowship, would seek to restore that personal relationship. In all likelihood He would reveal to men His purpose for creating them. If, after a short life on earth, men face an eternal destiny in His gracious presence or excluded from it, He would most probably tell them. A "very great probability" indicates that God would reveal His redemptive purposes to man.[28]

EVIDENCE FOR GOD'S REVELATION TO MAN

Although God could, and probably would reveal Himself to man, the question remains whether He did. If He did, what form would it take? God might appear to men in a human form (theophany), stimulate certain dreams and visions, quicken the minds of chosen men to write what He wanted written, or provide a personal embodiment of His divine character and will by becoming incarnate. Have such things actually taken place?

How could such supernatural revelations be attested if and when they occurred? Signs of supernatural power and wisdom could be displayed through miracles and prediction of events in advance. The only way to know whether such signs have confirmed alleged divine revelations is by examination of relevant evidence. In addition to sign miracles and fulfilled prophecy, other circumstances surrounding the origin of the Bible might be significant. And the character of the book itself should be examined. "If God *has* given a revelation, no amount of theorizing to the contrary can change the fact. The only

27. Ibid., p. 91.
28. Ibid., p. 100.

way those who do not believe God has given a revelation to man can prove their case is for them to show that the evidence for such a revelation is worthless."[29] Since the whole case rests on evidence, Hamilton asks these questions: Was the witness competent? Was the witness reliable? Was the witness in a position to know the facts? Hamilton calls upon any man of average intelligence to sit on the jury. No special technical training is necessary to weigh this case. All may examine the evidence and decide for themselves whether the Bible is in truth God's revelation. No one is asked to believe in advance the very thing to be proved.

The extensive amount of detailed evidence Hamilton presents can here be only summarized. He is aware of revelation-claims in other world religions (Islam, Buddhism, Hinduism, Taoism, Confucianism, and Shintoism). Hamilton argues in each case that the origin of the religion can be accounted for by purely natural causes. In contrast, the origin of Christianity, he finds, requires a supernatural explanation. Christianity was not spread by force, political power, ritual, compromise, appeal to man's lower nature, identification of vices as virtues, or separation of morality from religion. Although Christianity prescribed moral regeneration, the offense of the cross, and the threat of persecution and death, nothing could stop its spread. Of course some natural causes may have contributed: a universal language (Greek), good roads, a stable Roman empire, and a natural appeal of Christianity. But "a mighty effect must have a mighty cause, and the only cause mighty enough to produce this effect is the power of Almighty God."[30]

Hamilton supports this thesis with many lines of evidence. In calling upon all men to assess the evidence, Hamilton knows the implications of this procedure. He says:

> To some this will seem like an abandonment of Christian presuppositions and inviting the enemy into the citadel of the Christian castle of faith. To banish such fears of evangelical Christians let us hasten to state that our belief in the trustworthiness of the *whole* Bible is so strong that we are not afraid of descending to the level of destructive critics of the Bible, for the sake of argument, confident that the Bible will stand every critical test that may be proposed.[31]

29. Ibid., p. 105.
30. Ibid., p. 135.
31. Ibid., p. 137.

In that spirit the Bible's *literary phenomena* are cited as evidence that it is the most remarkable book in the world. Translated into more languages than any other book, the Bible is the most widely read volume in the world. It has consistently sold more copies than any other book. It has inspired more books about it and more allusions and quotations to it than any other work. Its literary variety, contemporaneity, moral inspiration, and perennial interest to people of all types support the conclusion that it is the most wonderful book in the world.

Similarly it is argued that the Bible's *ethics* have the mark of God's hand upon them. In contrast to such systems as hedonism, utilitarianism, intuitionalism, and rationalism, the ethical system taught in the Bible is superior in several ways. It offers itself as an external standard of ethics which is unchangeable, it provides the motive power by which man's will can be directed to fulfill the standard. It comprehends all that is good in the other systems of ethics and its demands are remarkably high.

Another aspect of evidence is drawn from the Bible's *unity*. From beginning to end the Bible presents a unity of theme, structure, teaching, symbolism, and literary emphasis. The writers employed their own intellects, language, and style, and there is a certain growth in their teaching. However, the progression is not from wrong ideas to true, but from implicit to explicit, incomplete to complete, unclear to clear without contradiction. "The Bible thus becomes a unit, parts of which cannot be cut off without irreparable injury to the whole."[32] Though there are over forty different writers, the Holy Spirit is peculiarly the inspirer of them all.

Because the Bible is the *history* of man's redemption by the living Lord it must be tested historically. A book may be accurate history and not be inspired, but no book can be accepted as inspired which is found to be historically inaccurate. The Old Testament is said never to be contradicted by proved scientific fact. Its trustworthiness is shown generally from its topography, geography, ethnology, and chronology. Many Old Testament accounts have been confirmed. Abraham's times and culture, Chedorlaomer's campaign against Sodom (Gen 14), Joseph in Egypt, Israel's exodus, the conquest of Canaan, the capture of Jericho, the description of Michmash, David's

32. Ibid., p. 167.

capture of Jerusalem, the strength of the Davidic and Solomonic empires, Shishak's raid of Jerusalem, Ethiopian King Tirhakah's rule of Egypt, Sennacherib's invasion of Judah and his defeat caused by the death of large numbers in his army, Belshazzar's co-regency with Nabonidus in Babylon, and the Bible's transliteration and transmission of names of kings from many nations in the ancient world.

Similarly, the New Testament is accurate *geographically* and *politically*. Specifically, Quirinius was governor of Syria when Jesus was born and a census was taken. Fragments of the gospels confirm earlier rather than later estimates of their date of composition. When Paul visited Cyprus Paulus was not propraetor, but as Acts says, proconsul; Lysanius was tetrarch of Abilene, confirming Luke 3:1. And at Thessalonica magistrates were in fact called politarchs. These assertions documented by Hamilton are regarded "sufficient to establish the fact that wherever the Old and New Testaments can be tested by external evidence they are proved trustworthy documents."[33]

A question often faced by Christian apologists, but more frequently answered in Old and New Testament studies, asks whether the original writings have been transmitted through the centuries to us in pure form. Hamilton answers by summing up the findings of *textual criticism* in a chapter entitled "The Integrity, Genuineness and Authenticity of the Bible." That the Old Testament text has been faithfully preserved through centuries of copying is indicated by the substantial agreement of wording among such sources as: the Masoretic text handed down by the Jews for centuries and written about A.D. 500, citations in the Talmud A.D. 200, quotations of the Old Testament in the New Testament during the first century, extensive quotations in Ecclesiasticus 200 B.C., the Book of Jubilees containing most of Genesis, 200 B.C., the Septuagint translation into Greek between 300-100 B.C., the Dead Sea Scroll of Isaiah 200-100 B.C., and the Samaritan Pentateuch dating from the time of Nehemiah. Hamilton concludes: "We have shown that the text which Christ and the Apostles used was the text which has come down to us, and we have also shown that this text is historical and trustworthy."[34] He then briefly alludes to Christ's authority. Since Christ placed His stamp of approval on the Old Testament as we have it, he who rejects it, neces-

33. Ibid., pp. 196-97.
34. Ibid., p. 207.

sarily questions either the omniscience or honesty of the Lord. Confidence that we have substantially the New Testament text as it came from the hands of the original writers is based upon the knowledge of textual critics from a study of 2,328 Greek manuscripts of the New Testament dating back to A.D. 200, versions in other languages, such as Syriac, Coptic, Latin, Ethiopic, and Armenian, voluminous citations by church fathers and the internal evidence of the documents themselves. No serious differences of doctrine or fact appear in all of these copies of the New Testament text. So we know what was in the original. It has been faithfully transmitted to us through the years.

Higher criticism examines the biblical books to determine their age, authorship, sources, and historical value. Such investigations need not result in rejection of the Bible as divine revelation, but often have. Higher criticism becomes destructive when it operates with certain presuppositions. A naturalistic bias presumes that nothing could have happened in the past that does not happen today. Any Scriptural indications of revelation from God, knowledge of the future, or miraculous power are immediately explained away. Also an evolutionary assumption reconstituted the biblical documents to support a development of Israel's religion from lower animistic forms to higher monotheistic forms. Any evidence to the contrary is altered or attributed to primitive sources.

> Now what we claim is this: No one has a right to make this assumption without providing (a) that all religion has undergone such a process of evolution, or (b) that God *cannot* found a religion on a different non-developmental basis, even though other religions may have gone through such a process, or (c) if it be admitted that He *could* found a religion by revelation if He wanted to, that Hebrew religion was *not* a religion founded in a way different from the way other religions developed.[35]

Furthermore, destructive critics assume without warrant that where biblical and non-biblical data differ, the Bible is wrong. And they take that interpretation of the biblical text which conflicts with other sources or contradicts itself. Alternative interpretations harmonizing the data are assumed wrong. The opinion of a scholar is preferred to the Bible's positive evidence.

The critical study which operated on these assumptions proposed

35. Ibid., p. 218.

sources (J, E, D, P, etc.) for the Pentateuch arranged according to the Graf-Wellhausen hypothesis. Hamilton finds this Old Testament criticism unwarranted by the evidence as it stands. Equally distortive is New Testament criticism, including Strauss' mythical theory, Baur's theory of second century reconstruction by conscious fiction, and more recent theories. The upshot? The destructive critics' attempt to remove all supernatural elements from gospel and apostolic history have failed. If they had succeeded, a merely human Jesus could not have founded the apostolic church. No alternative "explanation" accounts for Christianity's phenomenal origin in the first half of the first century. "There is no other way to explain the faith of the early Christians except to admit that the supernatural events of Jesus' life, death, and resurrection actually occurred and were the foundation of the belief in their occurrence in the Christian Church."[36] Christianity did not start by the proclamation of other worldly truths to contemplate, nor the assertion of a new code of ethics. Christians affirmed certain facts about the life, death, and resurrection of a person known to the Jews. If the facts were false they could have been exposed and the Christian church would never have started. But if the facts occurred, the origin of Christianity is easily accounted for.

Hamilton's extensive defense of the Bible's truth also considers evidence alleged to the contrary. *Apparent discrepancies* in the Bible are classified as follows: inaccurate reading of what the Bible says, misunderstandings of Bible teaching as a whole, an assumption that a brief record of an event or speech is complete, failure to appreciate an author's purpose, misinterpretation of chronological and numerical references in biblical cultures, and insufficient reckoning with different meanings of the same words in Hebrew and Greek usage. Doctrinal difficulties are treated in another chapter which includes explanations of the doctrine of the Trinity, Christ's two natures, His virgin birth, the atonement, predestination, and inspiration.

Three further lines of evidence complete Hamilton's case. First, the miracle of *Christ's resurrection* is defended against naturalistic explanations. Each of them lacks support or is contrary to evidence. Christ did not merely swoon, His body was not stolen by friends or

---

36. Ibid., p. 259.

enemies. He did not rise "spiritually." The appearances were not mere visions, optical illusions, or hallucinations. The conclusion?

> We have examined all possibilities and find that the only conclusion possible is that Christ actually rose from the dead. . . . His resurrection establishes beyond a doubt the truth of Christianity. But not only does it prove that Christianity is the one true religion. It also proves that all that Christ said and did was true, and this in turn proves that the Bible is the Word of God written.[37]

Second, *fulfilled prophecy* proves the Bible to be the word of God. The case here is based on the same illustrations as in Gerstner's treatment. Third, and also not significantly different from Gerstner's treatment is the argument from *Christian experience*. Christians of all ages, in all missionary situations have experienced changed lives through faith in the risen Christ upon the authority of Scripture as God's Word written. An appeal to submit the will to the truth of Scripture thus shown is based on Christ's words, "If any man is willing to do His will, he shall know of the teaching, whether it is of God or whether I speak from Myself" (Jn 7:17). So this case for the truth of Christianity closes with the invitation, "Taste and see that the Lord is good."

RATIONAL EMPIRICISM AND THE INVISIBLE GARDENER

Others who look at the weedy garden of the world may think it is uncared for. But Hackett and Hamilton assent to the truth of the claim that an invisible Gardener exists and has revealed Himself to men. They defend this belief on the basis of rational inferences from observed evidence. The garden itself exists, although everything in it is dependent upon other things in the garden for its existence. An infinite number of dependent causes and effects is inconceivable because "no series of particular and determinate entities could ever add up to infinity." If the whole series of causes is not infinite, it must end in a self-existent Cause. Furthermore the garden contains people with intelligence, purposeful action, and moral responsibility. The Cause of such effects must itself be intelligent, purposeful, and good. Evidence of the existence of the garden and its inhabitants is abundant. The principle of causality, furthermore, is an a priori assumption to all valid reasoning. Without it we cannot make any sense of

---

37. Ibid., p. 304.

the world. It is inherent to the rational processes of the human mind. Since the evidence and the inferential principle are both inescapable, the conclusion is demonstrated. A transcendent, intelligent, purposive, and good God is the only adequate cause of the garden.

Since God created the garden, there can be no a priori objection to the possibility of His continued activity in it. Divine revelation is not only possible but probable. Since God is personal it is highly probable that He would communicate with His personal creatures. Furthermore, according to adequate evidence, Divine revelation to people in the garden actually occurred. The evidence of supernatural wisdom is found in fulfilled predictions and the evidence of supernatural power is seen in the signs and wonders that accompanied the messages of prophets and apostles. No merely natural causes can account for the origin of Christianity, or the Bible's remarkable unity, ethic, and historical accuracy. Attempted naturalistic accounts of the Bible's literary phenomena and content have collapsed. Evidence conclusively supports the conclusion that the Bible has been preserved accurately through the centuries and that Jesus Christ came forth from the grave. So adequate evidence and sound reasoning demonstrate both God's existence and the Bible's truth. There is an invisible Gardener and the Bible is His revelation.

EVALUATION

Oddly enough, while all of us seek greater certainty in matters of religious belief, we immediately recoil from dogmatists who claim to have it. A premature finality in these difficult matters stifles investigation and seems inappropriate and unbecoming to finite, sinful minds. So the appeal to rational categories which hold out for greater certainty, may trigger an unexpected negative reaction. In some measure anticipating this, Hamilton has pointed out several factors complicating the knowing process, granting the validity of the mind's forms of thought: (1) A judgment may be false when the brain is diseased, or under the influence of drugs or intoxicating liquor. (2) External conditions may be abnormal and affect observation of data. (3) We may not have all the pertinent facts. (4) A judgment is false when, in spite of the person's intentions to be logical, it does not obey the laws of logic. (5) An imperfect memory may cause errors. (6) A hunch or hypothesis may be assumed true without sufficient testing.

(7) Accepted premises of deductive reasoning may in fact be false.
(8) And effects of emotions like hate may render reasoning less than valid.

In view of these complex factors in the human process of determining truth, Hamilton concludes that judgments based on experience "can be accepted only as tentatively true, provided they avoid all visible sources of error."[38] Surely Hackett and Hamilton would insist that these possibilities of error have been checked and found negligible. But inadvertently one may have escaped notice and so at best we can claim for the conclusions of rational empiricism, not demonstration, but tentative truth. Is this tentative truth so different, after all, from pure empiricism's probable truth?

Other qualifications upon the rational empiricist's "demonstrations" are also necessary. Hamilton indicates another when he says, "Unwillingly we are forced to admit that we cannot offer mathematical proof of the existence of God. All that we can offer is inferential proof, and yet this is not a matter of indifference to men."[39] So the truth of these apologists' conclusions is not direct. They do not claim immediate encounters with God Himself. They claim only causal inferences from finite things to the divine. Inferences from observable things to invisible things cannot claim the certainty of mathematical demonstrations.

Of course rational empiricists know tentatively and inferentially only a part of the truth. Hamilton also admits this, while stressing that the partial truth known is nevertheless truth. What nature reveals of God is held to be

> a finite revelation of the *true* God. It tells us much, but not all, about Him. It does give us *true* knowledge, though finite, of the infinite God as He has revealed Himself in the universe which He has created. We *do* claim that these arguments prove the existence of a personal God capable of producing the whole vast universe, and that a study of the facts of the universe gives us true and valid knowledge about the being of God revealed in creation.[40]

The word "prove" in statements like this is ambiguous. It sounds like it may mean mathematical demonstration, when in Hamilton's con-

38. Ibid., p. 12.
39. Ibid., pp. 35-36.
40. Ibid., p. 39.

text it must mean that these arguments though inferential lead to the tentative conclusion that God exists. Only in this way do we know some truth about God. The failure to give more prominence to these qualifications in the careful formulating of conclusions has led to a serious reaction against a kind of rational dogmatism which does not characterize Hamilton's qualifications. Apologists for any cause are tempted at times to overstate their conclusions. Apologists for Christianity, especially those not too long in the field, do not escape this temptation. Yielding to it, however, may produce a kind of reverse psychology. Those who were to be persuaded by our airtight demonstration may be repulsed. Oliver Cromwell's famous advice applies, not to the Scripture's own statements, but to our observations of our experience and our inferences from it, "By the bowels of Christ, I beseech you, bethink you that you may be mistaken."

If rational empiricism is not criticized for its dogmatism, it may be for its assumption of a priori laws of consistency and causality (as well as other categories). In the opinion of the writer the case for the law of non-contradiction is valid. Any objection to the law presupposes its validity. The case for the law of causality, however, is less compelling. Many fail to find a necessary connection between antecedent and consequent. If its necessity be granted, still its universal applicability may be challenged. And if it holds everywhere in time and space, it remains to ask whether it holds beyond the time-space world in a realm transcendent to our experience. Even when its necessity and universality are admitted, differences may arise in interpreting its requirements. What is an "adequate" cause for a given effect? What are the criteria of adequacy? With the causal principle's potential for so much dispute, it seems wiser not to make it the cornerstone of one's philosophy of life. At least it is worth considering whether there may be a less hazardous way of finding the truth about Christianity's claims.

The apologetic of Hamilton for the Bible as divine revelation raises some interesting questions. His argument is not so emphatically dependent upon the authority of Christ as is Gerstner's. John Gerstner first confirmed the historical trustworthiness of the Bible, then from those historical sources showed that Jesus was the incarnate Christ, and finally on Christ's word accepted the Bible as God's inspired Word to men. Although Hamilton alludes briefly to Christ's endorsement of the Bible, his major concern is answering objections and amassing independent evidences for the Bible's supernatural inspiration. Can an empirically minded apologist defend the Bible's authority directly in detail? Or should his case for Scripture be based on the authority of Jesus as God incarnate? Buswell said it made no difference where one started. Apparently he holds that with equal facility we could make a case for Christ's deity (without biblical authority), or for the Bible (without Christ's authority). Given the ideals of pure empiricism either might be possible. But complete objectivity is not possible in actual life. Furthermore, the conclusion that the Bible in its entirety is the inspired Word of God goes beyond the limits of any possible investigation in this life. As strict empiricists we could only conclude that as much of the Bible as we have investigated was inspired. If others accepted our criteria for that judgment, they could always raise questions about remaining passages.

Rather than attempt to answer every problem that can be raised against biblical authority, many like Gerstner feel it advisable to move directly from historical data about Christ to the claims of Christ. Several advantages are apparent. Interest in Christ's person may be greater than in the Bible as a book. Belief on Christ is the condition of salvation. Nowhere does the Bible demand that one believe in its inspiration as a condition of salvation. But when one accepts Jesus as both Lord and Christ, he ought to follow his Lord in believing the Bible as God's revelation. So while it is important to know that common critical objections to the Bible have an answer, as Hamilton shows, it is wiser when possible to deal first with the problem of salvation.

Today, however, there remains a serious question whether one can move from purely historical data about Jesus of Nazareth to a valid conclusion that God was in Christ reconciling the world to Himself. Historical data may be variously interpreted by people from different perspectives. The same events may seem to show very different things to Christians and non-Christians. Although Hackett and Hamilton seek to overcome this serious difficulty by the rational structure of the human mind, the problem remains. Hamilton admitted the determining influence of specific presuppositions when discussing those of the destructive higher critics. If they start with naturalistic and evolutionary assumptions they alter the biblical data to fit their presuppositions. On the other hand, those who start with theistic and revelatory assumptions can find the biblical data quite consistent as it stands. What constitutes evidence from one perspective is not considered evidence from the other. Can empiricists really find data independent of interpretive presuppositions that will convince the unconvinced? We shall see the systems of apologists who think they cannot. Before drawing final conclusions the student should examine presuppositional systems carefully. Meanwhile we simply note that many feel the evidence presented in rational empiricism is either inadequate to support the conclusions drawn, or that it is covertly interpreted in favor of those conclusions.

RESOURCES FOR RESEARCH

A. ON EVIDENCE AND A PRIORI PRINCIPLES OF LOGIC, CAUSALITY

Hackett, Stuart Cornelius. *The Resurrection of Theism: Prolegomena to Christian Apology.* Chicago: Moody, 1957. A thorough application of rational empiricism to the existence of God.

Hamilton, Floyd E. *The Basis of Christian Faith: A Modern Defense of the Christian Religion.* Rev. ed. New York: Harper, 1964. An application of rational empiricism to the defense, not only of theism, but also of Christ and the Bible.

Kant, Immanuel. *Prolegomena to Any Future Metaphysics and Critique of Pure Reason.* The primary source of Hackett's categories and a most influential modern philosophy.

B. ON EVIDENCES FOR THE BIBLE AS SUPERNATURAL REVELATION (EMPHASIZED BY HAMILTON)

Arndt, W. *Does the Bible Contradict Itself? A Discussion of Alleged Contradictions in the Bible.* St. Louis, Mo.: Concordia, 1946. A popular explanation and application of the law of contradiction to biblical materials.

Bowman, Allen. *Is the Bible True?* Westwood, N.J.: Revell, 1965. Succinct, well written chapters in defense of the Bible's truth.

Foster, Randolph S. *The Supernatural Book: Evidences of Christianity.* Vol. 3. *Studies in Theology.* New York: Hunt and Eaton, 1893. An older work of 439 pages gives a thorough defense of the Scriptures as true and of supreme, universal, and perpetual authority.

Margoliouth, D. S. *Lines of Defense of the Biblical Revelation.* New York: Edwin S. Gorham, 1902. Evaluation of higher critical attacks on the Scripture by a professor of Arabic from Oxford.

Pierson, Arthur T. *Many Infallible Proofs.* Vol. 1. Grand Rapids: Zondervan, n.d. A popular Bible teacher argues for the Bible's truth from fulfilled prophecy, miracle, its scientific accuracy, moral beauty, and sublimity.

Urquhart, John. *Wonders of Prophecy: The Testimony of Fulfilled Prediction to the Inspiration of the Bible.* Rev. ed. London: Pickering and Inglis, 1939. A classic on fulfilled prophecy.

Watts, Newman, *The Incomparable Book.* New York: Amer. Tract Soc., 1940. A London journalist writes attractively of the Bible's human interest, literary grandeur, sublime influence, perfect unity, amazing accuracy.

4

THE RATIONALISM OF
GORDON H. CLARK

THE TEST OF LOGICAL CONSISTENCY

VIGOROUSLY OPPOSED to testing Christianity's truth-claims empirically is Gordon H. Clark, professor of philosophy at Indiana's Butler University. Granted the Ph.D. by the University of Pennsylvania, Clark did additional graduate work in Paris at the Sorbonne. He has also taught at the University of Pennsylvania and Wheaton College. Theologically Clark is a conservative Presbyterian who has served as president of the Evangelical Theological Society. His three lectures on "The Postulate of Revelation," delivered at the Wheaton College philosophy conference of 1965, were printed in a Festschrift entitled *The Philosophy of Gordon H. Clark*, with thirteen other contributors. Clark has published many books and articles of significance in religion and the history of philosophy. Why does a man of his stature not defend his Christian faith by appeals to objective evidence?

THE FAILURE OF EMPIRICAL APOLOGETICS

Every attempt in the history of philosophy to derive principles of mathematics and logic from the observation of sense data has failed according to Clark. He argues that universal and necessary principles go beyond the limits of finite empirical investigation. Following Kant (like Hackett), Clark holds that the mind brings with it to the investigation of anything some innate categories of thought. For example, these innate concepts include the notion of a mathematical unit. Unless the child's mind knew what one was beforehand, he could not

100

recognize even one marble. Clark adds, "And since numbers are not marbles or anything sensory, it follows that arithmetic is not abstracted from experience."[1]

Similarly, Clark argues, the laws of logic are not drawn from the wells of experience, but constitute a bucket by which to draw water from experience. The law of non-contradiction allows for no exceptions; it is asserted for every proposition universally. But no investigator could check every proposition to see if this were always the case in all times. The law of non-contradiction not only holds universally, but also with necessity. However, the conclusions of inductive reasoning do not follow with unqualified necessity, but with a degree of probability. Since the laws of logic are universal and necessary, Clark concludes that they could not have been derived from observation, as Buswell and pure empiricists claim.

For similar reasons a universally necessary causal law could not be derived from experience. No one could examine every instance of causes and effects. If one could, it would not guarantee that the next effect would necessarily have an adequate cause. Hume showed that empiricists do not receive impressions of a *necessary connection* between causes and effects. Buswell might reply that the law itself is not necessary, but overwhelmingly probable and so could be employed in his theistic arguments from the observed world to probable conclusions. Then Clark would press him from his position of probabilism to the logical extreme of complete skepticism. Unable to examine every instance, Clark would give up the empirical quest for truth in exhaustion. Knowledge of truth would be impossible. The senses often deceive, and if there were no further court of appeal Clark could never be sure he was not deceived. So on empiricist bases Clark must always be skeptical about truth-claims. If we only know our impressions, do we ever know reality? Who, then, does the perceiving? And who does the thinking about the multitudes of different impressions? Why should the mind totally unfurnished with preconceived notions make one combination rather than another? From considerations like these Clark thinks that empiricism, as in Locke, Berkeley, and Hume, leads, not only to the impossibility of knowing whether God exists, but whether any proposition is actually true.

1. Gordon H. Clark, *A Christian View of Men and Things* (Grand Rapids: Eerdmans, 1952), p. 307.

Clark is also dissatisfied with Hackett's attempt to obtain knowledge of causes by finding a universal and necessary law of causality in the human mind-structure. Clark agrees that the mind has this innate principle of causality, but he thinks it does not help identify any particular cause. So it cannot confirm the claim that the biblical God is the cause of a given event. The category of causality simply means that every event has some cause or other. Such a general principle of uniformity does not enable us to pick out from the infinite number of preceding events the cause of the event in question. To illustrate, Clark cites Boyle's law concerning gases at certain temperatures. Under the same conditions, it is assumed, gases at other times will act in the same way. But when are the conditions identical in every respect? We can never know whether every condition is the same. Even granting an a priori category of causality, Clark cannot determine its applicability at any given time to demonstrate the particular cause of an event. If he could, he adds, the law of physics would be unalterable.

Gordon Clark's challenge of empiricism is, of course, an attack upon the scientific method. In spite of modern scientists' claims, their method, Clark contends, is not one of pure observation. Scientific laws do not describe the actual workings of nature. Others may claim that scientific observation is the sole gateway to knowledge. "On the contrary," says Dr. Clark, "a plausible analysis showed that science was incapable of arriving at any truth whatever."[2] In defense of that startling thesis, he published a paperback entitled *The Philosophy of Science and Belief in God*.

Tracing the development of scientific thought from the ancient world of Aristotle to that of Sir Isaac Newton (1641-1727), Clark then shows the contemporary reaction against Newtonian physics. He concludes that laboratory science does not exclude all non-observational and non-experimental authority, that the laws of mechanics do not describe how nature works, and that scientific laws are constructions rather than discoveries. Since Newtonian laws do not portray the actual workings of nature, they cannot be used to deny the possibility of God or miracles. The mechanistic picture of the world, as much as a theistic world-picture, is a matter of faith.

Professor Clark interprets scientific laws in terms of Percy Bridgman's operationalism. "In general, we mean by any concept nothing

2. Ibid., p 227.

more than a set of operations; the concept is synonymous with the corresponding set of operations."[3] Left to empiricism, Hume is right, "The ultimate springs and principles are totally shut up from human curiosity and enquiry." Since science is non-cognitive it cannot form the base for either a defense or a denial of Christianity's truth.

Despairing of any truth from empiricism, Clark has some advice for those who would give a reason for their hope. "Christianity should refuse to define reason as a body of general principles empirically obtained. . . . The history of rationalism and its outcome in irrationalism show that no such body of principles can be obtained."[4]

The inductive appeal to evidences fails, not only because of logical difficulties, but also because of moral problems. As J. Gresham Machen said to the modernists of his generation, "You cannot take account of all the facts if you ignore the fact of sin." Man is unitary personality, and man as a whole is depraved. According to Scripture and Calvinism, sin affects every human function.[5] Although God reveals his glory in nature, men do not perceive it. Sin "has so vitiated human powers that man can read neither the heavens nor his own heart aright."[6] But the more fully sin is pointed up, the harder becomes the empiricist's case for a God all-wise, all-good, and all-powerful. If we start with a special revelation of God's purposes in history, we may see His answer to evil. But natural theology cannot handle the problem of evil, and candid Christians, Clark emphasizes, ought to admit it.[7]

FALLACIES IN THE COSMOLOGICAL ARGUMENT

Clark finds the argument from observed finite existences to an infinite Cause to be invalid and irrelevant to proof of the biblical God. The argument is thought to be invalid because, first, as stated by Aquinas, it depends upon Aristotle's analysis of motion, which Clark thinks is circular. The cause of any movement, Aristotle taught, must actually be what the thing moved is potentially. But Clark finds both

3. Percy Bridgman, *The Logic of Physics* (New York: Macmillan, 1927), p. 5. Cited by Gordon H. Clark, *The Philosophy of Science and Belief in God* (Nutley, N.J.: Presbyterian and Reformed, 1964), p. 79.
4. Gordon H. Clark, *Religion, Reason and Revelation* (Nutley, N.J.: Presbyterian and Reformed, 1961), p. 109.
5. Ibid., p. 106.
6. Clark, *Men and Things*, p. 251.
7. "Revealed Religion," *Christianity Today*, December 17, 1965, p. 7.

actuality and potentiality undefined and the whole explanation of motion circular. Neither Buswell nor Hackett employs these Aristotelian concepts and so this criticism applies on the contemporary scene only to traditional Thomists.

Second, Clark thinks the attempt of Thomas Aquinas to rule out an infinite regress of finite causes assumes an unmoved Mover—the very thing to be proved. Such circular reasoning is not proof. Of course Hackett seeks to avoid this charge.

Third, the cosmological argument is invalid because it cannot be shown that the world is an effect. Within the world we may observe some causes and effects, but we cannot validly infer the universality of such causes, for we have not seen the universe as whole.

Fourth, the argument is invalid because one of its terms is used in two different senses. The word "exist" does not have the same meaning in the premise about the observed existence of finite things that it has in the conclusion about the existence of the infinite God. When finite things are said to exist they are said to have come into existence at a certain time, to grow, and after a time to cease to be. When from such temporal existences God's existence is deduced, suddenly existence implies no beginning, growth, or end. No logical argument can use the same term in two different meanings.

Fifth, the cosmological argument is not only fallacious, but also irrelevant to the God of Christianity. The universe, if an effect, includes a terrifying profusion of evils, disasters, and tragedies. If the cosmological argument proves the existence of a God, it does not prove the existence of a just and merciful God.

> To be sure, it allows, though it does not prove, the existence of a good God, but only on the assumption that he is neither omnipotent nor the cause of all that happens. But the cosmological argument was supposed to deal with the universal cause. As a recourse for Christian theism, therefore, the cosmological argument is worse than useless. In fact, Christians can be pleased at its failure, for if it were valid, it would prove a conclusion inconsistent with Christianity.[8]

Of course Clark believes that he can consistently account for evil in the world, but not on the basis of inductive reasoning from the world. From the evils of the universe one would reason to an adequate cause—an evil Deity!

8. Clark, *Religion*, p. 41.

Sixth, Clark thinks the cosmological argument, if it were valid, would prove a physical Deity. From the reality of physical motion one can argue only to a physical cause. Clark is unsatisfied with Aristotle's attempt to show that the unmoved Mover has no magnitude. But a physically extended unmoved Mover does not have the qualities of a transcendent personality. A neuter first Cause cannot be identified with the personal God of Abraham, Isaac, and Jacob.

Seventh, Clark thinks that the cosmological argument, if valid, supports a Deity of only finite power. Valid inductive reasoning cannot logically ascribe to the cause any properties not necessary to account for the effects. So the argument might give us a God sufficiently powerful to account for the things we have observed, but no more. "In spite of the remark of some orthodox theologians that that is already a good deal, one must reply that it is not the omnipotent creator described in the Bible."[9]

In sum, Clark finds the cosmological argument invalid because it involves circular reasoning, it includes universal assertions going beyond evidence actually observed, and it uses one of the key terms (existence) in two different senses. If it were logically sound, furthermore, he thinks it would not prove the existence of the Christian God. At best it could only prove the existence of a Deity evil as well as good, physical rather than spiritual, and of finite power rather than omnipotent. Because Clark's case is directed against the cosmological arguments of Aquinas specifically, the student will consider to what extent the considerations apply to the formulations of the argument by recent writers. Clark's attempts to distinguish the cause of existence from the Christian God, in this writer's judgment, are beside the point. The argument does not seek to show everything about the character of the Eternal, but only the existence of the Eternal. Other evidence is adduced to support the character of the eternal. But Clark's arguments against validity of causal reasoning from the cosmos effectively point up the fallacies in the cosmological argument.

The Problems of Christian Evidences

Clark can no more logically demonstrate the truth of the Bible or Christianity by appeals to evidence, than he can the existence of God.

9. Ibid., p. 40.

If he were to appeal to objective evidence, he could do little better than to appeal to the evidence of archeology. Some Christians, Clark says, have fallaciously argued that, because the Bible has been shown true in one hundred and one cases, it is therefore true in every case. Obviously the conclusion goes beyond the evidence. The conclusion may be true, but the evidence of archeology does not demonstrate it. Has archeology no value then? "It is valuable in refuting the claims of the destructive critics, and the more quickly their baseless claims are exploded the better. But Christianity has more subtle enemies than the destructive critics."[10]

What about the appeal to the evidence of fulfilled prophecy, miracle, and supremely, the resurrection of Christ from the dead? Do these not prove the truth of Christianity? In Clark's approach the declaration of these has a place in popular testimony to one's faith. But they do not constitute the first principles of one's apologetic. Apologetics has to do, not with the concerns of practical evangelism and the chronological order of approach to persons. Rather, it relates to the concerns of philosophical systems and the logical order of ideas in that system. Apologetics is to evangelism as theoretical mathematics is to practical engineering.

> Certainly there is a place for evidences in propagation of the faith. Certainly the resurrection of Jesus Christ should be preached and the testimony of the eyewitnesses recounted. But after we have published abroad His wonderful name, and after we have declared our faith, the auditors may ask us a reason. Apologetics has its place too, but in the temporal order it is a latter place.[11]

Christain evidences, then, serve the purposes of personal witnessing and answering specific attacks upon biblical assertions. Evidences, not apologetics, may consider particular difficulties such as where Cain got his wife, how Noah managed to get all the animals in the ark, or whether the Egyptian armies under Shishak ever surrounded Jerusalem. On the other hand, apologetics treats Christianity as a system of thought about the world. So it considers such themes as the existence of God, the problem of knowing God, demonstration and consistency, the logical starting point of thought about God, and

10. Gordon H. Clark, *A Christian Philosophy of Education* (Grand Rapids: Eerdmans, 1946), p. 34.
11. Gordon H. Clark, "Apologetics," in *Contemporary Evangelical Thought*, ed. Carl F. H. Henry (Great Neck, N. Y.: Channel, 1957), p. 140.

the understanding of His attributes (analogically, univocally, or equivocally).[12]

Some apologists insist that the conclusive evidence of Christianity's truth is the resurrection of Jesus Christ. Why does Clark not think that sheer evidence of Christ's resurrection can prove the truth of Christianity? He explains:

> Suppose Jesus did rise from the grave. This only proves that his body resumed its activities for a while after his crucifixion; it does not prove that he died for our sins or that he was the Son of God. While this line of anti-Christian argument contains certain misstatements, none the less the inference in the last sentence is valid. The resurrection, viewed purely as an isolated historical event, does not prove that Christ died for our sins, not only because Lazarus also rose from the dead, but also because sin is a notion which requires a particular view about God and universe, and on such questions archeology and history are incompetent.[13]

Christ's resurrection has a place in Clark's system of thought, but it is not a cornerstone that can stand alone. No individual event can be truly understood in isolation. Each particular thing is understood in its relationships to other things, and finally to his entire view of reality. Clark's view of reality, then, determines his assessment of a given event.

STARTING WITH CHRISTIAN PRESUPPOSITIONS

Every view of the world, Clark points out, contains certain presuppositions. If these are not made explicit, they are nevertheless implicit. The presuppositions of any religious or non-religious system are in the very nature of the case indemonstrable. Since they are starting points, they cannot be supported by any considerations more ultimate. Professor Clark explains:

> The situation is similar to the issue between Aristotle and Sophism relative to demonstration. If everything is to be demonstrated, the demonstration turns out to be either circular or an infinite regress. Both are unsatisfactory. Therefore some things cannot be demonstrated. These are first principles which themselves are the basis or beginning of argument; and if they are the beginning, they cannot have been previously argued.[14]

12. Ibid., pp. 137-61.
13. Clark, *Philosophy of Education*, p. 35.
14. Clark, *Men and Things*, p. 259.

Once such first principles are granted as true, then the whole system of thought may be deduced from them with syllogistic rigor.

Adopting this deductive approach to constructing a world view, Clark finds his chief analogies in geometry. The geometrician starts with unprovable axioms and then everything follows from them, not with probability, but with certainty. Those familiar with the history of philosophy recognize the similarity of Clark's approach to that of the modern French philosopher and mathematician, Renè Descartes (1596-1650). So the logical starting point of Christian apologetics is stated as an axiom.

The axioms with which to begin an apologetic must be specifically Christian. The only way validly to find Christianity in our conclusions, he argues, is to have Christianity in our premises. "Instead of beginning with facts and later discovering God," Clark says, "unless a thinker begins with God, he can never end with God, or get the facts either."[15]

The Christian axiom, as Clark puts it, is twofold, including the existence of God and the truth of His revelation in the Bible. His is no mere theism without a propositional revelation. Neither is the axiom to be confused with a deistic one which excludes biblical miracles. In agreement with Karl Barth, then, Clark holds that Christian apologetic does not establish revelation, but is derived from revelation.[16] Only if we begin with the presupposition of Christianity's truth can we defend Christianity's truth!

Immediately we cry out, "Circular reasoning!" Is not Clark's twofold axiom assuming the very thing to be supported? Part of Clark's reply to this charge is that every other system is equally guilty. "The non-Christian arguments regularly assume the point in dispute before they start. The questions are so framed as to exclude the Christian answer from the beginning."[17] So, if everyone has his own biases with which he begins, the apologist's task becomes worse than discouraging, it seems impossible. With the skeptics we must join hands; nothing can be proved. But if skepticism is true, something can be proved (skepticism). Because of this self-contradiction we cannot remain skeptics.[18] "Still it remains true that no demonstration of

15. Clark, *Philosophy of Education*, p. 38.
16. Gordon H. Clark, *Karl Barth's Theological Method* (Philadelphia: Presbyterian and Reformed, 1963), p. 99.
17. Clark, *Religion*, p. 27.
18. Clark, *Men and Things*, pp. 29-30.

God is possible; our belief is a voluntary choice; but if one must choose without a strict proof, none the less it is possible to have sane reasons of some sort to justify the choice. Ultimately these reasons reduce to the principle of consistency."[19]

THE TEST OF TRUTH

Clark tests conflicting first principles by the law of contradiction. He rejects as false axioms leading to a system which contradicts itself, and accepts as true the axioms from which the most consistent system can be deduced with the fewest difficulties. Why test proposed world-views by their consistency? He has shown that empirical tests do not succeed in demonstrating truth. But he cannot elude the demands of logic. The basic laws of logic are inherent in the human mind. Although Clark cannot agree with Kant's categories in detail, Kant's a priori view of logic is "inescapable."[20] Universally and necessarily we cannot affirm and deny the same thing at the same time and in the same respect. Such universality and necessity cannot be a probable induction from limited human experience. No claim to truth can satisfy the logically structured human mind if deductions from it lead to contradictions.

Clark's emphasis on logical consistency is often thought to exalt Aristotle (who classically stated the law of non-contradiction) above God. Clark replies that logic is not above God, but an expression of the way God Himself thinks. The relation of logic to God is seen in Clark's paraphrase of the prologue to John's gospel, "In the beginning was Logic, and Logic was with God, and Logic was God. . . . In Logic was life and the life was the light of men." If that seems objectionable, Clark challenges anyone to deny the validity of the softer translation, "In the beginning was Reason, and Reason was with God and Reason was God."[21] The softer translation accomplishes the same thing in Clark's judgment because he holds that nothing can be reasonable and be contradictory. And no contradiction can represent to us the mind of God on a subject. Only insofar as our entire system of thought is consistent can it be true. Truth is the same for God and man. Men do not know as much truth as

19. Clark, *Philosophy of Education*, p. 48.
20. Clark, *Men and Things*, p. 313.
21. Gordon H. Clark, "The Wheaton Lectures," in *The Philosophy of Gordon H. Clark*, ed. Ronald H. Nash (Philadelphia: Presbyterian and Reformed, 1968), pp. 67, 118.

God. "But if we know anything at all, what we know must be identical with what God knows. God knows all truth, and unless we know something God knows, our ideas are untrue."[22]

The test of contradiction, Clark also argues, does no violence to Scriptural teaching and practice. Scripture is not subjected to an alien norm when interpreted consistently. The Bible itself exhibits logical order. For example, Clark notes an enthymematic hypothetical destructive syllogism in Romans 4:2, a hypothetical constructive syllogism in Romans 5:13 and sorites in 1 Corinthians 15:15-18. Although many other examples could be given, Clark admits that much Scripture is not in the form of syllogistic deduction. Historical sections appear in narrative style. Even so, he argues, "every declarative sentence is a logical unit. These sentences are truths; as such they are objects of knowledge. Each of them has, or perhaps we should say, each of them is a predicate attached to a subject. Only so can they convey meaning."[23] Single Scriptural words, as well as sentences, exhibit the logical principle that a term must mean one thing and not its contradictory. When the Bible asserts that David was King of Israel, Clark insists it does not mean that David was president of Babylon or that Churchill was prime minister of China. A "libel" against Scripture says its meanings are infinitely elastic. If so, then the denial of verbal inspiration could be interpreted as the acceptance of verbal inspiration. Since that is impossible, it is equally impossible to interpret the virgin birth as a myth or the resurrection as a symbol of spring.[24] The Bible employs the laws of logic and is more simply interpreted according to the laws of logic. Consistency as a test of truth in no way undermines scriptural authority. The biblical stance is a logical stance.

Clark not only holds that the laws of logic are consistent with his axiom of God as revealed in Scripture, but also with the requirements of communication. "In all our conversation and writing the forms of logic are indispensable: without them discussion on every subject would cease."[25] If we are to be understood by others we cannot affirm and deny the same thing at the same time and in the same respect. Religious statements are no exception. If Christian claims are true,

22. Ibid., p. 77.
23. Ibid., p. 70.
24. Ibid., p. 71.
25. Clark, *Men and Things*, p. 308.

the system deduced from them cannot contradict itself. On the other hand, if non-Christian systems are contradictory their first principles cannot be accepted as true.

The Apologist's Negative Task

If Christianity is true, non-Christian systems should eventually contradict themselves. The task of reducing non-Christian positions to such absurdity (*reductio ad absurdum*) is called apagogic. To exemplify this method Clark singles out Logical Positivism, which holds religious statements to be meaningless because not verifiable by the senses. No statement about matters of fact are said to be meaningful if they are not verifiable. Clark comments that "this axiom of verification reduces to absurdity because it violates itself. The principle is not subject to sensory confirmation and hence is nonsense. Granted, this is not all a Christian evangelist should say to a Logical Positivist; it is not all that he should say about Logical Positivism; but the apagogic method must remain the basic apologetic procedure."[26]

John Dewey's behaviorism, Clark thinks, can also be reduced to absurdity. Dewey denied the existence of consciousness and then smuggled in all the advantages of consciousness. A merely physical organism is no more conscious of a sensation of red in a mental or "felt" awareness than a barn is conscious of its red paint. Clark also answers Dewey's instrumentalism. Dewey insisted that knowledge does not grasp antecedent reality, but simply outlines plans of action for the future. So Clark asks how he can consistently assert that there is an existence antecedent to search and discovery. Dewey admits a given— a buzzing, blooming mass of confusion. How can he assert, without all the difficulties Kant faced, an unknowable existence? The idea of the given is not a plan of action. Neither is historical knowledge of the past a plan of action for the future. Clark also shows how ambiguous are the key terms, habit and organism. Although Dewey himself did not discard the law of contradiction, he predicted that it could be changed in the future. The philosopher of change and flux could not have one changeless principle. But Clark argues that logic does not depend upon the changing states of science; rather, all meaningful speech in any field, however radical its development, depends on logic. Once the scientist seeks to stipulate away the law

26. Clark, *Barth's Theological Method*, p. 85.

of contradiction, intelligibility ceases. Instrumentalism would then mean it is contradictory, and be nonsense. Clark leaves the reader with a choice between unintelligibility and fixed logical principles. He goes on to argue that if thought has meaning, then there are eternal truths. Eternal truths, furthermore, require an Eternal Mind whose thinking makes them so.[27]

Clark's apagogic in relation to communism capitalizes on some skillful analogies. Engels' naturalism implied that the idea of number arises from counting our fingers. Engels explained that the ability to exclude from consideration all properties of objects other than their number is the product of a long evolution based on experience. Clark replies, "By so pushing a problem back in time and calling it solved thereby, Johnny in high school could argue that his proof of the theorem must be correct, for he took so long to do it." Communism's denial of any independent moral standards leaves the right of one class over another to be decided by force. The communist test of truth is pragmatic. Will communism produce the desired results? "If the proletariat can so arrange things that I can fish in the morning and hunt in the afternoon, then communism will be true." Clark also attacks the materialistic notion that the brain secretes thought as the liver secretes bile. On that assumption thought is simply the product of the brain, and no thought can contradict nature. "If all thought is thus natural, there is no logical reason to believe that some thoughts, ideas of dialectical materialism rather than of absolute idealism, are more natural, more true, or more valuable than others."[28]

How then does Clark reduce Kierkegaard's existentialism to absurdity? The stress on passionate appropriation or subjectivity apart from considerations of objective historical truth raises questions for Clark. If there is no objective truth, how can truth be distinguished from fancy? Why distinguish a suffering Satan from a suffering Saviour? Why not praise an inner, infinite, decisive appropriation of the devil as fully as a decision for God? Is it objectively indifferent whether one worships God or an idol? Does it make no difference whether God exists or not? Clark also asks existentialists why existentialism is to be regarded as more true than idealism or communism.

27. Gordon H. Clark, *Dewey* (Grand Rapids: Baker, 1960), pp. 41-61.
28. Gordon H. Clark, *Thales to Dewey: A History of Philosophy* (Boston: Houghton Mifflin, 1957), pp. 484-85.

Suppose now that there are serious flaws in Hegel's "System"; suppose too that the communistic mass-man violates the prerogatives of the moral individual; suppose in the third place that the Danish Lutheran church was formal, hypocritical, and dead; suppose therefore that S.K. has made some telling criticisms of his contemporaries. Does this then imply that the cure can be effected by a suffering or passion, a subjective feeling, to which objective truth and untruth are equally indifferent? If this were true, not only would an idol be as satisfactory as God, but Hegel or Marx would be as satisfactory as Kierkegaard.[29]

The entire history of philosophy, Clark finds, leaves the scholar with a choice between skeptical futility and a word from God. His extensive text, *From Thales to Dewey* concludes:

The history of philosophy began with naturalism, and so far as this volume is concerned it ends with naturalism. The Presocratic naturalism dissolved into Sophism, from which a metaphysics arose; and the metaphysics lost itself in a mystic trance (neoplatonism). Then under the influence of an alien source (Aristotle), Western Europe appealed to a divine revelation. In the sixteenth century one group put their complete trust in revelation, while another development turned to unaided human reason. This latter movement has now abandoned its metaphysics, its rationalism, and even fixed truths of naturalistic science. It has dissolved into Sophism. Does this mean that philosophers and cultural epochs are nothing but children who pay their fare to take another ride on the merry-go-round? Is this Nietzsche's eternal recurrence? Or, could it be that a choice must be made between skeptical futility and a word from God? To answer this question for himself, the student, since he cannot ride very fast into the future and discover what a new age will do, might begin by turning back to the first page and pondering the whole thing over again. This will at least stave off suicide for a few more days.[30]

Any Christian who so dismally evaluates history's finest philosophies will not make common cause with them at any point. Like Karl Barth, Clark thinks that any theologian who employs presuppositions common to non-Christian systems is descending the road to atheistic humanism.[31] The apologist's first task is not to find common ground with unbelievers, but to expose the fallacies in their thought.

29. Ibid., pp. 489-91.
30. Ibid., pp. 533-34.
31. Clark, *Barth's Theological Method*, p. 93.

THE APOLOGIST'S POSITIVE TASK

To show that non-Christian systems of thought were contradictory would not mean necessarily that Christianity is true. What is Clark's case for Christianity? It is simply an exposition of Christian ideas in order to display their inherent consistency. Clark likens the task to that of the geometrician. The theorems are reduced to the least number of axioms and their harmony disclosed. "Axiomatization" is "the perfecting and exhibiting of the logical consistency of a system of thought."[32] The Christian axioms of God and the Bible are not the starting point for non-Christians and so in principle there are no axioms in common. Starting with the God of the Bible, Clark seeks to spell out a revelational interpretation of every realm of human experience. "Christianity is a comprehensive view of all things: it takes the world, both material and spiritual, to be an ordered system."[33]

The consistency of Christian views of history and politics is sketched in *A Christian View of Men and Things*. In accord with the biblical axiom, history is held to be controlled by God, acted upon by God, and brought to its culmination by God. Government is a divine institution. Its authority derives, not from a social compact, but from God. God is the source of all rights. While non-Christian systems consider man's present condition normal, Christianity considers it abnormal because of sin. In a fallen world the state is not a positive good, but a necessary evil to administer justice. Humanistic principles lead to anarchy or totalitarianism, but Christian presuppositions justify civil governments with limited rights.

The contributions of Christianity in ethics and epistemology are also set forth in *A Christian View of Men and Things*. Biblical ethics provide an adequate scope for self-interest without endorsing selfishness, something non-Christian ethics have not succeeded in doing. Biblical admonitions like the Ten Commandments also provide specific guidance in the actual situations of life. On Christian axioms the existence of truth is consistently explained. Relativistic theories tacitly assume their own absolutism. If no propositions were changeless, no significant speech would be possible. Truth is always true; it is changeless. And it must be mental or spiritual, for it does not

32. Ibid., p. 95.
33. Clark, *Men and Things*, p. 25.

exist without a mind. If truth were some physical motion in the brain no two persons could have the same thought, and communication would be impossible. Neither could the same person have the same thought twice or remember it later. How could any motion connect two other motions that no longer exist? Christian presuppositions explain how truth is mental or spiritual and is eternally thought by God.

Christian presuppositions also account for language. God created beings who were not merely physical, but spiritual and intellectual, with an innate ability to think and speak. Language is not an evolutionary development from meaningless grunts and groans as those with naturalistic assumptions suppose. Language is not limited to referents in time and space. It enables intelligent beings to share non-physical ideas. It is adequate for communication between God and man in a written revelation, and in prayer. The Bible was verbally inspired, that is, its language was ultimately derived from God and given through the human writers. Clark's philosophy of language is found in *Religion, Reason and Revelation*.

If all knowledge can be systematized on the basis of revealed principles, one is bound to ask whether there is a Christian view of chemistry and physics. Clark answers:

> The axioms of faith are all-comprehensive and the sciences have no independent existence. This implausibility of theologizing arithmetic, chemistry, and biology, is, however, only initial. There is nothing more implausible in theologizing chemistry than there is in positivizing or hegelianizing it. Both are attempts to maintain the consistency of all truth. If the implausibility were read as an impossibility, one's word would be split in two, each with its own "truth," and each with its own schizophrenic logic.[34]

Although Dr. Clark has not emphasized metaphysics, some hints of his position appear. He does not adopt a mechanistic model of reality. "The world of physics drops into the secondary position of stage scenery, and instead of picturing hard pellets, the Christian view emphasizes a world of spirits or persons, or minds."[35] Unlike some personalists, Clark does not equate the physical world with the divine consciousness. All things and persons are brought into being by a free creative act of the sovereign Creator.

34. Clark, *Barth's Theological Method*, p. 97.
35. Clark, *Men and Things*, p. 322.

In ways like these briefly outlined, Clark seeks to exhibit the consistency of the system deduced from Christian axioms. Systematic theology would detail the matter further. The task of presenting a complete system is overwhelming indeed. Clark has not completed his own. Of course no one can achieve the all-comprehensive ideal. No one is omniscient. But the exigencies of life require a decision for some view of the world. In which shall we trust?

> If one system can provide plausible solutions to many problems while another leaves too many questions unanswered, if one system tends less to skepticism and gives more meaning to life, if one world view is consistent while others are self-contradictory, who can deny us, since we must choose, the right to choose the more promising first principle?[36]

In the choice of a system the whole man is involved. Clark rejects a faculty psychology which regards man a compound of three things, an intellect, a will, and an emotion. Rather, these are three activities of one individual. Sometimes a person thinks, sometimes he wills, sometimes he feels. So religion must make its appeal to the whole man.[37] In faith a person freely chooses a view which satisfies his intellect according to the laws of logic. Clark calls for a voluntary commitment to his deductive rationalism.

"There can be no volition without intellection . . . and conversely there can be no intellection without volition, for intellectual assent is itself an act of the will."[38] They are not to be considered two separate acts any more than two separate faculties. The mental act is equally volitional and intellectual. So faith as a volitional commitment is inherent in all knowledge. Christianity is not in a unique position at this point. "The use of logic requires a voluntary act of attention, as does every other belief. One may choose simply not to think; or, rather, if he thinks, he must choose to pay attention."[39] Thomism says you do not believe what you know or know what you believe. But Clark insists that: (1) all that we believe sensibly we know, and (2) all that we know truly we believe. Clark opposes a mere rationalism (either empirical or deductive) without faith and also a faith without reason, whether the faith of mysticism, Sören

---

36. Ibid., p. 34.
37. Clark, *Philosophy of Education*, p. 170.
38. Clark, *Religion*, p. 98.
39. Ibid.

Kierkegaard, Friedrich Nietzsche, William James, or Emil Brunner. Clark's treatment of these positions as well as his own occurs in a thorough chapter on "Faith and Reason" in *Religion, Reason and Revelation*.

An intelligent faith in Christianity is a repentant faith. When the non-Christian's system has been shown to be self-contradictory and the Christian's system consistent, "the Christian will urge the unbeliever to repudiate the axioms of secularism and accept God's revelation. That is, the unbeliever will be asked to change his mind completely, to repent. This type of apologetic argument neither intends deception nor does it deny that in fact repentance comes only as a gift from God."[40]

COMMON GROUND WITH NON-CHRISTIANS

The total difference between the Christian and non-Christian axioms does not keep the Christian from communicating meaningfully with non-Christians. "Unless everybody is to be included as a believer in the Church, we must admit the existence of unbelievers who actually even if inconsistently believe a few divine truths."[41] How does Clark explain this? Since people are inconsistent it is psychologically possible for an unbeliever and a believer to agree on a given proposition. Also, all human beings possess a common capacity for faith as a vestige of the divine image in man. Defaced but not annihilated, the image is "a psychological, mental, ontological reality. It is an existing part of human nature."[42] This capacity of itself cannot manufacture faith. It is not to be viewed in terms of modernism or Catholicism. But man does have "a capacity for faith not shared by a tree or a stone. . . . Faith is a mental activity and by definition presupposes a rational subject. Reason therefore can be considered to be an element in common to believer and unbeliever."[43]

Although no act of the depraved will in the unregenerate can be moral, intellectual arguments of the depraved mind can be valid. Undoubtedly the *use* of valid syllogisms is sinful, Clark thinks, but as such the syllogisms are logically sound. The doctrine of total depravity means that no function of man is free from the effects of sin, but not

40. Clark, *Barth's Theological Method*, p. 96.
41. Ibid., p. 103.
42. Ibid., p. 102.
43. Ibid.

that the image of God has been entirely annihilated. To show this, Clark stresses logic and reason. He says Christians could not preach the facts of Christ's death, burial and resurrection, much less their significance, if the non-Christian's mind were devoid of logic. The strictures which devotional writers put on human reason, Clark adds, are "pious stupidity."[44]

As a result of the capacity for reason and faith, as well as human inconsistency, Clark accounts for certain moral and theological beliefs among non-Christians. These beliefs are the basis of heathen responsibility before God. And "these beliefs, dimly and inconsistently held, often submerged and repressed, can be thought of as a point of contact for the gospel."[45] The Christian can count on these beliefs and capacities when engaged in his mission to pre-Christians. But apart from the supernatural agency of the Holy Spirit through the Gospel these beliefs never develop into faith in Christ. For redemption, proclamation of the Gospel in the power of the Spirit is necessary.

By admitting common moral and theological ground, has Clark not undermined his own stress on totally distinct axioms and systems deduced from them? The differences between the systems made clear in apologetics are as important to the Christian's witness as mathematics is to an engineer. Engineering

> is immediately concerned with an individual practical situation; its procedure is rough rather than rigorous; and everyone is satisfied if the bridge or building is serviceable despite some minor inconveniences. But the mathematics which the engineer used, the theory which he applied, was developed with utmost exactitude; and if Leibnitz and Newton had been preoccupied with bridges and buildings, they would never have invented calculus.[46]

Apologetics, in Clark's thought, provides the technically precise background and tools which may be applied in specific instances of conversation with non-Christian individuals.

Clark's Apologetic and the Invisible Gardener

Applying the system to one who does not believe in a Lord of history, we do not appeal to evidence or facts. Rather, the unbeliever

44. Nash, *Philosophy*, pp. 75-76.
45. Clark, *Barth's Theological Method*, p. 100.
46. Clark, "Apologetics," p. 140.

must be challenged to face inconsistencies in his own claims concerning his knowledge of "the garden." He may then be shown the consistency of the biblical view of the world. It accounts for the world's existence by creation, its thorns and thistles by man's fall into sin, its present purpose and future culmination by God's providence, its human government by a real, but limited authority from God, human morality by a healthy and prescribed basis of self-interest, and human knowledge with its elements of changeless truth by the creation of man's mind (categories) in the likeness of God's mind, and theological language by the creation of man to engage in communion with God. Every department of knowledge, including physics and chemistry, is consistently accounted for on Christian presuppositions.

Having seen the harmony of Christian knowledge, the unbeliever is called upon to repent of his non-Christian presuppositions and actions and believe in the God of the Bible, and the Gospel. Convicted by the Holy Spirit, he voluntarily accepts Christianity as the most rational account of the garden in its entirety. The test of Christianity's truth-claims is not their correspondence with facts, but their logical consistency.

EVALUATION

Suppose for the moment that consistency is the sole test of truth-claims, as Clark asserts. Admittedly Christianity's truth-claims cannot be proved by inductive evidence. But Clark chooses to believe their truth because Christianity, of all the systems men have known, is alone consistent. Notice what is necessary for Clark to establish that thesis. He must show the inconsistency of *every* other system in history and on the contemporary scene. He has done a phenomenal job toward this in the history of philosophy and in some measure among contemporary trends. At best, however, he can only assert that all non-Christian systems that *he has canvassed* are inconsistent, and *to the best of his knowledge* the only consistent system is Christianity. In other words he faces the same limitations he so frequently applies to the empiricists. The conclusion of an argument cannot go beyond the evidence. The finiteness of any investigator limits the findings necessary to support Clark's thesis that Christianity alone is consistent. One lifetime is too short to check all the other possibilities. If it were possible to check every other possibility to the present moment, he would have no basis on which to know what non-Christian system might be produced in the future. On similar considerations Clark requires the empiricist to admit mere probability. He must also admit to mere probability, however high or overwhelming, that he has shown Christianity alone to be consistent. He presses the most painstaking empiricist from probability to complete skepticism. If, as Clark says, a thesis that cannot be proved with certainty cannot be known to be true at all, then his own system may be reduced from probability to total skepticism. So we could not know from Clark's apologetic that Christianity is true.

On what grounds does Clark know that there could not be two or more consistent systems? He assumes that only one system could possibly be consistent. If proposed systems are not responsible to the data of experience, it would seem that perfectly consistent systems could be developed without limit—as in the making of rules for countless games. Is there a hidden axiom that only one consistent system could be developed? Does that make it so?

Sheer logical consistency is an inadequate test for truth. Contradiction is the surest sign of error, but consistency is not a guarantee of truth. For example, a consistent account of Christian Science might be given, but Christian Science truth-claims could not be accepted as long as it denied the reality of the all too prevalent facts of experience: sin, sickness, and death. Coherence with experiential data is necessary to show the truth of a proposed system, however consistent. Clark's test for truth cannot be interpreted as requiring the fitting of the facts. He has vigorously opposed any attempt to support truth-claims by empirical findings. Clark's test of consistency has negative value only. Many recent philosophers have preferred to refer, not as Clark does to the law of contradiction, but rather, to the law of non-contradiction.

It is difficult to agree with Clark's assertion that no knowledge is obtained from scientific observation. If scientific statements are merely operational procedures, why are some more operational than others? May it not be that they are closer to the truth about the world than others? Clark does admit as "facts," the path of the planets and acceleration of a freely falling body. But he will not call scientific laws or facts explanations. By explanation he apparently means an ultimate metaphysical explanation. Science, as distinct from scien-

tism, has not proposed that laws and facts are metaphysical ultimates. Scientific accounts of gravitation do inform us with an accuracy far beyond untested appearances of what in fact does occur.
Clark goes too far in saying that science is incapable of arriving at
any truth whatever. Science is not the only source of truth, and does
not produce a total world view, but it does yield some truth about the
world in which we live.

Of course scientific laws and facts change. But the grounds for the
changes are empirical, not metaphysical discoveries. Science, as distinct from scientism which Clark properly denounces, is self-critical
and self-correcting. When alterations are made in laws and facts, it
is because earlier inferences were drawn without sufficient evidence.
This does not mean that they can never be correct. Even the correct
views are stated in terms of high probability, not an alleged, but un-
supportable certainty. If views probable beyond reasonable doubt
are never true, then Clark's thesis for the truth of Christianity cannot
be true. Clark's demand for absolute truth, as we have shown above,
would rule out his own merely probable case for Christianity's truth.
Reasons similar to those Clark uses to show that science is non-cognitive would show that his case for Christianity would be non-cognitive.

Christian ontology, as Clark has said, views reality as primarily
persons, not pellets. But syllogistic reasoning alone is inadequate to
the knowledge of persons in their uniqueness. Syllogisms are invalid
if the middle term (common to both premises) is not distributed at
least once. It must refer in the same sense to every member of its
class. Clark can deduce things about Socrates insofar as Socrates
shares the characteristics common to all men—mortality, fallenness,
finiteness. But having limited himself to this one way of knowing,
Clark cannot know Socrates as an individual different from other
men. The only way to know a person in his uniqueness is through
direct experience of him, and his self-revelation to you, or indirect
testimony from someone who knows him personally. Experience, direct or indirect, is involved in coming to know persons as distinct
individuals. Premises of syllogistic arguments having to do with such
individuals in their uniqueness can be confirmed or disconfirmed
only by experience, or trustworthy reports of experience. Clark's
scriptural axiom in no way alleviates this requirement. From the
universal propositions in Scripture we can infer only universal traits

to men today. But on that presupposition I can never get to know Gordon Clark personally as a friend without the privilege of experience or correspondence with him. We know more than propositions and universals. Through true propositions we know particular men and things indirectly. But we can also have direct experience of men and things. We may then have to set forth our knowledge in propositional form to make it precise and to communicate it to others. But that does not displace the need for experience and the testing of our propositions again by their conformity with our experience, especially of persons in their individuality. Since Clark views reality as primarily personal—a personal Creator and personal creatures—this failure to account for knowledge of unique individuals is damaging indeed.

Over against these rather formidable criticisms of Clark's thought are some significant values. Young people seeking guidance in the critical evaluation of imposing figures in the history of philosophy will find it profitable to read Clark's works. He effectively exposes contradictions in the famous philosophers. In the fulfillment of the apologist's negative task he is proficient.

Furthermore, Gordon Clark is a first-rate philosopher who is at the same time a thoroughgoing Christian. Clark's positions and publications commend him to all who respect academic achievement. And his soundly biblical faith commends him to those who respect written revelation. Young people awed by certain non-Christian philosophers need to know about believers of this stature.

RESOURCES FOR RESEARCH

GORDON H. CLARK'S MOST RELEVANT WORKS
(in the order published)

A Christian Philosophy of Education. Grand Rapids: Eerdmans, 1946. Arguing the impossibility of a neutral education, Clark sets forth the educational goals and norms of Christian presuppositions.

A Christian View of Men and Things. Grand Rapids: Eerdmans, 1952. A reduction of alternatives to Christianity to absurdity, and an exhibition of the consistency of Christian thought on philosophy of history, politics, ethics, science, religion, and epistemology.

"The Bible as Truth." *Bibliotheca Sacra* 114 (April 1957) : 157-70. Clark compares his views with those of Van Til and Carnell.

"Apologetics." In *Contemporary Evangelical Thought*. Ed. by Carl F. H. Henry. Great Neck, N.Y.: Channel, 1957. A survey and evaluation of recent evangelical contributions focusing on the nature of apologetics, the cosmological argument, demonstration and consistency, the starting point, and analogy.

Thales to Dewey: A History of Philosophy. Boston: Houghton Mifflin, 1957. A discussion of the primary movements in the history of the problem of knowledge. The systems which fail to begin with propositional revelation from God are found to end in skepticism.

"Special Divine Revelation as Rational." In *Revelation and the Bible*. Ed. by Carl F. H. Henry. Grand Rapids: Baker, 1958. A chapter arguing against the contemporary view that special revelation is an irrational object of faith, and for the reformation view that finds the laws of logic implicit in Scripture as a meaningful revelation.

Dewey. Modern Thinkers Series. Ed. by David H. Freeman. Grand Rapids: Baker, 1960. A brief analysis of John Dewey's thought which argues that his instrumentalism does away with the law of contradiction and therefore all intelligibility, and so is literal nonsense.

"God." In *Baker's Dictionary of Theology*. Ed. by Everett F. Harrison. Grand Rapids: Baker, 1960. A discussion of biblical theology concerning God as creator and redeemer, and of philosophical theology.

"Truth." In *Baker's Dictionary of Theology*. Ed. by Everett F. Harrison. Grand Rapids: Baker, 1960. A brief analysis of philosophical and biblical meanings of truth.

Religion, Reason and Revelation. Nutley, N.J.: Presbyterian and Reformed, 1961. A denial that Christianity has any religious essence in common with other religions, followed by a discussion of faith and reason, inspiration and language, ethics, and the problem of evil.

Karl Barth's Theological Method. Philadelphia: Presbyterian and Reformed, 1963. A thorough evaluation of the first volume of Barth's *Church Dogmatics*. Clark agrees with Barth's repudiation of common ground all along the line. But he objects to Barth's refusal to accept an axiomatic system to maintain that total difference between Christianity and non-Christian systems. The chapter "Prolegomena and Apologetics" has particular relevance.

"How May I Know the Bible Is Inspired?" In *Can I Trust My Bible?* Chicago: Moody, 1963. Starting with the presuppositions of noncontradiction and the truth of the Bible's claims for itself as attested by the Holy Spirit, we can "see" that the Bible is inspired of God.

The Philosophy of Science and Belief in God. Nutley, N.J.: Craig, 1964.
Surveying the history of science, Clark concludes that it tells nothing
about the world, is non-cognitive, and merely operational.

The Philosophy of Gordon H. Clark: A Festschrift. Ed. by Ronald H.
Nash. Philadelphia: Presbyterian and Reformed, 1968. With Clark's
three Wheaton Lectures are chapters evaluating his thought by thirteen evangelical scholars. Clark replies to their criticisms in eight
chapters. See this work for a complete bibliography of Clark's works.

Historiography Secular and Religious. Nutley, N.J.: Craig, 1971. An expose of the philosophical presuppositions operative in the writing of
influential historians.

The Johannine Logos. Nutley, N.J.: Presbyterian and Reformed, 1972.
A case for faith as thinking with assent over against views of writers like
A. W. Tozer, who allegedly minimize belief and substitute for faith an
emotional or mystical experience.

Three Types of Religious Philosophy. Nutley, N.J.: Craig, 1973. An
evaluation of writings classified under the headings of rationalism, empiricism, and irrationalism.

5

THE BIBLICAL AUTHORITARIANISM OF CORNELIUS VAN TIL

THE TEST OF SCRIPTURAL AUTHORITY

AMONG THE MOST SIGNIFICANT contemporary apologists is Cornelius Van Til. Originally from the Netherlands, Van Til studied at Calvin College, Princeton Theological Seminary, and Princeton University. After a year of pastoring and a year of teaching at Princeton Seminary, Dr. Van Til went to Philadelphia's Westminster Theological Seminary where he has served since 1929 in the field of apologetics. Through the years he has developed several course syllabi and published numerous books and pamphlets.

Professor Van Til's purpose has been to devise an apologetic "consistent with the nature of Christianity."[1] All other attempts to defend Christianity, he thinks, fail to do justice to man's total depravity, to divine grace, to covenant theology, or to biblical authority. For Presbyterian Van Til, Christianity is best expressed in the Westminster Confession of Faith. With Benjamin B. Warfield, he thinks that Calvinism is "Christianity come to its own."[2] Readers who are not Calvinistic will nevertheless find the study of Van Til stimulating and profitable. His apologetic represents a position encountered with increasing frequency. How does he seek to show Christianity's truth?

1. *The Defense of the Faith,* p. vii. All works cited in this chapter are by Cornelius Van Til and all are published by Presbyterian and Reformed Publishing Company or the Craig Press. For dates of publication see "Resources for Research" at the end of this chapter.
2. Ibid., p. 88.

EVIDENCE CANNOT DECIDE

In agreement with Gordon Clark, Cornelius Van Til denounces an evidential approach to Christian apologetics. Christian-Theistic Evidences, as he conceives them, defend Christianity against attacks from science, where apologetics defends it against attacks from philosophy. Scientific attacks on Christianity are answered in one stroke. Scientific evidence can count neither for nor against Christianity's truth. How does Van Til arrive at this non-empirical conclusion?

Like Clark, Van Til thinks that Hume dealt the deathblow to a pure empiricism. The end result of sheer empiricism is sheer skepticism. Do Kant's categories as employed by Hackett save the day? Not for realistic knowledge of God Himself. The rational empiricist saves reason by divorcing it from experience. Arguments for theism based on a priori thought-forms end in a merely formal and empty concept of God. The God of such abstract reasoning is not the God of Christian experience. Furthermore, it is fatal to begin one's system with the human mind, however structured. Unless man first knows God he cannot truly know himself.

The principle of causality by itself is insufficient to lead us out of ourselves to anything beyond the mind. Although alleged to be universal, the hollow causal principle does not engage the real world. "No bridge of cause can be made from that which cannot be identified (the self) to something else that cannot be identified (the external world). The idea of causation cannot be taken as intelligible by itself in order by means of it to show that God has created the world."[3] From the beginning causality must be understood as dependent upon God's will, or it may be meaningless. So one premise of the cosmological argument is undependable if we do not first assume God's existence. But, when we do that, the argument is unnecessary. "If God has created the world, the idea of cause in the world must be determined from this its derivative nature. If it is first assumed to be working without God it cannot after that be shown to be working only in dependence upon God."[4]

Not only the cosmological argument fails; the moral and teleological arguments also fail. If either morality or purpose in the universe could function independently of God at the beginning, Van Til asks,

3. Ibid., p. 377.
4. Ibid.

why do they need God at all? Following Abraham Kuyper, Van Til rejects any neutral area of fact or principle common to believers and unbelievers. If such an area of common ground is employed simply to establish absolute divine authority, Van Til foresees that reason will never bow to God. "If reason is not challenged at the outset, it cannot fairly be challenged at all."[5]

Having dismissed a pure empiricism like that of Buswell, and a rational empiricism like that of Hackett and Hamilton, what type of apologetic will Van Til suggest? Not Clark's because the case against Hackett and Hamilton at the same time undercuts Clark's appeal to the law of contradiction. The Christian principle of authority is above man's mind or reason, but Clark's principle of contradiction is in the mind of man. The pre-Christian finds no difficulty admitting that all truth is relative to the rational structure of his own mind. But then "every form of authority that comes to him must justify itself by standards inherent in man and operative apart from the authority that speaks."[6] To reason with unbelievers on the basis of either facts or consistency, Van Til says, is "to beat the air."

> It is well to say that he who would reason must presuppose the validity of the laws of logic. But if we say nothing more basic than this, then we are still beating the air. The ultimate question deals with the foundation of the validity of the laws of logic. We have not reached bottom until we have seen that every logical activity in which any man engages is in the service of his totality-vision.[7]

The ultimate authority is neither science nor logic, but God, even when speaking to those who do not believe in God.

Systems Give Meaning to Facts

The key to understanding Van Til's approach comes from the idealistic reconstruction of thought which followed Kant. Idealists like Hegel, Bradley, and Bosanquet "think, and we believe think correctly, that every appeal made to bare fact is unintelligible. Every fact must stand in relation to other facts or it means nothing to anyone." Illustrating this point, Van Til says:

> We may argue at length whether there is a noise in the woods when a

5. Ibid., p. 382.
6. Ibid., p. 145.
7. *The Case for Calvinism*, p. 137.

tree falls even if no one is there to hear it, but there can be no reasonable argument about the fact that even if there be such a noise, it means nothing to any one. There is, therefore, a necessary connection between the facts and the observer or interpreter of facts.[8]

Idealists find it impossible to reason on the basis of brute (bare, uninterpreted) facts. From the beginning of meaningful observation there must be some principle of interpretation. "Everyone who reasons about facts comes to those facts with a schematism into which he fits the facts. The real question is, therefore, into whose schematism the facts will fit."[9] Van Til claims that authoritative Scripture provides the only schematism into which the facts will fit. At best any humanly devised scheme would be finite, and related to a limited number of precepts. These would in turn imply something beyond themselves. This points to the need of God whose scheme includes all possible precepts of his creatures.[10]

Kant showed that universals such as cause and effect, to have any validity, must be presupposed. Hegelian idealism showed that they must be all-inclusive. According to Bosanquet's illustration, we could not even count to number one if we came to the brute facts with a completely blank mind. "All counting presupposes and depends upon a qualitative whole." So Van Til, like Clark, endorses the view that "unless there were a numerical system as a whole we could not tell one number from another. If we are to add information to our store of knowledge, we need the system of knowledge in order to relate a new fact to the system of facts already known."[11] We cannot in any instance observe all the relations of one fact to all other facts, but we know that they must be so related. To hold that all facts—past, present, and future—are related, is to come close to maintaining an infinite mind containing the true significance of every event and thing. At this point Van Til ventures to ask, "Have we not presupposed the idea of God and shown that without this presupposition we could not know so much as a single fact?"[12]

On this idealistic showing Van Til is not limited to mere probability as are empiricists. "Without the existence of God as a system

8. *Christian Theistic Evidences*, p. 39.
9. Ibid., p. 40.
10. Ibid.
11. Ibid., p. 41.
12. Ibid., p. 45.

there would be no probable relation between any set of facts, none even between two facts. But with the presupposition of God's existence you have more than probability, you have absolute necessity." What is the best possible proof of God's actual existence? It is "the indispensable character of the presupposition of God's existence." You see, "If God does not exist, we know nothing."[13] No categories, no events, and not even the significance of possibilities and probabilities can be known apart from God's existence.

Van Til criticizes the idealists, however, because they have not begun with God in their reasoning, as logically they should. Instead they have attempted to derive the "Absolute" from experience. The inexplicable in experience then remains inexplicable in God.

> We must either make God surround that which is irrational for us, or we must make that which is irrational to us surround God as well as ourselves. God either includes the "negative instance" or the "negative instance" includes God. God either controls the devil, or the devil in some measure at least, controls God. Reality is either such that there is novelty for us, but no novelty for God, or such that there is novelty for God as well as for us.[14]

To the extent that the problem of evil is not related to the ultimate meaningfulness of all things, everything is threatened. The idealists, from whom Van Til has learned much, have failed to comprehend everything under the Absolute (the true significance of every thing and event).

> Bare fact still stares us in the face. Hume has not been answered. Bare possibility and probability are still thought of as the most ultimate concepts of philosophy. The future must be to us the womb of chance out of which anything may come; rationality itself is nothing but a correlative to the irrational. And no Christian apologetic can be based upon the destruction of rationality itself.[15]

Every man in quest of truth chooses the system within which he sees the significance of life. Christian apologists invite men to start all their thinking with Christian presuppositions. They alone give meaning to all our experiences.

13. Ibid.
14. Ibid., p. 48.
15. Ibid., p. 50.

Presupposing the Christian Scriptures

Van Til's system begins with two presuppositions. The first has to do with how we know truth, so it is epistemological (from the Greek *episteme*, knowledge). Only God knows the true interpretation of all facts. No man is omniscient. But God has chosen to disclose the meaning of experience in written form. The Bible provides the proper interpretation of things in their ultimate relations. Without this basic assumption we have no way of knowing what meaning events might have for God who sees all relationships. So Professor Van Til says, "we do not wish to hide the fact that in the last analysis we make every thought captive to the obedience of the revelation of God as it has come to us in the Scriptures of the Old and New Testaments."[16] This does not necessarily mean that every discussion must begin with explicit reference to biblical authority. But it does mean that, in principle, there can be no uncompromising union of scriptural authority and the authority of human reason.

Scriptural authority is compromised, Van Til thinks, by Roman Catholic and Arminian apologetic systems (as all others in this book) which assume the existence of neutral, or uninterpreted facts. The traditional argument for the possibility, probability and actuality of revelation allows for a sacred book, and even a superior book, but not an absolutely authoritative book.[17] Wherever facts may be found the apologist must challenge the natural man's presuppositions by arguing that "unless they are accepted for what they are according to the Christian interpretation of them, no facts mean anything at all."[18] The natural man who tries to find a meaning in facts apart from Christianity virtually ascribes to himself the attributes the Christian ascribes to God alone.[19] So the natural man must make a full surrender. He must reverse his entire position. He must accept or reject the whole Christian system. There is no middle ground.[20]

Van Til does not oppose experimentation and observation. He appeals to facts, but not brute facts. Experiential data do not become facts until biblically interpreted. *Every* hypothesis must be in accord with biblical teaching. "The ultimate test for the relevancy of our

16. Ibid., p. 54.
17. *Defense of the Faith*, p. 162.
18. Ibid., p. 164.
19. Ibid., p. 165.
20. Ibid., pp. 165, 167.

hypotheses is therefore their correspondence with God's interpretation of facts."[21] Van Til does oppose views consigning God to the leftover mysteries science has not yet penetrated. The scientist's ideal is complete comprehension without reference to God. No consignment of God to temporary gaps in scientific theory can possibly make room for the omnipresent God of Christianity. Neither Kant nor modern scientists who seek to make room for faith in this way, make room for orthodox Christian faith.[22]

The facts Van Til presents to unbelievers include: God's self-explained existence, God's creation of all things, man created in the image of God, an all-inclusive divine providence, man's fall into sin, and the redemptive work of Christ. Independent of these truths no other facts can be found. It follows that the only possible way to reason with the non-believer is by way of presupposition. We must say that unless the unbeliever will accept the presuppositions of Christianity "there is no coherence in human experience." Without hesitation Van Til adds, "That is to say, the argument must be such as to show that unless one accepts the Bible for what true Protestantism says it is, the authoritative interpretation of human life and experience as a whole, it will be impossible to find meaning in anything."[23]

PRESUPPOSING THE CHRISTIAN GOD

Van Til's second presupposition has to do less with how we know and more with what we know as real. The department of philosophy which examines the nature of ultimate reality has been called metaphysics (beyond the things of nature). The ultimate reality according to Van Til is not nature, man, reason, causality, or the law of non-contradiction. The ultimate reality is the triune God revealed in Scripture. He it is who sustains nature, man, and causality. Without His existence none of these reference points is meaningful.

Why does the causal principle not prove God's existence, but presuppose His existence? If no God existed, whatever causality may have been experienced until today might completely change tomorrow. As Heraclitus said, we could not step into the same river twice. A principle as dependable as causality might tomorrow be undependable. We cannot depend on causality whether or not God is. Rather,

21. *Christian Theistic Evidences*, p. 62.
22. Ibid., p. 79.
23. *Defense of the Faith*, p. 167.

we can depend on the causal principle only if God is and has revealed its validity. According to Van Til, "if the word cause is to mean anything to anyone, whether it pertains to things within the phenomenal or to things in the noumenal realm, there must be an absolutely unified experience in relation to Whom as a final reference point we may bring our predication of the cause and effect concepts."[24]

Apart from God all things could change into their opposites without notice. At any time "God is an existing Being" could change to mean "God is not an existing Being." The same could happen with assertions of all the theistic arguments: God is wise, purposeful, powerful, personal, and moral. Each could mean its opposite. So Van Til is willing to reduce all the theistic arguments to one argument from meaningful predication. That is, "unless this God exists, unless he is more than a concept in the mind of man, human experience would be meaningless."[25] God created man to engage actively in knowing things (as the subject of the knowing process). And God created the world to be known and ruled by man. So there can be no battle between the subject and object of knowledge. They are made for one another. "They do not merely happen to fit together somehow, but find their fruitful contact because they have been created in fruitful contact with one another by God."[26]

The concepts of existence, cause, and purpose can be applied to the things of the world in a proximate manner, but their ultimate reference is to God. The metaphysical question about ultimate realities requires the divine referent. On the proximate level, the meanings of such concepts are derivative and dependent on God. Apart from the presupposition of the Christian God, these limited references are meaningless. "To know truly, man's thought must be receptively reconstructive of the revelation of God."[27] The two presuppositions of a written revelation and the triune God are not independent of each other, but "mutually involved in one another and quite inseparable."[28]

If we must presuppose the existence of the God of the Bible, what are His self-disclosed characteristics? Frequently Van Til speaks of

24. *Psychology of Religion*, p. 50.
25. Ibid., p. 51.
26. Ibid.
27. Ibid.
28. Ibid., p. 52.

God as "self-contained." By this he means that "He does not depend in his being, knowledge, or will upon the being, knowledge, or will of his own creatures. God is *absolute*. He is autonomous."[29] Furthermore God is unchanging, eternal, omnipresent, and triune. In God the unity and diversity are equally basic and mutually dependent upon one another.[30] Whereas we are finite persons limited by principles of truth, goodness, and beauty beyond ourselves, God is not just less limited than we, but unlimited, an absolute person. "There were no principles of truth, goodness or beauty that were next to or above God according to which he patterned the world. The principles of truth, goodness, and beauty are to be thought of as identical with God's being; they are attributes of God."[31]

PARADOX AND ANALOGY IN LANGUAGE ABOUT GOD

Since Van Til stresses God's great difference from man, is it possible to speak of God in the same way we speak of men? Can we understand assertions about God univocally? Must our propositions about God be non-contradictory? Although Van Til finds the principles of truth in God's self-sufficient being, he does not find the law of non-contradiction there. That law of logic is "wholly independent" of divine revelation.[32] Differing with Buswell, Hackett, and Clark who considered the law of non-contradiction an expression of God's very being, Van Til charges them with idolatry. To enthrone the law of non-contradiction as they do is to reason from man's principle to God and so make God subject to human law. The rational man who employs his laws of logic to recognize the true revelation will also employ it to stand in judgment upon revelation. In one intellectual respect he will not submit himself to the judgment of revelation.[33]

God's revelation seems to be contradictory. God does not contradict Himself. But God's communique seems contradictory to man's finite intelligence. Antinomies result because human knowledge is never completely comprehensive. If every bit of that knowledge has somewhere a reference to God who is incomprehensible, Van Til reasons, we are "bound to come into what seems to be contradiction in all our

29. *Apologetics*, p. 7.
30. *Defense of the Faith*, p. 26.
31. Ibid., p. 28.
32. Ibid., p. 341.
33. *The Case for Calvinism*, p. 80.

knowledge." Furthermore our system is not deduced from a few axioms, but constructed from the disparate elements of revelation analogically. That is, the concepts of revelation supplement each other, but cannot be logically deduced from each other. The differences in the vast body of scriptural data appear to be contradictory.[34]

Where does the Bible assert and deny the same thing at the same time and in the same respect? Van Til finds a contradiction in the Bible's teaching on prayer and God's unchanging counsel. "We say on the one hand that prayer changes things and on the other hand we say that everything happens in accordance with God's plan and God's plan is immutable."[35] Is there another alleged contradiction? "That all things in history are determined by God must always seem, at first sight, to contradict the genuineness of my choice."[36] Furthermore, prior to creation God was perfect and in need of nothing, yet He created the world to glorify Himself. The "bucket" was full, but water is continually being added. So everything about time and space creation is involved in this contradiction. "The Christian, in particular the Reformed Christian, must not accord to 'reason' the 'prerogative of deciding whether a thing is possible or impossible.' "[37] Scripture, not logical consistency, determines whether anything is possible or impossible.

Van Til thinks the demand for non-contradiction, when carried to its logical conclusion, reduces God's truth to man's truth. Because God is greater than man, no coincidence of divine and human thought is possible. We must recognize that "the creature can only touch the hem of the garment of Him who dwells in light that no man can approach unto." Even the creeds are but approximations to the fullness of truth as it is in God.[38]

Like the demand for consistency, the claim to univocal understanding is said to reduce God's thought to man's. So Van Til rejects any univocal understanding of theological language. All our knowledge of God is analogical. Since we are unlike God, our knowledge cannot be comprehensive; since we are like God we nevertheless have truth. Van Til asserts that God is the "absolutely Other" but does not in-

34. *Defense of the Faith*, p. 180.
35. Ibid., p. 61.
36. *Common Grace*, p. 10.
37. *Defense of the Faith*, p. 298.
38. *Common Grace*, p. 11.

tend to eliminate a rational analogical relationship.[39] Man's thought is not identical with God's. God's thought is determinative; man's subordinate. God's thought is the original; man's the analogical copy of the original. So an alleged univocal understanding of God is non-Christian![40] Just as pure equivocation leads to skepticism, pure univocation leads to the identification of man with God.[41]

COMMON GROUND

Van Til is noted for rejecting beliefs common to Christians and non-Christians which could form a point of contact from which to begin an apologetic. Less attention is given his stress on factors common to believers and unbelievers. These should be considered first.

Both Christians and non-Christians are creatures of God who live and move and have their being in God. A point of contact appears in actual metaphysical dependence upon God for temporal existence. "For man self-consciousness presupposes God-consciousness."[42] Before the fall of man into sin, man's awareness of God was not dimmed. Ever since the fall, however, "no man can escape knowing God. It is indelibly involved in his awareness of anything whatsoever."[43] But fallen man suppresses his God-consciousness by seeking to interpret himself and his environment apart from God. In the suppression of God-consciousness, there is psychological common ground.

Morally and spiritually all men share a common rebellion against God. All sinned in their representative Adam when he broke God's covenant of works. And all responsible persons have themselves disbelieved and disobeyed God. The experience of violating God's law is common to us all. So we have common ground metaphysically, psychologically, morally, and spiritually.

In the realm of knowledge, Van Til emphatically denies common ground. The intellect is an instrument man uses to obtain knowledge. Like a saw, whether it will move at all, and whether it will move in the right direction depends on the man operating it.[44] The believer uses his reason to interpret divine revelation; the unbeliever uses his reason to suppress it or rebel against it. An unbeliever is not

39. *Defense of the Faith*, p. 58.
40. Ibid., pp. 56, 64-65.
41. *Christian Theistic Ethics*, p. 37.
42. *Defense of the Faith*, p. 107.
43. Ibid., p. 109.
44. Ibid., p. 98.

even in a position to judge the truth of revelation-claims. He will "certainly find the Christian religion incredible because impossible and the evidence for it . . . inadequate."[45] The reason of the sinful man "will invariably act wrongly."[46] The natural man will seek to reduce the contents of Scripture to a natural level. His own ultimacy is the basic presupposition of his entire philosophy. To ask him to judge the credibility of revelation is to ask him at the same time to believe and disbelieve in his own ultimacy.[47] Furthermore, "if the natural man's eyes (reason) enable him to see correctly in one dimension, there is no good reason to think that these same eyes will not enable him, without further assistance from without, to see correctly in all dimensions."[48]

Defense of the Christian faith cannot appeal to any capacity of discrimination in the non-Christian. Apologists cannot simply add to information unbelievers already possess. By nature his mind and will are incapable of arriving at any truth whatever. He is blind and dead in sin. On his own power and assumptions he can arrive at no Christian truth. He must be given new life and new sight by the supernatural act of the Holy Spirit. The whole person must be regenerated before the tool of the mind is used correctly. Until a sinner is regenerated he makes himself, rather than God, the principle of interpreting all things. To the jaundiced eye all is yellow. The sinner may use similar words, but his meaning is totally different. "There can be no intelligible reasoning unless those who reason together understand what they mean by their words."[49] The unbeliever may even construct proofs for the existence of God, as Aristotle did. But his God is the product of his own reasoning powers, not the sovereign Lord of his mind.

Existentially and psychologically oriented apologists of recent times have proposed that the case for Christianity should not start with theism, but anthropology. Could Christians not agree with non-Christians on their personal experience and their needs? Can apologetic begin with the nature and destiny of man rather than the existence of God? Although we have noted some common experiences, the natural man's view of himself is totally different from the Chris-

45. Ibid., p. 99.
46. Ibid., p. 100.
47. Ibid.
48. Ibid., p. 104.
49. Ibid., pp. 86-94.

tian view of him. "In the question of starting point it is all-important that we have a truly Christian doctrine of man."[50] Man's will is as incapable of right decision as man's intellect is of correct reasoning. Romanism and some evangelicalism mistakenly think human self-consciousness and consciousness of objects are to some extent intelligible without reference to God. So they consistently seek common ground. But common ground is impossible for Calvinists, Van Til thinks. Other Calvinists find the possibility resulting from general revelation and common grace. But Van Til finds only rejection of any supposed benefits through common grace. "There is no single territory or dimension in which believers and non-believers have all things wholly in common. As noted above, even the description of facts in the lowest dimension presupposes a system of metaphysics and epistemology. So there can be no neutral territory of cooperation."[51] *In principle* there can be no epistemological common ground, since the mind is but a tool of the depraved heart and misinterprets everything, including itself.

The total disparity between Christian and non-Christian, however, does not stand without significant qualification. In an important footnote, Van Til claims that "full recognition is made of the fact that in spite of this absolute contrast of principle, there is relative good in those who are evil in principle and relative evil in those who are good in principle."[52] The natural man has the possibility of truth relatively and also "proximately." Although ultimately he does not subordinate his concepts to God, he may apply truly to this world, such words as being, cause, purpose, and any other word.[53] On the proximate level the Christian does not have different laws of chemistry or logic. He simply gives them different ultimate significance. In the ultimate sense Christians and non-Christians have nothing in common, but in the proximate sense they have "all things in common."[54]

Epistemological common ground is also admitted formally and linguistically. "The intellect of the fallen man may, as such, be keen enough. It can therefore formally understand the Christian position." But the keener the intellect the more consistently will the truths of

50. Ibid., p. 89.
51. *Common Grace*, p. 85.
52. *Defense of the Faith*, p. 67.
53. *Psychology of Religion*, p. 51.
54. *Defense of the Faith*, p. 300.

Christianity be fitted into an exclusively immanentistic pattern. "The result is that however much they may formally understand the truth of Christianity, men still worship 'the dream and figment of their own heart.' They have what Hodge calls 'mere cognition,' but no true knowledge of God."[55] In talking with non-Christian philosophers, then, Van Til willingly employs their language, as did the apostles. He says, "We shall be obliged, to a large extent, to use the language of the philosophers or we shall have no point of contact with them. But we shall have to be on our guard to put Christian content into this language that we borrow."[56]

Even more concessively, Van Til admits that unbelievers may have much truth. Truth is a quality, not of mere form and language, but of meaning and content. Although the ultimate source of truth in any field is Christ,

> the world may discover much truth without owning Christ as Truth. Christ upholds even those who ignore, deny, and oppose him. A little child may slap his father in the face, but it can do so only because the father holds it on his knee. So modern science, modern philosophy, and modern theology may discover much truth.[57]

One begins to wonder whether Van Til's strictures upon any common ground have not died the death of a thousand qualifications. Van Til's evangelical opponents would claim no more than that unbelievers may discover much truth. When Van Til says that believer and unbeliever have no common ground, we must add, no common ground in principle, ultimately; but, however inconsistently, there may be much truth in common relatively, proximately, formally, and linguistically!

APOLOGETIC METHOD

The apologist's task is to unmask the sinner's suppressed responsibility before God. How shall he help a covenant breaker admit what he knows underneath to be true? Emphatically Van Til insists, "If there is no head-on collision with the systems of the natural man there will be no point of contact with the sense of deity in the natural man."[58] Any approach starting with the natural man's epistemology

55. Ibid., p. 91.
56. Ibid., p. 41.
57. *Case for Calvinism*, p. 148.
58. *Defense of the Faith*, p. 116.

will not do. We must start with explicitly Christian presuppositions. We must ask the non-Christian to accept the Christian's ultimate explanation, at least for argument's sake. He may then be shown that only upon such a basis do 'facts' and 'laws' appear ultimately intelligible.[59]

Van Til admits that his reasoning is circular. But he points out that all reasoning is. The scientific method begins by assuming the uniformity of nature, which it then "finds" in experimentation. In any system of thought "the starting point, method, and the conclusion are always involved in one another."[60] It is not strange then that Christians starting with the self-contained God as revealed in Scripture interpret everything by the inspired writings. Every method, including the allegedly neutral, presupposes either the truth or falsity of Christian theism.

Why start with Christian presuppositions rather than others? Not because the Christian system can be demonstrated conclusively by evidence or argument. "No proof for this God and for the truth of his revelation in Scripture can be offered by an appeal to anything in human experience that has not itself received its light from the God whose existence and whose revelation it is supposed to prove. One cannot prove the usefulness of the light of the sun for the purposes of seeing by turning to the darkness of the cave."[61] Scripture cannot be subjected to the scrutiny of reason "because it is reason itself that learns of its proper function from Scripture." The Bible "presents itself as being the only light in terms of which the truth about facts and their relations can be discovered."[62]

> If then appeal is made from the Bible to the facts of history or of nature outside the Bible recorded in some documents totally independent of the Bible it must be remembered that these facts themselves can be seen for what they are only if they are regarded in the light of the Bible. It is by the light of the flashlight that has derived its energy from the sun that we may in this way seek for an answer to the question whether there be a sun. This is not to disparage the light of reason. It is only to indicate its total dependence upon God. Nor is it to disparage the usefulness of arguments for the corrobora-

59. Ibid., pp. 117-18.
60. Ibid., p. 118.
61. Ibid., p. 126.
62. Ibid., p. 125.

tion of the Scripture that comes from archaeology. It is only to say that such corroboration is not of independent power. It is not a testimony that has its source anywhere but in God himself.[63]

The Bible is accepted, then, as self-authenticating. The Protestant "accepts Scripture to be that which Scripture itself says it is on its own authority."[64] The Bible's claims for itself are exegeted at length by B. B. Warfield in *The Inspiration and Authority of the Bible* for which Van Til wrote an extensive introduction. Van Til and his Westminster Theological Seminary colleagues also set forth the Bible's view of itself in *The Infallible Word*. So in his apologetic works Van Til does not expound the evidence again. And a false impression of the extensive amount of biblical data would be given if here we listed just a few passages. Students should consult these other books for evidence that the Bible claims to be true as a revelation of the ultimate significance of all things in the mind of God.

Granting that the Bible claims to disclose ultimate truth, there is nothing more ultimate to which to resort for support of the claim. The truth-claim must stand on its own self-attestation.

> The Reformed apologist throws down the gauntlet and challenges his opponent to a duel of life and death from the start. He does not first travel in the same direction and in the same automobile with the natural man for some distance in order then mildly to suggest to the driver that they ought perhaps to change their course somewhat and follow a road that goes at a different slant from the one they are on.[65]

The revelation in nature and God's revelation in Scripture, form "God's one grand scheme of covenant revelation of himself to man. The two forms of revelation must therefore be seen as presupposing and supplementing one another. They are aspects of one general philosophy of history."[66] And this Christian philosophy rests upon its own self-authenticating biblical claims.

Are there no considerations for accepting these biblical claims as true? Could we not establish convincing evidences for the resurrection of Jesus Christ and so supply evidence for accepting Christ's claims for Himself? Van Til answers that no proposition about his-

---

63. Introduction to *The Inspiration and Authority of the Bible*, by B. B. Warfield, pp. 36-37.
64. *Defense of the Faith*, p. 125.
65. Ibid., p. 130.
66. *Apologetics*, p. 28.

torical fact is presented for what it really is until presented as part of the system of Christian theism contained in Scripture. So when we speak of the resurrection of Christ, we refer to the resurrection of the Son of God, the eternal Word through whom the world was made. The event can be accepted only in terms of its biblically revealed meaning. And that is part of the whole system of thought. And what is true of the resurrection is true of every fact. The piecemeal approach of Christian evidences becomes meaningless. "A truly Protestant method of reasoning involves a stress upon the fact that the meaning of every aspect or part of Christian theism depends upon Christian theism as a unit."[67]

Can we not simply give a personal testimony of our own salvation experience in support of Scriptural truth-claims? In Van Til's article, "Why I Believe in God," the answer is negative. He says, "Your experience and testimony of regeneration would be meaningless except for the objective truth of the objective facts that are presupposed by it. A testimony that is not an argument is not a testimony either, just as an argument that is not a testimony is not even an argument."[68] If one's personal testimony is to be significant as an argument, it must be presented within the system flowing from Christian presuppositions. Those presuppositions cannot be even temporarily dismissed. "Arguing about God's existence," he says, "is like arguing about air. You may affirm that air exists, and I that it does not. But as we debate the point, we are both breathing air all the time!"[69] And Van Til has been "breathing" Christian presuppositions from childhood when he studied at a parochial school.

In a pamphlet entitled *Common Grace and Witness-Bearing*, Van Til explains:

> Surely the witness to the God of the Scriptures must be presented everywhere. It must be, to be sure, presented with wisdom and tact. But it must be presented. It is not presented, however, if we grant that God the Holy Spirit in a general testimony to all men approves of interpretations of this world or of aspects of this world which ignore Him and set Him at naught.[70]

Whether we should hope to start with considerations from the resur-

67. *Defense of the Faith*, p. 132.
68. *Why I Believe in God* (pamphlet), p. 16.
69. Ibid., p. 30.
70. *Common Grace and Witness-Bearing*, p. 26.

rection of Christ, personal experience, or a need of man, each of these is only understood if related to God from the beginning. But no one can speak of the whole Christian system at once. We must start somewhere, must we not? Indeed we must. Van Til's stress is on Christian theism as a unit, he says,

> does not imply that it will be possible to bring the whole debate about Christian theism to full expression in every discussion of individual historical fact. Nor does it imply that the debate about historical detail is unimportant. It means that no Christian apologist can afford to forget the claim of his system with respect to any particular fact. He must always maintain that the "fact" under discussion with his opponent must be what Scripture says it is, if it is to be intelligible at all. He must maintain that there can be no facts in any realm but such as actually do exhibit the truth of the system of which they are a part. If facts are what they are as parts of the Christian theistic system of truth then what else can facts do but reveal that system to the limit of their ability as parts of that system? It is only as manifestations of that system that they are what they are. If the apologist does not present them as such he does not present them for what they are.[71]

Do we then start with Christian presuppositions arbitrarily? Can no considerations support a system focused on God and the Bible in contrast to systems with contradictory presuppositions? If so, Van Til is not doing apologetics (as defined in chapter 1) but theology. For theological purposes one may assume Christianity's truth without supporting the assumption. But for apologetic purposes Christianity's basic truth-claims are at issue. Because Van Til does provide further considerations in favor of accepting Christian presuppositions, he has been included in this apologetics book. What are his distinctively apologetic considerations?

Negatively, to reject Christian presuppositions is to turn down the only ground of any meaning and truth. Acceptance of Christian presuppositions alone enables anyone to develop a system of thought. Every other position is atomistic, or impersonal. Empirical systems are limited by the present stage of finite observation. And absolute idealism which postulates an infinite knowledge of all things loses personality itself and knowledge of individuals. (For example Aris-

---

71. *Defense of the Faith*, p. 135.

totle's man knew nothing of Aristotle's God and Aristotle's God knew nothing of Aristotle's man.) So every other form of reasoning is challenged. "If man's necessarily discursive thought is not to fall into the ultimate irrationalism and scepticism that is involved in modern methodology we must suppose the conception of the God that is found in Scripture."[72]

Positively, acceptance of Christianity gives life meaning. True reasoning about God "is such as stands upon God as upon the emplacement that alone gives meaning to any sort of human argument." So, "unless you believe in God, you can logically believe in nothing else."[73] Non-Christian systems of thought leave something to the controls of persons or things other than God. But Christian theism, Van Til says, has an explanation of everything.

In advocating God's control of everything, Van Til does not mean to obliterate all second causes. Rather, he would insist that they be kept second. God is the ultimate, or first cause of whatsoever comes to pass. Van Til explains, "My interest is only to show that it takes an ultimate cause, God, if there are to be genuine second causes." That is true whether the second causes are impersonal forces in nature or the free will of man. "It is not a 'suffocating supernaturalism' to aver that secondary causes are meaningless without God, the Creator as primary or remote Cause." Suffocation of science and all human experience would take place if atheistic realism were true for a moment. "For then there would be no causes at all. All reality would be composed of irrational particulars. All would then be Chaos and Old Night."[74] Van Til's case for Christianity, then, argues that all other systems lead to irrationality and chaos; only Christianity gives meaning to life. For this reason we must accept the Bible's claims for itself, God and Christ.

Van Til and the Invisible Gardener

Why does Van Til believe an invisible Gardener cares for the world? Not because of objectively observed evidence. Not because every effect must have an adequate cause. Not because an independent principle of consistency is satisfied only by that belief. He finds in the garden a Bible which claims to give the ultimate explanation of

72. Ibid., p. 138.
73. "Why I Believe in God" (pamphlet), p. 18.
74. *Defense of the Faith*, p. 268.

the weeds, the plants, and the human observers of the garden—their existence, suppression of a divine awareness, and covenant-breaking conduct. Presupposing the truth of the Bible he can make sense of all of this. If the God of the Bible is not presupposed he finds no fixed reference point for our assertions. Even statements about the weeds in the garden might change their meaning in a world left to chance. Apart from God's existence neither "facts," nor thought-forms, nor causal principles could be counted on.

In seeking to convince another of the invisible Gardener, Van Til would deny any common ground in principle on the level of ulti-mate explanation. Proximately, however, and formally he might find that much truth was possessed. Taking a flame thrower to the im-manentistic explanations of the garden, Van Til would demand their complete abandonment and a beginning with the transcendent God of the Bible. On the Christian presuppositions life is no longer "a tale told by an idiot, full of sound and fury signifying nothing." Life is meaningful. And that meaning is attested internally by the witness of the Holy Spirit.

EVALUATION

Interaction with Van Til's apologetic is required by its highly con-troversial nature. If it is correct, every other writer considered in this book seriously compromises the Christianity he attempts to de-fend. If the other writers have some contribution, on the other hand, Van Til's approach is seriously overstated.

The question constantly arises as to whether Van Til speaks as an apologist or a theologian. For example, philosopher William Young in reviewing Rousas J. Rushdoony's *By What Standard?* (an analysis of the philosphy of Cornelius Van Til) said, "This is theology in a philosophical idiom rather than philosophy."[75] By and large this comment seems justified as those disciplines have been defined in this book. But somewhat less prominently Van Til does defend Chris-tianity's truth-claims and to that extent the criticism would not be entirely justified.

When more characteristically Van Til denies the ability of men to check revelation-claims, he opposes an inevitable requirement of hu-man existence. No one can miss the conflicting truth-claims made by

75. *Christianity Today*, November 23, 1959, p. 38.

the cults, world's religions, and philosophies by all the communications media. Similarly conflicting claims were heard by people in Old and New Testament times. If the Bible itself requires the testing of claims made by alleged prophets and apostles, we can hardly disqualify man's ability to test the truth-claims of alleged revelations today.

Obliged to obey the word of true prophets, the Israelites cried out, "How shall we know the word which the Lord hath not spoken?" The answer was twofold. First the prophet's sign-miracle must come to pass (Deu 18:22). Second, the prophet's teaching must be consistent with previous revelation (Deu 13:1-3). The New Testament tests were similar. Sign-miracles attested the claims of Christ and the apostles. And both defended the consistency of their teaching with previous revelation. As long as contradictory revelation-claims exist, it will be necessary to follow John's admonition and "test the spirits to see whether they are from God" (1 Jn 4:1-3). And the evidence that people in a state of incredulity did make such a test explodes any doctrine that denies them either the ability or right. Of course every system of thought has its presuppositions. But some presuppositions are true and some false. If Christian truth-claims are true, there must be some indication of it.

In spite of himself, Van Til has offered considerations in favor of starting his system with the God of the Bible rather than another God. Is the Bible's consistency one of these? On the surface it would seem not. He has cast out the bondwoman of logical laws. Or has he? His alleged contradictions are examples of complex causes, or merely first impressions which are harmonized after further thought, or indications of incomplete comprehension. These phenomena are admitted by the apologists who defend the law of non-contradiction. Complexity is not contradiction. Charges of contradictions in the Bible's teaching ought not be made loosely. To open the door to technical logical contradictions would be to undercut every statement in the Bible and the Westminster Confession. One would have to admit the truth of (1) all men are sinners, and (2) some men are not sinners, or (1) all Scripture is inspired, and (2) some Scripture is not inspired. Van Til opens the door for all this and more by his attack upon contradiction as a test of untruth. But he does not really want it to come to this.

Professor Van Til himself admits that it is not the law of contradiction that is at issue, but the use of it. "I do *not* maintain that Christians operate according to new laws of thought any more than that they have new eyes or noses. . . . The non-Christian uses the gifts of logical reasoning in order to keep down the truth in unrighteousness. The question is not that of the law of contradiction as a formal principle."[76] But if God is consistent, as Van Til teaches, then the law negatively applied does tell us what is impossible under God, although it may not help determine which of the non-contradictory alternatives may be true. Non-contradiction *cannot* be used to hold down the truth in unrighteousness. The truth is never self-contradictory. If it were, the unsaved man would have an excuse; he would not have any knowledge for which to be responsible. Van Til correctly says we must not accord to "reason" the prerogative of deciding whether a thing is possible, but he is wrong in adding "or impossible."[77] If a truth-claim is consistent it is not necessarily God's will (possible in that sense), but if it is inconsistent, it is not *God's* will, it is impossible.

Needless to say, Van Til everywhere assumes the validity of the law of non-contradiction. In arguing against Thomists and Arminians he constantly chides them for their inconsistencies. And he belittles the Reformed brethren who adopt a less consistent Calvinism. Indeed, the primary purpose of his apologetic is to set forth a method of defending Christianity which is consistent with his theology. And Reformed theology is notorious in its quest for rigorous consistency.

So it is difficult to take seriously his repeated charge that any appeal to consistency exalts reason above God. Apologists like Clark, Hackett, Buswell, and Carnell insist that logic is not above God; it is simply an expression of the divine nature. And the law of non-contradiction is not independent of God even though an unbeliever who employs it is unaware of the fact. Contradictory propositions cannot both be true. Inconsistency is a valid test of error for Christian or non-Christian, as Van Til acknowledges, at least in practice.

Does Van Til support his consistent Christian system with any other considerations? Often Van Til says that the apologist must deny the ability of the natural man to discern any truth whatsoever. Never-

76. *Defense of the Faith*, p. 296.
77. Ibid., p. 298.

theless he seeks to show the unbeliever that Christianity makes sense out of life. Is this really so different from the test of coherence or the fitting of the facts of human experience? As Van Til puts it, "The Christian-theistic position must be shown to be not as defensible as some other position, it must rather be shown to be *the position which alone does not annihilate intelligent human experience.*"[78] The coherence of consistent Christian presuppositions with all meaningful experience justifies Van Til's circle of reasoning as over against other circles of reasoning. With this interpretation of Van Til, James Daane concurs. His review of *The Case for Calvinism* ends:

> Van Til himself, however, does not escape what he calls the "autonomous man!" His purpose, he writes, is "to bring the challenge of the Gospel of Christ to modern man," because Christianity is modern man's only hope. "However," he adds, "this cannot be shown to be true unless it be made evident that Christianity not only has its own methodology but also that only its methodology gives meaning to human life." In making this "evident" Van Til himself appeals to something in man to which the truth of Christianity will hopefully appear "evident." And with this Van Til's "autonomous man" has returned.[79]

Christianity will hardly give meaning to the unbeliever's life if presented incoherently. With all of Van Til's protestations to the contrary, he himself employs non-contradiction and meaningful relevance to experience as tests of truth for all men.

We may learn from Van Til to make clear our presuppositions and always to be consistent with them. He wisely warns us of the dangers in compromising Scriptural truth in an effort to communicate with our contemporaries. Whatever one may think of his theology or apologetic, one cannot forget that an apologetic ought to be consistent with its theology and total system of thought.

While a system bordering on omniscience is ideal, none of us can attain it in this life. Of course we should continually strive for the ideal system, impossible as it is to achieve. Meanwhile, we must obey the great commission and reach men who have similarly come short of the ideal in their totality-outlooks. So for all the values of Van Til's apologetic between the Christian and non-Christian ideal systems in

78. Ibid., p. 197.
79. *Christianity Today*, September 25, 1964, p. 33.

principle it is of questionable value among men in flesh and blood. One wonders if Van Til has given "full recognition" to the fact that "there is a relative good in those who are evil in principle and relative evil in those who are good in principle."[80] Contemporary thinking has a deep devotion to the existing individual—his needs and problems. Must Van Til ignore the individual's relative good in speaking up for Christianity? Although he has admitted much truth in the unbeliever's thinking, he has given this no part in his apologetic strategy. It will be instructive to see less idealistic attempts to formulate a Christian apologetic in our day.

RESOURCES FOR RESEARCH
WORKS BY CORNELIUS VAN TIL

These are in order as produced. Books and booklets were published by Presbyterian and Reformed Publishing Company, Nutley, New Jersey.

BOOKS

"Nature and Scripture." In *The Infallible Word: A Symposium.* 3d rev. printing, 1967. Van Til's thesis is that there are only two positions on natural revelation: (1) his Reformed view that to interpret nature properly (by the principles of the Word) one must first be a believing Christian, and (2) the view of Plato, Aristotle, Aquinas, and Kant which reduces interpretation of the historic process to the dialectical movements of a reason sufficient unto itself.

Common Grace, 1947. As a result of the fall, all men receive, not a common grace, but a common condemnation. Unbelievers and believers who one day will be totally different, now do have metaphysical and psychological factors in common. But epistemologically they have no common ground. So it is impossible to convince a non-Christian of the truth of Christianity as long as he retains any of his non-Christian assumptions.

Introduction to *The Inspiration and Authority of the Bible,* by B. B. Warfield, 1948. The only apologetic consistent with Warfield's high doctrine of inspiration, Van Til argues, is his Reformed approach.

The Defense of the Faith, 1955. Van Til's most comprehensive statement of his apologetic, including over 200 pages of answers to his critics. The primary source for the study of Van Til's thought. The 1967 paperback edition omits most of the intramural debate with Christian Reformed writers.

Christianity and Barthianism, 1962. In a major work on contemporary theology Van Til argues that Barthianism, recent dialecticism, and the

80. *Defense of the Faith,* p. 67 n. 3.

new consciousness theology of Hans Ur Van Balthasar and Hans Kung, in spite of language like that of Reformed theology, are only higher forms of humanism.

The Case for Calvinism, 1964. Humanistic also are the systems of L. Harold De Wolf in *The Case for Theology in Liberal Perspective*, and William Horden in *The Case for a New Reformation Theology*. In the Westminster Press trilogy Edward John Carnell's *The Case for Orthodox Theology* stated the proper message, but undermined it by the method he chose for its defense. Against a sustained criticism of Carnell, Van Til sets forth what he considers to be a valid defense of orthodox Calvinism.

A Christian Theory of Knowledge, 1969. A major work expanding and supplementing *The Defense of the Faith*. Of special interest are the evaluations of Warfield, Kuyper, Buswell and Hamilton.

The Reformed Pastor and Modern Thought, 1971. An attempt to show a pastor how to proclaim and defend the Christian view of life for young people. Emphasizes Van Til's differences from Catholicism and Paul Tillich's approach.

SYLLABI

"Christian and Theistic-Evidences," 1961.

"Psychology of Religion," 1961.

"The Triumph of Grace." Vol. 1, 1962.

"Apologetics," 1963.

"Christian Theistic Ethics," 1964.

"The Protestant Doctrine of Scripture." Vol. 1 of the series of syllabi In Defense of Biblical Christianity, 1967. Van Til compares his view of Scripture with that of Roman Catholicism, neo-orthodoxy and Christ, mysticism, Warfield, Clark, Beegle, Hackett, and Berkouwer.

BOOKLETS

The Intellectual Challenge of the Gospel, 1953.

Christianity in Modern Theology, 1955.

The Dilemma of Education, 1956.

Barth's Christology, 1962.

The Later Heidegger and Theology, 1964.

Common Grace and Witness-Bearing, n.d.

Particularism and Common Grace, n.d.

Why I Believe in God, n.d.

Paul at Athens, n.d.

ABOUT VAN TIL

All were published by Presbyterian and Reformed Publishing Company, Nutley, New Jersey.

Marston, George W. *The Voice of Authority,* 1960. A popularization in 110 pages.

Rushdoony, Rousas J. *By What Standard? An Analysis of the Philosophy of Cornelius Van Til,* 1959. A sympathetic exposition of Van Til's thought in 209 pages.

———. *Van Til.* Modern Thinkers Series. Ed. by David H. Freeman, 1960. Fifty-one page paperback.

E. R. Geehan, ed. *Jerusalem and Athens: Critical Discussions of the Theology and Apologetics of Cornelius Van Til,* 1971. Essays by numerous scholars on Van Til's system. Includes my comparison of "Van Til and Carnell" and Van Til's "Response."

For Advanced Research

Students proficient in philosophy who wish to examine more extensive metaphysical implications of a position similar to that of Van Til may study the philosophy of Herman Dooyeweerd. Said Van Til, "I rejoice in the work of Christian philosophers like . . . Dooyeweerd."

Dooyeweerd, Herman. *A New Critique of Theoretical Thought.* Vols. 1-4. Trans. by David H. Freeman, William S. Young, and H. DeJonste. Nutley, N. J.: Presbyterian and Reformed, 1953.

———. *In the Twilight of Western Thought.* Nutley, N.J.: Presbyterian and Reformed, 1960.

Freeman, David Hugh. "The Neo-Augustinianism of Herman Dooyeweerd." In *Recent Studies in Philosophy and Theology.* Grand Rapids: Baker, 1962, pp. 33-63.

Nash, Ronald H., *Dooyeweerd and the Amsterdam Philosophy.* Grand Rapids: Zondervan, 1962. The most readable introduction to Dooyeweerd's thought.

Philosophy and Christianity: Philosophical Essays Dedicated to Professor Dr. Herman Dooyeweerd. Amsterdam: North-Holland, 1965. A tribute to the influence of Dooyeweerd by twenty-nine writers from different countries with essays on philosophy, philosophy of law, and philosophy of science.

Spier, J. M. *An Introduction to Christian Philosophy.* Trans. by David Hugh Freeman. Nutley, N. J.: Presbyterian and Reformed, 1954. An exposition of the thought of Dooyeweerd.

Young, William. "Herman Dooyeweerd." In *Creative Minds in Contemporary Theology.* Ed. by Philip Edgcumbe Hughes. Grand Rapids: Eerdmans, 1966, pp. 270-305.

6

THE MYSTICISM OF EARL E. BARRETT

THE TEST OF PERSONAL EXPERIENCE

REACTING AGAINST A WORLD gone sour people are turning to drug-induced "trips" in hope of finding reality. Disillusioned by rational attempts to discover the truth, they try an intense emotional experience. "Blowing their mind," they lose a sense of themselves as distinct from the ground of being, of time and its importance, of words and their meaning, and of all dualities and distinctions. Nevertheless, a good trip may leave them with the conviction of having encountered the ultimate reality. They think no other test is needed.

The characteristics of psychedelic experience are not essentially different from those described by mystics in various times and religions. The mystic lost himself in his Deity, usually minimized time and history, considered his experience beyond description in human words (ineffable), and felt certain that he had the highest and best experience of ultimate reality. For mystics, rational evidences or arguments seemed of little or no value. The test of religious truth was a self-authenticating, personal experience of Deity.

Many evangelical Christians would rather testify to their experience of God than appeal to biblical authority, logical principles, or scientific evidence. Two evangelical scholars in particular have made a personal experience of God the prime test of Christianity's truth. Warren C. Young, professor of Christian philosophy at Northern Baptist Theological Seminary in Chicago says that "the foundation stone" of apologetics is the Christian's faith-experience of the supernatural. Earl E. Barrett, professor in the division of religion and philosophy at Olivet Nazarene College, Kankakee, Illinois, calls his approach a "Christian mysticism." The experience-oriented thought of these men provides a stimulating contrast to that of the previous apologists. We must see whether a direct experience of God shows that Christianity is true.

DEFICIENCIES IN NON-MYSTICAL APOLOGIES

In *A Christian Approach to Philosophy* Professor Young puts his philosophical cards on the table. He appreciates the ideal of objectivity and seeks to be as objective as possible. But he admits that "no one is ever one hundred per cent objective, nor anything near that mark, as a matter of fact."[1] Adherents of all philosophies and religions have assumptions. Although they may change, at any given time they seem to be coherent and satisfactory. Since people with conflicting truth-claims believe themselves coherent, coherence can hardly be the criterion by which to decide between them.

No more successful is an appeal to facts. Naturalists put their supreme faith in the methodology of the natural sciences. As that method is defined it rules out any possibility of the supernatural. Idealists, on the other hand, test truth by a systematically consistent development of the empirical method applied to persons and values as well as things. By the same empirical method they come to conflicting conclusions. "Naturalists accuse the idealists of inconsistency; idealists charge the naturalists with inadequacy."[2] Will such differences be resolved by any appeal to facts? "It is not so much the 'facts' which determine philosophical systems as the perspective of the viewer. The naturalist, the idealist, and the revelationist do not differ essentially on their data but they interpret the data quite differently."[3] The coherent world-view a person holds is relative to a set of indemonstrable assumptions accepted by faith.[4]

THE DECISIVE EXPERIENCE

Just as various experiences contribute to the perspectives of non-Christian thinkers, a definite experience contributes to the perspective of Christians. Before believing in God, they had little interest

1. Warren C. Young, *A Christian Approach to Philosophy* (Wheaton, Ill.: Van Kampen, 1954), p. 34.
2. Ibid., p. 197.
3. Ibid., p. 37.
4. Ibid., p. 201.

in Christianity. Then God in the person of the Holy Spirit changed the Christian view "from a dead option to a living reality."[5] This encounter of a sinner with God's Spirit makes the difference between Christians and non-Christians.

The Christian experience of the new birth is a direct, unmediated experience of God Himself. The transcendent God then acts immanently in history. The experience is no projection of the human mind, but "the most real of experiences possible."[6] Unlike such mysticism, in Christian experience, God does not become a part of man, or man a part of God. In the cognitive act there is no identification of man with God. Christian mysticism, Young says, does not interpret all reality—divine and human—as one (Monism).[7] But the God who is distinct from men unmistakably meets men and transforms their entire outlook.

Like all mystical experience, Christian experience is "self-authenticating."[8] No additional proof is needed. And no rational proof is possible. The true God is known only when He takes the initiative and discloses Himself to the inner man. "The experience of the God who makes Himself known is the 'foundation stone' of Christian philosophy."[9] Because the truth is found only in response to God's initiative, human efforts to prove it are in vain. "To prove revelation would be to prove that there is not revelation. To experience revelation or the supernatural is quite another matter."[10]

Direct, self-authenticating experience of God produces no mere probability, but a certainty characteristic of all mysticism. Christian mysticism carries with it the conviction that it is grounded in the natural order, but that in it God Himself is working through His Spirit. The vital experience "is a matter of deepest possible conviction, never something optional which one views in an abstract or speculative fashion."[11]

Of what is a regenerated Christian so certain? He is certain that God has revealed Himself to him. The experience is not like many mystical experiences—ineffable, or beyond all description. The whole

5. Ibid., p. 204.
6. Ibid., p. 58.
7. Ibid., p. 71.
8. Ibid., p. 203.
9. Ibid., p. 204.
10. Ibid., p. 203.
11. Ibid., pp. 203-4.

man is confronted, including the emotional, volitional, and intellectual. The reason is not totally passive, but conscious and active in God's presence. "The emphasis is on the primacy of the faith-experience, but never to the exclusion of the rational faculty."[12] Christians enlarge the meaning of experience beyond the denotations given by naturalists or idealists, to include experience of God. And since this experience occurs in connection with the Bible and news of Christ's atonement, both the Bible and the experience are taken to be revelatory.

Young's experience of God is like mystical experience in other contexts in being immediate, self-authenticating, and convincing. It differs in that the mystic is not absorbed in God; God remains transcendent while active in human experience. Furthermore, God can be spoken about meaningfully as revealed in the living Word (Christ) and the written Word (the Bible).

THE CHRISTIAN POSTULATE

In order to account for his experience the Christian assumes the reality of "the God who has spoken to man through his written Word."[13] How do we know of God's existence? "We know of His existence because He has made himself known to us. The heart of revelation is to be found in Christ, the Word who became flesh, while the record of God's special disclosure is to be found in the written Word—the Hebrew Christian Scriptures."[14] Young's Christian assumption is similar to those of the other apologists—the God of the Bible and of Christ. On this presupposition Christians, like others, construct an integrated philosophy. This philosophy includes data of purpose, values, and the resurrection of Christ. But these are not employed as émpirical evidence.

THE CHRISTIAN WORLD VIEW

With the truth of the Bible in mind, we may coherently interpret experience. The contrast to a Buswellian type of empiricism may be seen in relation to the teleological argument. Young agrees with Buswell that God, who is outside the process of nature, works in it

12. Ibid., p. 208.
13. Ibid., p. 58.
14. Ibid., p. 201.

providentially and miraculously. "But that one can begin with natural theology, discover the presence of God, and in this way, prove or verify the fact of revelation, has no place in genuine Christian philosophy."[15] We cannot seriously think that we derive the idea of God's wise plan at the conclusion of the teleological argument. But with the concept of the Creator's wisdom in mind, and with our experience of God Himself in our hearts, we can then see signs of His activity in nature. "We know that God is at work in the world, not because we have discovered Him there, but because He has disclosed this fact to us."[16]

Similarly, Christian values flow from Christian assumptions. They are not supported by objective observation. Only when the eye of the soul is opened by the new birth can anyone "see" Christian values and live by them. For the Christian, values are not autonomous, but theonomous. "To value something for the sake of value is but the shadow of true value. But to value something for the sake of God is to value, not because one's own moral dignity requires it, but because it is commanded by God. True value, for the Christian realist, comes from above, not from below."[17] The central Christian value, for example, is self-giving love (*agape*). The Christian loves God because God first loved him. Having found the ideal of love in the New Testament and the source of love in the Holy Spirit, the Christian can live in faithful love. Apart from the new birth that is impossible.

What is true of teleology and values is equally true of "facts." As Christians we can point to the resurrection of Christ from the dead as a reason for our hope. When we do, Young explains, "We are not saying that men were saved because they were confronted with the resurrection, but that after they had come into a new relationship with God in Christ, the resurrection was presented as unanswerable evidence for the validity of their experience."[18] For believers with Christian presuppositions, Christ's resurrection is unanswerable evidence; for those without these presuppositions, it is no evidence at all! Young would not argue from history to Christ's claims and resurrection, but from the new birth to the God of the Bible and so to the resurrection.

15. Ibid., pp. 158-59.
16. Ibid., p. 157.
17. Ibid., p. 136.
18. Ibid., p. 208.

The Apologist's Task

Young skillfully formulates a Christian realistic world view as over against non-Christian alternatives. But the construction of a coherent view of the world, living forms, consciousness, values, purpose, and religion is not the answer to conflicting truth-claims.

> Let it be understood that our present task is not one of attempting to demonstrate to all comers that Christian realism is a more coherent world-view than those systems which other thinkers may have to offer. Our purpose is rather to state as concisely as possible what the Christian realistic philosophy is. Converts from one world-view to another are seldom made by demonstrating that one's own particular philosophy is more coherent than all others.[19]

The apologist's task is not to argue logically, but to witness to his experience and present the world view Christians hold. This announcement is totally ineffective to bring a sinner to faith. "The natural man is in no position to understand what the Biblical option is. Man is not self-sufficient according to the Christian realistic philosophy, so that it is of no use to present him with options as if he were."[20] If the effects of sin make an argument pointless, would they not render a statement of a viewpoint or perspective equally ineffective? Since perspectives are changed only by experience, one wonders what value there is in a witness to one's own experience, or a proclamation of the philosophy which is drawn from it. Before further evaluation, however, the position of Barrett may be surveyed.

Professor Earl E. Barrett's more extensive treatment of Christian mysticism is entitled *A Christian Perspective of Knowing*. The style of the book makes it difficult to systematize. Nevertheless we shall attempt to present the volume's major thrust.

Weaknesses of Rational Apologetics

"The common defect of all merely theoretical theistic proofs is their abstractness."[21] They attempt to go from an idea of God to His existence (ontological argument), or from nature to God. Instead they ought to move from experience of God to conclusions about God. "To try to determine the existence of a *religious* object by other than

19. Ibid., p. 200.
20. Ibid., p. 203.
21. Earl E. Barrett, *A Christian Perspective of Knowing* (Kansas City, Mo.: Beacon Hill, 1965), p. 71.

distinctive religious experience is just as unreasonable as to attempt to determine the existence of a *physical* object by religious experience."[22]

The traditional proofs do not produce belief; they are the product of belief. With Kant, Barrett says there are other and better sources of belief. The believer's faith ought not stand in the wisdom of men. During the first two centuries of church history, believers found no need for formal arguments. The Bible invariably assumes that it needs no proof. And men are religious before they are philosophical. The greatest values of life are experienced rather than proved. We can be no more satisfied with an inferred God than we could with an inferred friend.[23]

Rationalism offends whenever it assumes its own self-sufficiency, independent of faith in the testimony of others. Anselm believed before constructing the ontological argument. Similarly Descartes and Aquinas depended upon revelation for their idea of God. Whenever we have no experience of our own concerning an event we must rely on the testimony of one who has. So without faith, philosophy is impossible.

Rationalism is also considered inadequate to the extent that it "acts as though it were independent of feeling and will."[24] As William James showed, life exceeds logic, practical reason precedes our conclusions, and theoretical reason follows. Borden Parker Bowne, after dismissing the theistic arguments, concluded, "where we cannot demonstrate, we choose sides." The will to believe, Barrett thinks, is required by Hebrews 11:6, "For he who comes to God must believe that He is, and that He is a rewarder of those who seek Him." And the will to believe, Barrett says, need not degenerate into the will to make-believe.[25]

Rationalism fails to take account of sin. But sin cannot be left for consideration to theologians alone. And even though ignored, sin takes account of philosophers who may sin not only in deed but also in thought and word.[26] For example, Christian Wolff began with the reverent stand that all Christian truth can be demonstrated by reason, but irreverent minds inferred that what cannot be proved by reason

22. Ibid.
23. Ibid., p. 72.
24. Ibid., p. 74.
25. Ibid., p. 76.
26. Ibid.

is not true. The minds of unsuspecting brilliant sinners play such tricks upon them.

Rationalism also makes the mistake of thinking that the Gospel of Christ can be included in a single system. Like Kierkegaard, Barrett thinks Hegel's attempt as a system builder was too ambitious. Hegel tried to comprehend within a single system the whole realm of knowledge, putting Christianity within it. This is like putting new wine in old bottles. "Christ and His Gospel cannot be put into the narrow banks of any human system—they will overflow the banks. Christianity itself is a philosophy in the practical sense of a reasonable way of life, but it is very doubtful if there is any single philosophy that can be called *the* Christian philosophy."[27]

Add to these considerations the fact that rationalism commits the logical fallacy of reasoning in a circle[28] and that deduction alone gives us no information.[29] Barrett judges that rationalism alone is an inadequate method for defending the truth of Christianity.

Nevertheless, Barrett tries to maintain a place for certain insights of rationalists. From the days of Socrates and Plato the admonition to "know thyself" has turned men's eyes inward. Kant showed that the mind is not merely passive in the reception of precepts, but actively contributes its own concepts. Many rationalists starting with an analysis of the self, consciousness, and soul, realized their dependency upon changeless, eternal truths. During the Middle Ages these truths were recognized as divine truths in the Logos of God. From this followed one of the most valuable rationalistic insights, "that all knowledge in a sense is revelational. Truth is discovered, not manufactured by man. It is given, God-given."[30] Furthermore, rationalists believed in attaining certainty. They disallowed skepticism, agnosticism, and relativism. These elements of truth leave us indebted to the rationalists.

Weaknesses of Empirical Apologetics

Empiricism also has both strengths and weaknesses. Radical empiricism, as in the case of Hume, overlooked the existence of the knower. No self could unite the diverse impressions received by the

27. Ibid., p. 77.
28. Ibid., p. 74.
29. Ibid., p. 77.
30. Ibid., p. 79.

senses. Barrett insists, however, that "there is no experience without an experiencer, no knowledge apart from a knower."[31] And he seeks to protect his view against misinterpretations. "To be real, the self need not be a substance in the old sense of the term, but a simple, spiritual, separate, self-conscious, social, continuous, complex, causative, thinking, feeling, willing, active, and eternal being, whether called self, soul, or spirit." While Buswell holds that we did not have direct experience even of ourselves, Barrett says, "the most assured knowledge is that concerning the self. If there is no immediate experience of one's own self, there is no direct experience of anything."[32]

Various schools of thought, Barrett observes, have reacted against the empiricist's neglect of the self. This reaction is seen in the voluntarism of Schopenhauer, the intuitionism of Bergson, the pragmatism of James, the feeling (prehension) of Whitehead, the subconscious of Freud, the romanticism found in literature, the insights of the great religions, and the emphases of personalism and existentialism.[33]

Whether aware of it or not, "every person is the center of his world, the world *he* experiences."[34] This being the case, it is perfectly natural to begin in philosophy just where we are. To start with the self epistemologically and psychologically does not imply self-centeredness in moral and religious senses. To start with the individual as he is and move on to God, the world, and other persons is not a false autonomy. Augustine, Descartes, Pascal, and many other thinkers have quickly gotten from the self to God. And to be realistic, Barrett says, no orthodox Christian begins his thinking with the doctrines of the Trinity or any other doctrine. Is not the truth of Scripture a prior assumption? When we begin to read the Bible, it is not God who does the interpreting, however much help He may give. Although knowledge is objective and so needs to be mediated to us, the subjectivity comes in the end of the mediating process. The knower actively contributes to the learning process, or nothing is learned. The empiricists, insofar as they neglected the self who becomes knower, have erred.[35]

Not only is empiricism deficient in its view of the self, it is also narrow in its view of experience. On one hand extreme empiricists

31. Ibid., pp. 100-1.
32. Ibid.
33. Ibid., pp. 101-2.
34. Ibid., p. 102.
35. Ibid., p. 103.

have either ignored or minimized the experience of moral and religious values. Analytical philosophers "forsake experience and become rationalists when they deal with the arguments of others and
with the meanings of language instead of appealing to the experiences
of men in art, ethics, and religion."[36] On the other hand, existentialists are charged with nothing less than essentialism. "The existentialists have misappropriated the term and abused the verb 'to be.' They
are narrow in their concept of experience and encourage irrationalism, reductionism, distortionism, and pessimism."[37] We ought not
neglect objective aspects of experience with the existentialists, nor
subjective aspects of experience with the empiricists.

Empiricism also fails of its own weight. "The chief reason for the
essential inadequacy of empiricism as a theory of knowledge is this:
However it may be stated, it must include some general proposition
about the dependence of knowledge upon experience, and any general
concept is perceived, not by the senses, but by the mind."[38] So even
a moderate empiricism must acknowledge its dependence upon rationalism, an assumption not derived from sensory experience. Empiricism is a valuable source of knowledge, but cannot sustain its
claim to be the only source of truth.

Weaknesses of Revelational Apologetics

The chief weakness of reliance on authority is the danger of credulity. We ought therefore to exercise our critical powers in assessing
the alleged authority's credentials before accepting his truth. One
who is not convinced of the Bible's authority can hardly be expected
to yield to it blindly. Other books also claim to speak for God Himself. Which authority shall we follow? As Barrett says, "The Koran
is self-attesting for some. So an appeal to biblical authority cannot
justify a minimizing or discarding of reasoning or apologetics."[39]
Authoritarianism, Barrett here concludes, cannot be the *sole* method
of determining truth.

Barrett wants to include Scripture as an authoritative source of
truth. This he does because the Bible identifies itself as God's Word
and this truth-claim is corroborated by external evidence and the

36. Ibid., p. 104.
37. Ibid., p. 105.
38. Ibid., p. 106.
39. Ibid., p. 37.

internal witness of the Spirit. "The authority of Scripture, although self-sufficient, is not arbitrary; faith in Scripture as self-attesting is not necessarily a blind, irrational faith."[40]

THE PRIMARY SOURCE OF RELIGIOUS TRUTH

By what means of knowing can we determine whether Christianity is true? Experience is central in apologetics and the strongest of the evidences.[41] "Protestants in general hold that the final and strongest evidence to themselves and the greatest appeal to others is in an inner, direct experience of God."[42] Again, the greatest evidence of all for the existence of God is "personal acquaintance with Him."[43] Barrett calls this experience a religious empiricism or a Christian mysticism.

How is this Christian mysticism distinguished from other forms of experience? As intuitive, it obtains knowledge directly or immediately without recourse to reason or experience. Several forms of intuition may be contrasted with religious intuition. First, we intuit ourselves. The metaphysical starting point of Christian thought, for Barrett as for Augustine and Descartes, was the indubitable certainty that the doubter and the knower exist. Second, we receive sensory intuition. Perceptual intuitions encompass as a whole a number of parts, some of which are perceived by the senses, such as time and space. Third, the opposite of analysis which dissects, tears apart, and kills, is a synoptic intuition, feeling its way along in the attempt to grasp reality as a unit. Like painters, poets, and musicians, we intellectually intuit by looking not merely on the surface, but within, entering sympathetically into the process of life in motion. In the fourth place, we discern right and wrong and feel a sense of moral obligation. Moral intuitions, while subjectively ours, are not merely private judgments, but objectively valid as well. Fifth, religious intuition is defined as "the mystical certainty of spiritual realities."[44]

CHRISTIAN MYSTICISM AND KNOWLEDGE

What characteristics of Christian mysticism may be distinguished? First, and most emphasized in the discussions of Barrett is its *certi-*

40. Ibid., p. 53.
41. Ibid., p. 113.
42. Ibid., p. 196.
43. Ibid., p. 207.
44. Ibid., pp. 132-36.

tude. A psychological rather than a logical concept, certitude is an assurance at once "compelling and complete." In fact the immediacy of the experience is "self-validating."[45] Second, mystical experience is noetic or cognitive. It is not a discursive, analytic type of knowledge, but an insight that turns up, a way of wisdom, sudden, penetrating, and coercive. Barrett claims that mystical experience need not be completely devoid of knowledge content. The immediate experience is not exhausted in assurance *that* God exists; enough knowledge results so that we can identify *what* God is. "Although religious experience is basically feeling, it furnishes knowledge, as this feeling is cognitive-feeling."[46] So "the nonrational is a bearer of knowledge."[47] The *numinous* element of religious experience takes its rise primarily in the emotional life—not in bare feeling, but in "cognitive-feeling." "God is not reached at the end of a syllogism of reason, but is known in the immediacy of feeling."[48] As William James said, God is unseen, but not unfelt. "It is as if there were in the human consciousness a sense of reality, a feeling of objective presence, a perception of what we may call 'something there.' "[49]

This view of mystical experience, Barrett insists, need not become irrationalistic.[50] He rejects Emil Brunner's notion that God only actively reveals Himself to us as subject in an encounter, and never is the object of our knowing. "God can be known literally and positively. What a personal God says and does can be, and is, revealed to persons."[51] God "is not a logical entity, nor an ideal summing up of all the values of the universe, but a Person who may be known in interpersonal relations by acquaintance."[52] Acquaintance knowledge is like that of love and beauty. A person is directly presented in his activities. And "God *is* Personal Activity. (This is not meant to be an exhaustive statement, but true so far as it goes, and it goes a long way)."[53]

Mystical experience of God also need not be irrationalistic because

---

45. Ibid., p. 156.
46. Ibid., p. 46.
47. Ibid., p. 150.
48. Ibid., p. 122.
49. William James, *Varieties of Religious Experience* (New York: Longmans, Green), p. 58. Quoted by Earl Barrett, ibid., p. 122.
50. Barrett, ibid.
51. Ibid.
52. Ibid., p. 191.
53. Ibid., p. 196.

God is "not wholly Other."[54] "Of course God is beyond all ideas of God; every object of thought may be said to be beyond thought in the sense, at least of non-identity." So, "an infinite and transcendent God is 'beyond' the comprehension of man, but *not* beyond his apprehension."[55] This apprehension of God may be designated a personal encounter, a contact, a revelation, confrontation, and compresence.[56] Barrett agrees with Cherbonnier: to exclude a metaphysical description of God from one's philosophy is very dangerous. Contrary to many contemporary advocates of personal encounter, Barrett says it "does not break relation with God to describe Him."[57]

Although knowledge is possible, Barrett stresses that "the actual presence of God in human life, i.e., genuine contact with God, is of more importance than our rational explanations of it."[58] In line with this, Barrett says "Differences in theology among mystics are inconsequential. What is important is the awareness of union with spiritual realities, and the practice of the presence of God. The mystic does not feel called to teach theology; he is a witness, a witness to a life-shaking and life-shaping experience of union with reality."[59]

CHRISTIAN MYSTICISM AND THE BIBLE

Others who base their primary case for Christianity upon encounters often deny that the Bible is revelation, making it merely another human witness to revelatory experiences. Barrett claims that his Christian mysticism "does not displace the Bible as the primary base of religious knowledge, for it (the Bible) in turn is founded upon experience."[60] Job says, "I have heard of thee by the hearing of the ear; but now mine eye seeth thee" (Job 42:5, KJV). Isaiah saw the Lord "high and lifted up" (Is 6:1-8, KJV). "All the writers of the Bible had similar experiences, fitting them for their task."[61] "Of course Christ is the Mystic par excellence."[62] And "whatever the objective factors present in the conversion of Saul of Tarsus (and we accept the entire record), the features he emphasized later were sub-

54. Ibid., p. 191.
55. Ibid., p. 194.
56. Ibid., p. 143.
57. Ibid., pp. 125-26.
58. Ibid., p. 198.
59. Ibid., p. 157.
60. Ibid., p. 124.
61. Ibid., p. 113.
62. Ibid., p. 181.

jective: 'For God . . . hath shined in our hearts, to give the light of
the knowledge of the glory of God in the face of Jesus Christ' (II Cor.
4:6). In this sense all Christian experience is internal and cognitive."[63]

The Bible functions as conditioner of mystical experience both directly and indirectly. One who desires encounter with God should
follow its instructions as he would a laboratory manual. The Bible
mediates Christian mystical experience.[64] With all due respect for
conservative theologians who regard the Bible as the sole source of
Christian theology, Barrett challenges their belief. Admittedly "most
of our spiritual knowledge comes through faith in the testimony of
God, which is perfectly reliable."[65] But this cannot be the only source
of truth. Why? "This was not because we rejected divine authority,
but because we accepted it. For accepting God's Word as *final* authority, we turn again to the empirical method for support and supplement."[66] The Bible says, "Taste and see that the Lord is good"
(Psa 34:8). That means "experience for yourself," do not merely
rely on the Bible. "A thing is true because God has said it. But He
speaks both in the Bible and in the human heart."[67]

In beginning the Christian life, for example, it is not enough for a
Christian to point an unbeliever to a passage about salvation and rest
the case there. The sinner must genuinely repent. "No one is born
again until God speaks also in the soul of the *fully* repentant and
believing one, by the *direct* witness of the Spirit. This is not a matter
of inference as is the indirect witness—God speaking, for instance, in
the Bible. Experience does not supplant authority; it supplements
it."[68]

FURTHER MARKS OF MYSTICISM

In addition to the characteristics of certitude and knowledge, mystical experience involves ethical and voluntary union with God. Barrett rejects a metaphysical union which suggests actual absorption
in the divine in a more or less pantheistic sense.[69] Rather, in a the-

---

63. Ibid., pp. 194-95; cf. p. 182.
64. Ibid., p. 187.
65. Ibid., p. 203.
66. Ibid.
67. Ibid.
68. Ibid., pp. 203-4.
69. Ibid., p. 157.

istic perspective, the union is one of loving obedience. "Thus when the mystic speaks of union with God, he does not necessarily mean any interpenetration of personalities or loss of identity, for often self-consciousness is more vivid in the mystical experience."[70] While most fully himself the Christian in the mystical transport feels himself in complete harmony with God.

This experience is not publicly verifiable, but very personal and private. It is better felt than "telt." One must experience it for himself and it is nontransferable.[71] Because it goes beyond all description it may be characterized as ineffable. This does not mean, as in Walter T. Stace, that no sentence accurately asserts a predicate of God (that every proposition beginning 'God is . . .' is false, literally interpreted), as we have shown above. Rather, it means that all symbols (including words and concepts) are inadequate to the task of expressing the lived feeling involved in mystical intuition.[72]

Both humility and exaltation also accompany Christian mysticism. And mystics are known for their creative love in personal relationships. Enthusiastically mystics report that God is love. And the response of the whole man to divine love makes a difference in life. "Tests made by Robert Sinclair on college students reporting mystical experiences revealed a peculiar and practical inspiration present in them. They responded better to hints and promptings, were more socially and ethically minded than others. In effect, their experiences were satisfying and uplifting."[73]

Furthermore, Barrett stresses that mystical experience demands entire consecration and holiness.[74] To this important characteristic Isaiah witnesses. He "saw the Gospel dispensation with its demands and provisions for complete consecration and entire sanctification of heart and life. . . . he experienced a fiery cleansing, prophetic of the fiery baptism of the Holy Spirit."[75] H. Orton Wiley, author of a three-volume *Christian Theology*, regards entire consecration as the central idea of all mysticism. The experience demands and gets "internal sanctity of the heart, separation from the creature, and perfect

---

70. Ibid.
71. Ibid., p. 158.
72. Ibid., p. 159.
73. Ibid., p. 161; see also p. 179.
74. Ibid.
75. Ibid., p. 184.

union with God, the center and source of holiness and perfection."[76]
Barrett explains:

> Yet we would not narrow the definition of religious experience to
> mean only the initial contact with God in conversion and the second
> crisis experience, the baptism with the Holy Spirit. It is any experi-
> ence of God Himself. In the Christian perspective, it is any such
> experience received through the objective realities: Christ, the Holy
> Spirit, the Bible, and the Church; and the subjective realities of the
> reading of the Bible, meditation, worship and prayer, in which
> there is an awareness of God and His purposes and of His fellow-
> ship.[77]

OCCASIONS OF MYSTICAL EXPERIENCE

Granting experiences of this nature, what occasions bring them?
Several factors are mentioned. "For the effects found in immediate
religious experience, there are causes, divine and human."[78] First,
the environment may include a tradition of religious belief which
may evoke Christian mystical experience. A child growing up under
the influence of belief in the Bible and the church inherits beliefs
which need only to be translated into experience. Since the truth of
these beliefs may be tested, this tradition is not necessarily a restric-
tion or an imposition. Second, the Bible as "the Record of God's
self-disclosure . . . becomes the conditioner of God's revelation in
other lives, in the readers and hearers as well as in the writers."[79]

Third, imagination and the will are listed as conditioners of mystical experience. In most of us the power of imagination may be
weaker than the power of perception, but others may direct attention
to the power of imagination in the solution of problems. So imagination may be "a tool of faith in the approach to God." And since faith
is a voluntary activity, the will is a factor as well. Fourth, feelings
such as love, humility, and awe contribute. Finally, a person is conditioned by faith for experience with God. Based on the experience
of others including the Bible writers, men live not by sight but by
insight. Through faith as spiritual perception men come into contact with God.[80]

76. Cited by Barrett, ibid., p. 185.
77. Ibid., p. 121.
78. Ibid., p. 186.
79. Ibid., p. 187.
80. Ibid., pp. 187-88.

The immediate experience of God is also mediated by three methods of preparation. The experimental way exercises the capacity for direct intuition of the spiritual environment. The purgative way seeks cleansing, or holiness as a preparation for communion with God. And the illuminative way through meditation seeks the enlightening presence of God.[81]

TEST FOR TRUTH

How then do we know that Christianity is true according to Barrett? Although the mystical experience brings with it a psychological certainty, may we obtain a logical certainty? We may seek a logical certainty as well for the sake of those who have not had the experience and because the experience is preceded by ideas which mediate it and is succeeded by reflection. "Reason must play on this subjective material to aid in making it objective or public, and also to show that it is valid by meeting certain tests."[82] These tests are three.

The first test is pragmatic. "Any hypothesis can be *known* to be true only because it works." In the laboratory that which works is true. So with James and Dewey, our religious ideas must direct us to concrete experience. Approach to God cannot be merely theoretical. Our religious ideas also are "tools for action." They justify their usefulness in the discovery and practice of factual truth. To the objection that not all that works is true, Barrett points not merely to personal and immediate satisfaction alone, but the social and long-range view. This test is met by mystical intuition, Barrett maintains, because the individual who communes with God has a powerful force in his active life. He is contemplative, practical, and altruistic.[83]

The logical test of Christianity's truth requires coherence. "Neither private nor public evidence can be found to substantiate a real contradiction." A coherent view of all the relevant facts is the form Barrett's synopsis of authoritarian, rational, empirical, and mystical elements adds to the psychological certainty "a high degree of logical certainty." It "should appeal to all thoughtful people, those open to hear new evidence."[84]

Included in the criteria of truth is a necessity, logical and moral.

81. Ibid., p. 158.
82. Ibid., p. 213.
83. Ibid., pp. 213-14.
84. Ibid., pp. 214-16.

Belief in God is logically necessary as "an essential condition of all
reasoning." In language reminiscent of Van Til's, Barrett says that
God's existence, "while ultimately not an inference from any premise
(i.e. to the one who has directly experienced God), makes possible
all inference." Again, "if there be no Rationality, no Logos, no Ultimate Explanation at the heart of the universe, then human reason,
groundless and 'explanation-less,' could have no confidence in itself."
Furthermore, "belief in God is morally necessary for deliverance
from sin." The experience of that deliverance renders necessary the
theistic explanation.[85]

Christianity is held to be true, then, because it has worked in the
personal experience of many, and gives a coherent explanation of
mystical experience, logical assertion, and morality. That must be
made emphatic to a person questioning Christianity's truth-claims.
But primarily he must be given the witness of Christian mystics.
"Mystics from many parts of the world and from many periods of
history, as well as from many religious viewpoints bear solid and coherent witness to this phenomenon."[86] This may evoke a similar
immediate experience in the hearer. And "one personal contact with
God is sufficient for permanent certitude concerning His existence,
although not for full knowledge of His nature."[87] Psychological certitude of God's existence will be enjoyed only as the result of personal
experience of God. Logical demonstrations and faith in another's
authority cannot provide the same assurance.

BARRETT AND YOUNG ON THE INVISIBLE GARDENER

To help sum up the apologetic of Christian mysticism we may ask
again why some people believe in the care of the world by an invisible Gardener and others do not. The primary reason for belief in the
Gardener, Young and Barrett answer, is a person's very personal and
direct experience of God Himself. Independent of such an experience all empirical, rational, and authoritarian arguments for His existence are futile. After a mystical experience, however, a person is
unshakeably convinced of Christianity's truth-claims. The Christian
mystic's psychological certainty is not, therefore, united to intellectual
absurdity. With Christianity's basic presuppositions corroborated

85. Ibid., pp. 216-17.
86. Ibid., p. 206.
87. Ibid., p. 212.

by pragmatic experience, the believer can see their logical consistency, and their explanatory power in relation to such phenomena as Christ's resurrection, mystical experiences, meaningful logical assertion, and deliverance from man's moral predicament. The Christian's primary task with an unbeliever is to witness of his own direct, intuitive experience of God. The unbeliever will not "see" the coherence of Christianity until he has himself met God.

EVALUATION

We must commend Young and Barrett for stressing an aspect of experience other apologists have not made as explicit. They properly decry a mere system divorced from authentic commitment. Barrett sees that Protestant orthodoxy tended to adhere to the written Word apart from the personal Word, Christ. "Without Him and the inner witnessing Spirit . . . the result was an empty Word and a dead orthodoxy, a state of affairs that faced the Wesleys when they began to emphasize religious experience."[88] Barrett seems to be right that "man is not satisfied with merely a mediated knowledge of God, His thought, and His will for man. Man desires self-disclosure, self-evidence, and an intuitive knowledge resulting from the manifestation of God within his own spirit."[89] Our generation, like Augustine's, will find no rest until it rests in God Himself.

And we must commend these men for seeking a balance between experience and its rational explanations. They have emphasized Christian experience while trying not to depreciate a coherent world view. However, the way is paved for others to minimize a systematic understanding of theology. Barrett's unqualified statement, good in itself, is, "The actual presence of God in human life, i.e., genuine contact with God, is of more importance than our rational explanations of it."[90] A better balance might be achieved by saying that among all life's experiences none is more important than experience of God; among all the mind's beliefs, none is more important than belief in clearly revealed doctrines.

Our primary concern is to know whether Christianity is true, and if so, on what grounds. If we support its truth-claims primarily from mystical experience, we are immediately faced with a problem. En-

88. Ibid., p. 112.
89. Ibid., p. 139.
90. Ibid., p. 198.

thusiastic testimonies of mystics support religions with truth-claims contradictory to Christianity's. The immediate encounters of Hindus, Buddhists, and innumerable cults pragmatically "work" for them: If the attempts of Barrett and Young to unite their mysticism with sound doctrine were successful, they would escape this difficulty. But when the decisive factor in settling conflicting truth-claims is a self-authenticating experience, no further checks and balances are really in order. If the mystical experiences of Christians and non-Christians are not self-authenticating, then a more ultimate criterion of truth deserves a more thorough explication than they have allowed.

An ambiguity in Barrett's work may illustrate this point. On the one hand he claims a certitude that is immediate and non-inferred,[91] instantaneous[92], compelling, complete and self-validating,[93] impregnable, unshakeable, and imperturbable,[94] unchallengeable,[95] indubitable,[96] and permanent.[97] On the other hand, Barrett admits that "intuitions need to be checked and supplemented" because it is easy to claim as an intuition a hunch or feeling that does not pan out in the whole of life.[98] For such reasons as these, "the true mystic insists that his intuitions should be tested by other experience and by the Word of God." Furthermore, "intuitive apprehension should not be regarded as assured knowledge until it has been verified by observation and reason."[99] How can one experience, at the same time and in the same respect, be self-validating and not self-validating? It can hardly be both ways. If the claims for mystical certainty are sustained, it authenticates contradictory religious truth-claims. If not, then mystical intuition is but one datum of experience among many others to be accounted for, but not the "foundation stone" in settling issues of truth.

As Barrett says, however, "There is no getting around a fact of experience." And he alludes to the man who said, "Brother, when an honest-to-goodness Methodist tells you that he has had an experience,

91. Ibid., p. 140.
92. Ibid., p. 143.
93. Ibid., p. 156.
94. Ibid., p. 186.
95. Ibid., p. 197.
96. Ibid., p. 211.
97. Ibid., p. 212.
98. Ibid., p. 208.
99. Ibid., pp. 208-10.

you don't argue with him."[100] Statements like these overlook a crucial distinction between the experience as given, and the experience as taken, or interpreted. The element of truth is that no one can deny that mystical experiences as psychological phenomena have occurred. But the fallacy is the implication that therefore no one can challenge a particular interpretation of the experiences. After all, fundamental differences of interpretation appear among the mystics themselves. W. T. Stace, who writes very sympathetically of mystical experience, points out that mystics may misinterpret their experience just as those who "see" an event with the physical eyes may misinterpret their experiences.[101] So he says:

> I think the question has to be raised whether we are bound thus to accept blindly and without criticism whatever report the mystic gives us of his experience. Not that we shall doubt his veracity. But there is always the psychological possibility that he may be mistaken as to what in fact he did experience.[102]

As a classic example of possible misunderstanding of mystical experience, Stace alludes to the influential Jewish philosopher, Martin Buber. The author of *I and Thou* interpreted a religious experience of his in two distinct ways. His earlier explanation said he lost the bonds of personal nature in an undivided unity with God. Buber later questioned this pantheistic interpretation, however. Plainly the experience is one thing; the interpretation of the experience is another. And on the matter of interpretation, even a Methodist could be wrong!

A similar ambiguity lurks between frequent references in Christian literature to knowledge by acquaintance. Here again we must distinguish what is presented in experience from our view of it or attitudes toward it. Paul F. Schmidt recommends that we not speak of knowledge by experience, but of acquaintance experience. That experience may be a source of religious claims about experience. And "it can generate attitudes, but in itself, cannot justify them so as to provide knowledge about attitudes."[103]

---

100. Ibid., p. 198.
101. W. T. Stace, *Mysticism and Philosophy* (Philadelphia: Lippincott, 1960), p. 18.
102. Ibid., p. 128.
103. Paul F. Schmidt, *Religious Knowledge* (Beverly Hills, Calif.: Free Press of Glencoe, 1961), p. 136.

Here, then, is one primary source of confusion in questions about Christianity's truth. Some employ "truth" of interpretations of experience, others of the experience as given, and only in a pale and secondary sense of conceptual interpretation. We may rightly question an idealist emphasis upon a system of interpretation which minimizes experiential givens. But we need as well to avoid the other extreme of discrediting interpretations of encounters.

Little is gained by claiming that experience is far more important than reasoning, if experience is misunderstood. Those who think that apologetics is rendered unnecessary by a simple witness to what God has done overlook this inescapable point. The interpretations of religious experiences, including Christian conversion, are numerous. A. J. Ayer, who wrote *Language, Truth and Logic*, says that those defenders of Christianity's truth who "fill their books with assertions that they intuitively 'know' this or that moral or religious 'truth' are merely providing material for the psychoanalyst."[104]

Not all interpretations are quite as extreme. But they are not necessarily more complimentary. The German writer Goethe held that mystical phenomena required no belief in a supernatural being, but could be explained by an overmastering intrusion of feeling into the operations of the intellect. Others explained it as the intrusion of the subconscious into consciousness voluntarily (Du Prel) or involuntarily (Hartman). No amount of enthusiasm in witnessing to an experience will of itself impress naturalists who maintain that "imitation, social education, and individual suggestion furnish a quite sufficient explanation for all the phenomena of mysticism."[105] Is not some evidence of another kind also of value in answering the conviction that mysticism does not point to a transcendent God? Mystically inclined apologists must not only set apart their hearts to Jesus Christ as Lord, but be ready to give an answer to every man who asks, a reason for the particular interpretation of the experience to which they witness.

As Gordon H. Clark pointed out, Warren C. Young has asked the wrong question. "Instead of asking, Who decides? he should have

---

104. A. J. Ayer, *Language, Truth and Logic* (New York: Dover, 1946), p. 120.
105. J. B. Pratt, *The Religious Consciousness* (New York: Macmillan, 1928), p. 443.

asked, On what grounds can a decision legitimately be made?"[106] That is the apologetic question. Mystical intuitions may be part of the answer, but by themselves are not, in fact, self-authenticating. What shall be said to those who, having experienced the new birth and the second blessing, still ask whether Christianity is true?

RESOURCES FOR RESEARCH

Barrett, Earl E. *A Christian Perspective of Knowing*. Kansas City, Mo.: Beacon Hill, 1965. A defense of Christian mysticism by an evangelical who taught philosophy and religion at Olivet Nazarene College.

Braden, William. *The Private Sea: LSD and the Search for God*. Chicago: Quadrangle, 1967. A newspaper reporter and serious student of philosophy and theology sees a relationship between the trend to psychedelic experience and the death of God theology.

Brunner, Emil. *Truth as Encounter*. Philadelphia: Westminster, 1964. A new edition, much enlarged, of *The Divine-Human Encounter*. Religious truth is neither fact nor system, but a meeting between two active persons. Truth comes to us. God is not a passive object of our autonomous investigations which we can possess. Truth is loving responses to the living Lord as He communicates Himself (neo-orthodox).

Buber, Martin. *I and Thou* 2d ed. New York: Scribner's, 1958. One of the most influential sources of contemporary emphases on a direct and immediate relation with God expressed in personal language by a Jewish thinker.

Butler, Dom Cuthbert. *Western Mysticism: The Teaching of Augustine, Gregory and Bernard on Contemplation and the Contemplative Life*. 1922. Reprint. New York: Harper Torchbooks, 1966. "Mysticism" did not become current until the latter middle ages, so the Roman Catholic discusses experimental perception of God in terms of "contemplation."

Freemantle, Anne, ed. *The Protestant Mystics*. New York: Mentor, 1964. Contains the testimonies of sixty-seven Protestant mystics, although W. T. Stace said there were none, and "Calvinists, *en masse*, thought that even if there were mystics, there shouldn't be any."

James, William. *The Varieties of Religious Experience*. New York: Modern Libr., 1902. A psychologist examines the testimonies of mystics (chaps. 16-17).

Jewett, Paul King. *Emil Brunner's Concept of Revelation*. London: James Clarke, 1954. A responsible interpretation finding that Brunner, in the end, verifies the truths of revelation along mystical lines.

106. Gordon H. Clark, "Apologetics," in *Contemporary Evangelical Thought* (Great Neck, N. Y.: Channel, 1957), p. 151.

Montgomery, John Warwick. "Constructive Religious Empiricism: An Analysis and Criticism." In *The Shape of the Past.* Ann Arbor, Mich.: Edwards, 1962, pp. 257-311. An evaluation of attempts to discover religious truth from subjective religious experience, empirically examined. A plea for utilizing the empirical method on the more objective data of history, such as Christ's resurrection.

———. "A Critique of William James' *Varieties of Religious Experience.*" In *The Shape of the Past.* Ann Arbor, Mich.: Edwards, 1962, pp. 312-40. A summation of the merits and demerits of James' classic work, psychologically and philosophically.

Nicoll, Wm. Robertson. *The Garden of Nuts.* New York: A. C. Armstrong, 1905. Robertson interprets the Song of Solomon (from which he takes his title) as an allegorical portrayal of mystical experience of God.

O'Brien, Elmer. *Varieties of Mystic Experience: An Anthology and Interpretation.* New York: Mentor-Omega, 1964. Roman Catholic witnesses to a direct confrontation of the Ultimate in a way different from either sense perception or reasoning.

Otto, Rudolf. *The Idea of the Holy: An Inquiry into the Non-rational Factor in the Idea of the Divine and Its Relation to the Rational.* Trans. by John W. Harvey. New York: Oxford U., 1958. Another of the most influential sources of contemporary religious thought, arguing that "to *know* and to *understand conceptually* are two different things, are often mutually exclusive, and contrasted."

Pratt, James Bisset. *The Religious Consciousness: A Psychological Study.* New York: Macmillan, 1928. A valuable discussion of mysticism (chaps. 16-20) from a psychological and philosophical point of view.

Ramm, Bernard. *The Witness of the Spirit.* Grand Rapids: Eerdmans, 1959. A perceptive work relating evangelical Christian experience of the Holy Spirit to evidences.

Rose, Delbert R. *A Theology of Christian Experience: Interpreting the Historic Wesleyan Message.* Minneapolis: Bethany Fellowship, 1965. The professor of biblical theology at Asbury Theological Seminary expounds the teachings of Joseph H. Smith (1855-1946) who held that knowledge of God is personal and experimental rather than theoretical or philosophical, and sought to minister his experiential knowledge to others.

Schmidt, Paul F. *Religious Knowledge.* Beverly Hills, Calif.: Free Press of Glencoe, 1961. An analysis of truth-claims in Christianity, Judaism, Hinduism, Buddhism, Confucianism, Taoism, and Islam, critical of claims to "knowledge" by acquaintance although sympathetic to acquaintance experience.

Stace, W. T. *Mysticism and Philosophy.* Philadelphia and New York: Lippincott, 1960. A noted philosopher seeks to clarify the philosophical significance of mysticism, convinced with Bertrand Russell that the greatest philosophers have felt the need of both science and mysticism.

Stiansen, Peder. "Church Reform in the Late Middle Ages." *Bibliotheca Sacra* 105 (July-September 1948) : 341-63. An author of unassailable orthodoxy argued that the highest type of mysticism is found in the Christian religion.

Underhill, Evelyn. *Mysticism: A Study in the Nature and Development of Man's Spiritual Consciousness.* 1910. Reprint. Cleveland and New York: World, 1955. A comprehensive attempt to relate mysticism to psychology, theology, symbolism, magic, voices, visions, and the unitive life.

Warfield, Benjamin Breckinridge. "Mysticism and Christianity." In *Biblical and Theological Studies.* Nutley, N. J.: Presbyterian and Reformed, 1952. The noted Calvinist argued that "the history of mysticism only too clearly shows that he who begins by seeking God within himself may end by confusing himself with God." The mystic subordinates the Bible to his experience as a source of truth about God, whereas the evangelical Christian interprets all religious experience by the normative scriptural revelation.

Young, Warren C. *A Christian Approach to Philosophy.* Wheaton, Ill.: Van Kampen, 1954. Although Professor Young does not call his position mysticism, the Baptist philosopher of religion determines Christianity's truth primarily from personal experience of God. Subsequent to that experience the believer may obtain a coherence in philosophical teaching.

7

THE VERIFICATIONAL APPROACH OF
EDWARD JOHN CARNELL: FACTS

The Test of Non-Contradiction, Evidence and Experience

FROM THE PERSPECTIVE of the late Edward John Carnell (1919-1967), the previous tests of truth are like separate pieces of a stained glass window. The former professor of ethics and philosophy of religion at Fuller Theological Seminary sought to put the pieces back together again.

Carnell had picked up the pieces during his student days. From Cornelius Van Til at Westminster Theological Seminary he took his starting point, the existence of the triune God of the Bible. However, this tenet is not an unquestioned presupposition for Carnell, but a hypothesis to be tested. His test of truth is threefold. At Wheaton College in the classes of Gordon H. Clark, Carnell found the test of non-contradiction. The test of fitness to empirical fact was championed by Edgar S. Brightman at Boston University where Carnell earned his Ph.D. The requirement of relevance to personal experience became prominent during Carnell's Th.D. research at Harvard University in Sören Kierkegaard and Reinhold Niebuhr.

These pieces began to fall into place to form a single picture in 1948 when Carnell published his prize-winning volume, *An Introduction to Christian Apologetics*. The argument of this book is fundamental to the understanding of Carnell's later writings.

Starting Point

Where does Carnell start in order to test Christianity's truth-claims? He begins conversations where people's interests happen to

176

be. So Carnell's *temporal* starting point is a person's experiential conditioning. But this is common to all men, whatever their outlook. The question is how men with different biographical experiences can begin to test truth-claims heard from childhood. What is the *logical* starting point in apologetics?

Carnell cannot agree with Young and Barrett that the logical starting point is a direct experience of God. The feelings of the heart, Carnell admits, are a strong force in man, and the number of reporters testifying to immediate experiences of God is immense. Nevertheless, he argues that feelings are incapable of criticizing themselves, and result in devotion to many different gods: polytheistic, pantheistic, and unknown. If experience of God is really self-authenticating and beyond rational examination, theology as an informative discipline is impossible. Ethics would also be left adrift without meaningful standards. Although feelings produce strong psychological certitude, they cannot serve as self-authenticating tests of truth. All too often they not only serve contradictory causes, but deceive.[1] They may take you on a "bad trip" from which there is no return. Religious experience has an important place in Carnell's thought, but it is not his primary point of departure.

Analogously Carnell has a place in his approach for empirical evidence, but perception of the physical world is not his starting point. The attempt to come with a blank mind to nature does not end in knowledge, but skepticism. Like Clark, Carnell reasons that the best a pure empiricist can do is to describe a series of disjointed impressions. No universal or necessary laws can be derived from nature. Without a universal and necessary law of cause and effect pure empiricism cannot prove or disprove the existence of God. Rational empiricism also fails to show God's existence. Granting innate causality, all one needs to explain a finite universe is a finite God. Admittedly a cause may have more perfections than its effect, as the watchmaker possesses more attributes than the watch. If the cause of the universe is greater than the evidence indicates, however, empiricists have no way of knowing it. Since none of the inductive arguments prove an infinite God, it is possible that the finite God of one argument is not the finite God of another. There is room for thou-

1. Edward John Carnell, *An Introduction to Christian Apologetics* (Grand Rapids: Eerdmans, 1948), pp. 49-50; 74-82.

sands of finite gods. The god alleged is not the Almighty God unless ideas beyond empirical evidence are read into the conclusions of theistic arguments.[2]

The starting points of personal testimony, sense data, and rational principles all fall short of ability to confirm or disconfirm truth-claims about one infinite, wise, and loving God. Where then can one start his investigation of the biblical God's existence? "The logical starting point is the coordinating ultimate which gives being and meaning to the many of the time-space universe. For Thales it was water; for Anaximines it was air, for Plato it was the Good; and for the Christian it is the Trinity."[3] The logical starting point for testing Christianity's truth-claims is the hypothesis that the triune God of the Bible exists. Philosophers who explained everything from one thing like water had difficulty explaining the diverse character of the world. And those who started with a multitude of atoms or elements had difficulty accounting for the unity of the universe. The Christian answer to the unity and diversity of the world is a God who exists as three persons in one essence. The ultimate explanation of all things is itself a multiplicity in unity. Starting with the hypothesis of the Trinity's eternal existence it is possible to account for multiplicity and unity everywhere in the universe.

Without the Scriptures we could not know the Trinity, so Carnell includes the Bible along with the triune God in his initial postulate. While God is the ground of the Scriptures, the Scriptures are the means through which God is apprehended. The ontological and epistemological assumptions go together. Their inseparability is expressed in the single hypothesis—the God who has revealed Himself in Scripture. That hypothesis is the logical starting point of Carnell's apologetic.

Both Clark and Van Til also began by presupposing the God of the Bible. The difference is that Carnell does not regard this starting point an axiom or an unquestionable presupposition. For Carnell it is a hypothesis to be checked out by non-contradiction and experience. Hypotheses are not self-evident truths. Hypotheses are not known to be true by some flash of intuition. They are not true because worthy people say they are with authority. They are true only when verified as not contradictory and as adequate to account for all relevant data

2. Ibid., pp. 129-34.
3. Ibid., p. 124.

of experience. Carnell's "hypothesis" is by no means synonymous with Clark's axiom or Van Til's presupposition. Clark allowed the testing of axioms by the law of noncontradiction but not experience. Van Til permitted no testing of his presupposition by logic or experience. Carnell subjects his hypothesis to both logic and experience.

WHY A HYPOTHESIS?

Carnell argues that hypothetical reasoning is by far the more characteristic type in everyday life, in science, and particularly in philosophy. We define a problem, gather information about it, form hypotheses or tentative conclusions, test those conclusions, and in terms of our evaluation arrive at a decision.[4] Every Monday morning the laundress (without an automatic dryer!) faces the problem of drying her clothes. She looks out at the sky and listens to weather reports in order to form a hypothesis. The clothes can get dry before it rains. She has tested this conclusion on other days with a similar sky. Upon the basis of her evaluation of her experience she hangs up the clothes. If after hanging out the clothes they are drenched in rain, she has acted on a faultily construed hypothesis.

The scientist simply refines the housewife's procedure. Watt conceived the idea of the engine by watching the escape of steam from a teakettle. Archimedes figured out the law of water displacement when he stepped into a tub full of water and saw the water run over. Carnell reasons, "All hypotheses are but patterns of meaning which are thought out by the mind of the investigator to explain the configuration of data which it faces. The hypotheses that work well are called 'theories,' and theories that stick are called 'laws.' But let us not forget that these laws are but good hypotheses."[5]

Philosophers seek to give meaning to more than the problems of everyday life or the distinct fields of the sciences. Philosophers look for the significance of everything in the universe. Thinking about the universe in a certain way is inescapable. Even one who says the character of the universe cannot be known proposes that the universe is an affair unknowable to man. That is a hypothesis which must be checked. Plato's world of ideas is not assumed independent of ex-

---

4. For a well-illustrated introduction to the logic of hypothetical reasoning, see W. Edgar Moore, *Creative and Critical Thinking* (Boston: Houghton Mifflin, 1967), pp. 1-56.
5. Carnell, p. 93.

perience, but is proposed to explain the phenomena we see. In order to solve the problem of knowledge Kant proposed the forms of time and space and the categories of the understanding. To solve the metaphysical and epistemological problems the Christian proposes the existence of the biblical God. With this hypothesis he can explain, not deny, experience. The Christian hypothesis is no more ostentatious than that of the naturalist who denies the existence of God as the sine qua non for interpreting reality.[6]

Two dangers must be avoided in the making of hypotheses: the fear of proposing hypotheses at all, and the complete lack of fear. One must go beyond the facts if he is ever conceptually to know anything. Knowledge is the meaning of data, not the data itself. Huxley rightly said that he who does not go beyond the facts will seldom get as far as the facts. Logical positivists illustrated the danger of staying so close to the data that they lost its significance. In the other direction are "hypothesis-happy souls" whose imagination sets forth hypotheses too extensive to be verified. The geometrizing of reality by rationalists is a case in point. Rationalists forget that the imagination must be relevant as well as free. A good hypothesis is free enough to *explain* the facts, and yet restricted enough to explain the *facts.*[7] The rationalistic truth-claim is heroic and free, but is not relevant to the human situation; the positivistic truth-claim is relevant, but is not a solution. Knowledge involves two elements: the given, ineffable presentation (facts), and the conceptual interpretation which represents the mind's response.[8] Presuppositionalists are not sufficiently close to the given; empiricists have inadequate interpretive principles.

Hypotheses should be formulated in as simple a way as possible. The simplest hypothesis is most logically consistent, has the fewest ultimate principles, and the least number of special cases unexplained. Without the aid of additional hypotheses, it can exhibit the logical connections in the chosen domain.[9] The positive strength of a hypothesis is to make good what it claims. "So, in Christianity, its first test is to see if it can live up to its lofty claims by giving a basis of personal hope in immortality, a rational view of the universe, and

6. Ibid., pp. 95-96.
7. Ibid., pp. 98-99.
8. Ibid., p. 92.
9. Ibid., pp. 99-100.

a solution to the problems of truth."[10] On the negative side it is necessary to consider what one is left with if he gives up the hypothesis. With Clark, Carnell concludes that non-Christian systems lead to skepticism.

There are no holds barred in the forming of hypotheses. Non-Christians are invited to produce any they wish and only to allow the Christian the same freedom in setting his forth. The golden rule applies to hypothesis making. If the Christian wants a non-Christian to listen to his case, he must return the favor. And a non-Christian who wishes a Christian to take his world view seriously should attend as carefully to the Christian's world view.

COMMON GROUND

On what basis can Christians and non-Christians even discuss their different hypotheses as to the nature of the world? Admittedly Christians and non-Christians have radically different metaphysical systems. Although their concepts of ultimate meaning are diverse, the facts to be explained are the same.

Carnell distinguishes three levels of meaning. First, on a purely personal level, a fern plant from grandmother's funeral is more significant to a grandchild than to someone who did not know her. On this level of personal tastes no issue of truth or common ground arises. Second, on a scientific level, common ground exists. Take the plant to the laboratory and the fern is observed factually and classified in the order of *Filicales*. In terms of a botanical definition there is no difference of meaning for the Christian and non-Christian. Factually they share common ground. Third, when the ultimate meaning of the fern is in question, no common ground exists. The Christian regards it as a unit of being originally made and now sustained by the Almighty. It shares a place in the wisely planned and governed world of order and purpose. For the non-Christian the fern is an accidental development in a world without purpose or point.[11]

A naturalistic scientist may fail to stay within the limits of his field and state a world view. In so doing he speaks not as a scientist, but as a philosopher and metaphysician. His non-Christian system differs everywhere from the Christian world view. But, when he speaks strictly as a scientist, Christians share common ground. H_2O has the

10. Ibid., p. 97.
11. Ibid., pp. 213-15.

same qualities for Christians and non-Christians. Against such facts both may check their hypotheses. These hard facts are not subject to unlimited manipulation by theorizing. They are not wax noses changed by any whim of a religious or non-religious person.

Not all common ground is derived from the senses. Both Christians and non-Christians are assured of their own existence. With Descartes they must conclude that they exist because they think, or with St. Augustine, that they exist because they doubt. Consideration of Descartes' "I think, therefore I am," refutes the notion that there is nothing in the mind not first in the senses. Even one who is skeptical of all sense perception must admit this. Furthermore, we know that we are finite, dependent, and wretched. Our shared imperfection will lead us both to death.[12]

Upon further inspection of the mind, certain innate and changeless principles of truth, goodness, and beauty appear in Christians and non-Christians. The law of non-contradiction is not derived from experience. Without its a priori validity we could not have meaningful sense perceptions, truth, or significant speech. The universality and necessity of non-contradiction need not be labored since it has been argued by most of the previous writers.[13]

All men also know by nature the difference between right and wrong, the obligation of virtue, the responsibility for character and conduct, and the culpableness of evil deeds. Each person has a conscience and so all fear the consequences of wrongdoing, however repressed the fear may be. People everywhere and in all times have had ethical codes. Every tribe and nation has been governed by moral laws. However different the ethical norms may be, all seek the good in distinction from evil. In moral issues there is a basic and obvious difference between man and animal. Both enjoy sense perception, but only in the one case is there moral responsibility. It is universal and necessary and unaltered by varieties of circumstances. Cultural rationalizations of mass murders are inexcusable. Murder will be wrong on every tomorrow.[14] The most naturalistic scholar also respects intellectual honesty as a norm binding upon all men everywhere in all times. The highest of all ethical principles is love for others. Humanism recognizes the universal necessity of loving our

12. Ibid., pp. 158-61.
13. Ibid., pp. 161-64.
14. Ibid., pp. 164-66.

neighbors. But there are no empirical oughts. Humanism cannot validly derive this, its fundamental norm. If we know nothing but relativistic mores of different cultures, why *ought* we love and serve mankind?

Principles of aesthetics may be even more debatable, but Carnell argues that all human beings do talk about the beautiful and the ugly, and unless all culture is to be destroyed and man reduced to a beast, there is such a thing as art. Mozart is better than a chorus of cats, and the Golden Gate Bridge is prettier than a crushed cigar box.[15] Elton Trueblood argues that classics in art evidence some common standards of aesthetics recognized by people of varied circumstances and ages. Taking into account a long span of time, he claims that there is far more agreement in aesthetics than there is in science.[16]

Any world view must account not only for sense data, but also for truth about one's conscious existence and the principles of logic, ethics, and aesthetics. In presenting and defending the Christian hypothesis, the apologist can count on these realities. If non-Christians do not admit them explicitly, they are present implicitly. One cannot reason in defense of total absurdity unless these principles hold. Before showing the relevance of the Christian hypothesis to these inner principles the apologist may need to help make them explicit in another's thinking. Men do not begin with a blank mind to demonstrate the existence of God from sense perceptions of nature, but from a mind structured with these changeless principles (*rationes aeternae*). Carnell agrees with Hackett and Clark on the categories programming the human mind.

In his preface to *The Kingdom of Love and Pride of Life,* Carnell explains his utilization of this common ground. "I have consistently tried to build on some useful point of contact between the gospel and culture." In *An Introduction to Christian Apologetics* the appeal is to the law of non-contradiction and fact; in *A Philosophy of the Christian Religion,* to values; in *Christian Commitment,* to the judicial sentiment; and in *The Kingdom of Love and the Pride of Life,* to the law of love. Carnell calls these facts and principles his synoptic starting point. These internal points of contact are not in-

15. Ibid., pp. 167-68.
16. D. Elton Trueblood, *Philosophy of Religion* (New York: Harper, 1957), p. 125.

effable mystical intuitions, but effable principles related to other knowledge. Such internal effable experience is as real to all rational men as external experience.[17]

THE TEST FOR TRUTH

Many conflicting hypotheses are proposed to explain human experience. On what basis can the decision be made between atheism, Islam, Buddhism, existentialism, Mormonism, and Christianity? We cannot decide on the basis of instinct, custom, tradition, feeling, sense perception, intuition, or pragmatism. These criteria support contradictory hypotheses, so they must in turn be checked by a more ultimate test. The correspondence of our ideas with reality fails, because in our minds we can only compare one idea of reality with another idea of reality. Sheer logical consistency is also insufficient since a system of ideas might be perfectly consistent but have no relevance to the data of experience.

The criterion by which to distinguish true from false hypotheses is twofold. A true hypothesis must be noncontradictory and it must fit the facts of experience, both internal and external. Consider the first part of the test, noncontradiction. A contradiction is "our surest test for the absence of truth."[18] Contradictory hypotheses or implications of one hypothesis cannot both be true. One or the other, or both, may be false! When contradictions appear in a system of thought, one cannot even determine what is being proposed. The very thing that is asserted is denied. So nothing meaningful is communicated. In order to speak meaningfully, the law of noncontradiction must be valid. Even an attempt to argue against the validity of the law carries meaning only if the law is valid.[19] A paradox is an apparent contradiction, a literary device to attract attention. When logically analyzed it does not assert and deny the same thing at the same time and in the same respect. If the two sides of a paradox did that, they would render each other meaningless. For each side of a paradox to carry meaning, the law of noncontradiction must hold.

On the previous considerations the law of noncontradiction is a necessary part of the test of truth apart from distinctively Christian

17. Carnell, pp. 124-25.
18. Ibid., p. 57.
19. Edward John Carnell, *Christian Commitment* (New York: Macmillan, 1957), pp. 39-40.

assumptions. From the Christian perspective it is also justifiable as an element of the criterion of truth. The logical principle is not above God, independent of God, nor imposed upon Him. Rather, it is an expression of God's nature. "God is not a man, that he should lie" (Nu 23:19), He will neither lie nor repent (1 Sa 15:29), He never lies (Titus 1:2), indeed, it is impossible that God should prove false (Heb 6:18). God's method of dealing with sinners may vary according to their repentant faith or lack of it, but God does not contradict His changeless nature or purposes. Since God does not violate the law of noncontradiction, the Christian "is not afraid to apply the law of noncontradiction to God's revelation in word and fact."[20]

Carnell's test for truth requires more than consistency. It calls for systematic consistency. A "systematic" hypothesis fits all the relevant facts of experience. Two equally consistent hypotheses could account for a broken window: it was hit (1) by a trailer truck, or (2) by a shot from a B.B. gun. Upon examination, however, only one of these hypotheses fits the facts—there was just one tiny hole in the window! Our experience brings to us certain givens. These data cannot be irrelevant to our formulation of truth about the world. An acceptable truth-claim fits the facts covered by it. All the facts are consistent with one another. It follows that all true hypotheses must likewise be consistent with one another. The "world-viewish"[21] hypothesis cohering with the greatest number of facts with the fewest difficulties is most systematically consistent.

The criterion of fitting the facts makes sense from a Christian perspective. The Creator orders everything in the universe according to a good and wise plan. The discrete facts of the material universe are related to each other, not by demonstrable necessity, but by God's free purpose. No deductions about what is the case can be accepted without evidence. Only facts tell us what God actually chose to do. When we have properly construed the meaning of facts we have discovered the purposes of God. "Truth is correspondence with the mind of God."[22] We know we have God's mind on a subject to the extent that our thought about it is noncontradictory and fits all the

20. Carnell, *Apologetics*, p. 60.
21. For this term I am indebted to Professor Arthur Holmes, Chairman, Department of Philosophy, Wheaton College.
22. Bernard Ramm, *Protestant Christian Evidences* (Grand Rapids: Eerdmans, 1954), p. 33.

relevant data of experience. The Holy Spirit's work is to insure a proper response to evidence, not to create evidence or render it meaningless. The Old Testament people of God tested the claims of alleged prophets by the consistency of their teaching (Deu 13:1-5) and the factual occurrence of their signs (Deu 18:21-22). Similar criteria tested the claims of apostles to be spokesmen for God in New Testament times (Gal 1:8-9; 2 Co 12:12).

The use of systematic consistency may be illustrated from the field of biblical hermeneutics. Acquainted with different interpretations purporting to give the meaning of a given passage, the student gathers as much relevant data as possible: the literary genre, the grammatical structure, the author, date, purpose, cultural setting, and the immediate and broader contexts. The true meaning of the passage is the interpretative hypothesis which consistently fits the greatest amount of this data with the least distortion.

Systematic consistency may be employed by detectives to solve a mystery. Three men are suspected of a murder. Suspect number one is not guilty although he possessed a weapon and was in the locality. He had no motive. Suspect number two had a motive and a weapon, but was out of the country at the time. Suspect number three was seen in the vicinity, the bullet was traced to his gun, and he had a motive. Since there is nothing contradictory about considering suspect three guilty, and since this hypothesis fits the greatest number of facts, the detective finds it highly probable that it is true. An extensive trial checks out contrary hypotheses and finds the evidence to converge on hypothesis three, so the verdict is reached. Suspect three is guilty beyond reasonable doubt.

VERIFICATION OF THE CHRISTIAN HYPOTHESIS

If the hypothesis affirming that the God of the Bible exists is true, it must be in harmony with the laws of logic and the order of the experienced world. Contrary world-viewish hypotheses are shown to be contradictory or less capable of explaining all types of facts. If Christianity is coherent with logic and all types of facts, it is verified beyond reasonable doubt.

Does Christian teaching contradict itself? It contains mysteries, enigmas, parables, figures of speech, involved individual and social relationships, complex human and divine relationships, and apparent contradictions, but no logical contradictions. The illustrations of paradox frequently used by contemporary logic-haters miss the mark. In logical terminology they illustrate sub-contrary relationships, not contradictory relationships. Kierkegaard's chief example of paradox is the incarnation. How can God be man and man be God? As understood by the Christian church, the data is correlated without contradiction. The one person has the attributes of God and the attributes of man. In other words, some of Jesus' characteristics are truly divine; some are truly human. To be contradictory the doctrine would teach that all of Jesus' attributes were divine and some were not divine, or that all of Jesus' attributes were human and some were not human. These contradictions are no part of the biblical or church doctrine. Jesus possessed the essential attributes of God and man. Complexity is involved, but not contradiction. Systematic theology displays the harmony of Christian teaching on all its major topics.

It is not enough for Carnell to show Christianity's consistency, he must show its congruence with fact before it is verified as true. Because his *Introduction to Christian Apologetics* majored on the methodological problem, it did not present an extensive discussion of the facts that the Christian hypothesis fits. It did argue generally that Christianity fits the facts of sense data and of the mind's thought-forms. In Carnell's later works (to be considered in subsequent chapters) he treats extensively the relevance of the Christian hypothesis to internal experience. His more limited consideration of external experience may be conveniently supplemented by D. Elton Trueblood's evidence confirming the theistic hypothesis in his *Philosophy of Religion* and Bernard Ramm's evidences for a distinctively biblical theism in his *Protestant Christian Evidences*. Ramm's book was quite apparently influenced by Carnell's stress on hypothesis and verification. Beforehand Carnell profited from the earlier statement of Trueblood's approach entitled *The Logic of Belief*. Their books can be helpfully correlated without doing violence to the approach of each. Although Trueblood does not explicitly defend the truth of all that the Bible teaches, his theistic hypothesis is clearly a Christian theism. His case is useful as far as it goes. Both Carnell and Ramm find the evidence to support the hypothesis of the Bible's complete truth.

Ramm first seeks to answer the bias of antisupernaturalists who refuse even to consider the factuality of the hypothesis of "an infinite, all-wise, all-powerful, all-loving God who has revealed Himself by means of natural and supernatural in creation, in the nature of man, in the history of Israel and the Church, in the pages of Holy Scripture, in the incarnation of God in Christ, and in the heart of the believer by the gospel." No discovery of science has rendered this hypothesis inconceivable. Science is not competent to pronounce on all matters religious and philosophical because its method is limited. Only scientism attempts to reduce all qualities to quantities, all events to predictable regularities, all reality to observables, and all phenomena to general principles.[23] Such a reductive naturalism fails to explain the totality of human experience. For example, it fails to account for man's power of self-transcendence. Reason cannot be reduced to neurology, Ramm argues, morality transcends stimulus, memory transcends time, and psychological freedom cannot be reduced to sheer causal behavior. "To say that behavior observes behavior is meaningless. Only a conscious mind with powers of memory, rationality and meaning can observe behavior and give it scientific interpretation."[24] The Christian hypothesis is inconceivable only to arbitrary reductionistic scientism. Those who understand the limits of genuine science, however, do not rule out a priori the possible explanatory power of the Christian hypothesis.

Ramm's first line of evidence demonstrating Christianity's tangency to given facts comes from the Bible's predictions. While prediction of events may be an occasional phenomenon of non-Christian religions, it is integral to Christianity. Fulfilled prophecy was part of the means by which the Old Testament religion and Christianity were established. It pervades the entire Bible. Biblical predictions are detailed, given far in advance, clear and beyond any possibility of human forecast. Ramm answers attempts to escape the significance of the prophetic evidence. While forthtelling is a major task of the prophets, foretelling is also prominent. The minor prophets predicted details concerning Israel, Judah, the day of Pentecost, Tyre, Sidon, Syria, the Assyrian and Babylonian captivities, the birth of the Messiah in Bethlehem, Nineveh's destruction, the rebuilding of the Temple in Jerusalem, the Messiah's triumphant entry into Jerusa-

23. Ibid., pp. 50-51.
24. Ibid., p. 68.

lem, and the messenger to precede the Messiah's coming (John the Baptist). Ramm's exegesis of these and other predictions with the help of the leading linguistic authorities leads him to conclude that there is sufficient evidence of a knowledge and wisdom beyond the writers of these books. Limited human beings knew the detailed future of individuals and nations hundreds of years in advance. Naturalistic hypotheses cannot account for this. The hypothesis of an omniscient Lord of the universe does.[25]

Numerous miracles occurred under a variety of circumstances and over a long period of time. Often they were performed in the public eye and in the presence of unbelievers. We have the testimony of the cured. Miracles brought Israel into existence, Christ into the world, and the Church into history. In other religions little is lost by denying miracles, but without miracles we lose all that is distinctively Christian. The claims of the superstitious and fraudulent discounting some alleged miracles cannot logically support the generalization that all miracles are spurious. In spite of brilliant efforts to do so, no adequate evidence against the biblical miracles has been presented. Opponents of Christianity, strangely enough, have shown knowledge that Christ performed miracles: Celsus, Hierocles, and Julian the emperor.[26]

The biblical miracles cannot be read out of existence by the disciples of an a priori scientism. Responsible science does not throw out evidence. Historical criticism increasingly shows that time was lacking for an alleged naturalistic evolution of the life of Christ, the gospels, the rest of the New Testament, or the early church. As Albertus Pieters put it, legends like mushrooms grow best in the dark, out of stuff that has had time to decay. In the case of the New Testament records there was insufficient time and too much light! The apostles' integrity is confirmed by their fidelity to historical, geographical, personal, and cultural detail.[27]

Neither philosophy nor psychology has succeeded in discounting the evidence for miracles. Philosophical systems constructed in ignorance (willful or otherwise) of this evidence are inadequate grounds for defining miracles out of existence. Proposed philosophies must fit all the facts. A world view which accounts for these ineradicable

25. Ibid., p. 124.
26. Ibid., p. 144.
27. Ibid., pp. 146-55.

events deserves greater respect than one which does not. Psychology, like philosophy, cannot alter the facts, nor provide systematically consistent non-Christian explanations. Some biblical healings may have been psychosomatic faith-cures, but not all. The psychosomatic hypothesis does not account for the healing of congenital blindness and leprosy, the raising of the dead, or nature miracles. Psychological skepticism about human testimony has not succeeded in ruling out the reports of witnesses in courts of law. To throw out all testimony is irresponsible. To allow for the validity of credible witnesses is to allow for the validity of biblical witnesses. They are numerous, reliable, and competent. On the hypothesis that the omnipotent God of the Bible exists, justice can be done to these facts.[28]

While accounting for miracles, Christianity also accounts for a major scientific assumption. Science assumes the regularity of nature. Given the same conditions for an experiment the same result will occur. The order of days and nights and seasons remains the same. While scientists must merely assume this pattern without justification, Christianity offers an account of the world's orderly processes. The Creator and sustainer gave His word: "While the earth remains, seedtime and harvest, and cold and heat, and summer and winter, and day and night shall not cease" (Gen 8:22). So Carnell says, "The Christian is able to guarantee for the scientist that there will be maintained that order of sequence which the latter requires for the success of his method."[29]

Christianity also accounts for the universal and necessary propositions (in logic and ethics) which make significant inductions possible. Without the changeless law of noncontradiction no scientific conclusion would hold meaning.[30] The scientist is concerned for intellectual honesty. Such a moral demand cannot be accounted for on a naturalistic hypothesis. It is no mere suggestion of a temporary culture, it is a binding obligation upon all men everywhere who report the findings of their investigations. The scientific awareness of universally binding norms of conduct has soared with the mushroom clouds of atomic fall-out. The Christian hypothesis supplies the standards by which to use scientific inventions.[31]

28. Ibid., pp. 155-62.
29. Carnell, *Apologetics*, p. 230.
30. Ibid., p. 231.
31. Ibid., pp. 232-33.

The very existence of science is best explained on Christian assumptions. "The most amazing fact about scientific knowledge is the evidence which it provides that there is an actual correlation between the mind and the natural order which it apprehends,"[32] that our world yields its secrets to men who observe and reason with precision. The order of nature and of the mind coalesce. When scientific predictions under controlled circumstances are checked, they are confirmed perfectly. The hypothesis that best accounts for the kinship between man's mind and nature asserts the existence of God, the Creator of the natural order and of man's mind. The correlation between science and nature is simply explained if God created the world and man to know and subdue it. At the same time the impenetrable mysteries of man and nature are consistent with man's finiteness and sin.

The Christian hypothesis also fits the exacting details of archeology which painstakingly researches past histroy. Carnell cites a few of the discoveries: the high place at Gezer, Solomon's stables, Jeroboam's seal, David's wall, Hezekiah's tunnel, Sargon's inscriptions, Sennacherib's exploits, and Nineveh's downfall. The apologist concludes, "We do not say that there are not problems remaining, for there are; the spade has much more dirt to turn over. We only say that archeology is remarkably confirmatory of the Bible accounts, not hit or miss; this is what we should expect if Scripture has been inerrantly preserved [given?] by God."[33]

What if the biblical hypothesis is put to the test of scientific information about evolution? Does the teaching of Genesis fit these facts? Carnell argues that it does. The facts include a similarity of structure and function among many animals and man. These facts can be accounted for by the similarity of the Creator's plans. A considerable body of data shows that species are not fixed. From development of some different species from common ancestors, naturalists may extrapolate a theory of the development of all species from a common ancestor. That hypothesis of complete evolution goes beyond the facts as much as a Christian hypothesis. Which accounts for the totality of the data? Christianity can account for the actual evidence of development. The biblical limits to reproduction are not called species, but "kinds." The kinds are very general: herbs yielding seeds,

32. Trueblood, p. 95.
33. Carnell, *Apologetics*, p. 110.

trees bearing fruits, birds, cattle, creeping things and beasts, and man. Within the limits of these "kinds" no actual evidence of evolution contradicts Genesis. The biblical view can account for the evidence of development, and the origins of the great kinds where evidence of development is lacking. Since the Bible does not give a date for the creation of the world or of man, there can be no discrepancy with fact at this point. The age of man cannot be determined by the genealogies since they skip vast stretches of time, as research has shown. Work remains to be done in these areas by both biblical and scientific scholars. Should the age or alleged organic evolution of man be regarded a difficulty, it is incidental compared with the problems of alternative world views. A world view cannot be chosen on the basis of one realm of experience alone. All fields of knowledge must be taken into account. "A rational man settles for that position which is attended by the fewest difficulties, not one which is unattended by any."[34]

Higher criticism has been considered an area of particular problem to biblical Christianity. Do the facts related to the author, date, sources, and composition of the biblical books fit the hypothesis of the Bible's truth? Many higher critics approached the biblical books with the assumption that the unaided mind of man could know all that there is to be known, that God is abstract principle, and that nature is uniform to the exclusion of all miracles. What separates the evangelical from these scholars is not facts, but assumptions. Nonevangelicals, however, often recast documents, redated predictions, denied all the testimony to miracles, and discounted entire books of the Bible, in order to make the data fit more naturalistic assumptions. Without tampering with the data as it stands, the hypothesis of the Bible's truth fits. Minor difficulties may be expected because of the complicated character of reality, our own finitude and ignorance, and the parallel limitations in science. Considering all the radicals of the Christian faith, the evangelical hypothesis fits the undistorted evidence better than any other.[35]

Granting the genuineness of the biblical books as they originated, how well has the original writing been preserved to this day? Textual criticism of extant copies shows that the Bible has been preserved

34. Ibid., p. 111.
35. Ibid., p. 209.

with remarkable care. Through thousands of years of hand copying and printing, the variations of wording and spelling do not alter any major biblical teaching. Carnell quoted the introduction to the Revised Standard Version of the New Testament (1946), "out of the thousands of variant readings in the manuscripts, none has turned up thus far that requires a revision of Christian doctrine." Through unbelievably difficult circumstances of many centuries, the truth of the Bible has been kept intact. The evangelical hypothesis fits these facts.[36]

On the same hypothesis, Bernard Ramm argues, we can explain the "external phenomena" of the Bible. It has gripped the human soul more fully than any other volume. Against the competition of all the greatest writers in history, this Book has been the continuous best seller. Its circulation is in inestimable millions of copies. Comparatively few books have been translated into three or more languages, but the Bible has been translated into most influential languages in the world. The demand for the Bible has made it the most retranslated book in the world as well. In the English language, as well as most of the major European languages, it has been translated again and again.[37]

The Bible's influence upon culture is difficult to explain apart from its claims for itself to be the Word of God. Its impact is evident in the classic and modern world's literature, oratory, laws, politics, philosophy, ethics, and art. The Bible has also inspired a massive amount of literature about itself. From the Apostolic Fathers to the present time flows a massive river of Bible dictionaries, Bible encyclopedias, Bible lexicons, Bible atlases, Bible geographies, and books on the grammar of the biblical languages. Vast bibliographies are available of literature directly influenced by Scripture; commentaries, philosophy of religion, apologetics, evidences, church history, theology, religious education, missions, homiletics, religious biography, and devotional guides. Countless religious journals, periodicals, weeklies, monthlies, quarterlies, and annuals appear. Many publishing houses print nothing but religious works. And a great array of slides and moving pictures have grown up along side the published materials.[38]

36. Ibid., p. 207.
37. Ramm, pp. 227-30.
38. Ibid., pp. 227-28.

As remarkable as the external phenomena are the internal phenomena of the Bible. The Genesis account of creation is unequaled. Where is the equivalent of the Ten Commandments? No other treatment of suffering compares with Job. Devotional literature never replaces the depth and piety of the Psalms. For practical guidance what matches Proverbs? The prophets' zeal for justice and equality before the law is unsurpassed. No discussion of happiness compares with the Beatitudes. Has ever a prayer compared with the Lord's prayer? What religious teaching compares in simplicity and purity with Jesus' parables? Our world is becoming more and more aware of the profundity of Paul's doctrine of sin. With all the stress on love in psychology and humanism no one has improved upon Paul's portrayal of love in 1 Corinthians 13.[39]

The scope of Scripture sweeps from eternity to time, through the course of history to its meaningful climax and on to the eternal state. "Here is a universal, comprehensive history, human and divine, cosmic and terrestrial, angelic and demonic, from Alpha-eternity to Omega-eternity which for scope, grandeur, and tangency to so much historical fact, is unparalleled in the complete annals of human history."[40] Historical to the core, the Bible traces sin to the fall of the first man and woman, exhibits faith in the historical Abraham, finds redemption through Christ's death, and the new birth through Christ's historical resurrection.

The Bible is also realistic. Neither prudish nor obscene, it refers realistically to sex and sin. The Bible cannot fairly be charged with asceticism, fanaticism, or extreme mysticism. Soberly it emphasizes the true, the good, and the holy. Its heroes are men of all different characteristics and their weaknesses are not hidden.[41]

Scriptural doctrines are mysterious, but at the same time remarkably pungent and relevant to human need. The biblical doctrine of God combines the concept of the Highest, the transcendent, and the holy, with that of immanence, love, pity, compassion, wisdom and grace. Although written by some forty men over about 1600 years, the Bible teaches one doctrine of God, man, sin, and salvation by grace through faith. Any other collection of books as varied in origin would not reveal so profound a unity. "The sum total of the phenom-

39. Ibid., pp. 242-43.
40. Ibid., p. 244.
41. Ibid., pp. 245-47.

enology of the Bible is a witness to the divine breath in the Bible."[42]

Any view of the world must somewhere account for the life Jesus lived. The most examined records in the world consistently indicate that the man of Nazareth was sinless, a magnificent teacher, a dynamic personality, a miracle-worker, a model of love, a most truly human being. All the writers of the New Testament testify to the same Christ. They did not have the time, the deceit, or the inventive genius to fabricate such a picture. If God were to become incarnate, these are just the qualities we would expect. On this biblical hypothesis the data of His life become meaningful. On any other hypothesis some of the data remains unexplained: His purity, His wisdom, His power, His love, or His deeds. But the hypothesis of the incarnation and the witness of the gospel record are in amazing agreement.[43] The same hypothesis is required to make sense of Jesus' claims. He who possessed nothing claimed to be equal with the Father. If He is not God, He is an inexplicable madman. But He cannot be madman, Carnell reasons, for the sublimity of His teachings is incontestably secure. His claims as well as His life attest the truth of the incarnation.[44]

Death did not end the story of Jesus Christ. Predicted by the Old Testament writers and Jesus Himself, the resurrection is reported in each of the gospels, in each of the sermons recorded in Acts, and throughout the rest of the New Testament. Paul's great discussion of the resurrection in 1 Corinthians 15 reports resurrected appearances to Peter, the twelve, more than 500 at once (most of whom were still alive), James, and Paul. These witnesses verified that it was the Lord they had personally known by sense perception. They saw Him, heard Him, touched Him, walked with Him, and ate with Him. Luke's trained research concluded, "To these He also presented Himself alive, after His suffering, by many convincing proofs, appearing to them over a period of forty days, and speaking of the things concerning the kingdom of God" (Ac 1:3).[45]

To deny that Jesus' resurrection from the dead is a fact one must dismiss as unreliable all four gospels, Acts 1, the sermons in Acts, 1 Corinthians 15, and references in all the other epistles. One would

42. Ibid., pp. 244, 247-49.
43. Ibid., pp. 163-83.
44. Carnell, *Apologetics*, p. 110.
45. Ramm, pp. 190-92.

also have to believe that the Jerusalem church grew by preaching this fabrication in the very place it could have been disproved. Paul's exceptional witness would also be totally debunked. "If there were no resurrection it must be admitted by radical critics that Paul deceived the apostles of an actual appearance of Christ to him, and they in turn deceived Paul about the appearance of a risen Christ to them."[46] Given the hypothesis of the God of the Bible, however, this cumulative testimony to the resurrection can be accepted without distortion.

The same hypothesis also explains the fact of Christian experience. Hundreds of thousands in all walks of life are conscious of living in a double environment. In addition to the sensory universe is the spiritual universe which includes intellectual, moral, aesthetic, and spiritual principles and objects. As the naturalist experiences sensory objects "out there," the Christian experiences God "out there." God, Christ, and salvation and forgiveness appear to the Christian consciousness as objective and real. As a result of this common experience of God and His grace, Christians have sympathetic rapport. Their experience indicates a common source.

Christian experience fits the facts of man's deepest needs. It promotes personal respect, dignity, freedom, purposive living, and a sense of reality and certainty. It solves the most persistent human problems: the problems of guilt, fear, and motivation. Christian experience renews moral energy, transforming the personality and giving a new power to live in self-sacrifice. If the God of the Bible exists we can explain how it is that this experience "meets the daily and practical needs of human nature; the deep enduring thirsts of the soul; and provides comfort for the sorrowing, courage for the faltering, inspiration for the despairing, challenge for the aspiring."[47]

The Christian hypothesis accounts for all the facts which fit with other hypotheses and in addition the remarkable facts of: fulfilled prophecy, miraculous events, the success of scientific methods, archeological discoveries, any actual evidence of evolution of species, the undoctored data of higher criticism, the multiplicity of manuscripts examined by lower criticism, the Bible's continuous best-selling circulation, its remarkable impact upon culture, its unequaled content, its breadth, its realism, its relevance, the life of Christ, the claims of

46. Ibid., pp. 193-207.
47. Ibid., pp. 208-23.

Christ, the resurrection of Christ, and the persistent phenomenon of Christian experience. Christianity pertains to reality by reason of its factuality. It is congruous with: (1) physical facts such as geographical places, historical events, and cultural phenomena, (2) miraculous facts in connection with Israel, Christ, and the founding of the Christian church, and (3) experiential facts from Enoch to Paul and from Paul to Billy Graham.[48]

Professor Ramm's emphasis subsequent to his *Protestant Christian Evidences* has stressed the internal witness of the Holy Spirit. But he has not abandoned his evidential approach as many contemporary theologians have. In *The Witness of the Spirit* Ramm made a significant contribution to understanding the internal personal encounter with God. But he made it clear that the Spirit does not illumine a vacuum. The Spirit brings about assent to the content of Scripture and evidences.

> Evidences in themselves cannot create faith, for faith comes only by the action of the Spirit. But the Spirit works in conjunction with evidences. The evangelist must give good reasons for becoming a Christian; and if the reliability or credibility of certain matters be questioned, he must give an adequate defense. Thus if the Spirit illuminates the mind of the sinner, he will immediately see the credibility of the evidences.[49]

Many contemporary theologians decide either for evidence or for the Spirit's witness. Bernard Ramm wisely observes that conviction of Christianity's truth is born of both evidence and the Spirit's witness.

A cavalier attitude toward evidences, according to Ramm, shows a failure to understand the total complex of Christian revelation. "The *testimonium* validates one's personal participation in redemption; evidences validate the objective religion of the gospel."[50] Apologetics as a science investigates the objective truth of Christianity's claims. Apologetics as an art seeks also the Spirit's internal attestation of the truth and personal applicability of the case for Christianity. Apologetic reasoning does not displace the need for the Holy Spirit to open blind eyes of the intellect and to free sin-enslaved wills. On the other hand, the Spirit's renewal of mind and heart does not displace the

48. Ibid., pp. 16-17.
49. Bernard Ramm, *The Witness of the Spirit* (Grand Rapids: Eerdmans, 1960), p. 118.
50. Ibid., p. 119.

need for sound arguments based on adequate evidence for the new abilities to accept. As Ramm says, "The *testimonium* is not the proof of the divinity of Scripture. It is not the *ground* of the authority of Scripture. . . . The testimonium enlightens the eyes of the mind . . . to assent to the *indicia.*"[51] The Spirit who witnesses to Christianity's claims is a liar if no facts are involved.[52]

PROBABILITY AND CERTAINTY

How certain a conclusion is possible if Christianity is tested by systematic consistency? Theoretically the case cannot rise above rational probability. "Probability is that state of coherence in which more evidence can be corralled for a given hypothesis than can be amassed against it. The more the evidences increase, the more the strength of probability increases."[53] Rational certainty might be possible if the Christian hypothesis had to do with a merely formal realm of logic or mathematics. But the Christian hypothesis concerns unique individuals as well as particular events in history. No historical event, however recent, can be demonstrated beyond a degree of probability. So it would be inappropriate to expect verification of Christ's resurrection, for example, to rise to the point of logical necessity.

> The admission that Christianity's proof for the resurrection of Christ cannot rise above probability is not a form of weakness; it is rather an indication that the Christian is in possession of a world-view which is making a sincere effort to come to grips with actual history. Christianity is not a deductively necessary system of thought which has been spun out of a philosopher's head, wholly indifferent to the march of human history below it; rather it is a plan of salvation, a coherent solution to the persistent problem of man, "What must I do to be saved?"[54]

A second reason why Christianity cannot be rationally demonstrated is that it is a system of moral values. Judgments about the value of one soul in relation to the world, and the seriousness of sin, may go contrary to the heart of the natural man. Moral values cannot be demonstrated; they are either seen or not seen. But this fact need not lead to an irrational faith.

51. Ibid., p. 107.
52. Ibid., p. 140.
53. Carnell, *Apologetics*, p. 113.
54. Ibid., p. 115.

Absolute rational certainty is not necessary to subjective certitude or moral assurance. By moral assurance Carnell means "that apprehended strength of evidence which causes us to be convinced of the truth of a given meaning-pattern, and to act upon its strength."[55] We are morally assured, for example, that there was a president of the United States named George Washington, although the rational evidence for his existence is only probable. Similarly, although the rational case for Christianity is only probable, it is more probable than any alternative hypothesis. Upon that basis the Holy Spirit produces a moral certainty. So the Christian acts upon his conviction of the truth of the Christian faith. Between mystical certainty and moral certainty there is no difference. The mystic's account of his experience is unable to rise above rational probability and it may be far less probable than that of the one who takes into account the totality of experience.

To the objection that a probable apologetic makes Christianity tentative, Carnell replies that for any individual it is. If in fact Christianity were not systematically consistent, in all honesty he would abandon it. The system may be final, however, even though our proof for it is but probable. True revelation is as immutable as its Giver. Establishing the fact that it is a valid revelation is an inescapable work of finite men.

FAITH IN THE GOD OF THE BIBLE

Having found that the Christian hypothesis accounts for more of the evidence with fewer difficulties, in other words, that Christianity is true, a person believes the truth. Some people think we believe what we cannot know, but Carnell maintains that we believe only what we know. Faith is limited by knowledge. With Charles Hodge, Carnell says, "If a proposition be announced to us in an unknown language, we can affirm nothing about it. We can neither believe nor disbelieve it."[56] We do not believe anything on the basis of faith (our belief!). Faith is not a synonym for ignorance. Although faith is to be childlike it is not to be superstitious. A child does not act without knowledge. He can tell his parent from a gorilla. When Christ invited children to come to Him as an example of faith, it was not to

55. Ibid., p. 117.
56. Ibid., p. 65.

display their ignorance, but to show the alacrity and simplicity with which the kingdom of God ought to be received.[57]

To avoid trust in a counterfeit Christ or Satan himself, Carnell suggests two tests for faith. The internal test is the witness of the Holy Spirit to the believer's heart. By causing our hearts to burn within us (Lk 24:27, 32), God authenticates His own Word. But an external test is needed when the objective truth of the gospel is called into question. All truth is God's truth and so faith must be placed in that consistent hypothesis for which there is sufficient evidence. "If what is being believed makes peace with the law of contradiction and the facts of experience, it is a faith which is prompted by the Spirit of God."[58] Psychologically the assurance of faith often precedes the testing of faith. Nevertheless wise men cannot fail to put their faith to the test. Many conflicting faiths claim an inner certitude. The decree of ecclesiastical authorities is insufficient evidence. So are decrees based on subjective feelings alone. Faith is the resting of the mind in the sufficiency of the evidence.

Although faith includes knowledge it is not limited to an intellectual process. One who knows that the living God has spoken in the Bible realizes the demand of God upon his entire life. Faith involves commitment of one's whole existence to that which is true. Carnell's definition does justice to faith as assent to truth and to faith as personal trust. Faith is "a whole soul trust in God's word as true."[59]

THE SIGNIFICANCE OF RELIGIOUS LANGUAGE

On Carnell's approach, the biblical language about God is informative as well as evocative. Since it is accepted as true, it cannot be interpreted equivocally or merely analogically. God's mind, will, and being are not something totally meaningless to human understanding. God is not totally different from everything man can think and assert. God created man in His image to think His thoughts after Him. God renews fallen man in His likeness intellectually (Col 3:10). Our truth is God's truth. The biblical truth is not merely analogical in such a way as to rule out any univocal meaning. If an analogy has no univocal element in it, it is simply meaningless equivocation. Without a single meaning at some point we might as well compare "woofle-

57. Ibid., p. 82.
58. Ibid., p. 70.
59. Ibid., p. 66.

wumps with ear-pitchers: no meaning is conveyed." Should we tell an uncivilized people that "a steamship is like a canoe, they can understand the analogy only for the reason that there is a univocal element present—'force propelled conveyance for water transport.' . . . Without meaning there is no truth, for truth is properly construed meaning."[60]

Those who only know something analogous to God do not know God. If God's essence cannot be known, we do not know of what we speak. Those who claim to know Him, but cannot assert any propositions about Him, face a serious difficulty. What is the *Him* to which they refer? If we do not first know *Him,* how can we possibly establish any relation between the *Him* and the as-He-appears-to-us God? If we do not know God's essence as it is in itself, it does not seem meaningful to speak of this essence, for we have no known means of ascertaining what the meaning of the term "God" is. Without meaning, we repeat, truth is absent, for truth is systematically consistent meaning.[61]

Pure empiricists face the problem of interpreting all language about God equivocally. If nothing is in the intellect which was not first in the senses, then nothing can be known about an invisible Spirit. Did we possess no innate principles of logic and ethics, and no hypotheses drawn from the Bible, we could never obtain meaningful assertions about God. It is futile to say that God is in some way analogous to sensory objects without any univocal point of identity. "Where, in the whole gamut of our sensory experience, can we find that univocal element which a successful analogy requires, that we may use it in making a comparison between God and man? . . . The intellect may be Oh so active! but it certainly cannot take from sensory experience what is not there."[62]

If, on the other hand, we have certain universal and necessary principles of thought and life as part of the image of God we have a ground for interpreting assertions about God in accord with them univocally. And if we find the hypothesis of biblical revelation cohering with evidence, we have reason to understand its propositional assertions about God in a univocal manner. God made man's mind like His, and God has communicated meaningfully with man. Where

60. Ibid., p. 147.
61. Ibid., p. 150.
62. Ibid., pp. 147-48.

the disclosure employs analogies, analogous language is admitted, of course. But the point of the analogy, it must be remembered, is univocal.

SYSTEMATIC CONSISTENCY AND THE INVISIBLE GARDENER

Does an invisible Gardener really care for our world? To answer that question we must consider two hypotheses: that He does and that He does not. Which of the two hypotheses without contradiction accounts for the greatest amount of evidence from man's internal and external experience? The hypothesis that no invisible Gardener exists may seem to fit the facts of sense perception and of evil in the garden. However it does not account for a great many facts that the invisible Gardener's existence would explain: the Bible's confirmation by archeology, the manuscript discoveries confirming the careful preservation of the biblical text, the inability of responsible criticism to destroy the radical teachings of Christianity, the regularity of nature, universal and necessary principles of logic and ethics, the origins of the basic organic "kinds" where intermediate forms are missing, the rebelliousness of the human heart, the origins of the family, state, and church, the claims of Jesus Christ, the ability of the human mind to know the natural order, the purpose of life, the meaningfulness of history, the persistence of religious experience, man's powers of self-transcendence, self-consciousness, and logical reasoning, the Bible's fulfilled prophecies, biblical testimony to miracles, the unique personality of Jesus, the extensive testimony to Christ's resurrection from the dead, distinctively Christian experience, and the Bible's most remarkable internal and external phenomena. All of this data is consistently explained if the invisible Gardener exists. If God does not exist, all of it must be wrenched into unnatural shape. The cumulative weight of this evidence makes it overwhelmingly probable that the invisible Gardener of the Bible exists. Assured beyond reasonable doubt of the truth of Scripture, the inhabitant of the garden who follows evidence where it leads commits his entire life to the biblical God. What he knows to be true he believes with a whole soul trust. He then acts upon it in the face of all the pressures of life.

EVALUATION

A major charge against Carnell's apologetic must be faced. In allowing the natural man to test alleged revelations by criteria resident in himself, Van Til thinks Carnell puts autonomous human reason above God. Will a person ever bow to God's revelation if at every juncture he demands satisfaction of systematic consistency? The answer may be presented by way of illustration. Many medical doctors are listed in the phone book. They have varied backgrounds and qualifications. Before we submit ourselves to a surgeon we want to know that he has the proper credentials. Having checked out his training, experience, and present accreditation we then bow to his judgment. We do not make ourselves a higher medical authority than the physician because we want to verify his ability.

Analogously, when we insist on criteria for the truth of revelation claims, we do not ask God to confine Himself to our understanding. We do ask credentials, however, for books in human language claiming to speak for God. The sacred writings of non-Christian religions and cults cannot be accepted by "faith" any more than a quack surgeon. No claim of self-authentication can relieve a thinker from responsibility "to test the spirits to see whether they are of God." If biblical revelation stands accredited by the test, the Bible, not the inquirer, has accreditation as the mouthpiece of God.

Carnell explains:

> Since it is necessary that we first be assured that it is God, not the devil, that we are doing business with, we must apply the rule of the good to find God. But once the heart is satisfied that God is worthy of receiving loving trust, the abstract good is then set aside and the will of God becomes the standard of goodness.[63]

What Carnell here said of the good can be said of the noncontradiction and factual data. They test revelation claims, but do not thereafter stand in judgment upon revelation.

When an apologist has faced alternative truth-claims and has found that Christianity best accounts for the greatest amount of evidence, then he ought by all means to construct his theology with the judgment of Scripture as final. The Bible is then accepted as true. God's Word stands as the primary source and test of theological formulations. Theology derives not primarily from empirical observation, logical deduction, or merely human interpretation of religious experience. The primary source of Christian theology is the Holy Scripture.

63. Edward John Carnell, *A Philosophy of the Christian Religion* (Grand Rapids: Eerdmans, 1952), p. 315.

Wherever the biblical evidence leads the theologian follows. By sound exegesis the theologian determines the teachings of Scripture on given subjects. As these teachings are related to each other a system develops. A system of theology is not assumed a priori and read into Scripture, it arises from responsible interpretation of Scripture.

Although Van Til's authoritarianism makes sense for theological purposes, it does not answer the apologetic question. Why should we follow the Bible in its entirety and the Bible alone? Why not accept other allegedly sacred writings? Numerous other books claim to be the very word of God for these latter days. To be responsible before the Bible, the unbeliever must have enough judgment to know why he should determine his lifestyle by Scripture rather than the Koran or the Book of Mormon. The use of systematic consistency to distinguish the Bible from the Koran in no way detracts from the Bible's authority. It verifies the Bible's claim above all competitors.

Suppose, however, that in the near future someone succeeded in showing a non-Christian and non-biblical hypothesis to give a consistent account of more evidence with fewer difficulties than the Christian hypothesis can. Would Carnell give up his faith in Christianity? Very frankly, he declared he would. In reply to those who think this inauthentic commitment, Carnell might ask, "If Christianity were shown to be contradictory or contrary to fact would you continue to declare its truth?" Suppose for example that it should be shown far more probable that Jesus did not rise from the dead than that He did. Could an apologist be less honest than Paul who said if Christ be not risen, our faith is vain, we are yet in our sins and we are of all men most to be pitied? But a more consistent account of the complex fields of history, science, values, ethics, psychology, sociology, epistemology, ontology, Israel, Christ, Paul, Christian experience, and the Bible itself is highly improbable.

In all areas of personal and social existence we must accept and act on probabilities. Intellectually our finiteness and sinfulness make this inevitable. That this is so in relation to Christianity should not be surprising, for Christianity is concerned with life in its most profound and complex relationships. Intellectual probability, however, is compatible with moral certainty. The objective evidence is overwhelmingly probable; the internal experience born of the Holy Spirit brings total commitment and psychological certitude.

From a purely logical point of view it may be charged that the verification of the Christian hypothesis involves a fallacy. The form of the argument may be set forth like this:

1. If the God of the Bible exists, then non-contradiction and Christian evidences.
2. Non-contradiction and Christian evidences.
3. Therefore, the God of the Bible exists.

The consequent of the first premise is affirmed in the second premise. Hypothetical reasoning is logically necessary when the antecedent of the first premise is affirmed in the second. The conclusion does not follow with logical necessity when the consequent is affirmed. Aware of this, Carnell of course did not claim syllogistic necessity for his reasoning. He claimed only a high degree of probability.

Carnell's form of reasoning is common to critical scientific endeavor. The case for evolution goes like this:

> If some evolution, some fossils.
> Some fossils.
> Therefore, some evolution.

Whatever one thinks of the limited fossil record and the meaning of "evolution," the form of the argument commits the fallacy of affirming the consequent. How is it that science has gained such respect when its method of verification involves a logical fallacy? Answering that question, D. Elton Trueblood says, "We overcome the fallacy in great measure by committing it in a refined fashion, many times instead of once. . . . by affirming so many (resultants) we have a situation in which only a miracle of coincidence would the alternative to the validity of our induction."[64] Although the conclusion of such an argument fails to follow by virtue of logical necessity, it may in fact follow. A number of consequents begin to form a network of circumstantial evidence. W. Edgar Moore explains:

> It is ordinarily not the weight of a single proposition that demonstrates any high degree of reliability for a hypothesis, but rather the weight of a number of converging propositions. Converging propositions are somewhat like the threads with which the Lilliputians tied Gulliver. Gulliver could have broken any single thread with a

64. Trueblood, p. 64.

twitch of his little finger, but the network of threads rendered him helpless.[65]

The fit of the Christian hypothesis to the mass of evidence detailed by Carnell, Trueblood, and Ramm cannot responsibly be attributed to sheer coincidence. The many lines of evidence taken together leave no room for reasonable doubt. The addition of evidences not only adds, but multiplies the probability involved. The most brilliant minds have not developed a relevant world view with logical necessity. But this need not lead to despair so long as we can find ways to increase probability. The multitudinous kinds of evidence converge to render the case for Christian truth-claims beyond reasonable doubt. That is all that can be claimed for any world view related to actual human experience.

The strength of Carnell's case to this point should be carefully considered. A mere formal consistency without factual adequacy is empty and irrelevant. On the other hand an experiential relevance without consistency ends in chaos and meaninglessness. Systematic consistency, like Hackett's coherence, combines the formal and material aspects of human life. Loyalty to these standards delivers one as far as possible from religious dream castles, wishful thinking, rationalizations, and arbitrary whims. If Christianity meets these demanding tests, it cannot be dismissed as a projection of individual tastes. The retort, "It is all right for you but not for me," entirely misses the point. If Christianity answers to logic, evidence, and personal experience, it cannot be dismissed as a mere projection of a father image. It shares the same kind of objectivity as conclusions in a respected court of law. It is true beyond reasonable doubt.

A weakness on the amount of internal evidence outlined in this chapter may be detected. While considerable data from the publicly observable empirical realm has been set forth here and in other evangelical apologetics, more from the private experience of individuals might strengthen the case and be strategic for our times. According to James William McClendon, although Carnell understood what recent writers *said*, he showed insufficient awareness of how others in our era *feel*. Issues of epistemology are not settled by feelings, but existential feelings cannot be ignored by epistemologists. Aware of this need, Carnell attempted an emphatic identification with the

65. Moore, p. 57.

inward struggles of men in his subsequent works. McClendon's criticism can be evaluated only after study of those books, which we undertake in the next three chapters.

RESOURCES FOR RESEARCH

Carnell, Edward John. *The Case for Biblical Christianity*. Ed. Ronald H. Nash. Grand Rapids: Eerdmans, 1969. An anthology of relevant essays Carnell published in various journals and books on Niebuhr's criteria of verification, faith and reason, and other subjects.

———. *The Case for Orthodox Theology*. Philadelphia: Westminster, 1959. Chapter 6 on "Proof" presents Carnell's test for truth in nontechnical language. Formal truth requires harmony between judgments. And Christianity is consistent. Material truth implies a harmony between judgments and the order of things in the real world. Christianity answers to affairs of the heart (love, guilt) and affairs of history (Israel, prophecy, the resurrection of Christ).

———. *An Introduction to Christian Apologetics*. Grand Rapids: Eerdmans, 1948. Carnell's first volume, while majoring on the theoretical predicament, also acknowledged the practical human predicament. Perceptive chapters relating faith to truth are followed by the nature of hypotheses and the means of their verification.

Chapman, Colin. *Christianity on Trial*. Wheaton, Ill.: Tyndale, 1975. A comparison of the Christian alternative with others on truth, God, and Christ.

Dye, David L. *Faith and the Physical World: A Comprehensive View*. Grand Rapids: Eerdmans, 1966. With many similarities to Carnell, whose works he highly recommends, Dye helpfully compares scientific and Christian presuppositions. A Christian world view consistently accounts for physical and spiritual reality and satisfies the complex needs of the whole man, he argues. Scientifically Dye assumes: (1) physical reality exists, (2) logic applies, and (3) causality operates (not deterministically, but probabilistically).

McClendon, James William. *Pacemakers of Christian Thought*. Nashville: Broadman, 1962. In a chapter on "E. J. Carnell: Fundamentalist With a Difference," McClendon criticizes Carnell for a lack of empathetic identification with the native skepticism of our times. Admitting that Carnell is acquainted with what recent writers have *said*, the professor of theology and philosophy at Golden Gate Baptist Theological Seminary thinks Carnell's approach shows insufficient awareness of how others in our era *feel*.

Moore, W. Edgar. *Creative and Critical Thinking*. Rev. ed. Boston: Houghton Mifflin, 1967. An introductory logic textbook considering at greater length than many the hypothetical syllogism, evaluating evidence, forming hypotheses, testing hypotheses, and reliability and probability (especially chaps. 1-6).

Purtill, Richard L. *Reason to Believe*. Grand Rapids: Eerdmans, 1974. An analytic approach resting its claims upon the origin and order of the universe, objective moral laws, and the desire for happiness beyond the realm of time and space. Purtill seeks to show that his views are not only logically possible but also fit the known facts.

Ramm, Bernard. *Protestant Christian Evidences*. Chicago: Moody, 1954. While Carnell's *Apologetics* established the principle of verification, Ramm's *Evidences* may be viewed as applying it more truly. Ramm shows how the hypothesis supplied by the Bible fits the facts. Christian evidences, he says, demonstrate that Christianity is the religion which pertains to reality by reason of its factuality (p. 16). See also Ramm's entries in "Resources for Research," chapter 1.

Trueblood, David Elton. *Philosophy of Religion*. New York: Harper, 1957. Trueblood's approaches to faith, truth, hypotheses, and the process of verification are similar to Carnell's. Although Trueblood does not hold to biblical inerrancy he presents a well-written case for Christian theism. His analysis of paradox as a subcontrary, rather than a contradictory, relation resolves many recent disputes about paradox.

Van Til, Cornelius. *The Case for Calvinism*. Nutley, N. J.: Craig, 1964. While defending his own system, Van Til directs a sustained attack upon Carnell's apologetic. Here the issues between the two men, as Van Til sees them, are most sharply drawn.

EVANGELICALS ON THE APPEAL TO HISTORICAL EVIDENCES

Anderson, Charles C. *The Historical Jesus: A Continuing Quest*. Grand Rapids: Eerdmans, 1974. A valuable defense of a conservative view of the historic Christ of Scripture as "the most natural and logical solution to the problem, and the only one that guards against excessive subjectivism and ultimate skepticism."

Fuller, Daniel P. *Easter Faith and History*. Grand Rapids: Eerdmans, 1965. A thorough evaluation of problems faced in appealing to historical evidences for the truth of Christianity, as seen in the case of Christ's resurrection. After criticizing liberalism, dialectical theology, new quest of the historical Jesus and others, the dean of Fuller Theological Seminary argues for the necessity and conclusiveness of evidences intellectually, but recognizes the need for the illumination of the Holy Spirit volitionally.

Henry, Carl F. H., ed. *Jesus of Nazareth: Savior and Lord.* Grand Rapids: Eerdmans, 1966. Sixteen contributors consider different aspects of the relationship of revelation to history and to truth.

Ladd, George Eldon. *Jesus Christ and History.* Chicago: Inter-Varsity, 1963. While Professor Ladd acknowledges that the resurrection (etc.) took place in history, he holds that it was not wholly explained by history. God broke into human history transcending all historical causality and analogy. The significance of salvation events can only be received by Spirit-given revelation.

Moule, C. F. D. *The Phenomenon of the New Testament.* Naperville, Illinois: Alec R. Allenson, 1967. Seeks simply to display a selection of first-century phenomena which need to be reckoned with, and to ask, What do you make of these? Can you make sense of them as history without importing precisely the value-judgments to which the original Christians were led? Conversely, can you account for the value-judgment without the historical basis?

Tenney, Merrill C. *The Reality of the Resurrection.* New York: Harper and Row, 1963. Chapter 6 on "The Historical Evidences" helpfully summarizes the data supporting Jesus' death, His burial, the empty tomb, the appearances, and the historical effects of His alleged resurrection. All of this data can best be explained, Tenney concludes, by accepting the testimony of the New Testament.

8

THE VERIFICATIONAL APPROACH OF EDWARD JOHN CARNELL: VALUES

The Test of Satisfying Human Values

"So what?" That response may be evoked by empirical, rational, authoritarian, and testimonial apologetics. "What difference does all this make to me?" Comments like these may not express sheer indifference, but a quest for personal value as well as truth. Men cannot be convinced that a world view is true if it is not at the same time important. In *A Philosophy of the Christian Religion*, Edward John Carnell sought to show that Christianity is not only true, but most desirable for each individual person.

Carnell was convinced that "Christianity is by-passed by the contemporary mind more on the grounds of personal contempt than of Christianity's inability to unravel present problems."[1] Men will not drink the water of life until thirsty for it. And they will not eat of the bread of life until hungry for it. So Carnell attempts to arouse an appetite for Christianity. Over against unsatisfying alternatives he portrays Christianity's vital relevance for all sides of human existence.

Every person seeks his own well-being. The desire of self-preservation and enjoyment functions in the life of Christian and non-Christian. It is rock bottom common ground on which we may begin to build. Even one who seems to prefer his own unhappiness unconsciously finds satisfaction in a pretense of unhappiness. And the hero who sacrifices his life to save another points up the fact that human

1. Edward John Carnell, *A Philosophy of the Christian Religion* (Grand Rapids: Eerdmans, 1952), p. 44.

life is more than sheer physical survival. Invisible values may be prized more than visible values.

The values to which we commit ourselves may satisfy us partially or fully. A wise person chooses values that will satisfy every part of his being as long as he lives. It is foolish to choose values which are not lasting or are less fulfilling than others. For example, how should a student decide whether or not to quit high school and go to work? He should compare the value of his job and its possibilities throughout his life without high school graduation with employment opportunities throughout life as a high school graduate.[2] The Bible never argues that a person ought to act wisely. It presupposes that. The Bible shows how free decisions can be directed to attain a happiness that is whole.

The quest for fulfillment in life, therefore, should not overlook Christianity. Often caricatured or completely ignored, Christianity merits serious consideration. Faith in Christianity's primary sources— the books of the Bible— is not gullibility. Faith is trust in the veracious, valuable, and engaging.[3] No one can escape trust in something. "To trust no one is but a way of announcing self-trust."[4] The question is not whether or not to trust. The question is which authorities are most trustworthy. In research we trust those who display intellectual honesty and competence in their fields. When it comes to explanations of all of life, if there were a God, good and wise, He would be worthy of our trust. A communique from God would be most helpful in seeing the long-range implications of our commitment to certain values.

> Of course, the investigator will have to test carefully that it is God who claims to speak. All pretenses to revelation must be put through a scrutinizing test. Such testing, done in an honest effort to gain fellowship with the true God, is as wholesome to the individual as it is pleasing to God.[5]

The test of revelation-claims includes logical consistency and correlation with fact, but it also includes considerations of the heart. Otherwise the whole man is not convinced. "The heart knows a depth of insight which, while it may never be separated from rational consist-

2. Ibid., p. 21.
3. Ibid., p. 29.
4. Ibid., p. 30.
5. Ibid., p. 31.

ency, is yet not univocally identified with such consistency."[6] With the mind consider, then, which commitments of the heart will fulfill most permanently the greatest number of your desires.

LIVING FOR PLEASURE

Those who live for pleasure find it accessible, intense, and instantaneous. But it cannot last. It will let them down. What gives us pleasure the first few times inevitably bores us. We cannot long remain content with any pleasure or combination of pleasures such as wine, women, and song. Our capacity to imagine greater numbers of pleasures in innumerable combinations can never find satisfaction because of the limits of finite existence. As men we can always see beyond the confines of our present situation. Our boredom testifies to the presence of this ability to transcend ourselves. Because of that higher capacity in man, living for pleasure cannot permanently satisfy.

With boredom comes frustration and a sense of the stark hollowness of living to eat, drink, and be merry. Guilt ensues because our higher nature is violated. One cannot live like a thing or an animal and not destroy his human dignity. Carnell illustrates this from the pleasures of sex.

> In masturbation the free self supplies the partner through imagination. But (other things being equal) the result is always a feeling of incompleteness. Something within one cries saying, "You were destined for higher things." The homosexual finds a partner, and so need only impute to the other what is lacking through sexual likeness. But unless the day of grace has passed, there results a similar feeling of having cheated the self through a whole commitment to only partial conditions. In fornication the number and sex are complete; yet here each individual must supply a spiritual element missing in the other partner. Each has used the other as a *means*, whereas dignity cries out that others are to be treated only as *ends*. Each fondly imagines that there is a loving yielding of the one to the other, but reality affirms that the union is artificial and selfish. And as a consequence of such selfishness, each member thinks less of the other. . . . Fornication cannot continue indefinitely between the same two people. There will either be a break-through of love or a break-through of hatred and bitterness. The dialectic of sex points to the marriage relation as the only condition in which the whole

6. Ibid., p. 39.

person is wholly satisfied. Since both body and soul are yielded selflessly to the other, there is nothing to be regretted in the end.[7]

As long as physical strength remains, we may always hope that the next pleasurable venture will bring peace. But when that strength ebbs away the pleasure slips away. What then? "There is an irremedial finality to the ensuing despair."[8] Whoever seeks his highest fulfillment in physical pleasure will be disappointed. In the long run he will find boredom, frustration, guilt, exhaustion, and despair. Such common experiences have apologetic significance. Unless we are destined to nothing better, we may conclude that our higher nature may somewhere find lasting fulfillment. Whether or not there actually is anything beyond pleasure which can effectively satisfy mankind remains to be seen. If not, man is overendowed—tragically overendowed.[9]

LIVING FOR ECONOMIC SECURITY

Man's basic dissatisfactions arise from the lack of economic security of one large class of people, according to Karl Marx. Can we find enduring fulfillment by living and dying for the cause of a classless society? The cause presupposes that the material concerns of life are more basic than the nonmaterial. The hope is that when the economic needs of all are met, all man's needs will be met. Lasting satisfaction will follow in a utopia where all share everything in common. In an affluent society such a theory has tremendous appeal to young people deprived by educational costs of many luxuries. Here may be the answer to their restlessness.

However, the way to enduring satisfaction is not so simple. Should all our needs be met our power of transcending the present would manufacture other "needs." And suppose everyone had even more than he needed. Suppose all enjoyed the luxuries desired. Carnell points out, "The universal testimony of people *not* socially or economically discontented is that boredom goes right along with their station and place. Rancor and bitterness plague the wealthy."[10] Because of man's higher nature he can never be satisfied with economic security. All the deficiencies of immediate pleasure as a way of life

7. Ibid., p. 71.
8. Ibid., p. 77.
9. Ibid., p. 58.
10. Ibid., pp. 126-27.

afflict material security as a primary commitment. "If the classless society *is* attained, then the individual becomes bored. And if it is *not* attained, then the individual is frustrated. There is no way out of this dilemma—granted the ingredients of communism."[11]

The desire to help the deprived is commendable indeed. It is the promised solution to social injustice that is here challenged. Can we trust the authorities who claim mankind's problems will be solved by economic security? Is this truth-claim to be accepted? For communism, no world of unchanging truth provides standards by which to interpret history. Truth, allegedly, is made in the course of the historical process itself. "But because the process is controlled by the most active individuals, truth is made and destroyed as often as there is a shift in the centers of power in control. Whatever the ruler prefers becomes the truth."[12] Shall we determine truth by submitting to the authority of men whose power may be overthrown tomorrow? The truth-claims of communists and others are discredited by experience.

Take the experience of people leaving the communist party, for instance. They have testified to their disgust and disappointment when they realized that they were being sacrificed to a world of materialistic promises. Carnell, holding that man's power of transcending such situations shows his spiritual potential, comments, "Here is a martyrdom which is perfectly foolish: That a spiritually endowed individual should sacrifice himself for a materialistic system. Shall the greater be destroyed to establish the lesser?"[13]

LIVING FOR SCIENTIFIC DISCOVERY

Few would question the usefulness of the scientific method in the physical world. Experimental procedures have provided many valuable instruments for men to employ. The demand for verification of theories has removed unanswerable questions from serious philosophical investigation. The unquestioned values of science, however, have led some to devote themselves to scientism. They think no higher values are needed, and that life devoted to an empirical method will satisfy. Anything that cannot be reduced to quantitative analysis by some observable procedure is dismissed. But no experiment can verify a statement about the value of the scientific method. "The faith

11. Ibid., p. 98.
12. Ibid., p. 102.
13. Ibid., p. 111.

which binds the members of this cult together is the blinding creed that man was made for the scientific method and not the method for man."[14]

Can a human being rest in the hypothesis of scientism that all talk about right and wrong is noncognitive? In saying that stealing is wrong, are we simply saying that we do not happen to like stealing? Does a moral judgment only tell us about the subjective feelings of the one who makes it? Are individuals free to disrespect the dignity of other persons without suffering the consequences? Justice cannot be weighed and measured; shall we say injustice is simply a noncognitive matter of taste? Is it as acceptable to prefer error to truth? Shall we praise wickedness and despise the good? Values like these are too fundamental to require experimental verification. They are necessarily universally independent of sense data.

To live and die for a method which calls standards of truth and goodness, justice, and human dignity "nonsense" is indeed nonsense. Who would be around to check the results of experimentation on this sentence, "Destroying civilization through hydrogen bombs is a bad thing."[15] In view of the crucial issues facing all men on our shrinking planet Carnell concludes:

> The heart refuses to be troubled any further by an offer to live and die for the scientific method. It is a pretty poor bargain when one trades everything in life that counts for the anemic gain of being able to classify sentences.
>
> Whoever continues to repeat the stupid claim that sentences about justice, honor, chastity, self-control, piety, holiness and love are noncognitive, should be laughed at—laughed at good and hard. He shows not only a want of education, but also a want of common sense. There are standards so ultimate to all meaning that all else is judged by them. How then can they be judged by a subordinate method? If science is not *good*, what is it good for? If science is not true, why should one believe it?[16]

LIVING TO THINK

Shall we, like the Epicureans of old, seek our satisfaction in the long-term joys of the mind? We cannot deny the universality and

14. Ibid., p. 178.
15. Ibid., p. 169.
16. Ibid., p. 178.

necessity of the laws of logic. Without them we face meaninglessness. "Using logic to disprove logic is as foolish as catching rapid breaths while preaching that it is not necessary to breathe."[17] The law of non-contradiction is basic to sanity. Unfortunately, "the insane break the law of contradiction too frequently to remain socially tolerable."[18] Little wonder that philosophers have thought of man as a rational animal whose highest good is reasoning.

However, mental satisfactions cannot survive a divorce from non-rational satisfactions. We *choose* to think because we *enjoy* thinking. Thinking does not automatically produce pleasure. But thinking may occasion a kind of love which satisfies. When love vanishes, the value of everything including reason vanishes. "Love is the precondition of everything. We freely do only what interests us."[19] Reasoning, then, is not the highest value because it engages only a part of man and does not endure. Like the other immediate satisfactions, it suffers from boredom, and in the end there is insufficient strength to enjoy it. Furthermore, knowledge is impotent to take any initiative in support-ing the longings of the heart. If our love of wisdom is love of imper-sonal principle alone, it is an I-it relationship, less satisfying than an I-thou relationship. Rationalists always insert a middle premise be-tween themselves and their conclusions. But from acquaintance with persons we may draw conclusions directly.[20] So devotion to rationality is not our highest conceivable value. "The truth is that thinking is inferior to the act of promoting fellowship, since the latter engage-ment trips more abiding satisfactions in us than the former."[21]

Summing up the case so far, the rewards of pleasure, security, veri-fication, and syllogistic proof are immediate, but one-sided and tran-sient. In contrast, love involves the whole man endlessly. "Satisfaction in fellowship is a more intense pleasure than that found in chemistry or botany because like meets like in mutual sympathy. There is no boredom in love."[22] The lesser values, Carnell is careful to point out, are values. Their importance is acknowledged more fully than this survey may reveal. For example, while denying that reason is the highest human value, Carnell italicizes its role in checking truth-

17. Ibid., p. 184.
18. Ibid., p. 187.
19. Ibid., p. 211.
20. Ibid., p. 180, n. 1.
21. Ibid., p. 223.
22. Ibid.

claims. *"The primacy of fellowship as a value does not in the least cancel out the primacy of reason as a test for truth."*[23] Similarly, the priority of fellowship in no way removes the need for sense data to verify hypotheses concerning the physical world. Personal fellowship does not diminish, but enhances the shared value of pleasures and possessions.

LIVING FOR OTHERS

Humanism contends that our highest known value is love of man. Anything "less than devotion to living personalities is an affront to the dignity of man."[24] Since no higher power is known to exist, our problems and their solutions are entirely man's responsibility. Society's ills stem from our refusal to employ our natural endowments. Our problems will be solved by more advanced uses of reason and particularly the scientific method. The motivation for intelligent problem solving is love for man. Humanism significantly differs from previous positions in commanding men to love their neighbors as themselves. More fulfilling than love for things is love for persons. So men *ought* to preserve human values above all else.

In this cynical age we may well ask, "Why *must* we seek to conserve human values?" If this counsel is not merely an expression of individual taste, the proposal for our acceptance should have some support. But the scientific method cannot verify it by any appeal to sense data. Even so we are not really free to approve destruction of humanity by nuclear energy. We ought to preserve mankind. Granted, but not on the basis of the scientific method. This norm for all men everywhere is discovered independent of sensory experience. If one such meaningful proposition is true a priori why may we not discover others? "Either one must break with science on the finality of human values, and so destroy the ideal of humanism; or he must at least leave open the possibility of God's existence."[25]

Other problems with humanistic love for mankind present themselves. Service to humanity is service to an abstraction. An abstraction does not challenge sacrificial self-giving. "Humanity," Carnell says, is "an abstract, impersonal entity, lacking the organs of response needed to appreciate the meaning and worth of a delicate act of self-sacri-

23. Ibid., p. 215.
24. Ibid., p. 229.
25. Ibid., p. 243.

ficing."[26] Will we be motivated to serve the unlovely when our own
security is not endangered? Even if life and death for the collective
ego were adequate motivation, humanism could not provide a power
so that vacillating and capricious men could do it. In order to fulfill
the humanist ideal man needs a power beyond himself. The second
greatest commandment must be rooted in the first—love for God.
(God's love is free from all whimsicality and enjoys complete power
over prevailing conditions).

Inevitably humanism leads to serious dissatisfaction with ourselves.
Granting that we should love mankind, however unscientific and abstract it may sound, we do not always love our neighbors as ourselves.
To admit the validity of the law of love is to stand guilty before it.
"One is not an individual if he dissents from the law; yet he becomes
an immoral individual the instant he does assent."[27] Just such a sense
of guilt for unloving relations with others is disclosed by psychiatrists
in many lives. Humanism's ideal is not disputed; but the guilt that
ensues calls for a ground of forgiveness. Just as our experience cries
out for a timeless obligation to serve men as ends rather than means,
it cries out for a timeless love that forgives.

LIVING FOR GODS THAT CANNOT FORGIVE

God alone can satisfy man's quest for personal fellowship, meaningful standards of love, and forgiveness for our unloving conduct. These
values are not provided by a God like Aristotle's unmoved mover.
The deist's completely transcendent God is equally irrelevant to the
human venture. Is the pantheist's deity more significant? Not to
personal fellowship. As exclusively immanent the pantheistic God is
not sufficiently distinct from men to fellowship with them. Against a
liberal theology of immanence, neo-orthodoxy saw that if God were to
be relevant to human need, He must be distinct from human history
and Lord of it.

Because of the problem of evil some suggest that God must be finite,
struggling against evil with our help. If finite, we cannot place in
Him unreserved trust. He might lose the war against evil. Fullness
of fellowship, however, requires unreserved trust. The finitists in
their concern about evil overlook the most awful datum of human
experience—sin. Going about the problem backwards, they want God

26. Ibid., p. 248.
27. Ibid., p. 260.

to remove natural evils such as earthquakes before they fully trust Him. But they must trust Him and confess their sin in order to enjoy fullness of fellowship. "When one seeks to gain his way into the heart of another person . . . he does it first by disavowing his own desert. Love enters only after pride exits. The boy who disclaims his worthiness of the girl's love is first to receive it."[28] We know we have come short of the law of love. "Shall we trust a God who is able to take away our sins, or shall we trust a God who is nobly struggling against evil, but has made no provision for the forgiveness of sins?"[29]

LIVING FOR A GOD WHO FORGIVES ALL

Some cannot rest in a divine salvation that leaves anyone out. To them universalism seems the highest value. Love leaves the ninety-nine sheep to recover the one outside the fold. Would God's love be perfect if He did not bring back every last one? So the doctrine of hell seems intrinsically immoral. Fatherly love always welcomes the prodigal home. If God would ever withdraw His mercy, He would be unworthy of our trustful love. Karl Barth in at least one strand of his thought teaches that election reaches to all individuals. And Nels F. S. Ferré argues that "God, being *agape,* will pursue all men with his call to repentance until all are saved. The love of God will empty hell." While human *eros* is particularistic and selective, divine *agape* selflessly takes no thought of intrinsic worth in its object. Sin is very real, and sin must overcome. Ferré's is not a mere sentimentalism. God will continue in eternity what He has here only begun. Men who have not repented here will repent after death. The ultimate *agape* will not give up until all have been brought to self-despair and divine fellowship. "Heaven can be heaven," Ferré insists, "only when it has emptied hell."

In contrast, Carnell points out, "It is the consistent witness of all the writers (of Scripture) that since the mercy of God is extended to man within a day of grace, the opportunity to embrace this mercy is limited to this life only. Death seals man's eternal condition."[30] The issue with universalism becomes explicit, then, "Does God possess a right to withdraw his mercy and yet retain *agape* love? Or does an

28. Ibid., pp. 320-21.
29. Ibid., p. 321.
30. Ibid., p. 333.

analysis of the term *agape* force one to the necessary conclusion that all men will be saved?"[31]

The most high is not an abstract *agape* principle, it is God. Of course God is love. Does it follow therefore that God could never withdraw His mercy from undeserving sinners? Keeping in mind that we are men and not God, and that we have offended divine justice, we must remember that God alone can measure justice and freely dispense His grace. Illustrating the lack of decorum when the guilty demand mercy in the name of their rights, Carnell says:

> When the wayward husband returns to the wife, and disclaims all right to receive her forgiveness, he is the very one who quickly receives mercy. But when he arrogantly demands to be forgiven on the ground that justice stands on his side, mercy is quenched.[32]

Granting that God freely offers mercy, does it follow that His love forbids Him ever to withdraw it? "Nothing could corrupt the tension of moral struggle quicker than the announcement that there is no time limit for repentance. If one has eternity in which to perform, why watch and act?" In love the mother sets a time for meals. She does not say, "My little one, I shall stand vigil over your dinner plate forever and forever."[33] If a professor in *agape* assigned a term paper with no deadline for submission it would not be written. If we had eternity in which to repent, we would never overcome our moral inertia and repent. Since it is universally characteristic of sinfulness to postpone moral decision, it is questionable whether an eternity of opportunities would be any more effective than those of time. "If everything else worthwhile can be appropriated only within a day of grace, why should the principle suddenly break down when the most important value in life is in question?"[34]

Universalism enthrones an abstract notion of *agape* and banishes the teaching of Jesus Christ, *agape* incarnate. He it is, not the church's ministry or membership, who is responsible for the doctrine of an end to the day of grace, and a judgment which distinguishes the eternally saved from the eternally lost. Jesus said that the weeds would be gathered and burned with fire, that evildoers would be thrown into the furnace of fire where men would weep and gnash their teeth, that

31. Ibid., p. 352.
32. Ibid., p. 357.
33. Ibid., p. 359.
34. Ibid., p. 360.

body and soul could be destroyed in hell, that it would be better to enter the kingdom of God with one eye than with two eyes to be thrown into hell where the worm (of fellowship lost) does not die and the fire is not quenched (Mt 13:40-42; 25:12; 10:28; Mk 9:47-48).

To accept universalism is to reject the teaching of Jesus Christ. We can hardly commit our destinies to one who either knew better and deceived, or did not know the implications of *agape*. And "the more one ponders the attempt to retain trust in the Father's person, while rejecting it in the case of the Son, the more suspicious he becomes of this type of solution." Between the Father and the Son there was absolute trust. Jesus constantly acknowledged the Father's will, power, teaching and fellowship. And through Christ's ministry the Father's approval was upon him. He taught that his nature was consanguineous with that of the everlasting Father and made no effort to check the ambitions of those who worshiped him. To lose faith in the person of Christ is to lose faith in the person of the Father. "The instant we subordinate the historical Jesus to the abstract rule of *agape* we lose God's fellowship altogether, for the Father placed his approval upon all that the Son did and taught as embodying the perfection of his will for man."[35] But to forfeit fellowship with the Father is to find ourselves inescapably in the humanistic predicament.

Accepting Christ's teaching we know that the Father, in spite of the heinousness of sin, paid an incalculable price to be just while reconciling alienated sinners to Himself. Jesus Christ, the God-man, offered Himself, the just for the unjust, that He might bring us to God. On the cross He suffered the sinner's spiritual death—banishment from the Father's fellowship. "In sum, Christ descended into hell. Nor was it simply a passive want of the Father's fellowship which made the fury of hell unbearable; it was also that the hatred of the Father for sin was personally directed against him so that in his own heart he felt what it meant to be opposed by heaven, having the breath of an angry God on him."[36]

Can we continue to question the Father's prerogative to offer and withdraw mercy at His will? Not when we realize that "the price which the Father paid in sacrificing his Son on the cross was so unthinkably painful to heaven, and so incomprehensible for the sinful heart on earth to perceive, that one can only marvel that God has

35. Ibid., p. 373.
36. Ibid., p. 383.

made mercy available to man even within a day of grace."[37] Love
never demands mercy, it only patiently waits to see if mercy is there.
Our hearts find final rest when they rest not in an abstract *agape,* but
in God Himself. Concrete *agape* is not defined formally and imposed
upon God; it is what God does. If we cannot accept Christ's demonstration of *agape* and explanation of its significance, we are left with
another formal immediacy. We can no more have fellowship with the
principle of *agape* than we can with sex, money, or a method of knowing. *Agape* cannot be our most high. Our ultimate trust is in God.

Our danger lies in neglecting God's mercy during the day of grace
which is with us yet. "When a man denies God's right to punish
recalcitrant sinners in hell, he likewise must reject the Father's prerogative to punish his own Son through the second death on the
cross." But if Christ did not atone for our sins, how shall they be put
away? How else can we be reconciled to God's holy love? "If the
doctrine of hell is a hard doctrine to hear, universalism is even harder.
And when the modern mind seeks to know whether it is better to
suffer for the person of Jesus Christ or formal agape, it must be remembered that the gaining or losing of an absolute fellowship hangs
in the balance."[38]

LIVING FOR AN INSTITUTIONAL GOD

Having failed to love God and man as we ought we are delighted to
hear that there is hope in a noted institution. Grace for the guilty
comes, we are told, through the Roman Catholic Church with its
papal head, the vicar of Christ on earth. This institution attracts us to
its claims in many impressive ways. At first sight we are moved by its
cathedrals and art, its universality and ecumenicity, its age and con-
tinuity, its tradition and authority, its officialdom and ceremonies, its
scholarship and literature. Awed as we may be, however, we must
examine those claims before committing ourselves to it as our supreme value. And our competence to decide must not be discounted
if the Catholic apologist hopes to convert us.

Catholicism's imposing evidences from its antiquity, authority,
unity, and power are unconvincing. Antiquity has no intrinsic merit,
since people can perpetuate error as easily as truth. The church tra-

37. Ibid., p. 385.
38. Ibid., p. 390.

dition may simply preserve some of the errors into which people fell in the first century. Is the authority unchallengeable because of the pope's unique *ex cathedra* infallibility? Hardly, since fallible people must determine when popes did and did not speak officially. If every pope had explicitly indicated when he spoke infallibly, still fallible people would have to interpret his pronouncements. "At some point the individual must exercise his private right of interpretation, or no meaning is conveyed. Where, then, has our unique authority gone?"[39] The unity of the church, so evidently incorporating great diversity, does not of itself guarantee truth. People can and do unite around error. "Power? A neutral value capable of either good or evil. Grandeur? An irrelevant criterion."[40]

In spite of the inconclusiveness of the traditional evidences, Rome's claims could be supported by Christlike love in theory and practice. God is love. Without love we are nothing, although we may have prophetic powers, understand all mysteries, and have great faith (1 Co 13:2). By the standard of love, can we conclude that the priest has power to forgive sins, excommunicate members and interpret God's will infallibly for others? Is this institution a continuation of Christ's incarnation on earth? Do we hear God say, "This is my beloved church, hear you her?"[41]

Unfortunately Rome's doctrine of justification by works renders impossible the complete values of either righteousness or love. Universal selfishness and pride make personal attainment of righteousness impossible. Before the standard of God's love we can only be justified by the imputation of Christ's righteousness. That gift of free grace based on Christ's atonement is the sole ground of justification. What good works we may produce are the result, not the ground, of justification. In anathematizing that Protestant doctrine, the Council of Trent (Canons 11, 12) anathematized the teaching of Romans and Galatians. And so Rome disallowed the only ground of acceptance with God for men without perfect love.

Rome also misinterprets the role of God's moral law and so loses another necessary value. The commands to love God and neighbor, Rome infers, imply man's ability to keep them. If we could not keep the law, obligation would disappear. The inference that obligation

39. Ibid., p. 402.
40. Ibid.
41. Ibid., p. 404.

requires ability becomes Rome's highest value. But it is inconsistent with their view of infant guilt, and is not supported by the data of experience. Experience shows three things: (1) our assent to the law of love, (2) our natural inability to keep it, and (3) our responsibility for it, nevertheless. Because Rome's Pelagianism does not admit these facts, it is "not even good rationalism."[42] Rome does not see that God lays upon us the responsibility for holy love as a moral means by which to bring us to humility and repentance. By our guilt before God's righteous law we are driven to Him for mercy and grace. No abstract inference from the law can take precedence over what God has done. That is good because God did it. When forced to choose between Rome's justification by works and Romans' justification by faith, the epistle's is clearly the more excellent way to the highest value—fellowship with God.[43]

Since from a biblical perspective perfection is never attained in this life, Rome's claims are untrustworthy. Fallen man's best works are tainted by pride. But "we are responsible for its presence because we never disaffiliate ourselves from it with the consistency of which we are capable."[44] Ecclesiastical organizations are no more perfect than the sinners who make them up. The most saintly, furthermore, do not speak of their own holiness. In the Roman Church there may be individuals of great piety, but the Church has little reason to boast. She has pursued ways of "bloodshed, pride, intolerance, . . . hatred, and will-to-power which hardly have a parallel." In 1952 Carnell went on to say:

> If Christ had come to earth bearing the characteristic which Rome now bears—dealing with non-conformists with the same totalitarian tactics—the heart would scorn him as a blasphemer and impostor; for no man can claim to be consanguineous with God unless at the same time he exhibits a flawless perfection of love in his own person.[45]

In our search for the highest value we cannot freely commit ourselves to the Roman hierarchy because it refuses to be judged by divine law. "When an organization pretends that there is no voice of divine condemnation against its own sins—be it communism or Catholicism—one must take care. There is no sinfulness quite so in-

42. Ibid., p. 415.
43. Ibid., p. 416.
44. Ibid., p. 428.
45. Ibid., p. 430.

tolerable as that which pretends to enjoy divine approval."[46] Christ in holy love exploded against the Pharisees who claimed in His day to be the vicar of God on earth. The Pharisees interpreted God's Word for the people, multiplying endless details of legalistic requirements. So they missed the weightier matters of the law in the trivialities of ceremonial observances. Similarly Rome today keeps the common man from the true word and will of God.

"Because she arrogates to herself prerogatives of judging infallibly, while at the same time claiming exemption from divine judgment, the church of Rome is able to define the good as whatever promotes her security."[47] Her motives seem all too evidently far from altruistic. Her goals are not the highest. "The end she seeks is not a loving fellowship among Christians with Jesus Christ as mystical head, but a subordination of all men to the visible head, the pope. Catholic orders are united to advance Catholicism, not brotherly love and kindness to all."[48]

LIVING FOR LOVE OF GOD AND MAN

The importance of living in love, and not just theorizing about it, has been brought vividly to recent attention through Sören Kierkegaard's writings. In his native Denmark Kierkegaard opposed the institutionalism of the state church and the philosophical system of Professor Hegel. Thinking about Christianity and administering a church is not the same as being a Christian. We exist as Christians only when we passionately choose to express divine love (*agape*) in the complexities of life. No more consuming value could challenge us. In fact, the challenge is so great it transforms us.

Kierkegaard distinguished three levels on which people live. We do not naturally live for God and others, because of holy love. Instead we naturally live for aesthetic pleasures, neither suffering nor deciding for anything of eternal significance. Living for temporal pleasure, however cultured or "religious," is not living for the highest Christian values. Some are converted from the aesthetic level of life to the ethical. Speculation about right and wrong, even in terms of God's will, is not being a Christian. From this level people must be transformed. By a radical decision we must begin life all over

46. Ibid., p. 435.
47. Ibid., p. 431.
48. Ibid.

again. We are truly religious only when we have accepted the responsibility of carrying out the demands of love, and have despaired of ever realizing the truth in our lives. In each moment of existence there must be subjective concern for an unconditional surrender of self to the obedience of God by His grace. Only then can we become authentic individuals.

In Carnell's judgment, Kierkegaard thus made explicit what Christians have held implicitly. Saving faith is not merely intellectual assent to true doctrine. "Faith is cordial trust; it is a concerned, inward response to the person and work of Jesus Christ."[49] God desires goodness, not sacrifice. He looks for a transformed life of faith bringing forth works of love. Only a moment-by-moment existence in love by the grace of God enables us to become authentic individuals. And Jesus Christ exemplifies the eternal love incarnate in historical ambiguities. Kierkegaard has indeed pointed to the highest value in life.

Unfortunately, in stressing personal commitment, Kierkegaard thought it necessary to attack objective truth. For example, he said little about a ground of justification. "A great deal was said about the incarnation, and a little was said about the atonement; but one would need the lamp of Diogenes to find a systematic treatment of Christ's imputed righteousness."[50] This neglect may be attributed to a fear that the assurance of justification might have reduced the need for works of love. "If Kierkegaard was so dedicated to the existential necessity of good works that salvation by faith alone was impossible, then at this point in his thinking he was closer to Roman Catholicism than he was to Protestantism."[51] The value of personal fellowship is not hindered, but immeasurably helped by complete acceptance with God on the ground of Christ's atonement.

In order to focus on internal love Kierkegaard's writings also are criticized for "a very inadequate relation between the Christian religion and public evidences."[52] Carnell again seeks to analyze his reasoning. "He was so terrified by the prospect of complacency that he ended up asserting that faith is based on risk. He even went so

---

49. Ibid., p. 473.
50. Edward John Carnell, *The Burden of Sören Kierkegaard* (Grand Rapids: Eerdmans, 1965), p. 170.
51. Ibid., p. 171.
52. Ibid., p. 169.

far as to contend that the greater the risk, the greater the faith."[53]
In thinking that certainty and passion cannot go together, Kierkegaard opened himself to any kind of absurdity. Unless some test is
devised to distinguish mysteries from muddles our passionate commitment may be to something utterly unreal. "Certainty comes into
being whenever evidences are deemed sufficient. . . . The one and
only issue is the sufficiency of the evidences. All else is beside the
point." Pointedly Carnell continues, "A Christian *may* respond to
public evidences with passion, but passion has no more authority
to create evidences for the Christian religion than it has to create
evidences for the science of obstetrics. When all is said and done,
therefore, passion and certainty are friends, not foes."[54]

To the values of personal fellowship with God and justification by
faith we may add the value of evidences sufficient to make us willing
to act. The Christian enjoys values of the heart and the head at the
same time. Those of the heart without a test of error lead to fanaticism. A rational (evidential) test of error is not out of order.

> Since it happens that there is a univocal point of identity binding
> the eternal God and a finite individual together—for both God and
> man are *persons*—it is not true that the incarnation is an "absolute"
> paradox. . . . Since man is made in the image of God, therefore the
> intellect is *not* completely offended to learn that God has taken on
> his own image. The incarnation may be received by rational minds
> without self-betrayal.[55]

The incarnation is an incomprehensible mystery, but it is not a
logical contradiction (a square circle or loveless love).

A rational test of error is also necessary to avoid absurdities that
are not profound. Kierkegaard has no way to escape basing faith
on even greater absurdities than the incarnation. Carnell's fertile
mind suggested "that the Eternal became a naked red worm, appeared
to Joseph Smith, dwelt in Father Divine, or renders fallible popes
infallible! We can hardly decide between such commitments on the
basis of a "barometric reading of passion."[56] Furthermore, Carnell
effectively shows that "it is not psychologically true that passionate
concern increases in commensurate ratio to objective uncertainty."

53. Ibid.
54. Ibid., p. 170.
55. Carnell, *Philosophy*, p. 485.
56. Ibid., p. 487.

The cry, "Fire!" by a man of questionable seriousness of character does not evoke the concern that it would from a trusted friend against a background of smoke rising from the house. "Thus a faith based on rational evidences is able to nourish a healthy inwardness."[57]

On the ground of evidences sufficient to act upon, the Christian finds the highest values of loving fellowship, complete forgiveness before a God of holy love. At the same time he has nothing of which to boast. In grateful obedience he then seeks the well-being of men also created in God's image. Because he loves God, he loves those God loves. The soundest humanism is rooted in a biblical theism.

VALUES AND THE INVISIBLE GARDENER

Trust in the God of the biblical love and forgiveness more often than not is withheld because of misrepresentation. Inhabitants of the garden seeking pleasure think the Christian option is a merely negative way of life. The lover of bread imagines it cuts off his material rights. The positivist concludes that it is unscientific, and the rationalist that it requires blind submission to authority. The humanist supposes that it denigrates man, the finitist that it compromises goodness, the universalist that it short-changes love. The Roman Catholic presumes that it undermines authority, and the existentialist that it fetters his freedom.

But Christ has not come to rob us of anything but sin. He came to give us life, and life abundantly (Jn 10:10). Biblical Christianity recognizes the cosmic support of a love which cannot be exhausted in an eternity of creativity, and a freedom that is made perfect in love. Love for God enriches all other values. The Christian may enjoy pleasures designed for him in the earth which is the Lord's. He will have economic security if he works (2 Th 3:10). Knowing that the regularity of nature is sustained by God he pursues its revelation of the Lord's purpose with interest. His acceptance of biblical authority liberates him from merely human authorities and provides data for developing a system all-encompassing and consistent. Since Christ alone is master, no individual or institution has power to step in and destroy his fellowship.

Trusting Christ, a person engages reality as it exists and develops a system of truth in his mind. So he grows as a truthful, faithful per-

57. Ibid., p. 494.

son by combining all the values of existentially lived truth with essentially conceived truth. Admittedly Christianity has its unanswered questions, as every philosophy does. But it explains man's predicament in the "garden" and supports human values with fewer difficulties and greater coherence than other live options. Each of us must choose for himself. Until the day of our death we stand or fall before our chosen master. If the debris and rocks of misunderstanding which cluttered the way to personal faith in Christ have been removed, it only remains to trust the Lord. Christian apologetics cannot do that for you. Moved in your heart by the love of Christ and the conviction of truth by the Holy Spirit, you must accept Christianity's truth and live for Christianity's values.

EVALUATION

The defense of Christianity's values presupposes the metaphysical reality of God and the truth of biblically revealed Christianity. It is possible to prize certain things which in reality do not exist, or do not deserve the value given. Truth about reality in the final analysis must support our values or we shall be disappointed. Carnell wisely considers the defense of Chritsianity's values just one aspect of his apologetic. It can only be judged in terms of its limited purpose.

This axiological approach can gain a hearing among people with the interests discussed. More could be done to empathize with them. But the core of leading alternatives is accurately expounded and effectively answered. For those who want to know about the kind of things Christians consider important this presentation is significant indeed. One may begin with the things an unbeliever currently prizes highly, and show how Christianity includes those values and more. In a day of atomic power the human race desperately needs a ground on which men should respect and love one another. Carnell's approach in *A Philosophy of the Christian Religion* shows how love for one's neighbor can only be sustained under love for the God revealed in Christ and the Bible.

Since this approach is particularly crucial in our times we could wish for a fuller positive presentation of Christianity's values. The negative case against other options is adequate. The affirmative case seems less so. To some extent this need is fulfilled in Carnell's later works entitled *Christian Commitment* and *The Kingdom of Love and the Pride of Life.* To these we turn our attention in the following chapters.

RESOURCES FOR RESEARCH

Boyer, Merle William. *Highways of Philosophy.* Philadelphia: Muhlenberg, 1949. See chapter 13, "Values and the Philosopher as Man of Decision." The uniqueness of man is seen as he is a carrier and organizer of values by an author who seeks to be both philosophical and Christian.

Brightman, Edgar Sheffield. *An Introduction to Philosophy.* New York: Henry Holt, 1951. Chapter 7, "What Are Values?", discusses the objectivity or subjectivity of values and concludes that "religious faith is far more than enthusiasm about some special interest. It is confidence in the source of all values, expressed by worship and co-operation, and based on belief in what Hoffding calls the conservation and increase of values in the universe" (p. 172).

———. *Nature and Values.* New York: Abingdon-Cokesbury, 1945. A defense of theism over against naturalism in terms of values.

Carnell, Edward John. *A Philosophy of the Christian Religion.* Grand Rapids: Eerdmans, 1952. The major attempt of an evangelical to display the completeness of Christianity's values, as against the incompleteness of values in other options.

MacGregor, Geddes. *Introduction to Religious Philosophy.* Boston: Houghton Mifflin, 1959. Part 6 includes four brief chapters on "Value-Experience and the Idea of God" in defense of theism.

Macquarrie, John. *Twentieth-Century Religious Thought: The Frontiers of Philosophy and Theology, 1900-1960.* London: SCM, 1963. In chapter 5, "The Idea of Value in Philosophy and Theology," Macquarrie surveys attempt to limit religious statements to value-judgments in the Ritschlian school of theology.

Titus, Harold H. *Living Issues in Philosophy.* New York: American Book, 1946, pp. 367-71. A case for the existence of God based on man's sense of duty, the uniting of goodness and happiness, and the objectivity of values. Chapter 19, entitled "The Field of Values," emphasizes a relativistic interpretation of values.

Urban, Wilbur M. "Axiology." In *Twentieth Century Philosophy.* Ed. by Dagobert D. Runes. New York: Philosophical Libr., 1943, pp. 53-73. Argues that human values are meaningless if there is no purpose in the cosmos of which we are a part, and that axiology cannot be divorced from metaphysics.

9

THE VERIFICATIONAL APPROACH OF
EDWARD JOHN CARNELL: PSYCHOLOGY

The Test of Relieving Man's Deepest Anxieties

"I believe that if Christian apologists would rally their wits and make better use of love as a point of contact, great things might be accomplished for the defense of the faith."[1] In making that challenge, Edward John Carnell referred to love, not from the standpoint of ethics or values, but of psychotherapy or psychiatry. Taking his own challenge, in 1960 he wrote *The Kingdom of Love and the Pride of Life*.

Paul Tillich had suggested that Christianity answers the questions non-Christians are asking. In our age of anxiety and despair people are seeking a source of peace and acceptance. If man's search for meaning is relevantly answered by the gospel, the healing power of the gospel must be correlated with the needs of men estranged from God, one another, and themselves. Christianity has always taught that love is the law of life. Now the science of psychology has discovered as well that love is the integrating factor in a healthy personality.

Furthermore, psychotherapy has found it beneficial for people to see themselves through their own childhood. When people lose their early unconditional faith, they lose their happiness. Carnell says, "I think that Jesus would accept this Freudian insight, for he urged his own disciples to imitate the manners of a child. A happy child bears

1. Edward John Carnell, *The Kingdom of Love and the Pride of Life* (Grand Rapids: Eerdmans, 1960), p. 10.

231

witness to the release that love brings: release from anxiety, fear, and the dread of not counting."[2]

People in psychosomatic distress do not need so much to be told what to do, as to accept themselves and be accepted just as they are. Such an unconditional acceptance is offered in the gospel. It expresses God's love for the unloving. It tells of an individual's significance not only to others, but to the eternal God Himself. The healing of distress comes to those who are utterly honest with themselves. Similarly, the Lord would have us become as sincere as little children to enter the kingdom of heaven. That, of course, takes utter humility. Another mark of childhood is indispensable to reception of the truth about oneself and about God. Christians, then, may appeal to such points of contact with this generation as anxiety, insignificance, humility, sincerity, acceptance, and becoming as a little child in the search for a happy, integrated life.

As a literary vehicle to communicate this correlation of the gospel with human need, Carnell chooses one concrete instance. His book focuses on the ministry of Christ to the grieving at the death of Lazarus. The familiar story in the gospel of John (chap. 11) vividly portrays the Christian's resources in the face of distress. Of his use of the biblical account, Carnell explains, "I have not been bound by the details of the story, nor have I allowed myself to wander into the wastelands of speculation."[3]

The greatest threat to happiness is the loss of a loved one. No amount of poetry or song can make death lovely. The fear of death disturbs man's peace. Nothing more effectively shakes our faith in the future or dispels all hope. In the face of Lazarus' sickness, we cannot help but ask, "Do good people count, or do they not?"[4]

Children know that "a person is good when he is kind and truthful, and that in the end a good person has nothing to fear."[5] Both virtue and hope are brought out in the fairy tales, which reveal the very logic of life itself. In spite of all the evil in the fairy tales, their outcome is loving and virtuous. For children know that "if love is lost, all is lost."[6] Although imperfect children often quarrel, at the end of the day they rest in the securities that only love can bring. They know

2. Ibid., p. 7.
3. Ibid., p. 10.
4. Ibid., p. 18.
5. Ibid., p. 17.
6. Ibid., p. 19.

what adults may have forgotten, that security is gained not by power or influence, but love.

Adults may scoff at intuitions of the heart, but Jesus said we must humble ourselves as little children to enter the kingdom of heaven (Mt 18:2-4). Knowing something of the virtues of love, children know something of the virtues of the kingdom of heaven. Intuitively we know how to comfort the sick child. With a gift, a word, and a gesture we assure him that his life counts in the kingdom of love. At a funeral good people know that "if the dead do not count, then the living do not count, for the living and the dead form one unbroken fellowship."[7] In communicating assurances of hope to the bereaved we really say that the soul is immortal and God will overrule the verdict of death.

What keeps us from greater recognition of these convictions of the heart? The distractions and responsibilities of life make their contribution, but our underlying difficulty is our own pride. We refuse to become as a little child by insisting that we can complete our lives without the fulfillment of love. It is not that we must exercise uncritical judgment; that is not Jesus' intention. But humility must displace pride. "Pride draws us away from the kingdom of love, and thus from the kingdom of heaven, by tempting us to think that we can dispense with the duties of love."[8]

Science No Substitute for Love

After doing all they could for Lazarus, Mary and Martha sent for Jesus. He could be trusted because his actions were kind and his words truthful. "Jesus was the number-one citizen in the kingdom of love. Children came to him gladly, and so did all who were children in heart."[9]

Science, so beneficial as far as it goes, may keep us from the kingdom of love. But the interpretation and control of nature need not keep us from humbling ourselves before the Creator. He commanded man to rule it. The curiosity of a child discloses a spirit of scientific inquiry implanted in us by God Himself. Science may be warmly commended so long as it does not reduce rich human existence to mere formulae and statistics. Scientifically inclined people cannot

7. Ibid., p. 21.
8. Ibid., p. 22.
9. Ibid., p. 24.

afford to let a specialized interest alienate them from their own existence as human beings in love for God and others.

By making moral judgments the scientist recognizes knowledge attained apart from the scientific method. The scientist knows that he
must credit other men's research out of respect for intellectual honesty. Intuitively, the scientist as a human being knows that cheating
is wrong. "He will call no man good who is unkind and untruthful.
On the highway, in the market, or around the hearth, he expects
others to treat him as a human being. If his dignity is outraged or his
rights are defrauded, he instinctively judges the offending party
guilty."[10] In so doing he not only bears witness to the convictions of
the heart, but also to the limits of science.

The foundations of all decent society are to be found, not in quantitative scientific description, but in "the axiom that a man is good
when he is kind and truthful."[11] Our spiritual dignity does not allow
us to be merely academic when threatened by a malicious remark, an
unprovoked blow, or an atomic war. No one can be content with detached scientific objectivity alone when he arrives home to find a
hoodlum terrorizing his wife and children. In view of the world's
present moral struggle it is not the part of wisdom to limit knowledge
to the realm of scientific investigation. "Unless we recover a crusad-
ing zeal for righteousness, we may lose both the fraternity of science
and our way of life."[12]

When we trust a physician we show our respect both for science and
its limits. We look for signs of scientific competence and of personal
integrity. In subscribing to the Hippocratic oath, a physician acknowledges principles more ultimate than those of science. He must use his
skill for good, not evil. Unless he is a good man, he has no right to
call himself a physician. The scientist as a patient wants to know that
in the surgeon's heart his life counts. Carnell argues effectively then,
that "a physician is living proof that the convictions of the heart and
the scientific method can be blended in one dignified vocation."[13]

PHILOSOPHY INSUFFICIENT

Philosophy does not succeed in integrating a whole life either. Like

10. Ibid., p. 27.
11. Ibid., p. 29.
12. Ibid., p. 30.
13. Ibid., p. 35.

science, philosophy is valuable. The danger lies in failure to recognize signs of its limits. The intellectual awakening which takes place as we leave childhood brings its satisfactions but can play tricks on us.

For one thing, conceptual thought may lead us away from the realities we experience. Philosophers may argue that nothing moves or that everything moves. But a person with childlike simplicity remains close to reality, "he would know that some things are in motion, while other things are not. Rivers change, but the convictions of the heart remain the same."[14] We may not be able to fathom the mysteries of sleep or dreaming, but we nevertheless must go to sleep and we may dream. The problem of evil may be inexplicable, but it will not avail to deny that Lazarus was sick by any metaphysical subtleties. Socrates, so energetic in the search for conceptual definitions of virtue, denied knowledge of its essence himself. Why? Carnell interestingly suggests that though admittedly he could not conceive its universal definition, he knew it intuitively (in the "heart"). At least Socrates was wise enough not to deny what he could not conceive.[15]

Philosophers who did identify the good with a conception of it, forgot that the power of conception (like that of science) can be used for evil as well as good. "It did not occur to the Greeks that the intellect is often a willing servant of pride."[16] Assuming that the intellect is innocent and impartial, they failed to see the possibilities of rationalization according to one's will or affections. In the name of truth and eventual goodness, communists can gratify the resentments of those who seek the overthrow of capitalism.[17] In the midst of a quarrel even children think that power outranks love. They pretend they are defending truth; but they are really defending themselves. Knowledge alone never satisfies the whole man because it is impersonal. It lacks life and spirit. "The *experience* of being loved, not an intellectual account of love, is the substance of a happy life."[18]

Philosophy alone leads to disillusionment because it divests man from everything that makes him an individual. Greek philosophers, attempting to liberate men from the ambiguities of existence resorted to unchanging universals. In so doing, philosophy limited itself (like science) to the regularities characteristic of all men. But individuals

14. Ibid., pp. 37-38.
15. Ibid., p. 40.
16. Ibid., p. 41.
17. Ibid., p. 43.
18. Ibid., p. 44.

have unpredictable characteristics, freely disclosed or freely hidden. So the philosophers in their rarified wisdom became foolish (1 Co 1:20-21). By the assumptions of their method of knowing they had ruled out knowledge of a uniquely personal God, should He choose to reveal Himself. For we only know a person in his uniqueness when he communicates in the context of fellowship.

Carnell perceives a law in this regard. "The more we surrender our lives to one another in love and fellowship, the more intimately we know one another."[19] Love is an indispensable condition to knowledge of creative possibilities. It is richer than universal "manness" or natural law. While friends tell many secrets, lovers tell more. The language of love may be very brief. "Lord," Mary said, "he whom you love is ill." Detailed explanation is not called for at this point. A parent who hears his child is injured needs no further word. He knows all he needs to know. Detachment gives way to intimate concern. Since reality includes persons, reality cannot be limited to what is known by intellectual detachment. The secrets of persons, whether divine or human, cannot be inferred by inferences from universal premises. Unless human beings are to be impersonalized, world views based on universal and necessary deductions, laws, or categories, cannot be sufficient of themselves.

Love does not displace philosophy but makes it meaningful.

> As long as a philosopher remembers that he is a human being whose secrets remain his own until he chooses to reveal them, he will be delivered from the error of thinking that love has no role to play in the task of gaining knowledge. And how does a philosopher keep such a fact before him? By imitating the manners of a happy child, as Jesus advises. A child does not prejudice the possibilities of reality by intellectual detachment. He is content to accept things as they are.[20]

THE WAY OF LOVE

"Now Jesus loved Martha and her sister and Lazarus." Jesus had always gone about doing good. Acknowledging the dignity of individual man, he gave appropriate signs of respect. Discourtesy is one of the first signs of selfishness. Jesus disclosed in life the significance of unselfishness. "No man ever drew near to Jesus but that Jesus gave

19. Ibid., p. 48.
20. Ibid., p. 49.

gentle, spiritual signs that his life was precious in the sight of God."[21]

And Jesus, the exemplar of consideration, accepted people as they were. "Lazarus was a nonentity in the world, yet Jesus loved him."[22] Christ did not accept people on the basis of their power or influence. "Power brings admirers, but it does not make friends."[23] Lazarus did not have to put on airs. Jesus accepted his unaffected person for what he was. Previously Martha had vied for Christ's acceptance by outdoing Mary. Nevertheless, "Jesus would not let Martha shift the norm of acceptance from love to power. But he did this in such a way that Martha had no reason to wilt, nor Mary to gloat."[24]

A child rests in loving acceptance, except when it depends upon a greater daily achievement of which to boast. Then legalistic attainment of grades or neighborhood leadership replaces love. Unaccepted at home, such a child may find greater security in a gang. Rebelling against society for reasons he himself does not fully understand, he also rebels against the duties of love. He masks his insecurity behind brash talk and action to gain status in the gang. And his burning desire for power is fanned by ever-present propaganda asserting that power wins friends and security. Failing to achieve either by fair means or foul, he desperately flees from himself aided by narcotics, alcohol, or sex. These purported liberators in turn only enslave.

Often the "publicans and sinners" outwardly are more ready to acknowledge their sinful plight than the apparently respectable. So Jesus could say that tax collectors and harlots would enter the kingdom of God before the Pharisees. Before God, as before the psychotherapist, the demand is complete honesty. Christ's strongest invectives fell upon the ears of the self-righteous. More concerned with power than love, the hypocrites could not care less about those who fell along the way. In the parable of the Good Samaritan, the priest and Levite were too preoccupied with official duties to help a neighbor. "Even service to God can be corrupted into an excuse for serving self rather than God."[25]

How can these most serious tragedies in human life be resolved? People are so hungry for approval that psychic distress forbids hap-

21. Ibid., p. 53.
22. Ibid.
23. Ibid., p. 55.
24. Ibid., p. 54.
25. Ibid., p. 59.

piness and they can only find help in love. Freud "restored the symbolism of common grace by accepting the unacceptable. Neurotic
behavior evoked scorn from society, judgment from the church.
Freud rejected both attitudes."[26] He recognized the factors beyond
the individual's moral or rational control, and restored the ethic of
honesty to human relations. What they needed, he could see, was not
judgmental preaching but acceptance as persons. When they could
find one whom they could trust they could unburden the intimacies
of their hearts. How rare is the occasion for complete honesty in personal relations! The existing social order seems to be held together
by the adhesive of deception. With our closest loved ones it is difficult
to be completely honest.

Here then is our problem: complete happiness requires complete
honesty with ourselves before others. But whom can we trust not to
ridicule or tattle when he hears the inmost secrets of our hearts? Con-
fessedly Freud had no solution. He knew society could be dreadfully
cruel. "Freud could not articulate a philosophy of hope because he
could not break from scientific detachment. . . . it kept him from understanding the relationship between hope and the duties of love in
normal people."[27] He thought of love in terms of genital expression
rather than "a vital sharing of natures" and "accepting the unacceptable." So Freud failed to discover a prescription for the disease he so
ably diagnosed.

More recent psychologists have recognized a moral defect in man's
will and affections prompting him to do things he regrets. Is this not
sin? Sin, Carnell points out, "is much more serious than a conflict
between the pleasure principle and social restrictions. It is a spiritual
admission that the self is out of harmony with its own essence."[28]

The love Jesus manifests not only for neurotics, but for all men,
brings light and life to a world in need of honesty and grace. Jesus
received people as they were and made it easy for them to be honest
with themselves and God. He assures us that God who knows all that
is within our hearts loves and accepts us just as we are. In knowing
the sin of the woman at the well, and even in making it known to her,
He did not reject her or condemn her. Christ lovingly helped her

26. Ibid.
27. Ibid., p. 61.
28. Ibid., p. 64.

admit the truth about herself. Immediately she sensed the wisdom and love of the Messiah.

Convinced of God's love through Christ we can face the rejection of society. Acceptance with God, the assurance of His promises to the faithful, and the strengthening of the inner man by the Holy Spirit enable any forgiven sinner to bear misunderstanding with patience and hope.

LOVE AND THE PROBLEM OF EVIL

In such patience and hope Mary and Martha waited for Jesus, even after burying their brother. Most naturally they might have asked, "Why did you wait?" Why did you stay two more days where you were after learning of Lazarus' illness? Many and eloquent have been the anguished utterances about evil.

In the humility of a child, however, we shall not be skeptical, deny the reality of evil, or imagine it to be eternally as ultimate as good. Humility trusts the wisdom of God for mysteries not now revealed. Unless God chooses to tell us why, we cannot determine His purpose in detail. A childlike faith can endure the greatest problems so long as the end of the story is happy. In the end good people have nothing to fear. So trustful love does not worry about life but enjoys it.

The hearts of Mary and Martha could have hardened against God if they had made an all-controlling issue out of their brother's death. Then they would have been unmoved by the tender solicitations of love. Against such hardness of heart Jesus warned us when he laid down the requirement of becoming as a little child. He did not ask us to lay aside our trained critical faculties, but our unresponsiveness to love. Mary and Martha did not lose hope or refuse to await Christ's return. "Jesus was their friend, and as their friend he had a right to explain himself in a friendly atmosphere."[29] They did not judge Him in advance, but waited on the Lord.

LOVE AND ANXIETY

Although it meant facing the possibility of death from his enemies, Jesus went to Bethany. To his protesting disciples he finally said plainly, "Lazarus is dead." The ties of human dignity and love required that He and the disciples lose themselves in order to find

29. Ibid., p. 75.

themselves. In the service of others we may be delivered from excessive anxiety for ourselves.

But plagued with self-centered affections, we try to save ourselves by power rather than love. Each achievement calls for a greater one. No amount ever satisfies the self. So we nearly destroy ourselves trying to save ourselves. Then we try to escape from destructive anxiety about the reality by endless diversions. Either time, strength, or interest fails and boredom empties life of significance.

We should humble ourselves and become as little children. An alcoholic must. He must forsake unrealistic power drives and willingly accept anonymity. Honestly acknowledging his own inabilities, he seeks to help others. Then he is needed and wanted; he need not prove anything by displays of power. Overcoming pride he becomes again like a child who is content to be anonymous, since he does not identify life with power. Any of us may be as enslaved as the alcoholic to anxieties about things that belong to God, salvation, what others think of us, what shall we eat or wear. Trust in God's provision does not imply inactivity. Under God there is a time to rest and a time to work. Having done our part we must trust God to do His. If God did not dispense daily gifts we would perish. Trust in our heavenly Father is the remedy for destructive anxiety.

Another form of anxiety, however, may be intensified by associations formed in Christian love. Such constructive anxiety troubled the hearts of Mary and Martha who had cared for Lazarus to the end. All anxiety is not sinful resistance to the limits God set to creation. Without sin Jesus' great love caused Him to weep over Jerusalem and suffer in Gethsemane.

If anxiety necessarily plagues even a righteous and loving life, we must learn to cope with it. Anxiety will not get out of hand if we follow the direction of Christ and limit it to the troubles of the day. We may add too much to our burden by anticipating the troubles of tomorrow. Our task is to learn to trust God's mercies for today, with all of its difficulties. In spite of our repeated failures we must trust that God is longsuffering. Otherwise our love for God may occasion unnecessary destructive anxiety. Or our concern for the approval of a legalistic church also may produce a neurosis. If believers are forced to repress their true feelings for long periods of time, damage can result. Rather, the church should take the lead in stressing the ethic of honesty and the redemption of grace. "When we realize that we are subject to troubles on all sides, we can understand why it is just as necessary to trust God for present mercies as it is to trust him for everlasting life."[30] When we have learned that one lesson, the future will take care of itself. For the future can only come to us in present moments. So Christian faith overcomes destructive anxiety and properly channels constructive anxiety.

That same faith discovers an adequate ground of hope—even beyond the grave. Although the mind finds it difficult to explain the resurrection of decayed bodies, the heart cannot believe that loved ones perish like animals. Of the believer Jesus said, "Though he were dead, yet shall he live" (Jn 11:25, KJV). Martha reposed in these words from the Christ, the Son of God. At His word the lame walked, lepers were cleansed, the poor heard the gospel, and the dead were raised! As long as she knew that evil would not permanently triumph over a good man, she could rest. Christ's promise gave her a well-founded hope.

Martha's hope was not in the deliverance of Lazarus' soul from his body, but the resurrection of his body. Without the body a vital part of man would be lost to evil. The Greeks did not know the body would be divested from the consequence of sin and so did not anticipate the resurrection. But through special revelation we know that "when man is confirmed in righteousness, the conflict between soul and body will cease. The body will become the servant of the soul."[31]

Is a resurrection impossible? Not with God. "If God created man to enjoy the kingdom of love, why can't he recreate him to enjoy the kingdom of heaven?"[32] Fairy tales leave room for miraculous events without question.

> If miracles are needed to ensure a final triumph of goodness, so be it. In this case, miracles are as much a part of reality as trees and rivers. A child knows that it is much more difficult to accept the defeat of goodness than it is to accept the reality of miracles. If good people do not live happily ever after, then what difference does anything else make? The most important thing has been surrendered. Death has triumphed over life.[33]

30. Ibid., p. 91.
31. Ibid., p. 103.
32. Ibid., pp. 104-5.
33. Ibid., p. 105.

Love and Disunity

When Jesus saw Mary and her Jewish friends weeping, He was deeply moved. Standing with them at the grave of Lazarus, Jesus also wept (Jn 11:35). He who displayed divine attributes in stilling the waves and giving sight to the blind, also disclosed human characteristics in hungering, thirsting, and weeping. The tears of Jesus not only showed his humanity, but also symbolized the unifying empathy of His love.

> When the mourners gathered at the grave of Lazarus, they experienced perfect unity. Jesus himself was the rallying point for fellowship, doctrine and form: *fellowship* because the mourners were bound by cords of love; *doctrine* because the teaching of the Lord was normative; and *form* because the will of the Lord became the will of the group. The mourners were all of one mind.[34]

The church remained united until at Corinth a party spirit developed. To this day it has plagued the fellowship as considerations of doctrine and form exclude considerations of love. The Reformation succeeded in liberating the church from Roman formalism, only to find increasing disruption on doctrinal issues. Anglicans excluded from fellowship believers not part of the established church. Puritans made certain distinctive doctrines a test of fit fellowship. Scotch Presbyterians impaired fellowship by insisting that Presbyterian church polity was the only biblical polity. Lutherans linked the interest of the Church with the interests of race and soil. Against formalism Methodists stressed personal holiness, but the doctrine became a status symbol separating them from other believers. And their episcopal polity is "often more rigid and bureaucratic than Anglicanism."[35] Baptists and Congregationalists experience more and more encroachment upon the liberty of local churches and finally equate loyalty to Christ with loyalty to the institution. Separatists who wash their hands of all existing churches to start new ones become prey to novelty and enthusiasm and find no biblical answer to anarchy.

What can be done to unite believers in a fellowship of doctrine and form? We can frankly acknowledge the existing problem of disunity in an atmosphere of complete honesty. Some hope for unity in denominational mergers, but theologians will never come to full agree-

34. Ibid., p. 110.
35. Ibid., p. 115.

ment on polity, sacraments or ordinances, predestination, and degrees of sanctification. If fellowship is to be achieved, love must hurdle denominational barriers. Neither can the goal be achieved by reducing doctrinal considerations to an all-inclusive least common denominator. We cannot disparage correct doctrine without becoming indifferent to fit fellowship.

Pride that seeks status in form or doctrine without love must be humbled. "If we fail to radiate the love of God in our lives, our achievements in doctrine and form will profit nothing" (1 Co 13:2-3).[36] Our discipleship must be shown in love, "a gentle, outgoing charity that takes in all men, and especially those of the household of faith."[37]

In the love of Christ Christians find their identity. "If God has ordained that doctrine and form should be servants of the fellowship, then we should see that God's will is done on earth as it is in heaven."[38]

LOVE AND HUMAN WEAKNESS

Martha had made a good confession of faith in Christ, but now as He requested that the tomb be unsealed her trust faltered. She said, "Lord, by this time there will be an odor, for he has been dead four days." Jesus rebuked her saying "Did I not tell you that if you would believe you would see the glory of God?" (Jn 11:39-40). The great heroes of faith had clung to God's promises, undisturbed by what seemed to be taking place to the contrary.

Martha, like Paul, found that the good she would do, she did not perform, and the act of unbelief she sought to avoid came out. Like Paul she wanted to live a more perfect life and hated the imperfection. As shown in *Christian Commitment*, love is satisfied, although law is not, in a spontaneous doing of what is right, or a sincere expression of sorrow for having failed. So a child of God basically seeks to do the will of God, but when he fails, expresses his sorrow. An honest confession is no base for personal merit, but an occasion for forgiveness. The charge that such an easy way out leads to gross evil misunderstands the attachment of love.

> Martha may have regretted the manner in which her actions belied her confession. But a memory of this incident did not depress her.

36. Ibid., p. 120.
37. Ibid., p. 121.
38. Ibid., p. 120.

She knew that her standing before the Lord was not decided by degrees of legal righteousness. As long as she was actively struggling against the law of sin in her members, she proved that her dominant affections were holy. And in gracious relationships this is all that matters.[39]

EVIDENCES FOR FAITH, HOPE AND LOVE

"By the sheer word of his mouth, without secondary means, Jesus reversed the decree of death."[40] In response to Christ's call, Lazarus came out of the tomb. As Jesus concluded his public ministry he provided an objective indication to serve as a basis for trust during the hours of betrayal, trial, and death of the cross. So Jesus called upon the Father (Jn 11:41), focusing attention on the source of His power. Then He summoned Lazarus in a loud voice, symbolizing the open character of the Christian religion. "Everything necessary for salvation is revealed; nothing is reserved for a privileged caste. God expects no man to believe unless a body of sufficient evidences has been created."[41]

Evidences form the basis for belief in the person of Christ. He is now confronted "in and through the Scriptures, and the Scriptures witness to a body of redemptive events that are as much a part of history as the voyage of Columbus."[42] Those who do not accept Christ on the sheer authority of His words are invited to believe on the strength of His works.

Since our available records of Christ's words and works are in the New Testament, some might ask for evidence in addition to it. Since there is no counter-evidence from the times to call the reports into question, we have no reason not to believe them. Should we question the testimony of these reports to Christ's life we have ended all critical investigation. If assent is not proportioned to evidence, a person is free to accept or reject whatever happens to suit him. On sufficient evidence we believe that there was a man called Abraham Lincoln and we believe there was a man called Jesus Christ. "Historical claims are neither established nor refuted by science and philosophy. They

39. Ibid., p. 137.
40. Ibid., p. 138.
41. Ibid., p. 144.
42. Ibid., p. 145.

can only be judged by the sort of common sense that takes pleasure in submitting to things as they are."[43]

Belief in Jesus is supported not only by historical evidence but also the convictions of the heart. These convictions tell us when a neighbor is good or evil; they also tell us when a prophet is true or false.

> Since Jesus was always kind and truthful, he bears the mark of a true prophet. Truth *cannot* be called into being by an act of power. It is the property of a judgment (or the quality of an act) which accords with the real order of things. The convictions of the heart are part of this order, and Jesus accurately represented them.[44]

Jesus' law of love as an ethic has not been improved upon in all time. If a person claimed to represent God but advocated unkindness and untruth, indecency and irresponsibility we could not accept his claims. Jesus, on the other hand, honored the convictions of the heart by His teachings and His life.

While supporting justice and love, Jesus judged injustice and pride. In self-interest we esteem power above kindness and love. We tend to think we can find fulfillment in life without divine grace. Necessarily Jesus condemned that reasoning. "He assures us that if we will be honest with God, God will be gracious with us."[45] But if our pride keeps us from accepting God's grace on Christ's testimony, the fault does not lie with the testimony, or the gospel, or the sincerity of the divine summons. What then if we accept salvation by grace?

> With pride dethroned, we are able to accept a much more modest concept of the self. We are delivered from the error of thinking that we must prove ourselves all the time. Kindness and truth overwhelm us, for we are content to leave the work of salvation to God.[46]

CHRISTIANITY'S AMAZING ADEQUACY FOR MAN'S PSYCHOLOGICAL NEEDS

Also pioneering in a psychologically oriented apologetic is the president of Conservative Baptist Theological Seminary, Vernon C. Grounds. His Ph.D. dissertation at Drew University assessed the concept of love in the psychology of Sigmund Freud. In demand as a counselor and speaker on Christianity and psychology, Dr. Grounds

43. Ibid., p. 148.
44. Ibid., p. 149.
45. Ibid., p. 152.
46. Ibid., p. 153.

has also authored numerous articles in this field. His series of articles in *His* magazine (January 1963 - February 1964) was entitled "Psychiatry and Christianity." These considerations of the tensions between naturalistic psychiatric theory and relevant Christian teaching contribute significantly to understanding of the issue involved. These include rival views of reality (naturalistic and theistic), man, conversion, ethics, and therapy. The series presupposes the truth of Christianity and does not explicitly seek to defend its truth. Indirectly, however, it serves the apologetic purpose of removing unnecessary misunderstanding between the fields. For these two disciplines this is a highly important service.

A more explicit defense of the faith appears in some of Dr. Grounds' other contributions. "Christian Perspectives on Mental Illness," published by *The Journal of the American Scientific Affiliation* (December 1962), outlines Christianity's amazing resources for meeting the problems of mental health. For one thing, people suffering from an overwhelming sense of personal and cosmic irrationality will find in Christianity just the antidote they need.

First, Christians can have "a conviction of life's meaningfulness" and "a framework of orientation and devotion." Second, anxious people threatened by futility, guiltiness, and non-being may find in Christian faith courage to live and courage to die in the hope of a death-annulling resurrection. Neuroses-ridden people, in the third place, may exchange self-debilitating, neighbor-destroying hate for assurance of divine love which brings status and security and an outgoing love for others.

Fourth, Christianity's relevance to men's needs includes more than meaning, courage, and love. It also provides, as mental health demands, forgiveness as the antidote for guilt; fifth, fellowship for alienation; sixth, power for impotence and hope for despair. Can all of these ingredients be found in one prescription?

> Conveniently they are to be found in the Gospel exclusively—or at least with an adequacy that makes the Gospel an unrivaled antidote for neurosis. Dare I say that, if mental health and healing demand self-understanding, self-identity, self-acceptance, self-release, and self-investment, if this is their demand, then the Gospel of Jesus Christ

seems to possess extraordinary resources for alleviating mental illness?[47]

Similarly, "Psychology and the Gospel"[48] cites authorities on the necessary components of mental health and shows Christianity's amazing adequacy. It supplies an optimum of faith and insight so desperately needed by those suffering from neuroses.

Christian love is not an outdated, useless sentimentalism. Love is a relevant dynamic in today's world of competitive business and nuclear tension. In "Love: Poetry or Power" Grounds supports this thesis with authorities not prejudiced in favor of Christianity. Bertrand Russell, the English philosopher who wrote *Why I Am Not a Christian*, called upon the nations to have "love, Christian love, or compassion." He said, "If you feel this, you have a motive for existence, a guide to action, a reason for courage, an imperative necessity for intellectual honesty." And the noted anthropologist, Dr. Ashley Montague, concluded that a society doomed by the self-interest of criminally irresponsible adventurers can only survive if love survives. In his words:

> The dominant principle that informs all behavior which is biologically healthy is love. . . . Without love there can be no healthy social behavior, co-operation, or security. To 'love thy neighbor as thyself' is not simply a good text for a Sunday morning sermon; it is perfectly sound biology.

Similarly, Grounds quotes Harvard's sociologist, Pitirim Sorokin:

> Hate begets hate, violence engenders violence, hypocrisy is answered by hypocrisy, war generates war, and love creates love. Unselfish love has enormous creative and therapeutic potentialities, far greater than most people think. Love is a life-giving force, necessary for physical, mental and moral health.

The love men so desperately need today is offered freely in Christianity. Love characterizes the Creator (1 Jn 4:8). Love is the pivot of our relationship to God and men (Mt 22:37-40). Compared with anything else love excels (1 Co 13:1-3). It excels because it enables

47. Vernon C. Grounds, "Christian Perspectives on Mental Illness," *The Journal of the American Scientific Affiliation* 14 (December 1962): 111.
48. This and other articles by Dr. Grounds are available in the mimeographed study series at Conservative Baptist Theological Seminary, Denver, Colorado.

us to be what we could never be without it (1 Co 13:4-7), and it out-
lasts anything else (1 Co 13:8).

Faithful love is the prescription, not only for individual health but
also organizational soundness. Difficulties in churches and denominational fellowships arise for many reasons, but one of the most frequent factors is a lack of love. Drawing from the diagnosis of group
illness by Murray, Barnard, and Garland, in their *Integrative Speech*,
Dr. Grounds points out that groups become sick when members experience coldness, anxiety, and tension, bitterly criticize the leader in
private rather than in appropriate public debate, lack confidence in
the group's leadership, unrealistically overrate the organization's position and practices, divide up into cliques, leave active participation to
a few, become jealous, confused, and uncertain about the group.

What can Christianity do for a group in such a case? Members
must first acknowledge the illness for what it is. Its destructive tendencies are not ultimately of God, but are fleshly and satanic. All
leaders and members must recognize the ceaseless operation of original sin in the depths of their own hearts. And all leaders and members who would arrest a malignancy in their movement must recognize the priority of love in all their relationships and activities. This
love is combined with faithfulness to the platform which constitutes
the group's reason for existence. In these ways the breadth, balance,
and brotherhood of a group may be recovered.

Facing Difficulties Realistically

Now the questions rise on every hand. If Christianity has such
potential for relieving mental illness, why are so many Christians neurotic? If Christianity has the answer to the world's tensions, why,
after nearly two thousand years is the world still in such a mess? And
if the Gospel contains the solution to disunity among fellowships of
people, why is the church so divided and why are the denominations
so sick?

Dr. Grounds faces these probing questions in "Christian Perspectives on Mental Illness." We must recognize that "sainthood and
psychic soundness are not commensurables." The characteristics of
mental health, such as self-reliance, growth motivation, a unifying
outlook on life, independence of social influence, empathy, and a
creative capacity for love, work, and play, have not always accom-

panied even the most heroic faith in Christ. The relationship between Christian faith and psychic soundness is admittedly complex. Since conflicts, tensions, fears, guilt, scrupulosity, and aggressiveness may remain, care must be taken in stating the claim for Christianity as a panacea.

The difference between Christianity's potential and its realization may be traced in part to a misunderstanding of the Gospel.

> Will any honest evangelical deny that the Gospel is sometimes misinterpreted? Again and again sermons present the good news of redemption and release as gloomy, morbid, world-denying, puritanical, and repressive. God is frequently portrayed not as He really is, the God of Abraham, Isaac, and Jacob, the covenant-keeping God, the God and Father of Jesus Christ, the God of wisdom, power, righteousness, love and grace. He is portrayed instead as a sadistic monster, a legalistic tyrant, a cosmic egotist, obsessed with minutiae and taboos. It is no wonder, then, that the adherents of a misinterpreted Christianity fail to enjoy a larger measure of psychic health.

Furthermore, the gospel is often misapplied.

> An individual may profess faith in Christianity, but what if his faith never issues in a personal experience of the new birth? What if it issues only in formal affiliation with a church? What if it is never internalized? . . . What if, as William James says, it remains a dull habit? Under such circumstances we need not be surprised if our own unique faith, sadly misapplied, demonstrates little value, no value, or minus value with respect to healthymindedness.

The relationship between health and Christianity, Dr. Grounds maintains, is analogous to that between physical health and Christianity. Christians are necessarily concerned about the whole man's well-being, but their primary concern is neither for physical nor mental health, but for the individual's relationship to God. People may have physical and mental health but be alienated from God. On the other hand, illness, mental as well as physical, can occasion commitment, or deeper commitment to Christ. Ultimately, the primary issues are sin and redemption. In a choice between spiritual renewal and psychic recovery, Christianity unhesitatingly assigns priority to the spiritual dimensions of personality. Ultimately, health of mind and body are of value only as used to serve and glorify God.

WHEN CHRISTIANITY IS IMPERATIVE

To say, however, that the relationship between Christianity and mental health is complex is not to say that Christianity is in any sense unnecessary. Christianity's resources meet needs psychiatry can never meet. While appreciating the contributions of psychiatry, therefore, the Christian cannot ignore its limitations. Given the best in psychiatric competence, skill, and concern, we must consider "When and Why the Psychiatrist Can't Help You."

Under that title Dr. Grounds observes, in the first place, that "the psychiatrist cannot help us when we are up against the problem of *real* guilt." If we are distressed by incessant guilt feelings because of some trifling mistake, the psychiatrist can be of invaluable help. But when the cause of torment is found to be an actual violation of God's law, the psychiatrist may listen to the rehearsal of it, but he cannot forgive it. Forgiveness is precisely what the guilty need.

> For when a person faces his sin and sees it for what it is, he insists that somehow or other he ought ... to make right the wrong he has done. Somehow or other he ought to be punished; somehow or other he ought to suffer; yes, somehow or other he ought to atone. That explains why a neurotic often keeps on punishing himself. Frantically, and futilely he is attempting to atone for his wrongdoing.

Christianity's good news in no way minimizes evil acts or the real guilt of men. But it tells us that in mercy and grace Jesus Christ made right all the wrong we have done against ourselves, society, and God. As our substitute on the cross, He bore our penalty and provided an atonement infinitely adequate. For real guilt Christianity supplies a real atonement. And its power to remove guilt is received by real faith.

In the second place, the psychiatrist cannot help us when we are up against the problem of basic anxiety. He may assist us greatly when we are troubled with morbid anxieties, symptomatic of neurotic maladjustment. Unnecessary phobias may be relieved by the help of psychiatrists. But other anxieties are built into the very structure of existence. The most well-adjusted individual cannot escape them. They focus on the certainty and unpredictability of our own death. At any moment, we know not when, we may be catapulted out of time into eternity. Only the knife-edge of the present moment insecurely preserves us from disappearing from the present life. From this anxiety no psychiatric theory can deliver us. "When it comes to basic anxiety, we need a supernatural therapy. What we need is the Good News of our Saviour's death-shattering resurrection." We need to realize that neither death nor any other experience can separate us from the love of God, which is in Christ Jesus our Lord (Ro 8:38-39).

PSYCHOLOGICAL HEALTH AND THE INVISIBLE GARDENER

A believer and a unbeliever examine a garden with its weeds and flowers. Why does one believe in an invisible Gardener? He suggests with Carnell and Grounds that the two look at their own experience. Here they are, human beings who prefer health to sickness. They suffer, not only from physical illness but also mental illness. Some help is forthcoming from the psychiatrist, but basic existential and moral anxieties remain. For these very problems Christianity offers a diagnosis. Christianity, and Christianity alone, informs of Christ's completed atonement to remove their guilt. Christianity, and Christianity alone, reports the Savior's resurrection, removing the fear of death itself. Christianity answers these universal human experiences as no other philosophy of religion does. Christianity's truth-claims, therefore, may be accepted. Christian faith displaces irrationality with meaning, anxiety with courage, hate with love, guilt with forgiveness, alienation with fellowship, impotence with dynamic, despair with hope, and pride with humility. If truth about reality includes truth about man's psychological well-being, then Christianity is true.

EVALUATION

This psychologically oriented apologetic capitalizes upon a realm of high interest. Its relevance and communicative power are exceptional as publicity increases concerning psychosomatic illnesses and guilt feelings. Combined with the data from ethics and values, it shows how Christianity indeed ministers to the whole man. Since everyone in some measure experiences anxieties about himself, his significance in this life, and his survival in the next, the appeal of apologetic targeted to these needs can hardly be exaggerated. Unquestionably Carnell struggled inwardly with anxieties characteristic of our times.

Is the psychological apologetic sufficient by itself, however, to support Christianity's truth-claims? Experientially, of course, it may serve to answer the problems that certain individuals face, and so for them become the occasion of faith. But from a theoretical point of view, it is conceivable that a religion might alleviate people's anxieties with counterfeit promises. In fact, that is what some of Christianity's cultic deviations do. Adherents of groups who disbelieve the core of Christianity claim healings of mind (and body). Contradictory truth-claims cannot be accepted because they produce mental health. But the truth about the whole of life should promote mental health. The psychological evidence of Christianity's fitness to human experience when combined with the empirical and axiological evidence is an important contribution.

RESOURCES FOR RESEARCH

Carnell, Edward John. *The Kingdom of Love and the Pride of Life.* Grand Rapids: Eerdmans, 1960. Psychotherapy has shown that people who have lost the zest of the unconditional faith of childhood cannot regain happiness without love. And there is no love without humility. The Gospel of Christ, the apologist shows, is precisely the remedy that men need psychologically.

Grounds, Vernon C. "Christian Perspectives on Mental Illness." *Journal of the American Scientific Affiliation* 14 (December 1962): 108-13. Presents the newest apologetic for the gospel—its value in terms of mental hygiene—by outlining its amazing resources for helping to alleviate mental illness.

————. "The Hope of the Gospel and the Gospel of Hope." Conservative Baptist Theological Seminary Study Series. Mimeographed. Denver: Conservative Baptist Theological Seminary, n.d. In a day of increasing pessimism and despair Christianity offers hope.

————. "Love: Poetry or Power?" CBTS Study Series. Mimeographed. Denver: Conservative Baptist Theological Seminary, n.d. Christian love is no mere irrelevant sentimentalism, but a saving force and redemptive power that excels, enables, and endures.

————. "Psychiatry and Christianity." *His* 23-24 (January 1963-February 1964). A thorough analysis of the relation between Christianity and recent thought in psychiatry including articles on: "Tensions," "Rival Views of Reality," "What Kind of God?" "The Mystery of Man,"

"Tension Over Therapy," "Conversion," "Tension Over Ethics," and "Potential Allies."

———. "Psychology and the Gospel." CBTS Study Series. Mimeographed. Denver: Conservative Baptist Theological Seminary, n.d. Only the Gospel supplies the essentials of optimum personality health: faith, hope, love, and insight.

———. "Study for Skeptics" *His* 18 (April 1958) : 8-13. Unbelief as well as belief may be an infantile hangover emotionally motivated, the product of ignorant fear and social pressure.

———. "When and Why the Psychiatrist Can't Help You." CBTS Study Series. Mimeographed. Denver: Conservative Baptist Theological Seminary, n.d. With appreciation of psychiatry's values, Dr. Grounds points out that at its best it cannot supply an atonement for real guilt before God, nor a resurrection for the inevitable threat of death.

10

THE VERIFICATIONAL APPROACH OF EDWARD JOHN CARNELL: ETHICS

THE TEST OF RESOLVING MAN'S MORAL PREDICAMENT

AN "OPEN-MINDED" PERSON today frequently pays so much attention
to sense data from without that he closes his mind to moral data from
within. Edward John Carnell's *Christian Commitment* dares the
open-minded to take a careful look at themselves. Introspection,
Carnell thinks, discloses the fact that we are held by moral considerations that cannot be rationalized away. We may choose to ignore this
data, just as Christian Scientists choose to ignore the data of the senses.
But we do so to our own loss. Humility before the evidence is the
condition of all learning.

Facing up to the data of human morality, then, Carnell asks us
simply to analyze its components. He does not argue from the fact
of right and wrong by the principle of causality to a moral God.
Analysis is not inductive or deductive inference from experience to
something outside. Neither is analysis simply a phenomenological
description of our experiences. It is a reflective discrimination of the
various elements already present in our experience. It cannot be
done by proxy through what we hear from others. It is our own
unique experience that we are encouraged to analyze. And we simply
ask what, if anything, makes it meaningful.

CASE STUDY IN HUMAN CONDUCT

Trying his hand at examining an experience uniquely his, Carnell
fed pigeons in the city park. At the top of his notebook he wrote,

"To what am I committed as I freely choose to go to the city park?" But in investigating this simple question he sensed that he was responsible to know the implications of his action.[1] By going to the park he risked all the dangers that can happen to anyone out-of-doors. Is he responsible for the hazards of rain, lightning, disease, and being robbed? Carnell concludes that he is not responsible unless these things could have been anticipated by reasonable foresight.

Risks would not have been avoided by staying home, however. There he could have choked on a cracker or fallen downstairs. "All of life is organized against a legion of insecurities."[2] Although every freely initiated action is attended by risks, *"All men must act."*[3] This is the universal starting point for knowing one's self. No normal person could avoid activity.

If we are responsible insofar as we can anticipate eventualities of our actions, then nature must be regular. Just as meaningful speech implies the law of non-contradiction, meaningful action implies the law of uniformity. If relativists try to deny this truth, their action of standing confidently on the floor betrays their position. "There is no direct way to show this, of course. If relativists refuse to view the matter through the realities that already hold them, they will remain as blind to the law of uniformity as skeptics are to the law of non-contradiction (which makes their arguments for skepticism meaningful). Ultimates cannot be seen unless the heart is controlled by right affections."[4]

MORAL RESPONSIBILITY

Analyzing our personal actions, we find two kinds of responsibility. (1) When we buy an automobile we are already committed to uniform laws of nature. We must admit responsibility for knowing what is universally necessary to the driving of the vehicle. (2) We are also accountable for our particular driving. If arrested for violating a law, we cannot argue that we were unaware of it. We are responsible for laws governing safe driving. Our responsibility for the consequences of our driving is a judicial obligation. Allowing for conse-

---

1. Edward John Carnell, *Christian Commitment: An Apologetic* (New York: Macmillan, 1957), p. 34.
2. Ibid., p. 35.
3. Ibid., p. 36.
4. Ibid., p. 43.

quences of mere inconvenience, and honest mistaking of fact or law, the simple act of operating a moving vehicle implies moral responsibility.

The fact that any actions carry such responsibility reveals our belief in the possibility of moral uprightness ("personal rectitude"). Routine conduct reveals our belief in general being. Excited conduct mirrors our belief in values. Morally inspired conduct discloses our belief in uprightness.[5] So the actions for which we regard ourselves responsible are an index to our moral convictions. Because we are excited about these issues and may praise or blame ourselves for our decisions, it is difficult to be honest. Utter intellectual honesty, however, is a necessary condition of research, not only in the laboratory, but also in the inner man.

Human morality is vastly more complex than the scientific method suggests. At best a scientific tabulation of moral habits indicates only what others profess to hold, or choose to reveal. There is little reason to believe that the true convictions of a tribe appear in an empirical coverage of their moral habits. Do any people live up to their beliefs? On these matters is it not easy to deceive? Why do prophets speak against the mores of their cultures? And why did Socrates choose to die rather than to escape from prison? "The surface realities of a culture may only cloak a set of absolutes which are inwardly known and spiritually feared. 'For what can be known about God is plain to them, because God has shown it to them' (Ro 1:19)."[6]

The universality of moral standards is indicated by the fact that all men make comparative judgments. They judge that some courses of action are better than others. We must ask, better in relation to what? Without a standard we would not know which action was closer to it. To illustrate, if we did not know how long a foot was, we could not know whether two inches or eleven inches was closest to a foot. Because moral standards are present in all men, all are responsible for their judgments and conduct.

PERSONAL FELLOWSHIP

The presence of norms for right and wrong conduct is indicated also in our relationships with persons. Carnell asked, "To what realities am I committed when I freely stand in the society of others?"[7]

5. Ibid., p. 49.
6. Ibid., p. 54.
7. Ibid., p. 55.

Consider first the situation of meeting total strangers. A stranger requests directions to a given address. We feel no compulsion to comply unless he shows signs of respect for us. In thinking about experiences with strangers, it does not take long to realize that "we are powerless to trust others unless they give evidence of accepting the dignity of our persons."[8] Anyone who seeks fellowship must extend fellowship. But even if another is not friendly we are morally responsible to treat him, not as a thing, but a human being.

> If a person is so foolish as to deny either the law of contradiction or the law of uniformity, that is his private affair. But if he dares to deny the law of our dignity, we instantly abandon our detached attitude. Under no conditions, real or presumed, will we grant him the privilege of deciding whether or not he finds it personally interesting to regard us. This demand is a category of our spiritual life; it is a priori to the moral sense.[9]

Relationships between friends, upon analysis, disclose this rule: "The more spiritually intimate the relation is, or the more power a person has to threaten or support our happiness, the more we look for evidences that our dignity is being regarded."[10] The initial greeting may be a nod, a smile, a handshake, or an embrace, depending on the situation, the relationship, and the temperament of the people. But it must be sincere. The season of fellowship completes one's own life in and through the life of the other. "Fellowship looks for a twinkle in the eye, a cheery word, and a steady refusal to challenge the other's integrity, even though points of view differ."[11] A parting farewell assures that nothing will alter the unconditional obligation in trust.

Significant public communication also rests on a tacit moral contract. Who would trust a speaker who did not subscribe to the "absolute" that "one must say in word what he intends in meaning."[12] So a lecturer on relativity contradicts himself. He attacks all absolutes, but an absolute is indispensable to his being understood.

In all cases, then, a person *ought* to respect other persons. Respect for persons is a moral necessity. But it must at the same time be sin-

8. Ibid.
9. Ibid., p. 56.
10. Ibid., p. 57.
11. Ibid., p. 61.
12. Ibid., p. 65.

cere and free. How can we understand this paradox? We need not abandon either the necessity or the freedom. A moral act is free because it is natural, and necessary because issuing from the moral and spiritual environment.[13] Kant was not successful in his attempt to base personal respect on a need for self-consistency. Whenever people receive us because of respect for rational self-consistency, we are offended. We are not properly received if the sheer presence of our person fails to excite moral respect.[14] Professors who propound rational theories of ethics overlook the realities that hold them in their classes. "Rational conditions of validity are powerless to communicate a sense of moral duty. Rationalists are always embarrassed by the question, 'Why *should* a man be moral?' "[15]

Suppose it is argued that fellowship may be based on practical (pragmatic) motives. If we talk about things that interest other people and compliment them whenever possible, they will do nice things for us. "This may influence people, but it will never win friends; for the act has no moral value."[16] Unless one's real purpose is concealed, the relationship will not continue. A feigned sincerity is nothing but the worst kind of hypocrisy.

Sören Kierkegaard denounced a merely formal ethnic in favor of spontaneous moral decision. Unfortunately, however, his passionate ethical life clouded his intellect.[17] Passion must be guided by the seriousness of truth. We cannot wisely commit ourselves in personal relations, any more than in anything else, when evidence is insufficient. But with sufficient indications of respect we may freely trust people and so fulfill our moral responsibility to them.

WHEN HUMAN RIGHTS ARE VIOLATED

Continuing an analysis of inner experience, Carnell asks, "To what moral realities am I committed when those in the circles of nearness refuse to show signs of fellowship?"[18] Indifference is impossible when people violate a person's dignity or his rights in society.

> Even as dignity comprehends the secret essence of personality, so rights comprehend its social expression. . . . Freedom to express our-

13. Ibid., pp. 66-67.
14. Ibid., p. 68.
15. Ibid., p. 72.
16. Ibid., p. 69.
17. Ibid., p. 75.
18. Ibid., p. 85.

selves is not an adventitious element that can be added or subtracted without altering the essence of our dignity. It is as indispensable to our essence as the beating of the heart. An attack on our rights is an attack on our person.[19]

The question then becomes, "To what moral realities are we committed when our rights are violated?"[20] A clerk knowingly bypasses us to wait on someone who came into the store later than we did. We are offended. When any feelings of personal revenge have subsided, we can distinguish a moral issue from one of mere taste by this criterion: "A morally provoked feeling can be defended with the consent of our nobler faculties and the praise of men of character."[21] Our offended moral faculty judges people guilty for treating people as things, and denying them their human rights.

THE ADMINISTRATION OF JUSTICE

However, Jesus said, "Judge not." Christ's command forbids not our discrimination between right and wrong, Carnell reasons, but our vengeance upon those who violate our dignity or rights. We have no native right to enforce the law against the guilty. But our recognition of their liability before the law is the only thing that distinguishes guilt from a vague feeling of personal unhappiness. We are to blend self-love with duty. In self-love we may defend our rights, but in doing our duty we will not become self-appointed administrators of justice. "Ethicists usually make one of two capital errors. Either they deny man's concreated sense of dignity, and so end up with a formalistic ethic that outrages the heart; or they recognize the omnipresence of self-love, but fail to anchor it in a sense of duty."[22]

Although we have no authority to enforce moral law, we continue to judge culpability before it. An unenforced law, however, is inoperative. This law is operative in our daily experience. "Even as meaningful speech implies the law of contradiction, . . . so meaningful moral judgment implies the administrator of justice."[23] Unless all moral judgment is pointless, we are faced with the reality, not

19. Ibid., p. 86.
20. Ibid., p. 87.
21. Ibid., p. 90.
22. Ibid., p. 97.
23. Ibid., p. 103.

merely the possibility, of an omnipresent Administrator of justice. "Realities to which we are committed by existence itself need only be impressed not proved."[24]

Is the Administrator of human moral responsibility, then, a thing or a person? To be responsible means to be liable to give account to. We do not give account to things, but persons, not to an investment made in us, but to its benefactor. Similarly an account of moral behavior cannot be given to a thing, but must be made to a person. Is it then to the person offended? No, pride would delight to mete out justice, but then it would not be justice. Can we give account to people in general? Hardly. To the state? "The state is an impersonal entity, and it is meaningless to render account to a thing. This may not flatter dictators, but it is nonetheless the truth."[25] And the representatives of states may themselves violate the principles of morality. Neither can citizens surrender their rights to the state. "Men cannot surrender what they do not have. Freedom is a privilege accorded by God."[26]

Yes, the ground of our being as persons and the administrator of justice are one and the same. Other explanations failing, we cannot escape the fact that the omnipresence of God's person alone completes the picture. By "person" Carnell means "freedom expressed through moral self-consciousness." And by "God" he means "that person to whom violators of our dignity must give an account."[27] If men were morally autonomous, juridical decisions would be the expression of personal interest, not of law and right. Our system of jurisprudence protected itself against such expediency by requiring an oath in the name of God. Appreciating man's participation in the divine moral and spiritual environment, the founders inscribed on Harvard's Langdell Hall, *Non sub homine sed sub Deo et lege* (not under man, but under God and law). "That which is indispensable to a given condition cannot meaningfully be repudiated by one who stands within the privileges of that condition."[28]

So by analysis of moral experience we know that we must act, we are responsible, and we recognize a standard of uprightness. Violation of that standard results in guilt, and meaningful guilt requires

24. Ibid.
25. Ibid., p. 107.
26. Ibid.
27. Ibid., p. 108.
28. Ibid., p. 109.

a personal Administrator of justice. God is not the conclusion of Carnell's argument here, but a requirement of a meaningful analysis of morality.

PREPARING TO MEET GOD

Knowing that God exists, however, is no substitute for meeting God personally. Since God is a person, we may become acquainted with Him. God is not far from any one of us. He it is who invariably defends our dignity. In Him we live and move and have our moral and spiritual being. We may be very close to a person, however, and not enjoy fellowship with him. How do we begin acquainting ourselves with the person of God?

We may show signs of gratitude for His support of morality. When people recognize our dignity, we sense an obligation to acknowledge theirs. Nothing arouses the judicial sentiment more quickly than ingratitude. But the more we try to be grateful, the more we realize the insufficiency of our resources adequately to do so. Our expressions of thanksgiving may be anything but spontaneous before Him who sees our innermost thoughts. Paradoxically, "we cannot thank God unless we have fellowship with God; but our very want of thankfulness is itself a barrier to fellowship."[29]

Of course the assumption of these analogies between human and divine relationships denies that God is totally other than man. Because our judicial sentiment contacts a changelessly just Person, we know that God shares the same moral and spiritual environment (but not the same essence, as in pantheism). If there is no point of identity between God and man, "nothing significant can be known or said about God—not even that there is a God, let alone that God is a person."[30] "Because God is immanent, as well as transcendent, most of the debate about 'point of contact' is mere sophomoric quibbling. God is 'wholly other' only in a very special sense."[31] "A proud and overweening attitude blocks the flow of fellowship as effectively as insulation blocks the flow of electricity."[32] Fellowship with God is not possible when we are too proud for it. God reveals Himself to us "whenever the right moral conditions prevail."[33] Otherwise He

29. Ibid., p. 129.
30. Ibid., p. 137.
31. Ibid., p. 139.
32. Ibid., p. 150.
33. Ibid., p. 151.

would violate His own moral and spiritual principles. God does not require sacrifices and offerings, but humility (Mic 6:6-8). He opposes the proud and gives grace to the humble (Ja 4:6).

We may humbly seek fellowship for two reasons: because we have to and because we love to. No one appreciates forced respect, whether by a Kantian rational necessity or another. On the other hand, we may freely express "the law of the spirit of life" which always involves "a cordial pleasure in doing what is right."[34] Unless an act fulfills the law it is not moral; but an act fulfilling the letter of the law (selfishly or maliciously) also is not moral. Hypocritical humility before God is valueless.

THE ROLE OF REPENTANCE

Suppose that a person has been ungrateful for benefits received, what can he do to be received back into fellowship? For example, on a busy highway you change a flat tire for a lady only to meet an icy indifference. What condition must she meet to be received again into fellowship? She must sincerely apologize. An apology is sufficient when the offense is such a single specifiable incident. Then the offended person must forgive or he in turn is guilty. Whether the apology is accepted or rejected, the one who apologizes ends with reasonable security.[35]

When there have been repeated offenses, a simple apology does not release from guilt. For a habitual offender the only hope is genuine repentance. Admitting that he can never deserve forgiveness, he simply throws himself on the mercy of the "court." Despairing of finding a legal way out, the repentant person inquires whether the offended party can possibly forgive one unworthy of forgiveness. We find ourselves in this condition before God. By nature and by choice we have habitually failed to express spontaneous gratitude to God. We have proudly ignored His presence.

THE LAW OF CONSIDERATION

The meaning of repentance shows that there is more to morality than justice. Justice alone does not satisfy our moral and spiritual environment. Our judicial sentiment is often aroused when justice is met. "Although rectitude may never exist apart from justice, jus-

34. Ibid., p. 161.
35. Ibid., p. 165.

tice is not necessarily the same thing as rectitude."[36] People talking on a party line are asked to relinquish their first right to it because of an emergency. They have it first and so in justice may continue their conversation. But a higher concern now operates. The law of consideration is called for when an act of a person within his rights annoys us. We request him to stop the annoying act as a special favor to us. Convinced that he does not intend to offend us, we appeal to his consideration for others. "Society is held together by inconsiderate people who are willing to give and seek forgiveness."[37]

Although we desire to be considerate, often we are inconsiderate. Because of our human depravity we never do "directly meet the terms of law." When we fail to fulfill its standards of goodness, we may indirectly satisfy them by "being sorry for our failure to be good." Our inability to keep the law "in no way invalidates our responsibility to be sincerely sorry for our self-centered affections."[38]

THE LAW OF LOVE

Justice and consideration, however, do not exhaust the demands of morality. The law of justice applies to matters in which we are formally one with the whole human race. When we meet the terms of a contract, we expect the other party to do the same. We are satisfied that justice is received if we receive what all others would receive. When we reveal our particular differences from the race (allergies, perhaps), we pass from justice to consideration. But "justice and consideration only answer to as much of our person as we happen to reveal."[39] What about the mysteries we choose not to reveal? With all of justice and consideration our whole person has not been received. Much remains unrevealed and hidden. An obligation falls upon others by the sheer presence of our person. Here we have come to the pith and marrow of the imperative essence, the law of love.

A truly moral individual, Carnell concludes, "accepts our lives for what they are, both in the way they are revealed and in the way they are hidden." In other words, he loves. "Only love accepts another without forecast, interest, or calculation. . . . Love cheerfully limits itself by the mystery of the beloved; . . . it never challenges

36. Ibid., p. 176.
37. Ibid., p. 194.
38. Ibid., p. 200.
39. Ibid., p. 205.

or distrusts; it bears up under all phase changes, wishing nothing but good."[40] In this sense God is love; and in this sense humans must love their neighbors. "The one who abides in love abides in God, and God abides in him" (1 Jn 4:16). Since love is the most comprehensive expression of morality, an aroused judicial sentiment signifies a lack of love. An offense against love, in the final analysis, is an offense against God. Justice and consideration apart from love profit nothing. Love indirectly fulfills the law. By expressing the law of love the judicial sentiment is "the narrow point of contact between time and eternity."[41]

A paradox appears again in relation to love. Although we are responsible to love persons who simply enter the circle of nearness, we lack the power to fulfill this infinite responsibility authentically. We simply find it beyond our power to love all the drivers on the crowded highways, all the shoppers in the stores, all the neighbors in our community. But the very presence of their persons calls for more than justice and consideration, it calls for love. Since we are held by the law of love, we are in a perilous moral position before God.

> In sum, each time a person stands before us we are on trial before God. We can always do more good than we have in the past; more to relieve destitution and distress, more to guide, direct, and forgive. Being made in the image of God, we are already in contact with the essence of rectitude; for God is love. Moral uneasiness over selfishness is the voice of God speaking to and against our heart. The more perfect a man becomes, the clearer this truth becomes.[42]

Our guilt before God's law of love may be seen as well from the ambiguity of tragic moral choices. "A choice is tragic when one consciously chooses evil in order that a greater good may come."[43] In the complexities of life we cannot escape these choices, illustrated by the Greek tragedians. Does the loving physician tell the patient the seriousness of his disease? Does a guest tell the hostess the truth about his experience or confirm her pride? Is the ethical problem resolved by expressions of appreciation for the hostess' effort? Truth, Carnell points out, "pertains to what we know others *think* we intend, rather

40. Ibid., p. 207.
41. Ibid., p. 209.
42. Ibid., pp. 222-23.
43. Ibid., p. 223.

than to the strict semantical limits of our words."[44] We must evaluate appreciative statements differently, as Samuel Johnson saw, when they are called for and when they are spontaneous. Every preacher distinguishes the routine comments following his sermons from spontaneous expressions upon occasions which do not require support for his self-respect. Knowing how important it is that people feel appreciated, we find ourselves forever in these dilemmas. How can we be faithful to both truth and love?

Judging casuistical attempts to escape the dilemma a failure, Carnell concludes that we acknowledge moral claims when we hate the inescapably evil course we choose. So Paul recognized his own wretchedness (Ro 7:22-23). And this is why God could justify Rahab, the harlot who lied about hiding Jewish spies (Heb 11:31).

> What, may I ask, *should* Rahab have done? If she had forthrightly told the king that she was concealing spies, she would have abetted the murder of God's chosen people. Realizing that a choice between levels of good had to be made, she did what any moral person in her place would have done. 'We must obey God rather than men.' (Acts 5:29). God, who reads the heart, saw that she would have told the truth if she had been morally free to do so. She was a good woman because she hated the very thing she did.[45]

Between what we are and what we ought to be lies a great chasm. We cannot escape the insecurity of tragic moral choices. Our best attempts at loving our neighbors fail before moral law. We find it literally impossible to treat everyone with justice, consideration, and love.

Nevertheless, all normal human beings are morally responsible for living justly, considerately, and lovingly. Civilized or uncivilized, educated or uneducated, all of us know that it is wrong to violate the moral environment which holds us. "Whether or not one has right moral standards is irrelevant, for all men should be sorry for not doing the good as they know it."[46] In terms of the requirements of their cultures, people show that what the law requires is written on their hearts (Ro 2:14-16). God's judgment of all men is perfectly just. "And from everyone who has been given much shall much be required; and to whom they entrusted much, of him, they will ask all

44. Ibid., p. 226.
45. Ibid., p. 229.
46. Ibid., p. 238.

the more" (Lk 12:48). All men know that the good is to be done and the evil avoided. But just as clearly all men are guilty before God. In humility each of us must acknowledge his sin. We must repent. "One cannot legally thread his way through the labyrinth of human relations. Everything we do is morally ambiguous. Self-love taints all but the rarest expressions of sacrifice and courage."[47]

HOW TO BE JUST BEFORE GOD

Analysis of our moral environment can take us no further than the point of throwing ourselves upon the mercy of the divine court. General revelation, as the theologians call it, assures us that God cannot receive sinners apart from right moral conditions. These remain unknown. So in order to consider whether Christianity answers to moral reality, we must turn to its primary available source: written revelation. Since we have no claim upon God, if He has chosen to reconcile us to Himself, we should be the last to spurn His love. Even if we reject the biblical atonement, we ought to know what it is that we are turning down.[48]

How then can a sinner be just before God? God's judicial sentiment has been continuously offended. He can pardon only when that moral nature is propitiated. In amazing love for those who would not repent and could in no way justify themselves, the offended Deity sent Christ to die. So God turned away His holy wrath by the overwhelming act of His holy love. Christ propitiated the judicial sentiment in God by fulfilling all righteousness during His life and bearing divine wrath in His death as the sinner's substitute. On this basis God remains just and justifies those who are united to Christ by faith. We are reconciled to God, not by our wretched attempts to keep the law, but by our trust in Christ. So as we have been forgiven, infinitely forgiven, we should be always willing to forgive at the first signs of repentance. However, if we reject an offer of pardon, there remains no further way of forgiveness. An offer of pardon "does not include a pardon of the rejection of pardon."[49]

The pardoned sinner, though adopted into God's family as a righteous son, unfortunately remains sinful. Objections to Christianity because it regards a believer at the same time justified and sinful,

47. Ibid., p. 241.
48. Ibid., p. 249.
49. Ibid., p. 255.

overlook an important difference of respect. Their conduct continues to come short of the law's perfect requirements. But as God's love beholds them in Christ, their position is righteous. "A wife has an imperfect husband when judged by the law of ideal husbands, but a perfect husband when judged by love. Children are imperfect in themselves, but perfect as children."⁵⁰ God does not falsify the facts. A repentant sinner stands in a right relationship to divine law because he is rightly related to the cross. He then experiences the compulsion of love to grow in grace and knowledge. Genuine sanctification issues from genuine justification. But sanctification in this life remains incomplete. "The church is a fellowship of *forgiven* sinners, not a fellowship of *former* sinners."⁵¹ In a love that casts out fear, Christians either do the will of their Beloved, or express sorrow for having failed. In either event love is satisfied. "Just as lovers have no dread of divorce, so Christians have no dread of hell."⁵²

The faith with which this loving relationship begins is "a cordial trust in the person and work of Christ."⁵³ A person must have knowledge concerning Him, give assent to what He has done for him, and commit himself wholly to Him for deliverance from all the consequences of his sin. Cordial trust in the person of Christ does not rule out assent to knowledge about Him. Whereas traditional Catholicism neglected personal commitment, neo-orthodoxy neglected assent to true doctrine. Carnell rejects the popular distinction between "thou-truth" and "it-truth" as "an *ad hoc* invention of theologians." His crucial argument must be stated in his own strong words.

> Whenever a person enters the circle of nearness, he blends intellectual assent and spiritual commitment without any consciousness that he is leaving one realm of evidences for another. The individual before him is just as much a fact 'out there' as a bottle or a tree. The essence of personality is hidden from the eyes of science and philosophy, of course, but that is quite beside the point. Science and philosophy have no access to the essence of pain either. *Many* facts are known only as they are felt. But this does not change matters. Facts are facts, whether they are persons, pains or planets.⁵⁴

50. Ibid., p. 257.
51. Ibid., p. 260.
52. Ibid., p. 261.
53. Ibid., p. 267.
54. Ibid., p. 269.

Having been satisfied with the signs of Christ's person and work, we may approach Him in unconditional trust. Trusting Him, we gain a new perspective upon such difficulties as the problem of evil. Intimately, as a father talks with his son, God reveals His fidelity to uprightness in every respect. He leaves details for more mature stages of understanding, but reminds us of the cross, as the final answer to history's greatest evil. God's provision for our redemption could not be anticipated by human standards. But this we know, "Being good enough to receive sinners through the righteousness of Jesus Christ, he is good enough to be trusted for everything."[55] If we are not moved to thankfulness by His general goodness, we may be, by this overpowering display of His holy love.

CHOOSING A SYSTEM

All religious or philosophical systems are chosen, rather than forced. A person who thinks for himself is not forced to be a Marxist, atheistic existentialist, philosophical analyst, Muslim, Hindu, Buddhist, or a Christian. On what basis do we choose the ultimate presuppositions of one system as over against another? Carnell replies, "Systems are chosen or rejected by reason of their power to explain areas of reality that a particular individual finds important."[56] Christianity, as Carnell here considers it, solves the crucial moral predicament.

Is Christianity the true solution? Others have been proposed. How do we verify systems of thought? He answers, "Systems are verified by the degree to which their major elements are consistent with one another and with the broad facts of history and nature."[57] Christianity is true, therefore. Its major elements are consistent: the existence and personality of God, God's image in man, the moral and spiritual environment, love as the law of life, the spiritual defect in man's will and affections, and the necessity of repentance, the substitutionary atonement. Not only are these teachings consistent with each other, they harmonize with the data of our moral experience as persons with other persons. And the doctrine of substitutionary atonement alone resolves the predicament without offending our physical, rational,

55. Ibid., p. 282.
56. Ibid., p. 285.
57. Ibid., p. 286.

aesthetic, or moral environments. No other religion can give a consistent answer to this question: "How can a sinner be just before God?" All other religions support human sufficiency by suggesting that "man can resolve the moral predicament by arousing dormant virtues within him."[58] Christianity, in contrast, summons us to crucify personal pride and to live a life of repentant faith in Jesus Christ. If critics imply that other religions are thus dismissed too lightly, they are reminded that "when love is wanting, all else is inconsequential. . . . When a religious system is not founded on this truth, it is defective in its very core."[59]

Since love is central, thinking about it is insufficient. Thinking is necessary, but not enough. If a person in our presence merely thinks about us, he arouses the judicial sentiment. He does not rightly know us, respect our dignity, or fellowship with us. Similarly, it is not enough to think about loving God. Correct thinking does not constitute personal righteousness. Righteousness is achieved in life not by pharisaic law-keeping, but by spontaneous expressions of love. Thought can lead to the true Person with whom to fellowship. But the apologist cannot humbly bow in repentant faith for another. Each person in response to the divine Spirit must enter the dynamic of personal fellowship with God.

Christianity alone can resolve the individual's moral predicament. This thesis is argued also by Carl F. H. Henry in his *Christian Personal Ethics*. The former editor of *Christianity Today* contends that "Hebrew-Christian ethical realities alone can lift the Western world from the mires of paganism." And he adds, "We may soon find ourselves past the ability to break with evil, if we ignore biblical Christianity's known way of severance."[60] For a more wide-ranging exposition of Christian ethics this volume is recommended. Henry clearly sees that the Christian view "operates on its own distinctive and controlling ideas." But at the same time he insists that Christianity is "a coherent and self-consistent revelation of moral realities."[61] Only Christianity can adequately account for the present world of behavior, including: (1) the universal recognition of a right and wrong, (2)

58. Ibid., p. 294.
59. Ibid., pp. 301-2.
60. Carl F. H. Henry, *Christian Personal Ethics* (Grand Rapids: Eerdmans, 1957), p. 15.
61. Ibid., p. 150.

inability to do the right, and self-justifying efforts while rebelling against God.[62]

RESOLVING THE PREDICAMENTS OF SOCIAL ETHICS

Dr. Henry has not limited himself to personal ethics. More recently he has turned to the explosive issues threatening to destroy human society. In *Aspects of Christian Social Ethics*, Henry maintained that "for its validity and vitality social theory requires both scriptural standards and moral power."[63] Disillusionment awaits those who hope for other solutions to social enigmas. If Christians can show how their faith meets these urgent needs, little excuse will remain for challenging its relevance for our generation. Since society is made up of men who violate moral guidelines, the basic need of society is re-generated individuals. The apparent impotence of Christianity in the presence of social need, Henry asserts, stems from neglect of the potential for social change through lives responsive to supernatural impulse and motivated by spiritual concerns.

Compare the strategy of regeneration with other options. The communist theory of revolution calls for radical change of social patterns in their essential constitution through violence and compulsion. Christian tactics also express indignation over the *status quo*. However, "the former brings the whole socio-historic movement under the criticism of Marx in order to destroy it, and the latter under the criticism of Christ in order to renew it."[64]

Between the extremes of revolution and regeneration are reform and revaluation. Reform strategy builds on an evolutionary philosophy of emerging ideal society and so hopes gradually to amend particular abuses and improve prevailing social conditions. Reform strategy has two weaknesses. Because it must build on present society, reform strategy "lacks a deeply indignant criticism, and also any fixed criterion of judgment."[65] Revaluation, on the other hand, has a fixed criterion in transcendent moral norms discoverable in human experience. But it jeopardizes the norms by associating them with evolutionary theory and by failing to exhibit cosmic justification for them in the living God of the Bible.

62. Ibid., p. 151.
63. Carl F. H. Henry, *Aspects of Christian Social Ethics* (Grand Rapids: Eerdmans, 1964), p. 9.
64. Ibid., p. 18.
65. Ibid., p. 19.

While the other strategies make social issues the ultimate concern, Christians give place to theological issues. Christian leaders do not regard themselves primarily as social reformers, but as the bearers of God's entire revelation. From revealed principles the church derives her message for man's spiritual and material condition. The Creator-Redeemer's message "is basically one of supernatural redemption from sin, and the problem of social justice is placed in necessary relationship to man's need and God's provision of salvation."[66] So Christians wield a two-edged sword. They proclaim "the hard news that social evils contradict man's dignity and destiny by creation, but also the good news of a 'new heaven and new earth' assured in Jesus Christ."[67]

The dynamic of the Christian strategy for social action also vividly contrasts with the others. The revolutionary counts on brute force, the reformer on legislated morality or political compulsion achieved by democratic processes. Both of these think progress lies in changing the political environment and doing this by political action. But one seeks it more rapidly than the other. Changes of social environment apart from changes of the human perspective are insufficient. So revaluationists stress as media of social change: moral education, propaganda, conversation, and persuasion. Regeneration, on the other hand, aims "not merely to re-educate men (although it knows that the Holy Spirit uses truth—particularly the truth of the gospel—as a means of conviction), but to renew the whole man morally and spiritually through a saving experience of Jesus Christ."[68] Its dynamic is not that of force, law or education, but of Gospel. Preaching the Gospel must retain its priority. For the believer's spiritual renewal "vitalizes his awareness of God and neighbor, vivifies his sense of morality and duty, fuses the law of love to sanctified compassion, and so registers the ethical impact of biblical religion upon society."[69]

CHRISTIANITY, LABOR, AND MANAGEMENT

How then does the Christian strategy of regeneration apply to the problems of labor and management? It treats the underlying significance of a person's time. If the workweek be continually reduced and

66. Ibid., pp. 22-23.
67. Ibid., p. 23.
68. Ibid., pp. 24-25.
69. Ibid., p. 26.

the worker's life on and off the job remains meaningless, he has no challenge. "The collectivistic promise of status for the worker has become a tragic mirage. Not the worker, but his hard work, is glorified."[70] Communism has failed to provide a challenge for the worker. So has traditional Catholicism. In the Middle Ages Romanism limited the idea of vocation under God to the priestly class. "Such denial of the priesthood of all believers has two important consequences: it excludes the laity from divine service, and it elevates the priesthood above the world of labor."[71]

While Protestants have stressed the priesthood of every believer, they have often failed to see that in so doing they did not secularize the ministry but sanctified the laity. Fundamentalists modified the Catholic concept only partially, for God was thought to call only some believers to specific vocations. They were ministers, missionaries, and possibly teachers and medical doctors if tied to Christian education or missions. While fundamentalism did seek to encourage Christian attitudes on the job as an indirect witness, and the avoiding of questionable work, it "did not comprehend all work as divine vocation, as spiritual service to God and man."[72]

According to the New Testament, every believer has received God's call. All are to walk worthy of their vocation (Eph 4:1). So every Christian has reason to go beyond dutiful obedience to outgoing service. Without degrees of value or dignity, every Christian's job is "a medium in and through which the believer offers himself to God."[73] If the work obligates one to do evil, then the Christian is called to leave sinful occupations and seek a good work. And the church should encourage in positive ways its people to engage in such labor as they can pursue wholeheartedly with clear conscience. Then work would be no mere religious duty, but an opportunity for divine and human service. Dedication to such spiritual service must take precedence over salary, conditions, location, etc. "If work is primarily a means of service, and of self-giving, it ceases to be primarily a means of acquisition."[74] When Christ is Lord the ultimate concern is not the salary, but a "good work that promotes human good."[75] As G. L.

70. Ibid., p. 35.
71. Ibid., p. 36.
72. Ibid., p. 40.
73. Ibid., p. 44.
74. Ibid., p. 46.
75. Ibid.

Treglown said, "There can be no sense of purpose in making trash."

From the beginning, Henry shows, the Bible supports the dignity of work. Before the fall of man into sin, the Creator allotted Adam the task of dressing and keeping the Garden of Eden (Gen 2:15). So work is not a punishment for the fall. Work is further dignified by the example of God Himself. While in Greek philosophy thinking was higher than working and the creative acts were attributed to inferiors, the Bible teaches that God executed His purpose in heaven and earth. And He continues to do so in preserving and redeeming the fallen today. Jesus Christ incarnate also exemplifies the dignity of work. He said, "My Father worketh hitherto, and I work" (Jn 5:17, KJV). While using the carpenter's tools He grew in wisdom and stature and in favor with God and man (Lk 2:52).

But how, in a day of monotonous assembly line routines, can a person maintain this high view of work? The assembly line has been condemned by communists as a capitalistic evil and by Christians as an unchristian means of oppressing the laborer. But Henry answers that the assembly line is not a problem to capitalist economical structures alone. With all the improvements of conditions: noise absorbers, piped-in music, safety devices, and changes of assignments, the worker's life may seem meaningless without Christian purpose. How then can a Christian avoid being reduced to a mere cog in an impersonal machine? He can consider the fact that "whatever contributes to the elevation and good of mankind is worthy, even if it lacks romance and novelty."[76] Physicians specialize in order to enhance efficiency and skill. While a doctor could think of pieces of humanity coming down the line, in respect for his calling he considers each a private patient and the only patient he has. Is this not easier with persons than things? Indeed, "but no worker's responsibility is lessened simply because he serves an invisible neighbor. Many a life has been saved by a properly tightened screw, and many lost through an improperly tightened bolt."[77]

The real problem today lies deeper than machine-bound existence, assembly line routines, or the apparent insignificance of organization men! As long as the worker's commitment to God is qualified or lacking, his delight in his work will be less than satisfying. Estranged from the ultimate significance of his task, the laborer's life seems

76. Ibid., p. 59.
77. Ibid., p. 60.

pointless. Even the Christian who seeks God's glory in his work is less than satisfied if he does not give it his best. "To turn a screw with Job-like patience on an assembly line is no reproach if it represents one's highest level of creative ability. Such limitation is sinful, however, for a disciple of Christ who has greater potential for service."[78]

Christianity's relevance is challenged not only in relation to the impersonalization of assembly line work, but also the individual's apparent insignificance in terms of big business and organized labor. What can a worker do when management tells him to speed up and the union tells him to slow down? If the laborer finds himself in a union which continuously violates his principles as a faithful steward of God, he may find it possible to join the Christian Labor Association which promises opportunity to carry out one's conviction on the job. In unions where service, let alone service to God, is not primary, he may nevertheless cooperate whenever the purpose is not anti-God. His highest "boss" is God, and his highest brotherhood the body of Christ. Christians in management are subject to the same Lord and are members of the same brotherhood. Recognition of Christ's lordship does not destroy the functional distinctions between labor and management, nor make men perfect, but it does exclude "both the cringing worker and the tyrannical employer."[79] Furthermore it means taking pride in one's work and "a contagious sense of creative contribution and service." It lifts men beyond greed to seek God's justice and love.

THE CHRISTIAN AND THE STATE

Although Christians seek to transform society by regeneration and radically criticize the status quo, they do not find everything in society bad. In addition to seeking regeneration of individuals they seek the preservation of present social values. Not all Christians are agreed on ways and means but they can scarcely avoid some responsibility in regard to democratic forms of government. "Whatever we may think about the fact, political forces are indeed determining the future more and more."[80] While political programs will not solve all problems they have certain legitimate objectives which Christians can and should support. Christian citizenship is not fulfilled merely in attacking legislation which violates revealed principle. Christian

78. Ibid., p. 61.
79. Ibid., p. 65.
80. Ibid., p. 76.

citizens ought to promote legislation which is in accord with Scripture, and an atmosphere in which that can be done. The objective is not union of church and state, not favored prestige and power in the political realm, and not a universal Christian society (an alleged "kingdom of God"). Rather, the church seeks indirectly to promote "the welfare of society as a whole."[81] It emphasizes that "the political order does not exist for the enforcement of sectarian objectives."[82]

Numerous Scriptural injunctions call upon the Christian to promote public morality by personal example and a positive spirit. We must pray for (not against) rulers, honor them as ordained of God, render to Caesar what is "ideally Caesar's," support the state as a guardian of peace and justice, pay taxes, and call the state to account for its stewardship under God. Other reasons support responsible involvement, according to Carl Henry. When the Christian concept of government is not advanced, an incorrect notion is adopted. Such false and sometimes idolatrous notions must be dispelled. The urgency of world crisis cries out for the legitimate but limited authority of civil government. This is critical not only in the contexts of totalitarian tyranny but also in democracies weakened by relativism. "Where it is no longer held that the individual is somehow directly related to the eternal, it is scarcely possible to maintain that the State must secure the rights of the individual."[83]

The State as Servant of Social Justice

The church, then, cannot fulfill its calling in the world and fail to tell the world that the state is merely a servant of eternal justice.[84] The laws of any state will be increasingly disrespected as long as they are thought to be based on subjective judgment, the will of the temporarily stronger, or the momentary will of the majority. The only hope of recovering respect for civil law and order lies in its derivation from divine law and order. God's law is universally valid (Ro 2:14-15). It "makes social order possible; it not only judges man's disobedience of administered law, but also his willful surrender of absolute moral standards to subjective desires."[85]

From the Christian perspective then, the task of government is not

81. Ibid., p. 79.
82. Ibid., p. 80.
83. Ibid., p. 86.
84. Ibid., p. 89.
85. Ibid., p. 92.

to create human rights, but to preserve, without respect of persons, each citizen's God-given inalienable rights. Christian social action is not limited to cooperation with other Christians; we may associate with any who seek to preserve human rights, even though they do not share the same ultimate explanation of them. Human beings are not created for the state, but the state for the just and peaceful preservation of individuals. To support decency and order in society at large is a responsibility of the obedient church. It is necessary and crucial in its own right; it is also important for pre-evangelistic purposes. "Where the claims of justice and law are obscure, there the understanding of redemption will also be confused. On the other hand, a nation whose conscience is sensitive to the objective character of justice and law and morality provides an ideal climate among the citizens for the effective preaching of the Gospel."[86]

THE INDIRECT ROLE OF THE CHURCH

The problem of implementing the Christian position in political realms has seriously divided the church. But if Christianity has the solution to man's ethical dilemmas socially as well as individually, that solution must be spelled out and applied as effectively as possible. In attempting to show the social relevance of Christianity, some have merged the interests of the church with the interests of the state. Identifying the kingdom of God with a specific political program, they sought to transform society by political compulsion. Walter Rauschenbusch originally had insisted upon a basis for this in personal spiritual regeneration, but subsequent emphases often neglected conversion for social action. This approach enables one to be up and doing, and doing something specific to meet human need.

But the relevance of Christianity to man's social need is not to be identified with a specific economic or political program. There are several reasons for this, Henry carefully observes. Only minimal standards can be legislatively enforced upon any given society, and Christian responsibility is broader than that. Furthermore, Christian social action must spring from the heart of an individual who seeks to do his duty, not achieve benefits for a special interest. Reliance on governmental power to satisfy the interests of a group of (Christian) citizens inevitably calls for pressures from others (non-Christians) for

86. Ibid., p. 94.

a contradictory law. Consequently the alleged "kingdom of God" might enforce what is in fact not our duty at all. Beyond this, of course, Christians could be mistaken on a given piece of legislation. At best, lobbying before the lawmaking body can only readjust existing disorders along new lines.[87] Nowhere does the New Testament teach the regenerate to force their way of life upon unregenerate society. And nowhere does the New Testament confuse the kingdom of God with the state.

How then can Christians come to the aid of a needy society? Can anything concrete and specific be done? The formation of a Christian political party faces all the dangers of Christian legislation. Although such parties have been influential historically, they fail "to distinguish the Christian's sectarian objectives from his public support of universally valid principles of justice and morality."[88] It tends to identify the mission of the church with its particular political struggle. This makes opponents of the party opponents of the church as well. And it may call for loyalty to the party program above loyalty to Christian principle. Furthermore, to identify the church with a political party would inevitably make the church endorse causes of indirect if not antithetical concern. But the greatest difficulty, as Henry sees it, is the promotion of the officeholder as the church's representative in the political realm. "No political office ought to be viewed as belonging to any specific religion; all should represent the broadest community of interest."[89]

If Christianity remains distinct from government and political parties does it not lose significance for all practical purposes? How can the thesis be maintained that Scriptural position is necessary to social well-being? While the Christian impact upon society is indirect, it is nevertheless a most crucial factor in the long run. Preaching the undiluted Gospel is its prime reason for existence, but that is not its entire mission. The Lord of individual redemption is also the Lord of all creation. All men of every race and nation live and move and have their being in Him. He created all of one set of parents. Although all are not morally and spiritually brothers, all are by nature brothers under God's providential Fatherhood.

It is by no means irrelevant or ineffective, then, for the church to

87. Ibid., p. 124.
88. Ibid., p. 141.
89. Ibid., p. 144.

support the basic principles which must underlie social justice in whatever party, race, or nation it will ever be found. Some of these basic principles are: "the divine source and sanction of human rights; the accountability of men and nations to objective and transcendent moral law, and the servant-role of the State as a minister of justice and order in a fallen society; the permanent significance of the social commandments of the Decalogue; the inclusion of property rights as a human right. . . ."[90]

The church has been negligent in expounding these principles and exposing the error of their alternatives. Instead of

> openly challenging race discrimination and civil rights compromises, the evangelical churches ought to have been *in the vanguard*. They shared, in fact, the one great spiritual dynamic—personal regeneration and sanctification—which overcomes the inner dispositions of prejudice, but this resource was not effectively enlisted.[91]

Defending these principles against liberal and neo-orthodox defection, evangelicals nevertheless failed to preach them relevantly. Meanwhile those who denied them in theory responded existentially to the needs and rights of persons. Evangelicals ought to capitalize upon the strategy of indirect influence of legislation to conserve universal values.

The Christian apologist must seek not only to show the theoretical relevance of Christianity, but also to demonstrate its actual relevance within and beyond the church. While the church biblically cannot as such become identified with specific political ideologies, its members individually may be encouraged to participate with reflective compassion. Just as Christians may witness in the teaching profession they may be encouraged to work energetically in legal and political careers. There the Christian may serve justice above all partial and sectarian interests. And all Christians must be trained in revealed principles of universal justice and encouraged to seek their realization responsibly through every legitimate influence.

Christianity may be shown to supply the very qualities necessary to overcome the weaknesses of democratic government. In order to make the right decisions people must have access to relevant information. Granting the most effective methods of communication, men

90. Ibid., p. 124.
91. Ibid., p. 123.

nevertheless are preoccupied with selfish concerns and need moral motivation to do what is right. "Because inordinate selfishness and passion easily overwhelm one's sense of justice, self-government requires spiritual direction in order to suceed."[92] Those who will not conform to the likeness of Christ's self-giving love may be moved by the liability of all men to divine judgment. So "when properly comprehended and appropriated, the Christian message energizes those very virtues of community life which best contribute to social well-being."[93]

JUSTICE AND LOVE

The greatest Christian impact upon society will be made, however, only as justice and love are held to be equally ultimate in the character of God, and are not confused in the distinctive roles of the government and the church. Liberalism dissolved justice into love, cancelling any separate function for justice in God's dealing with men or the moral order. The attempt to apply *agape* everywhere blurred the distinction between justice and benevolence in the politico-economic realms as well. While Karl Barth in a way reinstated righteous wrath, even God's acts of judgment, in his teaching, turn out to be acts of grace. Barth's denial of any revelation in nature deprives him of a valid basis for universal law and justice. Of course he attempts to found social ethics on Christological revelation. But this obliterates the difference between Christ's rule of the world to come and the present world. Christ did not destroy civil law in order to promote redemptive mercy. Neither need the Christian impose the Christian ethic upon the world.

Attempts to implement Christian love in political and economic realms fail to provide either justice or love. We cannot be true to Scripture and overlook the radical difference between the city of God and the city of the world. The task of the government in the world is to preserve justice for all equally, by compulsion if necessary; the function of the church is to redeem some from the world, restoring individuals who will respond to Christ's love. From this perspective Henry questions whether human rights can be preserved if love is implemented politically.

92. Ibid., p. 132.
93. Ibid., p. 133.

While love as a government function would seem in theory to destroy the State's role of coercion, benevolence in state welfare actually becomes a handmaid of government compulsion rather than of freedom under God. According to the New Testament, the coercive role of the State is limited to its punitive function.[94]

Henry asks, "Has the Church any biblical basis for viewing *agape* as a government duty, or for making *agape* a citizen's rightful expectation from the state?" The contrasting question follows, "Is not the State's obligation in preserving justice to provide what is *due* (as corresponding to the *rights* of men) rather than to implement *agape* by acts of mercy or love?"[95] Can love be forced? Should the ethic of a few citizens be imposed on all? Justice has its fundamental place in the divine nature and the fulfillment of God's will in a fallen world. In justice God will one day judge the present world. The true nature of love cannot be appreciated until uncompromising justice is understood. Justice and love are indispensable and irreducible. "Justice deals with one's neighbor as a member of society as a whole, whereas love deals with him as a particular person."[96]

ETHICS AND THE INVISIBLE GARDENER

The apologist may help an investigator in John Wisdom's garden to analyze his own moral experience. He may be helped to see his responsibility to the demands of justice, consideration, and love. His accountability in these regards indicates that he is already held by a personal Administrator of these laws. But before the Administrator's tribunal he stands condemned. Reconciliation to God calls for sincere repentance for habitual lovelessness, inconsiderateness, and injustice, as well as ingratitude and pride. In other words, he must simply throw himself upon the mercy of the divine court. God displayed His love and satisfied justice by providing the atonement of Calvary. On that basis the repentant sinner is declared righteous. So he may live in an enduring fellowship of faith.

Life in the garden presents us not only with individual guilt, but also serious economical and political problems. For these Christianity alone provides a viable solution. The ineptness of other proposals may be pointed out in contrast to the strength of personal

94. Ibid., p. 160.
95. Ibid., p. 166.
96. Ibid., p. 171.

regeneration and its implications. A regenerate worker, for example, has a purpose for living and considers his job a sacred vocation given of God. So every laborer has a dignity under God and is motivated to creative service for God and men.

From the Christian perspective the state can never receive a person's ultimate allegiance. It fulfills a servant role as the minister of justice in a fallen world. So its services are limited and apply to all men equally, without respect of persons. The minister of consideration and love is the church. In redemptive love it offers benevolence. Without a clear delineation of these roles for the state and the church, difficulties multiply. But both are indispensable to alleviation of social injustice and human need. In the nature of God both justice and love are equally ultimate. So Christianity provides a just and loving solution to the ethical needs of people individually and socially. Christianity answers to the data of human experience morally.

EVALUATION

The strength of the ethical apologetic lies in its communicative power for people concerned about personal and social morality today. The existential urgency of such issues provides a hearing that epistemological debates will never gain. Too long evangelical Christianity has been charged with irrelevance. But while many neo-orthodox writers laud I-thou relationships, Carnell has skillfully analyzed them. And his existential analysis shows that personal fellowship is not antithetical to the propositional truths of the Gospel. Rather, ethical needs are such that they can be resolved only by the Word who became flesh, died for our sins, and rose again dynamically to provide a reconciliation with justice and love.

Admittedly, evangelicals have been slow to develop a social ethic. Carl Henry's work incompletely surveyed here is introductory. Much remains to be done in this field. But Henry's guidelines are soundly rooted in Christianity's scriptural sources and relate meaningfully to experience. By his approach an apologist can show that evangelical Christianity is not too otherworldly to be any earthly good. It does meet men where they are in both personal and social concerns.

To what extent does the ethical approach support Christianity's truth-claims? Conceivably a philosophy could answer to man's ethical needs and still be false on other grounds. Its notions of right and wrong, guilt and judgment, atonement and justification could be a mere projection of someone's dreams. Like a sugar pill, it might nevertheless bring a believer pragmatic benefits for a time. If so, it would not permanently support our appropriation of it with reality. The ethical apologetic does not stand alone. By criteria of consistency and factual adequacy, it is necessary to test truth-claims concerning the reality of God, Christ, and their revealed redemption for unethical men. A total philosophy of life must fit the facts of morality, however. The fitness of Christianity to ethical experience makes a most significant contribution to the cumulative case.

In sum, Carnell's apologetic finds the Christian hypothesis true because, without contradiction, it accounts for more empirical evidence (chap. 7), axiological evidence (chap. 8), psychological evidence (chap. 9), and ethical evidence (chap. 10), with fewer difficulties than any other hypothesis. The Christian hypothesis includes not only the existence of the triune God of the Bible, but also the truth of all that the Bible teaches. Carnell defended inerrancy in *An Introduction to Christian Apologetics* (pp. 196-198, 205-209) and in a letter to *Christianity Today* (October 14, 1966). Following Warfield, his letter argued that "a Christian has no more right to construct a doctrine of biblical authority out of deference to the (presumed) inductive difficulties in the Bible, than he has to construct a doctrine of salvation out of deference to the (actual) difficulties which arise whenever one tries to discover the hidden logic in such events as (a) the Son of God's assumption of human nature or (b) the Son of God's offering up of this human nature as a vicarious atonement for sin." Of course we are free to reject the Bible's teaching about itself, he added, but in so doing we demolish the procedure by which we determine the substance of any Christian doctrine. So Carnell concluded that we cannot pick and choose as we please within Scripture teaching. We have seen that a purely inductive method cannot in a lifetime establish the truth of every passage of Scripture. Rationalists cannot merely presuppose the truth of the Bible without assuming the very thing to be supported. Mystical encounters simply do not certify the truth of every biblical teaching. If the Bible is true, its truth can best be defended on Carnell's apologetic.

Evangelicals do well then to invite attention to the hypothesis of the Bible's truthfulness in all it teaches and to display the fitness of that teaching to man's inner and outer experience. The argument is that this hypothesis accounts consistently for the greatest number of facts with the fewest difficulties. Difficulties are not denied. But they are put in proper perspective. They are incidental in comparison with the problems of squaring the hypothesis of a fallacious Bible with the remarkable empirical, axiological, psychological, and ethical data considered in the four chapters surveying Carnell's thought. Accepting the Bible as true, we can account for its historical accuracy, its unity, its preservation, its fulfilled prophecies, its promotion of direct experience of God through the centuries, the claims of Jesus for Himself and for the Bible, the high sense of fulfillment in the lives of believers, their freedom from anxiety about life, death and guilt, their assurance of acceptance (in spite of moral infractions) with God through faith in Christ, and the relevance of the biblical guidelines to the complex social and political problems of our times.

RESOURCES FOR RESEARCH

Bennett, John C., ed. *Christian Social Ethics in a Changing World: An Ecumenical Theological Inquiry.* New York: Association, 1966. Twenty contributors from different countries and theological traditions agree that Christianity should transform the institutions and structures of society without distinction between the two realms of those within, and those outside the church.

Carnell, Edward John. *Christian Commitment: An Apologetic.* New York: Macmillan, 1957. In this work Carnell starts with an insightful analysis of the moral realities holding him during a simple walk in the park. The moral considerations, which we cannot escape, are best explained by the hypothesis of Christianity's truth and best met by repentant faith in the crucified and risen Christ.

Culver, Robert D. *Toward a Biblical View of Civil Government.* Chicago: Moody, 1974. Discusses political theory from the standpoint of a biblically informed world-and-life view.

Henry, Carl F. H. *Aspects of Christian Social Ethics.* Grand Rapids: Eerdmans, 1964. Elucidates the relevance of biblically revealed Christianity to the needs of man in society.

———. *Christian Personal Ethics.* Grand Rapids: Eerdmans, 1957. A critique of non-Christian ethical options and a thorough statement of a responsible Christian position. The apologetic thesis: Only Christianity can adequately account for the present world of moral behavior.

———. *Such As I Have: The Stewardship of Talent.* New York: Abingdon-Cokesbury, n.d. A discussion of ways Christian laymen can invest their respective talents to help the church minister more effectively to human need.

———. *The God Who Shows Himself.* Waco, Tex.: Word, 1966. Addresses on the difference the biblical God makes in the socio-political world, and the worlds of education and ecumenism.

———. *The Uneasy Conscience of Modern Fundamentalism.* Grand Rapids: Eerdmans, 1947. An exposé of weaknesses in the traditional fundamentalist neglect of social need.

Lewis, C. S. *Mere Christianity:* A revised and enlarged edition, with a new introduction, of the three books *The Case for Christianity, Christian Behaviour,* and *Beyond Personality.* New York: Macmillan, 1952. An inductive argument from right and wrong as a clue to the meaning of the universe. Although the form of the argument differs from Carnell's, the data are similar and may be helpfully correlated with his *Christian Commitment.*

Moberg, David O. *Inasmuch: Christian Social Responsibility in the Twentieth Century.* Grand Rapids: Eerdmans, 1965. Shows the consistency of contemporary social sciences and the values of Christian faith revealed in the Bible.

Ramsay, Ian T. *Christian Ethics and Contemporary Philosophy.* London: SCM, 1966. An attempt of analytic philosophers to clarify issues of morality and religion, duty and God's will, reason and authority in ethical decision.

Trethowan, Illtyd. *The Basis of Belief.* New York: Hawthorne, 1961. A volume of the *Twentieth Century Encyclopedia of Catholicism* arguing that an apprehension of God may best be achieved by an analysis of experience morally and personally. A helpful supplement to the approach of Carnell's *Christian Commitment.*

11

CONCLUSIONS

LIFE DEMANDS DECISIONS. At some point surveys must turn into evaluations and conclusions. Do we or do we not have reason to believe that God exists and reveals Himself to us in Christ and the Bible? Our answer depends upon the nature of reasons which seem convincing to us.

If by reason you mean observable data, Buswell speaks to the point. If reason means something more logically demonstrative, that may be found in Hackett's rational empiricism. If you seek a mathematical certainty, consider Clark's deductive rationalism. If it seems more reasonable to leave religious debates to a higher authority, Van Til's presuppositionalism may be more convincing. Many today find their convictions in personal experience and so may find most reasonable Barrett's Christian mysticism. Others, like Carnell, accept the world view which without contradiction fits the greatest number of facts empirically, axiologically, psychologically, and ethically.

Christianity has been effectively defended in all these classical ways of knowing. If all these approaches to the defense of Christianity are rejected, one wonders on what basis the non-believer accepts any belief. Thinking people from any one of these epistemological stances may know that God lives today. Of course not all the systems appeal equally to every individual. But responsible evaluations reckon with the basic points in debate.

Five issues call for careful consideration: (1) the logical starting point, (2) common ground or a point of contact with non-Christians, (3) the test for truth, (4) the role of reasoning, and (5) the basis of faith in God, Christ, and Scripture. The varied positions on these

SUMMARY OF APOLOGETIC SYSTEMS

ISSUES IN APOLOGETIC SYSTEMS	BUSWELL	HACKETT	CLARK	VAN TIL	BARRETT	CARNELL
Logical Starting Point	Empirical Data	Empirical data and rational principles	Axioms of: Logic God Bible	Presuppositions of: Autonomous Scripture and the Triune God	Testimony to Christian experience	Hypothesis of: The Triune God of the Bible
Common Ground or Point of Contact	All Facts	Facts and the mind's thought-forms	The mind's thought-forms	No common ground epistemologically in principle. Actually dependence on God, suppression of awareness of God, guilt	No significant common ground prior to conversion experience	Facts, Law of non-contradiction, the quest for values, laws of morality and love
Test for Truth	Integration (Correspondence)	Coherence	Consistency	Self-authenticating biblical claims	Self-authenticating experience	Systematic Consistency (Coherence)
Role of Reason	Pure Induction	Rational Induction	Pure Deduction	Interpretation of Scripture and confessions	Interpretation of experience	Verification of hypotheses by all inner and outer experience
Basis of Faith in God, Christ and Scripture	Intellectual Probability	Rational Demonstration	Syllogistic Certainty	Scriptural Authority	Psychological Certitude	Intellectual Probability and Moral Certainty

issues are outlined on the chart (p.286). It is the purpose of this chapter to assess the significance of these differences and draw some conclusions.

THE LOGICAL STARTING POINT

We must decide whether to initiate a test of Christianity's truth-claims by attending first to facts alone, facts and categories, indemonstrable axioms of Christianity, presuppositions of Christianity's truth, mystical experiences of God, or a tentative Christian hypothesis to be tested. In my judgment, the most pure empiricist cannot come to the facts with a completely blank mind. Ideally it might be well to start with mere facts, but realistically no one is completely objective. All bring to the facts perspectives gained from previous experience. The responsible mind also brings general principles of truth (logic), goodness, and beauty as Hackett, Clark, and Carnell have argued. It would be unwise to begin with these principles alone without integrating them with experience, for this might lead to otherworldly systems of no earthly relevance. Hackett considers the rational categories with empirical data the logical starting point. It remains questionable, however, whether he can ever reason convincingly from sense data and general principles to specifically Christian conclusions about God, Christ, and the Bible. He must stretch the principles of logic beyond the requirements of observed data to conclude that God is omnipotent, that Christ is fully divine, and that the Bible is true in all its teachings.

Van Til properly recognizes the need to have fully Christian concepts in mind in order to test genuinely Christian concepts. But the major strand of his system seems to assume the very thing in question. Starting with Clark's unchallengeable axioms or Van Til's unquestionable presuppositions short-circuits the apologetic question. Barrett's starting point of testimony to personal experience requires an interpretive point of view which either assumes the very thing to be supported or gives insufficient evidence to establish the truth of the evangelical perspective.

Carnell provides the interpretive principle necessary to test evangelical Christianity, but does not presuppose the point in question. He considers the biblical viewpoint a tentative conclusion to be checked out by its adequacy to the entirety of experience. Explicitly starting with the Christian hypothesis, Carnell acknowledges that he does not have a blank mind. That is realistic. He also makes it clear that Christianity is not true because he presupposes it to be true, or labels it an axiom. That avoids circular reasoning. His hypothesis, like everyone else's, must be verified. That is fair. It is also most useful in discussions. People who would not assent to axioms and presuppositions without evidence may consider the truth and the relevance of a tentative conclusion, at least for the sake of argument.

COMMON GROUND

Having begun to test Christianity's truth-claims, we wonder what court of appeal can hear the case. Can we check out these proposals by anything held in common between believer and unbeliever? Do all men, irrespective of Christian convictions, face similar observable facts, employ the same general principles of non-contradiction, and find themselves accountable to certain basic principles of right and wrong?

Buswell's empiricism properly stresses the publicly observable facts presented to all alert people independent of their religious perspectives. Hackett agrees, and adds that all men share some general forms of thought. Clark also finds the laws of logic to be programmed in the human mind. Carnell assents and adds a general sense of accountability to justice, consideration, and love. These men have made their case. Any world-viewish hypothesis must answer to empirical facts and to the principles of basic truth and morality.

Van Til's case against common facts and knowledge *in principle* does not succeed in ruling out all actual common ground. He admits that both Christians and non-Christians inconsistently share some truths. In addition, Van Til's point of contact with non-Christians lies in their suppression of their awareness of God. All men are covenant-breakers. A sense of fallenness and guilt is described by existentialists and uncovered by psychiatrists. But Van Til's interpretation of guilt feelings as derived from the breaking of God's covenant is hardly common ground. To say it is assumes the very interpretation of experience which needs to be supported. The non-Christian may explain the sense of guilt as a result of social pressure, family condemnation, or relativistic mores. He does not interpret his guilt feelings in Christian terms. In spite of the circular reasoning involved at the interpretive level of Van Til's position, it has a strategic point descriptively. We may count on it. No one honestly thinks he has always been the child, the parent, the citizen, the neighbor, the humanist, or the religionist he ought to be. The resources of Christianity to help individuals become more of a complete person can well be brought to bear upon the pervasive sense of fallenness and guilt.

Although Barrett does not discuss the question of common ground, his position implies that the presence of facts, principles, and guilt would not provide a ground on which to evaluate Christianity's truth-claims. Until a person has a direct experience of God, he cannot appreciate the truth about God. In effect, then, no common ground between the Christian mystic and the non-Christian is significant for apologetic purposes.

Carnell finds truth in most of the previous views, except the mystic's denial of common ground. The other positions are not mutually exclusive. Sense data does not present to observers certain givens without respect of Christian or non-Christian convictions. Meaningful thought and speech requires adherence to the law of non-contradiction for both. Ordinary decency, respect, and love also disclose some fundamental ethical norms among men in general, as well as their failure to live up to them. To these facts and principles Carnell appeals in testing the Christian hypothesis. The appeal of argument in the others is only to facts (Buswell), only to non-contradiction (Clark), only to a sense of guilt (Van Til), only to a testimony of one's own distinct experience (Barrett). Hackett, like Carnell, appeals to both evidence and changeless principles of thought. These reference points provide the most stringent data against which to test the truth-claims of a religion or a philosophical world view.

THE TEST FOR TRUTH

Granting a base of common ground in factual data, logical principles, and existential guilt feelings, by what criterion can a world view be shown to be true or false? Buswell's view that all ideas arise from empirical experience requires that all ideas be confirmed or rejected in terms of correspondence or integration with the data from which they came. But the data of experience seem to support contradictory theses and the law of non-contradiction cannot be abstracted from experience to deliver us from the quandary.

Hackett's coherence criterion demands that an idea be consistent with all other ideas alleged to be true, as well as in accord with empirical fact. Truth must cohere with the evidence and rational categories. This provides a better check and balance on truth-claims than evidence alone, but fails to include the facts of personal experience as fully as systematic consistency.

Clark thinks it futile to test truth-claims by their adherence to facts, but in this position seems to open the door to defending a system that has no relation to our world. The test of logical consistency is inescapable and useful as the prime test of error, but it cannot by itself guarantee truth.

Van Til's attempt to regard the Bible as true because it is self-authenticating does not work. Contradictory sacred writings also are said to be self-authenticating. On a different course Van Til says that the Christian Scriptures alone provide a meaningful view of the world. If this criterion of meaningfulness signifies more than "suits my taste" it must then appeal to standards of meaning in logic, fact, values, psychology, and ethics. Then Van Til's criterion of truth would amount to the criterion of Carnell.

Barrett claims that Christian experience is self-authenticating. This test also is insufficient. Contradictory positions claim their views to be authenticated by mystical experience. Integrated with other checks and balances, however, experience of God is an important datum to be accounted for on any world view.

Carnell's systematic consistency overcomes the limitations of the other criteria by a number of checks and balances. Truth does not violate the law of non-contradiction, and it fits with the data of man's entire inner and outer experience. Hackett's use of coherence stressed non-contradiction and the empirical world. Carnell's coherence adds to this a stress on the data of man's existential experience in his inner self. Internal effable experience of values, ethical guilt, and psychological anxiety also provide data to be explained by a view of our world. Because Carnell's test of truth-claims has the greatest number of checks and balances it is the best means of avoiding error and obtaining truth. A true opinion fits the facts covered by it. All the facts of reality are consistent with one another. So all true beliefs must be consistent with one another. The world view which consistently accounts for the greatest amount of data given in the world is true. Upon it we must act.

THE ROLE OF REASON

The problem of relating faith in Christianity to human reason is implicit in each of the apologists studied. The place of faith is discussed in the next section. In this section consider the role of reason. Exactly what can reason do to check out truth-claims? Assuming the test of truth adopted in each system, how does reason proceed?

According to Buswell reason observes sense data, infers the high probability of the law of causality and so induces the most probable causes of observable effects. This pure induction involves no Christian presuppositions or faith. Evidence alone establishes all principles of reasoning and the conclusions drawn with their help. On the basis of observed evidence and causal inferences, an eternal, independent, wise, and powerful being is found to be the cause of the universe, of the Bible, and of the unique life of Christ.

Hackett's reason observes evidence and draws conclusions about causes because of the innate principles of causality and non-contradiction. These universal and necessary principles enable a thinker to draw conclusions with demonstrable certainty. Such conclusions depend on both sense data and rational categories. Concepts without percepts are empty; percepts without concepts are blind. Entirely apart from Christian presuppositions or faith a person can examine the evidence and logically conclude that a powerful, wise cause of existence exists, and that He inspired Scripture and entered the observable world in Jesus of Nazareth. On the basis of this knowledge, he is responsible to believe and act.

As Clark sees it, reason cannot of itself discover the true meaning of sense data or argue validly to its cause. Reason operates solely on the basis of an inherent principle of consistency. Any view of the world is presupposed like a geometrical axiom. None can be proved by empirical evidence and causal inference. Reason's task is to see which of the fundamental axioms permits the deduction of a system which does not contradict itself. Reason's role is not that of pure induction or rational induction, but syllogistic deduction from basic, unproved axioms. Deductions from non-Christian axioms eventually involve one in contradictions. Deductions from the axiom of the existence of the God of the Bible are free from contradiction. Thus reason shows that Christian assumptions are more consistent than non-Christian assumptions.

According to Van Til's main trend of thought, reason cannot of itself discover the true meaning of sense data, or determine the most consistent view of the world. Fallen man cannot refer to facts or logic to test the words of God. Every thinker begins with some unproved presuppositions and so does the Christian. Presupposing the triune God of the Bible, Van Til simply seeks to set forth the Bible's teaching. Reason's role is not to check the validity of Scripture by evidence or noncontradiction, but simply to interpret the Scripture as accurately as possible. In its interpretative role reason is aided by those who have formulated the creeds of the Church—particularly the unrevised Westminster Confession. However, if Van Til is forced to answer why *this* Scripture and why *this* confession, he answers, "Because this presupposition alone makes sense of life." When all is said and done, reason must be capable of showing how Christian presuppositions are more meaningful than non-Christian presuppositions.

Barrett views reason as primarily interpretative also. In the first instance, however, Christian mysticism has reason testifying to the experience of God. But this experience is interpreted according to the Bible. Forced to answer why a Christian guide to interpretation, Barrett also resorts to the coherence of this interpretation with all human experience. Although the role of reason is frequently said to be that of a witness, reason must also select its fundamental interpretative principles. Both Barrett and Young set forth the consistency and adequacy of the Christian world view as over against other world views. Reason has a task beyond that of interpretation. Reason must discern or judge between conflicting world views on the ground of certain specifiable criteria.

It is Carnell who most explicitly recognizes reason's creative and critical task. Creatively, reason proposes hypotheses by which to account for experience. Critically, reason determines which of these hypotheses is verified. So reason proposes and disposes of hypotheses. In the case of the hypothesis of the God of the Bible, of course, reason creatively sets forth a truth-claim of divine revelation. Reason's creative task does not exclude the recognition of revelation if revelation occurred. In the face of conflicting revelation-claims, reason puts them to the test. The comprehensive teaching of Scripture can be adequately tested only by the totality of human experience, within and without. The scope of this task precludes complete logical demonstration, but is satisfied with a high degree of probability. By common grace fallen men are capable of confirming or disconfirming claims of other men and books to speak for God. On the basis of that ability they are responsible for their use of their minds in the judgment. When the discriminatory work of reason is done it has found its primary principles of interpretation and so can make proper sense of observed evidence and of religious experience. Reason's task of discriminating between truth and falsehood does not displace its task of interpreting the revelation once it is found.

For apologetic purposes then, reason's primary role is not that of making pure inductions from sense data (Buswell), not that of constructing rational demonstrations from sense data (Hackett), not simply that of spinning a purely deductive system from axioms (Clark), not simply that of interpreting a presupposed revelation (Van Til), not simply that of testifying to an allegedly self-authenticating experience (Barrett), but that of verifying or disverifying hypotheses in terms of a worthy criterion of truth.

THE BASIS OF FAITH

Upon the reasoning followed in each case these apologists feel justified in assenting to the truth of Christianity's basic claims and so in committing their lives to the realities they designate. In all these thinkers faith involves Spirit-born assent of the mind and total participation of life. The Holy Spirit's work is not independent of apologetic reasoning or in spite of the case for Christianity. People are called to relate their lives to God and Christ as revealed in Scripture because of the considerations given.

Buswell recognizes that acceptance of Christianity means a reorientation of a person's ethical alignments and loyalties, but he insists that cognitively we believe the truth of Christianity in the same way we believe any truth of science. Religious beliefs require neither a greater degree nor a different kind of faith. In both, examination of evidence leads to an overwhelmingly probable case for an inductive conclusion. On the basis of that evidence one believes the assertion and acts in view of the reality of its referent. On the ground of empirical evidence Buswell expects a person to assert the existence of God, the truth of the Bible, and the Deity of Jesus Christ. Such a genuine belief leads to authentic trust in God Himself, His truth, and His Son. For Buswell reason precedes faith.

For Hackett belief in Christianity's truth is established not by high probability alone, but rational demonstration. Granting a valid use of innate principles of reasoning, the cognitive conclusion follows with logical necessity. That does not rule out faith. Just as one believes the conclusion of any sound reasoning, he believes the conclusion of the cosmological argument. He also believes the conclusive evidential case for the Bible and Christ. Mental assent leads to total commitment or responsibility for it. Hackett also has reason precede faith.

Clark reacts against reason preceding faith as much as he does reason without faith or faith without reason. Clark calls for faith in the primacy of truth over error. Then he asks for assent of the will to Christian axioms as the logical starting point for obtaining truth. On the grounds of the consistency of the logically necessary system deduced he calls for life-commitment. Faith is not placed in the irrational. For example, if all men are mortal and you are a man, you are mortal. Your impending death is not believed less because the necessary conclusion of a valid syllogism. You believe what you know and act in terms of the possibility when driving through intersections and taking out life insurance. You know what you believe and believe what you know. Faith and reason are as inseparable as a person's functions of mind and will.

Van Til asks us to believe not what we can confirm or infer, but what God says because God says it. Faith in God, Christ, and Scripture is not the result of our assessment of evidence or logical facility, but the appropriate response of the creature to the Word of his Creator. To Scriptural authority the intellect gives assent. On that basis a person repents of his covenant-breaking self-sufficiency and begins to live before God. Faith in divine authority precedes every valid use of the intellect. Apart from this faith no one makes sense of life.

In Barrett's thought the total commitment of faith is evoked by a psychological certitude resulting from a mystical encounter. The acceptance of empirical, logical, and authoritarian arguments does not precede, but follows this personal experience of God. Reason does not lead to faith, but faith to reason. This order sounds pious, but can support faith in all the contradictory notions peddled in the name of God and religion. In Barrett it does not do this, for one strand of his thought calls for intellectual testing of the allegedly self-authenticating experience and intellectual confirmation of the psychological certainty.

Carnell's approach calls first for a willingness to consider the Christian hypothesis for what it is. A genuine sense of inquiry precedes the effective use of man's mind. So a tentative belief that Christianity is at least worth considering precedes effective testing of its truth-claims. One who does not believe that there could conceivably be a God disclosed in Christ and the Bible will never see sufficient evidence for God. Humility before creative hypotheses and evidence precedes knowledge. Granting a willingness to consider Christianity's truth-claims, reason then examines them according to the explicit test of systematic consistency. Since no one can examine all inner and outer evidence, the best result of reason is a high probability. In many cases, however, it is so high that only a fool would withhold assent. The overwhelming probability of Christianity leads to moral certainty—a responsibility before the evidence—and to a psychological certainty—a conscious assurance of assenting to the truth about reality. Consequently one places his whole soul-trust in the God of the Bible. A tentative faith precedes reason; intellectual confirmation precedes total commitment.

Although I see values in each of the systems studied, I confess that Carnell's seems most realistic. I found it meaningful when I studied it under Carnell during my senior year in college. Christianity's ability to fit the facts was underscored during seminary days. As I tested non-Christian options during doctoral work in philosophy I failed to find a non-Christian interpretation of the world with greater consistency fit more facts. As I teach waves of college graduates year after year I have found no more challenging perspective from which to answer their searching questions. I am open to any facts wherever they may be found (1 Co 3:21-23). I can without loss of integrity become all things to all men that by all means I may win some (1 Co 9:22). At the same time I have a convincing reason for my own faith in the God who acts miraculously, knows the future, speaks, judges evil, raises the dead, redeems the unlovely, and welcomes them to an endless fellowship with Himself.

APPENDIX

Other Recent Approaches

THE DAWN OF EXCITING DEVELOPMENTS in Christian apologetics is breaking upon the horizon. Followers of Jesus Christ live in a new era of challenge to their faith from other eastern religions, Christian cults, occult powers, political pressures, social needs, medical complexities, ethical decisions, scientific perplexities, and philosophical question marks. Ecological concerns vividly demonstrate the fact that no part of life can be exploited without consideration for other parts of earth's life-support system. In a new way Christians see the dangers in increasingly diversified specialization and the values in a system of thought. The need for systematic approaches in apologetics was never more pressing.

Among the essentials that must be interrelated in an apologetics system are the defender's logical starting point, common ground or points of contact with non-Christians, his test for truth about reality, the role of reason and the basis of faith. This chapter seeks to introduce the thought of a number of recent writers on these issues that have been focal points through the book. Not all the men here surveyed write on each of these points explicitly, or desire to be called authors of apologetics systems. Nevertheless, their contributions merit attention. This chapter seeks to sum up their perspectives and compare them with systems previously discussed.

FRANCIS SCHAEFFER

One of the most popular defenders of the faith today is Francis Schaeffer, a man who prefers not to be judged the producer of just another system. His concerns focus upon the communication of the faith to non-Christians. With full recognition of their practical intent and value, his writings reflect a characteristic stance on the issues inherent to a system of apologetics. His readers necessarily seek to relate his different writings to one another systematically. Hopefully his thought (and that of others surveyed) is not studied as an end in itself, but a means to fellowship with the living God and to effective service for Him in a world of conflicting religious claims. We share Schaeffer's concern in this regard, and hope we do not do his perspective an injustice by including him here. A greater injustice would be done by omitting reference to his effective approach.

In *Escape from Reason* and *The God Who Is There,* Schaeffer traces the roots of contemporary non-Christian thought. He seeks to point out some of the turning points in the history of philosophy leading to shattered beliefs in the validity of logic, ethical norms, world views, and objective truth. He properly regards epistemological issues as the key to this sense of unreality and to a renewed sense of Christian reality. In spite of the verbal mysticism (ambiguity) so prevalent today, he calls people to decide between reality and unreality, truth and falsehood, right and wrong.

Schaeffer's presuppositional starting point frequently sounds like that of his former professor, Cornelius Van Til. In many passages Schaeffer insists upon the need for starting with Christian presuppositions concerning God's existence as the source of the world's existence, God's personality as the source of the significance of man's personhood, and God's righteousness as the source of moral absolutes.[1] Apart from Christian presuppositions man fails to know reality from unreality, man from animal, and right from wrong. People with non-Christian presuppositions sometimes borrow or steal from Christian ones, but they must be pressed to consistency with their adopted assumptions. Schaeffer sees his presuppositions not as ending conversation with people, but opening up meaningful communication.[2] There is little use talking with others today about a plan of salvation if we do not take into account their especially crucial presuppositions concerning the nature of truth and the method of attaining truth. When the presuppositions are clear, then press a non-Christian to the logical conclusions of them, point up his tensions with God's world or

1. Francis Schaeffer, *The God Who Is There* (Downers Grove, Ill.: Inter-varsity, 1968), pp. 121-24.
2. Ibid., p. 126.

his own identity, and so help him see his need for the gospel.[3] "The truth that we must let in first is not a dogmatic statement of the truth of the Scriptures but the truth of the external world and the truth of what man himself is."[4]

Starting with the Christian presupposition that an infinite-personal God made man in His image, Schaeffer is not surprised that man has worth and that his unique gift of verbalization has meaning with others and with God. Christian belief in a Creator led scientists to look for objectivity and order in the universe. Now that the presuppositional base is dismissed, science has been reduced to mere technology and another form of sociological manipulation. But on Christian presuppositions, God made the external universe and man's mind so that a correlation between man's mind and nature, and man's mind and Scripture is not surprising. Thus one can meaningfully understand the possibility of real truth, and similarly, real morality. In *He Is There and He Is Not Silent*, Schaeffer argues that apart from Christian presuppositions man can find no meaning. Only on the Christian presupposition of the Bible's truth can anyone know anything or communicate anything.[5]

But how do we know that our presuppositions are true? Presuppositions, as Schaeffer uses them, "are bases and we can choose them."[6] Why should we select Christian presuppositions of the infinite-personal God who has spoken in Scripture? "The strength of the Christian system—the acid test of it—is that everything fits under the apex of the existent, infinite-personal God, and it is the only system in the world where this is true."[7] While the stress on presuppositions sounds like Van Til, the meaning of those statements is more like Carnell's hypothesis, for they are subject to testing by the coherence criterion of truth. Schaeffer had earlier set forth his answer to the question, "How do we know it is true?" in *The God Who Is There*. Proof in religion follows the same rules as proof in science and philosophy. Verification has two steps: the theory must be non-contradictory and must give an answer to the phenomenon in question, and we must be

3. Ibid., pp. 127-28.
4. Ibid., p. 129.
5. Francis Schaeffer, *He Is There and He Is Not Silent* (Wheaton, Ill.: Tyndale, 1972), pp. 15, 88.
6. Ibid., p. 65.
7. Ibid., p. 81.

able to live consistently with our theory.[8] Here he argues that "Christianity, beginning with the existence of the infinite-personal God, man's creation in His image and a space-time fall, constitutes a non-self-contradictory answer that does explain the phenomena and which can be lived with, both in life and in scholarly pursuits."[9] Christianity is true because it is consistent, factual, and viable. Or, in Carnell's words, because it is horizontally self-consistent and vertically fits the facts, not only external, but internal (values, moral norms, and guilt and psychological need).

The role of reason, according to Schaeffer, is to "open the door to a vital relationship to God."[10] It serves two purposes: defense of the faith and communication of the faith to each generation in terms it can understand. In defense of the faith, in addition to verifying its claims, reason pushes the non-Christian to the logic of his presuppositions until he sees his need for grace. Reason shows the non-Christian the truth of the external world, what man is in himself as a moral rebel, God's existence, and Christ's work on the cross.[11] In Scripture the Holy Spirit's work is not separated from knowledge and knowledge precedes salvation. But all this does not mean that the Christian is rationalistic. A Christian does not "try to begin from himself autonomously and work out a system from there on. But he is rational; he thinks and acts on the basis that A is not non-A. However, he does not end with only rationality, for in his response to what God has said his whole personality is involved."[12] Reason has an important role in Schaeffer's approach, but it is not the sole principle apart from revelation.

What is the basis of faith in the God of Christ and the Bible? Faith is not an irrational leap in the dark. The invitation to act is given in the Scriptures only after an adequate base of knowledge has been given.[13] That adequate base includes not only good and sufficient reasons for belief in the infinite-personal God, the external world, and the importance of man in the world, but also good and sufficient evidence that Christ is the Messiah. Only the faith which believes God on the basis of knowledge is true faith. Knowledge precedes faith.[14]

8. Schaeffer, *The God Who Is There*, p. 109.
9. Ibid., p. 111.
10. Ibid., p. 112.
11. Ibid., pp. 119-30.
12. Ibid., p. 113.
13. Ibid., p. 141.

"Accepting Christ as Savior can mean anything. . . . We are talking about objective truth. . . . Biblically based experience rests firmly on truth. It is not only an emotional experience, nor is it contentless."[15]

Hopefully Francis Schaeffer will shake off hesitations about system-making and while skillfully communicating the faith find time to formulate a full-blown system relating the content of all his relevant publications and taped lectures. Until that is done, of the systems studied, Schaeffer's approach seems closer to that of Carnell's with its "presuppositions" or hypotheses verifiable on the ground of logic, facts, and viability. The Carnellian stance is greatly enriched by the communicative skills and relevance Schaeffer has developed.

Os Guinness

An associate of Francis Schaeffer at L'Abri, Os Guinness, in his *Dust of Death*, provides a perceptive critique of the counterculture and the establishment, and offers a third way. This third, Christian way is a proposal that is subject to verification or falsification. If there is any question about Schaeffer being in the camp of verificationists, there can be none about Guinness. In his major chapter presenting the Christian option, Guinness asks, "Can Christianity be verified?" It can, he answers, and for the possibility of verification to be meaningful as Anthony Flew argued, there must also be a meaningful possibility of falsification. Guinness does not arbitrarily limit all meaningful assertions to the verifiable or falsifiable. But he writes, "The Christian claims that wherever God's self-disclosure touches the world at these points, it is not only open to falsification but in fact is not falsified; rather it answers questions where no other revelation, hypothesis or guess can probe."[16]

God's disclosure of Himself, Guinness insists, must be tested in the areas of both general and special revelation. General revelation comprises the external universe and the personality of man. Special revelation comprises primarily Christ and the Bible. Scholastic attempts to do apologetics on the basis of rationalistic premises alone have failed. So have many Protestant attempts to defend the faith on

---

14. Ibid., p. 142.
15. Ibid., p. 144.
16. Os Guinness, *The Dust of Death* (Downers Grove, Ill.: Inter-Varsity, 1973), p. 345.

the basis of Christ and the Bible apart from general revelation. In both realms historic Christianity has been characterized by openness to examination.[17]

The Christian view of the universe stresses both its rationality and reality. Christianity accounts for the uniformity of natural causes at the frequency level and the possibility of some knowledge of reality. All knowledge is not deceptive; the world is not unreal (maya). Christians are not the only ones to maintain the reality and rationality of the universe, but Christianity gives a basis for living in the universe in a way man needs in order to be meaningful.[18]

Having earlier shown something of the failure of humanism, determinism, and Hinduism in their final ability to explain man adequately, Guinness argues that Christianity best explains man's sense of individuality, alienation, and striving for communication and love. Again, the argument is not that only Christians are loving, but that only Christians have a sufficient basis for living the way all men must live for life to be meaningful. Apart from the Christian basis, man is not fulfillable and is destined to alienation.[19]

The life of Jesus was open to observation, including the fulfillment of prophecies, the consistency of His life with His claims, His death, burial, and resurrection. As Paul said, the Christian's faith is null and void if Christ has not been raised from the dead. Historic Christianity and biblical faith allow no discontinuity between facts and faith, between credence and credibility. Such faith must not be reduced to anything less than full conviction of truth. In subjecting his presuppositions concerning God, Christ, and the Bible to verification, Guinness is far closer to Carnell's system than Van Til's. Guinness, like Schaeffer, exhibits a fresh communicative skill and his work shows careful systematization.

CLARK PINNOCK

Another apologist influenced by Schaeffer, Clark Pinnock, disclosed his potential for developing a system in defense of the faith in a brief, but forceful work, *Set Forth Your Case*. Showing acquaintance with Van Til and Rushdoony, Pinnock nevertheless calls his starting point

17. Ibid., pp. 346-49.
18. Ibid., pp. 349-51.
19. Ibid., pp. 351-54.

a hypothesis[20] or postulate.[21] When he uses "presupposition" he does so in the context of challenging the validity of non-Christian assumptions and offering better ones.[22] In Pinnock's usage, presuppositions can be verified or falsified. "We must challenge the non-Christian to suspend his prejudice against Christianity for the time it takes to examine fairly the evidence for the Christian faith, to take up a proven method for ascertaining truth, the empirical method, and apply it to the biblical records. No one is imprisoned within an iron cage of presuppositions."[23]

It seems clear that Pinnock's points of contact with non-Christians include empirical data and the empirical method of research. More explicitly, he says, "The cultural point of contact for the gospel lies deep within man himself, as one created in the image of God." Although atheists may deny this, they cannot live consistently with their denial of man's given nature. "A person can profess disbelief in gravity but living consistently with that profession is quite another matter."[24] Just what the image of God means for logical categories of thought is not explained in this brief work.

Pinnock's test for truth stresses empirical verifiability. "The beauty of the gospel in the avalanche of competing religious claims is precisely the possibility we have of checking it out historically and factually."[25] That factual matters can be confirmed only to a degree of probability is of no serious consequence. "That it is only probable does not mean that it is worthless, however, for all legal and historical decisions are made upon a basis of probable judgment in terms of the evidence. Since the whole of life proceeds on such a basis, it is not a weakness that Christian evidences should rest on it too."[26]

Religious experience has no place in Pinnock's verification procedure. "The attempt to establish religious truth by an appeal to the data of comparative religious experience has proved a failure. The uniqueness of the Christian message is not found at the point of experience at all, but in the incarnation datum."[27] Dismissing the experiential approach, Pinnock returns to historical data for the life,

20. Clark Pinnock, *Set Forth Your Case* (Nutley, N. J.: Craig, 1967), p. 68.
21. Ibid., p. 74.
22. Ibid., p. 86.
23. Ibid.
24. Ibid., p. 32.
25. Ibid., p. 44.
26. Ibid., p. 45.
27. Ibid., p. 47.

death, and resurrection of Jesus Christ. Of the latter he concludes, "The resurrection is the only hypothesis which will make peace with all the facts."[28]

Reason has more than an interpretative function. It also serves to verify conflicting claims to the meaning of the universe. "There are checking procedures for testing the Christian clue, and it is the task of apologetics to present the fruits of them cogently."[29] This task falls in the area of pre-evangelism.[30] It is one of validation.[31] Can the natural man's reason function accurately in respect to a message against which he is biased? Pinnock holds that the unbeliever's mind is finite and sinful. "His reason is not ultimate in the universe. His mind is also fallen and twisted. . . . It will be forever impossible for man to explain the meaning of reality starting from himself alone."[32]

But man's sinfully distorted mind does annihilate the hypothesis-verification role of the intellect. "All men employ the rational function. They are capable of receiving data and evaluating data. Because of the noetic effects of sin, however, the non-Christian is unwilling to allow the truth of the gospel to have its persuasive effect on his life. The miracle of regeneration coincident with the presentation of the gospel is required in order to convert him to Christ. The faith which the Spirit creates in the hearer is an intelligent faith, and we must fulfill our role of bringing to the attention of people the grounds of faith."[33]

What, then, is the basis of faith? "Faith is not believing what you know to be absurd. It is trusting what on excellent testimony appears to be true."[34] Even more precisely, "Faith is based upon credible evidence which people can recognize as trustworthy in accord with proper criteria for truth."[35]

On these points of comparison with the systems previously studied, Pinnock's approach seems closest to the hypothesis-verification apologetic of Carnell. Pinnock's potential for a relevant statement of this

28. Ibid., p. 68.
29. Ibid., p. 4.
30. Ibid., p. 8.
31. Ibid., p. 40.
32. Ibid., p. 83.
33. Ibid., p. 85.
34. Ibid., p. 49.
35. Ibid., p. 3.

approach is enhanced by his strong biblical scholarship and interest in developing a cultural apologetic.[36]

JOHN WARWICK MONTGOMERY

Another vigorous defender of the faith, John Montgomery, has published numerous articles in defense of Christianity and several collections of them in book form. Because of the diversity of purposes and times of writing, there is difficulty in systematizing his specific position and doing justice to his thought. He comes to the field with a rich background, including a major emphasis upon history and historiography.

The logical starting point in some articles seems to be empirical data[37] and in others assumptions or gestalts.[38] These could be viewed together in a manner like Carnell's logical starting point (hypothesis) and synoptic starting point (data, etc.). This interpretation seems justified by Montgomery's article entitled "The Theologian's Craft" which skirts both induction and deduction in favor of "retroduction" or "abduction." In that approach the success of a theory (hypothesis) depends upon its ability to fit the facts.[39] In his article on "Inductive Inerrancy" he does not stress the evidence alone, but the evidence and gestalt (a total view supplied by Scripture in this case).[40]

Montgomery strongly opposes a presuppositional approach which precludes investigation of evidence, although he recognizes the importance of methodological assumptions. "Properly we should start not with substantive content presuppositions about the world (e.g. the axioms of revelation), which gratuitously prejudge the nature of what is, but with heuristic, methodological presuppositions that permit us to discover what the world is like— (and equally important) what it is not like."[41] More than methodological assumptions, however, are immediately evident in the same context when he

---

36. Clark Pinnock, "The Secular Wasteland," *His* 30 (May 1970): 27-28; 30 (June 1970): 17-18; "Cultural Apologetics: An Evangelical Standpoint," *Bibliotheca Sacra* 12 (January 1970): 58-63; "For Those Who Don't Despair," *His* 33 (December, 1972): 2-3.

37. John W. Montgomery, *The Shape of the Past* (Ann Arbor, Mich.: Edwards, 1962), p. 141.

38. Ibid., p. 241.

39. John W. Montgomery, "The Theologian's Craft," *Concordia Theological Monthly*, 37 (January 1966): 76.

40. John W. Montgomery, "Inductive Inerrancy," *Christianity Today*, 11 (March 3, 1967): 48.

41. John W. Montgomery, *Where Is History Going?* (Grand Rapids: Zondervan, 1969), p. 179.

adds, "Proceeding on the basis of empirical method as applied to history, one can inductively validate the Christian revelation-claim and the biblical view of total history."[42] These different emphases for different purposes point up the need for a system of apologetics. Until that is developed, a reader may attempt to synthesize the elements by affirming that Montgomery holds a methodological presupposition and a contentful hypothesis to be tested. He is neither a pure empiricist nor a Van Tilian presuppositionalist, but closer to Carnellian verificationist, in his treatment of his starting point.

On the matters of a Christian's common ground with non-Christians, Montgomery emphasizes observable data publicly available for the observation of all. More than data are available to all men, however, for so are their meanings. Historical events, he says, do not in themselves display a level of equal non-importance. Neither are all explanations equally plausible. "The conviction that historical facts do carry their interpretations (i.e. that the facts in themselves provide adequate criteria for choosing among variant interpretations of them) is essential both to Christian and to general historiography."[43] Without further defense of this highly debatable point, he asserts, "When the historical facts of Christ's life, death, and resurrection are allowed to speak for themselves, they lead to belief in His deity and to acceptance of His account of the total historical process."[44]

Although extensive common ground is found in external events, little is found in internal experiences. Montgomery says, "I am convinced that the empirical investigation of subjective religious experience has an almost negligible probability of yielding religious truth."[45] That conviction results from the difficulty of distinguishing what is religious experience from what is non-religious experience on subjective grounds, the problem of determining what religious experience will verify what hypotheses of religious truth, and the problem of obtaining exactly the results presupposed by those whose investigation of subjective experience is littered with a priori assumptions. In contrast to Carnell and closer to Buswell, Montgomery finds no inner categories of thought in the human mind. A law like that of causality is said to be no more than "an empirical, synthetic construct

42. Ibid.
43. Ibid., pp. 163-64.
44. Ibid., p. 166.
45. Montgomery, *Shape of the Past*, p. 269.

which is employed ad hoc to deal with historical facts."[46] Apparently the laws of logic are similarly invented. So there seems to be no common ground except in external, publicly observable evidence that carries with it its meaning.

As for Montgomery's test for truth, his writings are clear that hypotheses must fit the objective facts, but are not so clear with respect to harmony with the law of non-contradiction. An article in 1961 said objective empirical evidence for Jesus Christ and His message is the only truly valid Christian apologetic possible. Internal consistency and the external fitting of the facts do not prove a sacred book to be God's revelation.[47] But a 1962 publication says, "It seems that a claim to written revelation could be tested by its systematic consistency. . . ."[48] In *The God Is Dead Controversy* he appeals not only to the historicity of the resurrection and the facticity of biblical miracles, but also to "the internal consistency of holy writ."[49]

Nevertheless, in opposition to the position of Gordon Clark, Montgomery explains how to test the spirits. "Not by internal consistency (the devil is an exceedingly coherent logician as are all great liars), but by empirical comparison of doctrine with the objective, historically given Scriptures. Thus we are brought back again to the absolute necessity of an objective historiography, for without it we can establish no scriptural testing-stone."[50] In order to harmonize this with the earlier uses of consistency, I infer that he overstates the negation of non-contradiction as a test while intending to attack only Clark's use of consistency apart from empirical data. Montgomery apparently does not mean to deny the validity of the logical criterion in association with empirical tests of hypotheses. Possibly Montgomery is saying that the Scriptures are substantiated by empirical data alone and after that consistency with their teaching is a test of truth. However, the laws of logic apply to every statement made by pure empiricists as well as others. Surely contradictory interpretations of the data could not both be true. So this does not seem to be a successful way of seeing the consistency of Montgomery's statements regarding

---

46. Montgomery, *History*, p. 170.
47. John W. Montgomery, "The Apologetic Approach of Muhammed Ali and Its Implications for Christian Apologetics," *The Muslim World*, 51 (1961:) 111-122.
48. Montgomery, *Shape of the Past*, p. 287.
49. John Montgomery, *The God Is Dead Controversy* (Downers Grove, Ill.: Inter-Varsity Press, 1967), p. 59.
50. Montgomery, *History*, p. 178.

the criterion of non-contradiction. Until Montgomery does his readers the service of providing a more comprehensive and systematic treatment of apologetics, it seems that one would be justified in holding that in spite of some statement apparently to the contrary, his test for truth includes both logical non-contradiction and the fitting of the objective, empirical facts. His difference with Carnell is not so much at the point of consistency as the attempt to fit the hypothesis to external and internal data of man's subjective experience.

Montgomery's view of the role of reason in apologetics involves the verification or falsification of revelation-claims. In the outworking of his case for the resurrected Christ and the truth of Scripture his steps are similar to Gerstner's (above). Six steps are involved: (1) The gospels are tested critically and found historically trustworthy. (2) From these sources Jesus is known to have historically exercised divine prerogatives and made divine claims resting them on his forthcoming resurrection. (3) All four gospels attest His resurrection which evidences His deity. (4) The resurrection fact cannot be discounted by a priori definitions. (5) If Christ is God, He speaks the truth concerning the Old Testament, the New Testament, His death, and the nature of man and history. (6) So all biblical assertions bearing on philosophy of history are to be regarded as revealed truth and all human interpretation must harmonize with them.[51] Reason has far more of a role than that of interpretation. It critically assesses historical data and verifies claims for Christ and the Bible.

The basis of faith in Montgomery is the conclusiveness of the case based on adequate data. The purpose of his argument for Christ's resurrection is not to force anyone into the Christian faith. "The argument is intended, rather, to give solid objective ground for testing the Christian faith experientially. . . . The Scriptural Gospel is ultimately self-attesting, but the honest inquirer needs objective grounds for trying it, since there are a welter of conflicting religious options and one can become psychologically jaded through indiscriminate trials of religious belief. Only the Christian world-view offers objective ground for testing it experientially; therefore Christ deserves to be given first opportunity to make His claims known to the human heart."[52]

51. Montgomery, *Shape of the Past*, p. 341 ff.; *History*, pp. 179 ff. Cf. *History and Christianity* (Downers Grove, Illinois: Inter-Varsity, 1964-65), pp. 5-110.
52. Montgomery, *Shape of the Past*, p. 140.

The solid ground offered by Montgomery's argument at best establishes a high degree of probability. Historical evidence cannot yield apodictic certainty. This is not a weakness, Montgomery argues, for probability is the sole ground on which finite human beings can make any decisions. Apodictic certainty stems from self-evident axioms involving no matters of fact. In matters of fact probability is unavoidable and does not keep us from making decisions in nonreligious realms so it should not immobilize us when religious commitment is involved.[53]

Does the probability of the argument for Christianity mean the probability of every Christian doctrine? Montgomery points out that the epistemological route by which one arrives at biblical truth does not determine the value of what one arrives at—any more than the use of a less than perfect map requires one to reach a city having corresponding inadequacies. "The empirical, historical evidences in behalf of Christian revelation are not absolute (no synthetic proof can be), but they are sufficiently powerful to bring us to the feet of a divine Christ who affirms without qualifications that biblical revelation is trustworthy."[54]

Montgomery's system with its stress on methodological presuppositions, objective evidence, the fitting of the facts, an inductive use of reason, and the ground for faith in high probability, is a noble attempt at a pure empiricism, similar to that of Buswell and Gerstner. But insofar as he allows for hypotheses as starting points and abduction rather than induction, he has tendencies in the direction of Carnell's hypothesis-verification scheme. Even, then, however, he seeks to account for his gestalts, principles of causality, and logic as inductions from data, not internal principles given in the nature of the human mind. And so his thought may not be as Carnellian as at first it appears.

NORMAN L. GEISLER

John Montgomery's case is built largely upon Christ and the Scriptures, while that of Norman Geisler is directed in his *Philosophy of Religion* almost exclusively to the existence of God. Both Montgomery and Geisler seek to begin with human experience, as pure empiricists. Geisler does not talk about his methodology, but from

53. Ibid., p. 144.
54. Montgomery, *History*, pp. 180-81.

his procedure it is not too difficult to infer his answers to the issues on which we have compared the various thinkers.

Geisler's starting point is not presuppositions, biblical authority, or hypotheses about experience. However, the experience with which he begins is not limited to sensory data. "Experience," as Geisler defines it, "is the state of consciousness of an individual who is aware of something as other whether or not it is really other."[55] What, then, is religious experience? Religious experience "involves two basic elements: an awareness of the Transcendent and a total commitment to the Transcendent."[56] The most basic dimension of religious experience is man's fundamental drive to get beyond himself. It is a transcendent thrust.

The strategic point of contact with non-Christians, then, is this universal urge toward self-transcendence. In the history of thought Geisler finds that this transcendence has taken at least seven directions: "among the primitives transcendence was backward to the Origin; the Neoplotinians transcended upward to the highest possible reality; and other mystics sometimes transcend either Outward or Inward. But due to demythologization, many modern religious men have been unable to transcend in these traditional directions and have transcended either forward to the final End or downward to the Ground of all that is. Others, who deny religion, nevertheless transcend in a Circle."[57] Man is found to be incurably religious. The history of mankind, sacred or secular, supports the thesis that by nature man has an irresistible urge to transcend himself.

What then is the test of truth of assertions concerning the reality of a transcendent object of experience? Is there a transcendent reality with independent and objective existence? "One needs evidence to know that there is a God there, but he needs faith to commit himself to the God which the evidence indicates is really there."[58] So Geisler seeks to utilize the emphases of both verifications and fideists.

Geisler's basis for believing that there is a God depends upon the premise: "What men really need really exists." This is an inference from evidence, rather than evidence. And it is an inference based on an analogy to food, drink, etc. "Experience shows that even though

55. Norman L. Geisler, *Philosophy of Religion* (Grand Rapids: Zondervan, 1974), p. 13.
56. Ibid., p. 39.
57. Ibid., p. 63.
58. Ibid., pp. 73-74.

basic human needs are not always actually fulfilled in the case of given individuals, nevertheless, needs are characterized by fulfillability. . . . Some men may *think* that there are real but unfulfillable needs, but few men (if any) will really *believe* it, and no man can consistently *live* it."[59] "The need for God shows that there is a God somewhere to meet that need, and the fulfillment of the need for God in some men indicates that an experience with this God is actually achievable."[60]

The problem with atheism is that it admits man's need to transcend but it allows no object to fulfill this need. Not only is atheism "existentially cruel" but it entails the assertion that some men have been deceived about the reality of God, and that indeed all religious men who have ever lived have been completely deceived into believing there is a God when there really is not. If even one religious person is right about the reality of the Transcendent, then there really is a Transcendent. "Now it seems much more likely that such self-analyzing and self-critical men like Augustine, Pascal, and Soren Kierkegaard were not totally deceived than that total skepticism is right. It is simply unbelievable that every great saint in the history of the world, yes, even Jesus Christ himself, was completely deceived about the reality of God."[61]

As discussed above, Geisler reflects his commitment to a criterion of fitting the data of human experience. In addition, he works with the law of non-contradiction, defended at some length in discussion of the question, "Is the rationally inescapable real?"[62] But the law which determines what is logically possible is not the sole test of truth. "Not everything logically possible is real, e.g. centaurs and mermaids."[63] But reality cannot be contradictory and so the rationally inescapable is the real.[64] Whatever experiential data the test of truth may include, it clearly involves a non-contradictory account of that experience. But whether the principle of non-contradiction is an empirical construct or an innate idea is not discussed.

Reason's role is the philosophical substantiation of beliefs[65] or the giving of good reasons for one's beliefs.[66] The good reason for belief

59. Ibid., p. 80.
60. Ibid., p. 81.
61. Ibid., pp. 81-82.
62. Ibid., p. 97.
63. Ibid., p. 98.
64. Ibid., p. 99.
65. Ibid., p. 93.
66. Ibid., p. 95.

in God is primarily the cosmological argument for God's existence. The teleological is found to be based upon it, in that it assumes a cause for the design of the world.[67] And the moral argument assumes that an objective moral law requires a cause and so goes back to the causal (cosmological) argument.[68] The ontological argument is invalid without the assumption that something exists. But when the argument becomes something exists, therefore God exists, it reverts to the cosmological argument.[69]

Restating the cosmological argument from a context of logical necessity based on the principle of sufficient reason, Geisler begins with limited existence and by the use of the principle of existential causality proceeds to an unlimited cause of all existence. In brief, "If any finite being exists, then an infinite being exists as an actual and necessary ground for finite being."[70] The argument is not the ground for God's existence, but for the truth of a statement about God's existence. It is a logical argument based on reality, which rationally explains why limited being must be caused.[71]

Geisler's basis of faith lies in the logical possibility and existential probability of God's existence. On that basis he calls for faith in the God believed to be there. As he illustrates it, "It would be an insult to one's wife to demand reasons for loving her. But it is not an insult to her to demand that one have evidence that it is really she (and not the neighbor's wife) before one kisses her."[72] Similarly, "It is unworthy of God to believe in Him for the sake of the evidence. For if there is an ultimate value in the universe, then it ought to be believed in *for its own sake*. On the other hand, it would be unworthy of a reasonable creature to examine the evidence that there is an ultimate value before he makes an ultimate commitment to it."[73] So Geisler concludes, "Verification demands that one look before he leaps, that one makes sure that it is his wife before he embraces her, and that one is assured God is here before he believes in Him for His own sake."[74]

Geisler's approach seems most similar to that of the pure empiricists (Buswell and Gerstner) with a concept of experience broader than

67. Ibid., pp. 116-17.
68. Ibid., pp. 130-31.
69. Ibid., pp. 161-62.
70. Ibid., p. 224.
71. Ibid., p. 225.
72. Ibid., p. 74.
73. Ibid.
74. Ibid.

the more positivistically inclined empiricists would want to admit. But Geisler has utilized very well much significant literature in the field of religious experience and deserves a careful reading by those who hold this pure empiricism and those who reject it. As yet, granting his revision of the cosmological argument, he has only established the existence of God. It is to be hoped that he will complete his apologetic for Christ and the Bible.[75]

GEORGE I. MAVRODES

Ground is cleared for a defense of Christianity by professor of philosophy, George Mavrodes, in his *Belief in God: A Study in the Epistemology of Religion.* In that brief work, he acknowledges the significance of the task here undertaken, "I think the most important question that one can ask is, 'Is it true?' " Mavrodes disclaims providing an answer to that question, "I will not have very much to say directly about the truth of these (religious or Christian) beliefs."[76] How does he view his purpose? "What I hope to do is to carry out an investigation that is now, for many people, a required preliminary to usefully engaging themselves in the question of the truth of religious beliefs. But it is only preliminary and so it would be unfortunate if one's intellectual excursion into the realm of religion were to end where this book ends."[77]

Mavrodes appears to make somewhat separate comments about problems of knowing and believing, the difficulty of finding one solution convincing to all, ambiguities in the question, "How do you know?" (biographically, the content of the truth-claim believed or the grounds for that belief), the meaning of "proof," the termination of an infinite series of arguments, how to go about proving anything to another person, etc. An attempt will be made to convey some of his most significant points for the present comparative purpose.

The activity of knowing for ourselves and of convincing someone else is both person-oriented and content-oriented. Activities of knowing, believing, proving, solving, or experiencing are not merely epis-

75. In Geisler and Nix, *A General Introduction to the Bible* (Chicago: Moody, 1968), some problems of inspiration, the canon, and text have been answered extensively, but an evidential apologetic for the Bible is also needed to complete the system begun in *Philosophy of Religion.*
76. George I. Mavrodes, *Belief in God: A Study in the Epistemology of Religion* (New York: Random, 1970), p. viii.
77. Ibid.

temological questions, but also questions having to do with a certain person's attitude or disposition in relation to the content and its evidence. A large part of Mavrodes' book attempts to distinguish objective concepts from the subjective beliefs. He thinks a large part of the confusion engendered by epistemological discussions arises from the failure to recognize the mixed character of crucial epistemological concepts.[78] The mere fact that a given statement is true entails nothing at all about what any person's attitude is toward that statement.[79]

Mavrodes presents a simple argument for the existence of God:

> Either nothing exists or God exists.
> Something exists.
> Therefore God exists.[80]

The form of the argument is valid. It is formally impossible for the conclusion to be false if the premises are true. Are the premises true? The second premise seems obvious, though a person may not believe it. Is the first premise true? One's belief or disbelief in it does not make it true or false. It is true if it is the case that God exists and false if it is not the case that God exists. The argument cannot be rejected unless a person takes the stance of an atheist and denies that God is, metaphysically and theologically. A mere agnosticism leaves open the possibility that God does exist and the argument remains sound. If one must defend every statement, then the atheist must prove his atheist position. Neither Hume nor Kant proved that there are no sound arguments for God's existence. An argument may be sound or cogent, but a person may not know it to be cogent, and so for him it is not convincing. Cogent arguments are not always sufficient to prove their conclusions in the sense of convincing someone. One is convinced only if an argument is cogent, he knows it to be cogent, and he knows that each of its premises is true without having to infer them from the conclusion, or inferences from it. On this analysis, we will have proved a statement to a person only if we succeed in convincing him.[81]

A person may come to know the truth of a premise through obser-

78. Ibid., pp. 112-14.
79. Ibid., p. 38.
80. Ibid., p. 22.
81. Ibid., p. 34.

vation or experience or other means than argumentation. Since there may be other ways of knowing that God exists than by means of theistic argumentation, the question of proof by arguments is not crucial. On the other hand, valid argumentation is one way in which we extend our knowledge and so theistic arguments may not be unimportant either.[82]

One other way in which a person could learn of God's existence is through a competent authority. "One of the most important and far reaching consequences of the human capacity for rational communication is that the individual does not have to recapitulate in his own intellectual life the intellectual history of the race."[83] Most of our scientific and political knowledge has been learned through a single, competent, and reliable authority. In these cases, however, the possibility of a person's following the experiment for himself or examining the records for himself remains. "For any statement that can be known to be true an argument that is convincing for someone can be constructed."[84] But it is held to be unlikely that something could be proved to everyone by some argument or other. If that were possible with respect to God, then everyone would have to know something that entails that God exists and each person would have to know the requisite logic. Mavrodes finds no reason to think that all people could be convinced by any such logical argument.[85]

If there is any knowledge at all, then there must be some source of knowledge other than argumentation. The truth of the first premise of the argument for the existence of God may be derived from direct experience. This is Mavrodes' starting point and it has some similarity to that of Barrett and Young. The experience of God intended is not a purely psychological entity, like a pain, but an independent entity with His own existence. Experiencing something, furthermore, is more than receiving an input from it or being affected by it. "Experiencing something is a cognitive activity involving a conscious judgment. The judgment may be mistaken without thereby precluding the experience with which it is associated, but if there is no judgment at all then there is no experience. There is at most effect or response."[86]

82. Ibid., p. 42.
83. Ibid., p. 44.
84. Ibid., p. 45.
85. Ibid., p. 47.
86. Ibid., p. 62.

A mystic's claim to an immediate ineffable experience of God, on Mavrodes' analysis, testifies to his psychological sense of directness, but not to an unmediated experience. He is like an experienced railroad dispatcher working the trains through a television picture of their locations. The experienced person in the use of television for this sort of work would tend to omit reference to the mediator of the information and simply be directly concerned with the trains. He would make no reference to telecasts, electronic equipment, or the relations between them and trains. Similarly the directness of thought and judgment that claims "immediate" experience of God overlooks the intermediate inference and argument.[87] Many a person in a long distance telephone conversation does not stop to think through the many factors in the mechanics of the receiver and speaker, the electrical lines, but thinks he immediately hears the voice of another person.

Similarly, events or things may serve as media for the experience of God. We may hear the voice of God in a biblical passage, a remembrance of a remark made by a friend, a question we put to ourselves, the ringing of a bell on New Year's Eve, etc. God is known in conjunction with some other object that mediates His presence. There is no object or event in the natural world that could not serve as the mediator of His presence. It follows that whenever anyone is experiencing anything he *might* be experiencing God. It would, however, be a mistake to conclude that whenever anyone is experiencing anything he is experiencing God.[88]

How can such religious experience be verified? Mavrodes seeks to give a practical and existential reply, rather than a theoretical answer. It does follow that if a person claims to have an experience of God that his claim is true. Can it be known to be true if there are sufficient checking procedures? Mavrodes' analysis stresses the difficulties of checking on such a simple thing as seeing a piece of paper by yourself or others. Is it simply the possibility of carrying out verification procedures that is required? Then the possibility of experiencing God could be held even though it had never happened. Or the possibility might be derived from the judgment about the reality and independence of the experienced object, rather than the other way around. One who claims an experience of God can claim that He could be

87. Ibid., pp. 65-66.
88. Ibid., pp. 66-70.

similarly apprehended by others, or He might reveal Himself in quite different circumstances. If verification procedures are difficult for a piece of paper, they are much more so for a wolf in the Rocky Mountain National Park. A person who cannot be persuaded to tread lightly and sit patiently may never see the wolf. But a person who has seen a wolf would be foolish to deny having seen it just because the majority of his colleagues have not seen it.

At the same time, a person who has experienced God does not imagine himself infallible and does compare his claims with contemporaries and others. "A well-formulated religion such as Christianity, has much material (Bibles, creeds, etc.) against which the believer is urged to check his own experience. A large part of this material is the distillation of the accounts which previous believers have given of their experience."[89] Although Mavrodes seeks to minimize epistemology and technical tests of truth, the following statement is difficult to distinguish from a coherence (systematic consistency) criterion. "The final judgment that a person makes over the whole range of the experience of his life and of those testimonies that seem to him to have 'the ring of truth' is, of course, both subtle and complex. I do not know of any algorithm for such a judgment. But I suppose that the judgment in the end should answer the question: What is it that, in the light of my whole range of experience and thought, makes the best and the fullest sense?"[90] If "best" were defined, it would most likely include "non-contradictory"; if "fullest" were defined, it would quite naturally include all types of data from one's internal and external experience.

Verifying one's own experience is one thing, but verifying the experience of another, in which you begin with his report, is another. A person's report is sometimes taken as strong evidence that he has had such experience and sometimes it is not. Our judgment, Mavrodes explains, is guided by three considerations. First, we decide in terms of the importance of being right and the risk involved in making the judgment one way or another. When the risk is very high we tend to be more critical. Second, we judge by the credibility of the witness, a composite of many factors such as his moral character, his reputation as an observer, his readiness to act on his own observation,

89. Ibid., p. 80.
90. Ibid.

"the look in his eye," the number of such witnesses, their independence of each other and their agreement with each other on essential points.

Third, we judge another's report of an experience by the initial probability we attach to the possibility of such an experience. This is of great importance in assessing experience claims. For many people, claims of religious experience have a low probability because they assign a low probability to the existence of God. If they became convinced of His existence, then they might be much more sympathetic to the experience claims. Rather than trying to resolve the theoretical problem of God's existence first, Mavrodes suggests that a person who is interested, but doubtful of the experience claim may think of resolving these doubts by seeking such an experience himself. By way of illustration, I may go to the basement, flashlight in hand, to look for the traces of termites with my own eyes. By doing so, a person seeks a better basis for, and perhaps a change in the probability assigned to the hypothesis of termites being there. Such a search is particularly apppropriate in religion, and especially Christianity, for it has traditionally stressed the possibility of each man's own fellowship and communion with God.[91]

What can Christians do to try to make experience of God more accessible to another person? Although he has no guaranteed procedures, Mavrodes suggests three ways to proceed. One is to point up circumstances similar to those we were in when we had the relevant experience. When a friend cannot see the parade, we say, "You can see it from over here." We customarily assume that what has worked for us will work for other people. Though obvious and natural, this procedure, as Mavrodes admits, is often overdone. Every entity in the world is dependent upon God, and whatever a person is interested in is the workmanship of God. There are many factors that determine the degree of obviousness of the theistic features, and persons vary greatly. So it does not follow that what is convincing for one person will be so for another.[92]

A second way to invite people to experience God is to tell the person what to look for. Even though this procedure may lead to mistakes, it is important to help a person see a man among the trees in

91. Ibid., pp. 82-83.
92. Ibid., pp. 83-84.

a forest or the point of a scientific experiment. So we may not only mention the things or events in which the theistic features are prominent, but come right out and tell them what we hope they will discover by looking at these things and events. So the first and second procedures are frequently combined.[93]

The third procedure provides "an extensive conceptual framework which exhibits the meaning of the particular experience, or at least provides a place for it, by integrating it with a large range (ideally, the whole range) or other experiences." Providing a man with a conceptual framework in which he can see his whole life as being lived in the presence of God is like teaching a man to read a strange script. We can give him the key, a sort of Rosetta stone, by telling him the meaning of one particular inscription. If he believes us he can understand that inscription. But the test of whether he has really learned to read the script, and the confirmation that the translation we gave him was accurate, comes when he encounters all the other inscriptions that are scattered throughout the world. If "he finds that he can read the new inscriptions, if they make sense, if, in fact, he can correspond with those who write that language, and communicate with them, then he has learned that language. And every successful communication increases his grasp of it and also his confidence in it."[94]

The theologian provides us with a sort of key to what God is doing in the world, His moral demands, sin, guilt, judgment, redemption, forgiveness, Christ's incarnation, the Bible, the church, prayer, death, and eternal life. "All this may seem cumbersome, and singularly ill-supported. But if some part of it makes contact with some element in our experience so that each one illuminates and makes sense of the other, then we will take a new interest in that theology. If it goes beyond this, if it serves to light up broad ranges of our experience so that we begin to see a kind of sense in our lives, then perhaps we will be more than interested. Most important, if the terms and doctrines provide a clue as to how to respond, and if, as we try that response, we find our experience continuing to make sense, then we are likely to say that the key was a true one and that we also have heard God speaking to us."[95]

93. Ibid., pp. 84-85.
94. Ibid., pp. 86-87.
95. Ibid., p. 87.

Wisely, Mavrodes warns Christians against the dangers of over-simplifications in their representations of the "web woven of experience, inference and testimony" leading people of diverse backgrounds, personalities, and interests to faith.[96] At the same time, there is another temptation toward generalities that misses the distinctive essence of the evangelical Christian faith, such as the heart of the gospel and the distinctive experience of regeneration. Even a preliminary work such as his might suggest that while there are differences among Christians there are also certain essential similarities that make Christianity the uniquely distinct religion that it is.

We must also beware of the temptation, Mavrodes says, of supposing that another person's web must be just like our own. That well-taken counsel is one of the reasons for the present book. It has seemed that many apologists have assumed that there is but one system or approach to the defense of Christianity and all others are wrong. While Mavrodes says we should recognize different patterns, the present text practices his counsel in a way his own does not. Hopefully this comparison of apologetic approaches, including that of Mavrodes, will lead to the achievement of his expressed desire—to acknowledge varieties of approaches or "webs."

Mavrodes has attempted to avoid epistemological approaches in favor of experience and analysis in ordinary language. But experience involves interpretation, as was shown in the chapter above on direct experience. And judgment, as Mavrodes holds, decides whether a "state of affairs" is, or is not "the case," or whether an explanation does, or does not, "make sense." A reader looks for some definition of these key terms in his book, but fails to find it. Could it be that definitions would include the very epistemological concepts he is attempting to sidestep? Would not "making sense" call for logical noncontradiction? And would not being "the case" amount to fitting the facts? Mavrodes has helpfully shown that the issues are not merely epistemological, but call for experiential data. However, he has avoided the usual epistemological concepts at the cost of a lack of precision.

Arthur F. Holmes

The analytic approach of Mavrodes typically pays little attention

96. Ibid., p. 89.

to pre-analytic philosophical thought. Arthur Holmes' writings, on the other hand, are primarily involved with the contributions of thinkers in history. Holmes expounds the major philosophies and assesses strengths and weaknesses from his Christian perspective. He calls his approach more of a historical or philosophical dialogue than an apologetic argument.[97]

Like several others we have surveyed, Holmes disclaims a system and intends only to clear away some preliminary matters to a defense of Christian thought. His *Christian Philosophy in the Twentieth Century*, he says, is "propaedeutic to other tasks."[98] *Faith Seeks Understanding* is a guidebook "by no means complete." A guidebook, he explains, "maps out alternative paths, and rests its recommendations on the experience and evaluation of those who like the writer have explored those paths a little for themselves."[99]

What Holmes resists is a kind of approach which imagines itself capable of a complete and conclusive system.[100] But of course his views are consistent throughout his writing and he develops a position (limited system?) which "mediates between rationalistic or scientistic dogmatism on the one hand, and relativistic scepticism on the other. I find it impossible to be either extremely pessimistic or extremely optimistic about the outcome of philosophical investigation. At the same time I have tried to show that existentialism and analytic philosophy are not completely antithetical and that cognitive understanding and existential self-knowledge are not mutually exclusive."[101]

The term Holmes prefers for his metaphysical stance is "perspective." "Metaphysical descriptions are 'confessions' about the nature of things as seen from a particular perspective. . . . A metaphysical system is confessional. It includes both a *kerygma*—the proclamation of a world-view in articulate symbols—and an *apologia*—a persuasive appeal to look at the adequacy of its descriptions and the coherence which its language discloses."[102] Since Holmes' "perspectival ap-

97. Arthur F. Holmes, *Faith Seeks Understanding* (Grand Rapids: Eerdmans, 1971), p. 5.
98. Arthur F. Holmes, *Christian Philosophy in the Twentieth Century* (Nutley, N.J.: Craig, 1969), p. ix.
99. Holmes, *Faith*, p. 7.
100. Ibid., p. 37.
101. Holmes, *Christian Philosophy*, p. x.
102. Ibid., p. 208.

proach" incorporates an examination of the adequacy and coherence (an *apologia*) of a world view, it should not be out of place to consider it in a survey of systems of apologetics. Indeed, it would be an injustice to omit it.

What, then, is Holmes' starting point? It is his personal, subjective perspective, a Christian perspective. He has no apology for starting with a point of view, for "philosophy is 'perspectival,'—all philosophy, not just the work of Christians. Philosophizing is an intensely personal activity in which one's basic beliefs and values are inevitably revealed."[103] In his judgment, metaphysics objectifies and evaluates the guiding perspective subjectively embraced. "That subjectivity is not lost when it becomes self-critical, but only examined and refined and weighed. Objectivity and intellectual honesty are not the same as neutrality. 'Know thyself,' not 'forget thyself,' is the touchstone of philosophical integrity."[104]

Many philosophers draw the "root-metaphors" of their perspectives from some common area of human experience, often leading to natural theology. An explanation of this sort fits metaphysical systems that use mechanistic, idealist, or organismic models. For the Christian, meaning is disclosed most fully and clearly, not in some universal form of ordinary experience, but in a unique event—the incarnation. "Jewish theism was articulated by poets and prophets who reflected on the works of Jehovah. In Jesus Christ this is brought to fulfillment, and the New Testament writings elaborate an enriched conception of God and of man and history that is made possible by his coming. It is this perspective, subjectively embraced in believing, that the Christian philosopher deliberately confesses in his metaphysical explorations."[105]

Just as Holmes' perspectival starting point is parallel to Carnell's hypothetical starting point, so Holmes' has some points of reference in human need similar to Carnell's synoptic starting point or common ground. Holmes says, "Let us take as our starting point the Christian's belief that 'men need God'." By "men" he means the total personality of people, and by "needing God" he does not intend Hume's customary belief or the need to accept as a fact the existence of God. To "need God" involves far more than this. It involves logi-

103. Holmes, *Faith*, p. 6.
104. Ibid., pp. 46-47.
105. Ibid., p. 47.

cal, ethical, religious, and emotional needs. He confesses, "Logically I need God in order to account adequately and consistently for man and the universe. This is where traditional theistic evidences come in. Ethically, I need God in order to understand man's moral sensitivities, and in order to acquire that moral dynamic which is lacking. Religiously, I need God as an objective, personal Supreme Being, whom to worship. Emotionally, I need One on whom to rely when all else gives way. The full explication of the meaning and legitimacy of these needs and the relevance of Christian theism thereto is the task of apologetics."[106]

Incompatible traditions persist in answer to these needs of men in spite of criticism and dialog. We are left with the problem of deciding which world view is true. What are the criteria by which we should choose between conflicting metaphysical perspectives? The logic of world view decisions is neither that of mathematics nor that of empirical science. Because Holmes seeks an understanding which grasps things as an intelligible whole and gives meaning and authenticity to his life, he uses neither an inductive nor a deductive logic, but a more informal "lived-logic" geared to world view thinking.[107] Its criteria of truth are implicit in the quest for understanding, and involve three norms.

First is the criterion of personal disclosure value. Metaphysical belief is a function of a life-perspective. In taking the viewpoint I do, Holmes says, I act as a person and accept responsibility for the decisions I have made. I must be true to myself as well as to the facts as I see them. I must take the perspective that illuminates experience and frees me from the threat of meaninglessness. If this factor does not operate at all consciously or unconsciously, a philosophical view is held inauthentically, in an impersonal and detached way, as a result of an unthinking response or biographical accident. To call this criterion "existential" is to relate it to the personal, historical situation of the philosopher, to stress that it transcends the detachment of sheer objectivity by involving the subjectivity of the knower as a person. "Existential" value does not relegate the decision to the emotions and detach it from legitimate questions about the rational justification of

---

106. Arthur F. Holmes, "The Nature of Theistic Apologetics," *Bulletin of the Evangelical Theological Society*, 2 (Spring 1959): 4.
    107. Ibid., p. 53.

belief. So this criterion is not sufficient as a test for objective truth. Empirical and logical considerations must be added to it.[108]

Second is the criterion of empirical fit. The perspective one lives with must do more than give personal disclosure value, it must fit the facts and fit them well. It must be able to encompass all relevant data without cramping them; it must have adequate scope. It must also be precise, applicable to particulars.[109]

The criterion of empirical fit depends upon the definition of experience. Natural experience is both wider and richer than sense-empiricisms have supposed. Not only the sciences, both of nature and of man, must be taken into account, but also the humanities. "Here the pulse of human experience beats more loudly than in the sciences, for experience is pervaded by interests and purposes, by evaluation, reaction, and interpretation. Aesthetic, cultural, social, moral, and religious experience must all be faced, for metaphysics bears responsibility to them all."[110]

The third criterion is that of logical coherence. A philosophical perspective must have power to integrate, to reveal the oneness in the many and the intelligible order in diversity and change. Self-consistency is necessary here, for, however difficult it may be to establish the logical law of non-contradiction on logic alone, it remains essential to any intelligible unity. Yet coherence is more than consistency, for wholly unrelated propositions may be consistent but quite incoherent.

The demand for intelligibility is a demand for ordered unity. But that unity need not be limited to that of a deductive system in which every proposition is logically implied by the premises, nor a causal account that traces connections between events. A work of art coheres around a common theme. We speak of unity in the lifework of an author or composer, or even a school or tradition. A family is cohesive by virtue of the values that bind its members together, and the same could be said of other social groups. All these examples and other instances of unity may help us see the coherent picture.[111]

Holmes brings a particularly helpful irenic spirit and insightful articulation to criteria of truth (existential authenticity, empirical

108. Ibid., pp. 53-55.
109. Ibid., p. 55.
110. Ibid., p. 56.
111. Ibid., p. 57.

adequacy, and rational coherence) that are similar to those of Carnell and Schaeffer. Holmes' constant interaction with the philosophical alternatives makes his contribution especially valuable for people with philosophical backgrounds.

In discussion of the role of reason, Holmes' breadth is evident. Reason is not limited to deductive syllogistic reasoning or inductive amassing of hard data. He is willing to appeal to anything that helps him see what makes the perspective in question do the job. "The history of thought can help by revealing how a position that has been variously expressed, or a tradition that has had various formulations, achieves coherence. Dialogue with other traditions forces self-criticism through a rigorous exposure to other points of view. Analysis helps in sorting our related questions and explicating connections, in mapping the use of words and showing their surprising scope, in detecting logical and linguistic relationships that have been overlooked. Symbol, analogy, metaphor, and paradox help in painting provocative pictures, pointing directions, suggesting new angles, and disclosing obscure relationships. All of this helps us to see things whole."[112]

The perspectival use of reason does not start with neutral data and develop impersonal, Thomistic style arguments for God's existence. Neither does it join the Barthian refusal to consider the demands of logical consistency, nor the existentialist separation of an authentic kerygma from historical fact. Furthermore, perspectives are not presuppositions that produce a closed system independent of empirical and rational criteria. Truth is more than a quality of propositions; it is also a property of a person in relationship to the source of all truth, God. Individual truths can be isolated from this context, but only as fragments torn from the whole. Reason has a task larger than that of traditional correspondence of ideas to facts or of consistency. It does justice to both of these and to existentialist insights. One must be true to himself as well as to theoretical understandings, be "in the truth" as well as "know the truth."[113]

What then is the basis for faith? Faith is not mere mental assent to a syllogism, it is an existential response of the whole person to God through the Christ of Scripture. Faith is not a leap in the dark. Holmes asks, "Does the Jesus event grip a man with faith and hope apart from the redemptive history of which it is the culmination? Or

112. Ibid., pp. 57-58.
113. Holmes, *Christian Philosophy*, p. 239.

does it derive its existential power from the history of sin and grace in which it stands? Does any historical event trigger authenticity in isolation from the context which makes it important? Does existential disclosure occur in isolation from our understanding, or does it occur rather in the dynamic interrelation of event and context, of fact and meaning, of subject and object?"[114] The answers are obvious.

How does Holmes apply his approach to the fact of Christ's resurrection? "That the tomb was empty on Easter morning and that Jesus appeared to his followers are historical phenomena to be supported by historical and literary evidence. That God raised Jesus from the dead is a causal explanation of the historical phenomena, whose validation depends on theistic presuppositions and requires us to exhibit the superior empirical adequacy and rational coherence of this explanation over alternative hypotheses. That God raised him for our justification is a still further account given in Scripture, whose plausibility is seen by its coherence within the whole pattern of Biblical theology. That Jesus Christ is therefore Lord, that we owe him our faith and devotion, and that our knowledge of God reaches fulfillment in knowing him, is a further inference that depends on the larger theological pattern."[115]

In addition to all these bases of faith, Holmes notes that faith and devotion are not coerced by argument. They are rather elicited by the witness of God's Spirit to the bearing of Jesus Christ and Gospel on the felt needs of a man. If we are to give good reasons for the faith, we must see that religious language is not modeled on the verifiable statements of empirical science, but on world views and personal discourse. It must interpret life as a whole and bear witness by history and precept and paradox and symbol and every literary form possible to the mystery of God revealing Himself and redeeming men. "If we are to communicate religious truth to others, it is equally essential to do so in a personal context of mutual trust and love that will help them see by way of analogy what it would be like to know God himself. But if a man is to know God for himself, it will be a response to God's personal disclosure which goes beyond the communication and attestation of truth to the application of divine grace to man's deepest need."[116]

114. Holmes, *Faith*, p. 76.
115. Ibid., p. 161.
116. Ibid., pp. 161-62.

It is to be hoped that Holmes will go beyond these "preliminary matters" and develop a thorough defense of Christianity in accord with these principles so effectively articulated in his present works.

Josh McDowell

Evidence that Demands a Verdict: Historical Evidences for the Christian Faith makes no attempt to develop a philosophical system, but to show in extensive detail how Christianity fits the facts.[117] This work supplies an abundance of support for all the apologists who insist that Christianity is superior to other systems because of its empirical fit. Josh McDowell, utilizing a team of researchers, has brought together a vast compilation of quotations from specialists in the examination of evidence related to belief in the truth of the Bible and the deity of Jesus Christ. Although the authorities selected support his position, and one could collect a like body of quotations from liberal scholars, the evidence to which McDowell's authorities refer is important. He has done a real service in bringing it all together in one volume.

The book seeks to avoid philosophical apologetics, but that is hard to do. In the organization of that much material certain methodological assumptions become evident. The overall structure reflects an approach of pure empiricism (similar to Gerstner and Montgomery) in that it presents evidence from history and archaeology for the reliability of the Bible and then considers Jesus as a man of history. From the historical evidence concerning His claims and characteristics a case is made that He was God's Son. Further confirmation is cited in His fulfillment of Old Testament predictions and His resurrection from the dead. Then a chapter on other fulfilled prophecies confirms the fact that the Bible is more than a history book and could not have been produced by merely human minds. (Since prior to this point in the argument the deity of Christ has been supported, the Lord's view of the Bible is often added.) Fulfilled prophecies show also that God

---

117. Josh McDowell, *Evidence That Demands a Verdict* (San Bernardino: Campus Crusade for Christ, 1972). See his second compilation, *More Evidence That Demands a Verdict* (San Bernardino: Campus Crusade for Christ, 1975), which challenges the assumptions and arguments often presented as assured results of modern scholarship for the documentary hypothesis of the Pentateuch and form criticism of the Gospels. In his book, see my appendix applying a verificational approach to the criticism of the Gospels: "A Comparison of Form Criticism and Classical Criticism of the Gospels," pp. 335-40.

is at work in history. His activity in people's lives is then supported by numerous testimonies of conversion from people of diverse backgrounds. Josh McDowell adds his own witness and concludes with Bill Bright's "Four Spiritual Laws."

Although the overall structure is similar to that of pure empiricism, some of the chapters start, not with evidence, but with hypotheses from which to choose on the basis of the evidence. Chapter 7 presents several options (hypotheses) concerning Christ: Lord, liar, lunatic, good man, or great prophet. Authorities quoted say the evidence rules out all the hypotheses except the one that He was Lord. Chapter 8 uniquely gives a structure to the argument for which the evidence is utilized. And the argument form is hypothetical. "*If* God became a man, *then* what would He be like?" The qualities of God then included in the hypothesis are observed in the life of Christ. Although no conclusion is drawn, the intent is to the effect that the hypothesis of His deity fits the facts. This argument is drawn from Bernard Ramm's *Protestant Christian Evidences* which was in turn significantly influenced by Carnell's *Introduction to Christian Apologetics*. McDowell continues to write in this field, and it will be interesting to see which starting point becomes most prominent. (His latest book is *More Evidence That Demands a Verdict,* San Bernadino: Campus Crusade for Christ, 1975.)

Bernard Ramm

Another able writer in apologetics is Bernard Ramm. His *Types of Apologetics Systems* surveyed historical systems and his *Protestant Christian Evidences* has been utilized above for evidential support of the existence of the triune God disclosed in Scripture. Has Ramm provided a new approach in *The God Who Makes a Difference?*

His major chapter, "An Outline of a System of Apologetics" indicates the direction his thought is taking. His logical starting point emphasizes the freedom to survey options and choose a proposed hypothesis after exploring what one is committed to in accepting it. "All progress in knowledge of any kind is possible only if from facts we go on to postulation, namely suggesting some theory or hypothesis that integrates and explains the facts."[118] So his logical starting point is not essentially different from Carnell's.

118. Bernard Ramm, *The God Who Makes a Difference* (Waco, Tex.: Word, 1972), p. 32.

The content of his Christian postulate is similar, but more detailed. "The Christian religion is the redemptive and revelatory work of the Holy Spirit which reaches its highest expression in revelation and redemption in the Incarnation of God in Christ; and this religion is preserved for all ages and is witnessed for all ages in the inspired Holy Scripture." To make his hypothesis even more explicit, he adds, "The truest expression of the Christian religion is the Reformed faith which seeks to preserve the best of Christian theology from the end of the Apostolic Age to the Reformation, and which cast the faith of the Reformation in its most biblical form."[119]

The seeds of a more creative contribution appear in relation to Ramm's analysis of three concentric circles of verification, representing three stages in the process of verification which shows on what grounds Christianity is held to be true.[120] While this distinction may often have been assumed by apologists, I think Ramm's explanation may dispel misunderstanding of the apologist's task by others.

In Ramm's first circle, a sinner hears the Gospel and is persuaded through the illumination of the Holy Spirit that it is true, and applies to him. Every believer is so illumined, even though he is unaware of the Spirit's activity. So each has a sense of the Gospel's truth as revealed in the Word, a sense of sonship, and a sense of certainty that he belongs to God. This is "a spiritual verification in that the primary verification of religion must be of this order else the case is deeded away to a method of verification alien to religion."[121] The first stage of verification is that of the persuasion and witness of the Holy Spirit. This is not a subjectivism in which what a person believes is true simply because he believes it or because of his own unique experience. But it is truth that is inward. It is not subjectivism, but subjectivity.

A second stage of verification is called for in relation to Christianity because the Scriptures contain objective elements. The maturing Christian does not limit his belief to the Gospel simply as it applies to him, but learns in the Scriptures of the living God who is at work in the world and has been active in history. The God who saves is the God who created, called Abraham, and led Israel in usual and un-

119. Ibid., p. 33.
120. Ibid., p. 38.
121. Ibid., p. 44.

usual ways. The most exceptional acts of God provide the clearest test of Christianity's truth-claims. Hence evidentialists have focused upon miracles and fulfilled prophecy, the prime example being the resurrection of Jesus Christ from the dead. "Evidentialists [Ramm's term for those appealing to the usual Christian evidences (prophecy and miracle) the action of the living God in creation, revelation and redemption] believe that the evidences do establish the divine origin of the Christian faith."[122] The supernatural event validates the theological claim. A revelation is tested by reason. Reason recognizes the presence of God in the supernatural.

The function of Christian evidences is to create a favorable attitude toward the gospel; they are not the Gospel. They are not the Spirit. They do not change man's nature, nor do they put him in the kingdom of God. But they do show that "the God of Israel, and the God and Father of our Lord Jesus Christ, are not empty religious concepts or barren theological notions. This God does come into our time, our history, our space, our cosmos, and make a difference. Because God makes this difference, we know that we are believing truth and not fiction or mere religious philosophy."[123] Circle two—the action of God in creation and history thus delivers Christians from the charge of subjectivism—is consistent with the appeal to verification of claims in Scripture by miracle and prophecy and in fact shores up, in its own way and in its proper place, the veracity of Holy Scripture.[124]

The Christian is convinced of the truth of his faith first by the witness of the Spirit to the Gospel, second by the actions of the living God which make a difference in the cosmos, and third by the adequacy of the synoptic vision Christianity provides of humanity, the world, and God. In the third stage Christianity is found to be true because on its principles one can make the most sense out of life in this world. Eventually people leave the microscopic study of facts to take a look at life as a whole. By "vision" Ramm means a pattern, configuration, model, picture, complex diagrammatic chart by which he can synthesize his discipline into one unified theory or interpretation. "That pattern or that picture which has the most appeal to him, that puts things together for him the most meaningful way even with the lack

122. Ibid., p. 55.
123. Ibid., p. 57.
124. Ibid.

of a great number of important data, is the one he chooses. That is his synoptic vision."[125]

The lack of a synoptic vision on the part of people from the churches is one of the main reasons, Ramm thinks, for the defection from Christianity among high school and college students. Previously these students received only bits and pieces of Christian teaching, but not a systematic theology, or system of apologetics. Hence their faith resembles a patchwork quilt.

The Christian synoptic vision is not alone in the world. As a young person is brought face to face with convincing presentations of non-Christian synoptic visions, on what basis does he make a choice? Synoptic visions are not to be arbitrary choices but responsible choices. Some sort of specific criteria must be considered to help distinguish true from false philosophies of life on planet earth in our universe.

Ramm's test of truth remains similar to Carnell's and others and does not require further elaboration. "A responsible synoptic vision must have reckoned with a measure of factual support. The mere choosing of a synoptic vision does not make it true or free from measurement from some kind of criterion. A synoptic vision may be false as in the case of idolatry. Synoptic visions must show some interaction with concrete data or facts or the realities of the cosmos."[126] "A responsible synoptic vision must have a measure of internal coherence."[127]

Ramm's clarification of the three circles of Christians in terms of their concern for Scripture verses alone, evidences, and a synoptic perspective, hopefully will enable people who needed only one of these factors in coming to faith and justifying their faith against non-Christians, to respect and understand those who require two or all three. In effect, he is saying the Christian "is convinced of the truth of his faith by the witness of the Spirit. He is convinced of the truth of his faith by the actions of the living God in the cosmos which make a difference. And he is a Christian because he believes that the Christian faith gives him the most adequate synoptic vision there is with reference to man, humanity, the world, and God."[128]

125. Ibid., p. 60.
126. Ibid., p. 63.
127. Ibid., p. 67.
128. Ibid., p. 61.

Does the Christian have this conviction on the basis of a high probability or a full certainty? Ramm has some helpful counsel on this persistent question, including a distinction between certitude and certainty. " (1) In view of the divine revelation in Scripture and the internal witness of the Holy Spirit, a Christian may have full spiritual certitude. He believes with full certitude that God is, that Christ is his Lord and Savior, that he is a child of God, etc. He does not add to these convictions the word *probably*. (2) In that so much of the Christian faith is a matter of history, ordinary or sacred, the logical status of Christianity is that of probability. Historical facts cannot be known with full certainty. Therefore on its historical side Christianity can never be known with certainty (that is, as if it were a purely symbolic system; or, that it has a probability status of 1). But it can be known with a high degree of probability. (3) The Christian apologist then says that spiritually, inwardly, convictionally he rests his faith in full certitude; in reference to the objective historical, factual, etc., basis of the Christian revelation, he believes with a high degree of probability."[129]

C. S. Lewis

A survey of recent apologetics would hardly be complete without reference to the popular apologetic of C. S. Lewis (1898-1964). The gifted English author, who emphasized the richness of human experience in different literary styles, did not produce a formal system of apologetics. But he did recognize the priority of epistemological questions. "What we learn from experience," he said, "depends on the kind of philosophy we bring to experience. It is therefore useless to appeal to experience before we have settled, as well as we can, the philosophical question."[130]

How then does C. S. Lewis resolve the questions of logical starting point, common ground, test for truth, role of reason, and basis of faith? And how does his perspective compare with the systems studied above?

It seems justifiable to consider Lewis's starting point to be philosophical hypotheses and finally the hypothesis of orthodox Christianity's view of God, Christ, and Scripture. Upon occasion he calls the

---

129. Ibid., p. 73.
130. C. S. Lewis, *Miracles* (New York: Macmillan, 1948), p. 11.

alternative philosophies under consideration "hypotheses."[131] He
rejects a deductive methodology because "we do not know in advance
that God might not."[132] The different hypotheses are presented as
he experienced one after another in his own intellectual pilgrimage.
The naturalistic explanation of the world is evaluated in *Miracles*
over against the supernaturalistic explanation. In the process he
assesses different "theories" of nature's laws. The humanist variety
of explanation is found to be "polishing the brass on a sinking
ship."[133] The hypothesis of Eastern religions posed an attractive
alternative, but he failed to find in Hinduism the help he needed.[134]
His materialism was more disturbed by Spiritualism, Theosophy and
pantheism. Finally he moved to theism and then Christianity.[135]
Clearly, C. S. Lewis tested different logical starting points from which
to account for the world.

As a Christian defending his faith, did C. S. Lewis find common
ground with non-Christians? His writings reflect at least five points
of contact with outsiders. The first element in common is facts: "It
will be agreed that, however they came there, concrete, individual,
determinate things do now exist: things like flamingoes, German
generals, lovers, sandwiches, pineapples, comets and kangaroos. These
are not mere principles or generalities or theorems, but things—
facts—real, resistant existences."[136] Lewis spoke of "the father of fact-
hood," God, as "the eternal Fact."[137] Describing his apologetic task,
Lewis said, "All I am doing is to ask people to face the facts. . . .
I wish it was possible to say something more agreeable. But I must
say what I think true."[138]

A second element of common ground with non-Christians is the
laws of nature. These "laws give us only a universe of 'Ifs and Ands':
not this universe which actually exists. What we know through laws
and general principles is a series of connexions."[139] For there to be

131. Ibid., p. 42; C. S. Lewis, *The Pilgrim's Regress* (Grand Rapids: Eerdmans,
1943), pp. 37-38.
132. Lewis, *Miracles*, p. 21.
133. Lewis, *Pilgrim's Regress*, p. 108.
134. Ibid., p. 143.
135. Ibid., p. 164; C. S. Lewis, *Surprised by Joy* (New York: Harcourt, Brace and
World, 1955), pp. 197-238.
136. Lewis, *Miracles*, p. 105.
137. C. S. Lewis, *The Great Divorce* (New York: Macmillan, 1946), p. 44.
138. C. S. Lewis, *Mere Christianity* (New York: Macmillan, 1952), p. 25.
139. Lewis, *Miracles*, p. 105.

a real universe concrete particulars must be fed into these patterns. They have to have something to be true *about*. The principles themselves cannot create anything or do anything. "They produce no events; they state the pattern to which every event—if only it can be induced to happen—must conform." "To think the laws can produce it is like thinking that you can create real money by simply doing sums. For every law, in the last resort, says 'If you have A, then you will get B'. But first catch your A: the laws won't do it for you."[140]

In the third place, Christians share with non-Christians the laws of thought. On this assumption, Lewis attacks naturalism by showing its inherent self-contradiction. Naturalism poses as a rational theory, but if true, it is itself the product of nonrational causes. God Himself cannot violate the law of non-contradiction. Is not God able to do anything? "He cannot do what is contradictory: or in other words, a meaningless sentence will not gain meaning simply because someone chooses to prefix to it the words 'the Landlord (God) can.' "[141] Although we often say that a certain thing is impossible *unless* conditions change, Lewis says, "I know very well that if it is self-contradictory it is absolutely impossible."[142]

Fourth, Lewis appeals to common laws of morality. These explain why human beings do not fight like animals but argue about the rightness or wrongness of their actions. In order to quarrel, both parties recognize a law of right and wrong that they know by nature. Those who deny such a law may acknowledge its existence by claiming that they have been treated unfairly. Such a law of decent behavior alone makes possible judgments that the world is getting better or worse. This is a real law above and beyond the ordinary facts of men's behavior—a real law, which none of us made but which we find pressing upon us. If there exists such an absolute goodness, it must hate most of what men do. Only after realizing the reality of the Power behind the law and that we are in wrong with it can Christianity begin to make sense.[143]

A fifth element in common among all human beings is an experience of intense longing for an Object that is never fully given nor can be fully given in the present mode of subjective and spatio-temporal

140. Ibid., pp. 71-72.
141. Lewis, *Pilgrim's Regress*, p. 181.
142. C. S. Lewis, *The Problem of Pain* (New York: Macmillan, 1948), p. 15.
143. Lewis, *Mere Christianity*, pp. 3-25.

existence.[144] This desire for the transcendent cannot be fulfilled by aesthetic experience, sexual experience, or any other state of human experience. No feeling whatever will appease us. What we desire is no state of ourselves at all, but something Other and Outer.[145] Lewis finds similarity to this longing for the transcendent in the attraction of far away places, mountains, fantasies, magic, occultism, and other things. But he confesses, "I have myself been deluded by every one of these false answers in turn, and have contemplated each of them earnestly enough to discover the cheat."[146] Beneath these desires is a deeper longing for the joy God alone can give to every human heart.

On the issue of common ground, C. S. Lewis finds facts, laws of nature, laws of logic, laws of morality, and a longing for happiness with God. Given these realities common to all people, meaningful discussion of alternative world-views are possible.

What, then, has C. S. Lewis to say about a criterion of truth? A true hypothesis about the world must consistently account for these givens in all human experience. "A complete philosophy must get in *all* the facts."[147] All reality should be "consistent and systematic."[148] When C. S. Lewis read Chesterton's *Everlasting Man,* he saw for the first time Christianity's coherence. He saw "the whole Christian outline of history set out in a form that seemed to me to make sense."[149] He became a Christian because Christianity was factual, consistent, resolved the moral problem, and led to the transcendent Other. But the major criteria were factuality and consistency. "No thought is valid if it can be fully explained as the result of irrational causes."[150] An invalid truth-claim resulted from the unwarranted association of mere ideas; a valid truth-claim was established by sound inference from observed facts. Truth is well informed by the data. Mystical experience alone does not validate any religion in which it happens to occur. The true religion gives value to its own mysticism, not vice versa. Lewis likened mystical experience to a sea voyage. All the people who leave the port of ordinary consciousness find the same things at first. But the important question is where they land at the end

144. Lewis, *Pilgrim's Regress,* pp. 7-10.
145. Ibid., p. 129.
146. Ibid., p. 8.
147. Lewis, *Miracles,* p. 52.
148. Ibid., p. 74.
149. Lewis, *Surprised by Joy,* p. 223.
150. Lewis, *Miracles,* p. 27. Lewis's italics.

of the voyage. Where does the trip take the voyager?[151] Lewis stressed consistency as well as fitting the facts in his test of truth. He attacked as nonsensical the idea that mutually exclusive propositions about God can both be true.[152] At the same time, the application of the law of non-contradiction did not mean "pronouncing all other religions to be totally false, but rather saying that in Christ whatever is true in all religions is consummated and perfected."[153]

What, then, is the role of reason in the approach of C. S. Lewis? Reason does not merely interpret an alleged revelation or religious experience. Reason tests alternative world views to determine not whether they are pleasing or whether they work but whether they are true. For him the basic issue in apologetics is showing Christianity's truth, not its relevance. Speaking to ministers and youth workers, C. S. Lewis said, "The great difficulty is to get modern audiences to realize that you are preaching Christianity solely and simply because you happen to think it is *true:* they always suppose you are preaching it because you like it or think it good for society or something of that sort."[154]

The spirit of the age, Lewis thinks, is not too rational. The problem is that "The Spirit of the Age wishes to allow argument and not to allow argument." He explains: "If anyone argues with them they say that he is rationalizing his own desires, and therefore need not be answered. But if anyone listens to them they will then argue themselves to show that their own doctrines are true." What is the antidote for this? "You must ask them whether any reasoning is valid or not. If they say no, then their own doctrines, being reached by reasoning, fall to the ground. If they say yes, then they will have to examine your arguments and refute them on their merits: for if some reasoning is valid, for all they know, your bit of reasoning may be one of the valid bits."[155]

As against other views such as naturalism, reason shows that they are illogical (denying the validity of reasoning and so cutting their

151. Kathryn Ann Lindskoog, *C. S. Lewis: Mere Christianity* (Glendale, California: Regal Books, 1973), p. 210.
152. C. S. Lewis, *God in the Dock* (Grand Rapids: Eerdmans, 1970), p. 102.
153. Ibid.
154. Ibid., p. 91.
155. Lewis, *Pilgrim's Regress*, pp. 71-72.

own throats) or unplausible (accepting a picture of things which no one believes) .[156]

In establishing his case for Christianity, Lewis is not worried about reason destroying one's faith. The battle is not between faith and reason but between faith and reason on the one side and emotion and imagination on the other. He insists, "I am not asking anyone to accept Christianity if his best reasoning tells him that the weight of evidence is against it. That is not the point at which faith comes in."[157] Reason shows the high probability of the Christian answer, as in the instance of the doctrine of creation. "I do not maintain," Lewis says, "that God's creation of Nature can be proved as rigorously as God's existence, but it seems to me overwhelmingly probable, so probable that no one who approached the question with an open mind would very seriously entertain any other hypothesis."[158]

Reason, furthermore, must show that the deep longing for the infinite in humanity has an object. Critics charged that being hungry did not prove that they had bread. Lewis reasoned, however, that these critics missed the point. "A man's physical hunger does not prove that that man will get any bread; he may die of starvation on a raft in the Atlantic. But surely a man's hunger does prove that he comes of a race which repairs its body by eating and inhabits a world where eatable substances exist. In the same way, though I do not believe (I wish I did) that my desire for Paradise proves that I shall enjoy it, I think it a pretty good indication that such a thing exists and that some men will. A man may love a woman and not win her; but it would be very odd if the phenomenon called 'falling in love' occurred in a sexless world."[159]

What then is faith and how is it related to the basis provided by reason? In the first sense, faith means "accepting or regarding as true the doctrines of Christianity."[160] In this sense assent to a proposition thought to be highly probable leads to a psychological exclusion of doubt even though there is not a logical exclusion of dispute. Reason evaluates the evidence and leads to the door of faith.[161]

156. Lewis, *Miracles*, p. 43.
157. Lewis, *Mere Christianity*, p. 107.
158. Lewis, *Miracles*, p. 42.
159. C. S. Lewis, *Weight of Glory* (Grand Rapids: Eerdmans, 1965), p. 6.
160. C. S. Lewis, *Christian Behavior* (New York: Macmillan, 1952), p. 59.
161. Richard B. Cunningham, *C. S. Lewis, Defender of the Faith* (Philadelphia: Westminster, 1967), p. 81.

During his own pilgrimage, Lewis saw the inconsistencies and inadequacies of non-Christian hypotheses and came to the place where he "was to be allowed to play at philosophy no longer."[162] Ideals of virtue now became commands. What had been a concept of God now demanded total surrender, all or nothing, simply all.[163] He finally committed himself, he says, to the "unrelenting approach of Him whom I so earnestly desired not to meet. That which I greatly feared had at last come upon me. In the Trinity term of 1929 I gave in, and admitted that God was God, and knelt and prayed: perhaps, that night, the most dejected and reluctant convert in all England."[164] Faith as belief in true doctrines had become trust in the One of whom the doctrines speak. *Fides* became *fiducia*. Not everyone need go through the intellectual and moral struggle C. S. Lewis endured; some may achieve total commitment more easily through the help of "Mother Kirk" (the church). But faith required both (1) assent to truth and (2) commitment to the realities of which it speaks.

A third use of faith is important to the continuation of the Christian life. Once a person decides that the weight of evidence is for Christianity, he may expect testings in the next few weeks. He may receive bad news or get in trouble with those who do not believe the gospel. Emotions may rise up to carry out a sort of "blitz" on his belief. "Or else there will come a moment when he wants a woman, or wanted to tell a lie, or feels very pleased with himself, or sees a chance of making a little money in some way that's not perfectly fair; some moment in fact, at which it would be very convenient if Christianity were *not* true." These are not moments at which new reasons against Christianity turn up. Those have to be faced in a different manner. "I am talking about moments when a mere mood rises up against it."[165]

"Now faith, in the sense in which I am here using the word, is the art of holding on to things your reason has once accepted, in spite of your changing moods. For moods will change, whatever view your reason takes."[166] The rebellion of your moods against your real self is going to come. "That is why Faith is such a necessary virtue: un-

162. Lewis, *Surprised by Joy*, p. 227.
163. Ibid., p. 228.
164. Ibid., pp. 228-29.
165. Lewis, *Mere Christianity*, p. 108.
166. Ibid., p. 109.

less you teach your moods 'where they get off,' you can never be either a sound Christian or even a sound atheist, but just a creature dithering to and fro, with its beliefs really dependent on the weather and the state of its digestion."[167] So one must train the habit of faith. There is a silly idea about, that good people don't know what temptation means. Quite the contrary, "No man knows how bad he is till he has tried very hard to be good."[168]

Faith is not just an action but becomes a quality of life as people are properly related to God. It is paradoxically related to works. "A serious moral effort is the only thing that will bring you to the point where you throw up the sponge. Faith in Christ is the only thing to save you from despair at that point: and out of that faith in Him good actions must inevitably come."[169]

Faith is (1) belief based on sound reasoning from sufficient evidence, (2) trust in God, and (3) persistence in both belief and trust in spite of fluctuating moods and situations.

C. S. Lewis, then, is a practitioner of a verificationist apologetic similar to Carnell's. He did not stop to put the elements together in a system of apologetics, but he has skillfully utilized the approach in his writings. He illustrates the fact that the most popular approach to apologetics should have an implicit, reliable system. And he remains a challenge to the most technical systematizers to "translate every bit of your theology into the vernacular." C. S. Lewis's valuable suggestions on how to do this may be found in his address on "Christian Apologetics."[170]

I have tried to follow C. S. Lewis's counsel in applying the hypothesis-verification approach nontechnically in several different areas (albeit without his inimitable literary style) . The claims of Latter-Day Saints for *The Book of Mormon* are tested by the criteria of consistency and fitting the facts in *Confronting the Cults.* On theological issues, *Decide for Yourself* presents alternative hypotheses and challenges the reader to accept the one that consistently accounts for the greatest amount of biblical data with the fewest problems. A similar approach is taken in *Judge for Yourself* on popular problems in apologetics, such as "Is Christ the only way to God?" and "Does Chris-

167. Ibid.
168. Ibid., pp. 109-10.
169. Ibid., p. 115.
170. Lewis, *God in the Dock*, pp. 89-103.

tianity really work in today's world?" This does not necessarily assume acceptance of the Bible as God's fully inspired Word, if a person is open to consider the teaching of Christianity on these issues from its primary sources (a standard principle of graduate study). Most recently the hypotheses of Maharishi Mahesh Yogi have been compared and contrasted with those of Christianity in *What Everyone Should Know About Transcendental Meditation*.[171]

May God enable every reader in his distinctive way to present his approach to the masses, who need a meaningful and reliable word in behalf of the Christian faith!

171. Gordon R. Lewis, *Confronting the Cults* (Nutley, N.J.: Presbyterian and Reformed, 1966), *Decide for Yourself* (Downers Grove, Ill.: Inter-Varsity, 1970), *Judge for Yourself* (Downers Grove, Ill.: Inter-Varsity, 1974), and *What Everyone Should Know About Transcendental Meditation* (Glendale, Calif.: Regal, 1975).

GLOSSARY

ANALOGICAL. Meaning based on analogy. Resemblance in some particulars between things otherwise unlike; e.g., a man's mind is like God's mind (not totally different—equivocal meaning—or identical—univocal meaning).

ANXIETY, BASIC. Not neurotic phobia, but a realistic concern about the inescapable experience of death (Grounds).

APAGOGIC. A method of argument which reduces an opposing view to absurdity (Clark).

APODICTIC. Knowledge of what must occur, as opposed to knowledge of what might occur or is capable of occurring or is actual or occurring.

APOLOGETICS. The science and art of defending Christianity's truth-claims.

A PRIORI. Knowledge of universal principles whose validity is logically independent of particular things observed by the senses. Sometimes used in a derogatory way to mean prior to critical evaluation—uncritical. In contrast to *a posteriori* knowledge whose validity depends on experience of things observed by the senses.

AXIOLOGY. The theory of values (all).

AXIOM. A self-evident truth with which to begin a system of deductive thought (Clark).

AXIOMATIZATION. A method of argument which exhibits the logical consistency of a system of thought (Clark).

CATEGORY. A general form of thought employed in all reasoning (Hackett).

CAUSE. Whatever produces an effect; a person or thing that makes something happen (sooner or later).

CAUSALITY, LAW OF. The principle that every effect must have an adequate cause, that everything that happens has an explanation sufficient to produce it, a sufficient condition to account for it.

340

CIRCULAR REASONING. Argument involving in the premises the point to be proved, assuming the thing to be established.

COGNITIVE. Meaning which asserts something and hence is either true or false. Such theoretical meaning is not merely expressive of the emotions of the speaker or writer. Assertive meaning.

COMMON GROUND. Knowledge available to all men (non-Christian as well as Christian) on the basis of which Christians may reason with non-Christians in defense of their faith. Knowledge not dependent upon faith in God, Christ, or Scripture.

CONTRADICTION. Two propositions asserting and denying the same thing at the same time and in the same respect (all).

COSMOLOGICAL ARGUMENT. Either something must be eternal or something comes from nothing. Something does not come from nothing. Therefore something is eternal (Buswell).

DEDUCTION. Inference from a general rule or principle to particular cases. Starts with a general principle that is accepted as true and applies it to a particular case. The conclusion is true if the principle was true; e.g., All people are sinners. X is a person. X is a sinner. Contrast "induction."

DUALISM. A world-view which admits that there are two independent and mutually irreducible ultimate beings, usually one good and one evil. In contrast, monism maintains that there is but one ultimate Being.

EFFECT. Any finite thing or event; fact.

EMPIRICAL. Knowledge based on experience, starting with sense perception.

EMPIRICISM. The theory of epistemology that all knowledge is derived from and based on experience. No knowledge is derived from mental processes independent of experience because without the data of the senses the mind is a blank tablet (*tabula rasa*).

EMPIRICISM, PURE. The mind, of itself a blank tablet, obtains no knowledge independent of experience (Buswell).

EMPIRICISM, RATIONAL. The mind, structured by rational categories, obtains all its knowledge through experience (Hackett).

EPISTEMOLOGY. The division of philosophy which examines the sources and tests of human knowledge (all).

EQUIVOCAL. Meaning which is vague and ambiguous because it has two entirely different meanings; e.g., man has a mind, God has a mind; but *mind* is used in two entirely different ways. See "analogical" and "univocal."

ESSENCE. That in virtue of which a thing is what it is; intrinsic nature.

ETHICS. The branch of philosophy and theology that studies conduct that is right or wrong; what people ought and ought not to do; morality.

EXISTENTIALISM, CHRISTIAN. A view of life maintaining that Christianity is to be passionately appropriated by sheer faith even though it is an implausible offense to the human mind (Kierkegaard).

EXISTENTIALISM, NON-CHRISTIAN. A view of life maintaining that individual existences, not essences or forms, make up reality. Since universal patterns of meaning cannot be found, life appears to be absurd and meaningless (Sartre).

EXPLICIT. Clearly and fully expressed or formulated, the absence of ambiguity or the need for inferring what is meant.

FAITH. (1) Whole soul trust in an unseen reality on the ground of sufficient (seen) evidence (Carnell). (2) Assent to the truth of an unprovable presupposition (Clark and Van Til). (3) A passionate leap into the dark (Kierkegaard).

FINITE. Having limits or bounds; a limited nature and existence because of location in space and time. See "infinite."

GNOSTICISM. A pre-Christian and early Christian school of religious thought distinguished by the conviction that matter is evil and that emancipation comes through a hidden or secret knowledge (Greek *gnosis*).

GUILT, REAL. Accountability, not for trifling mistakes or necessarily to civil law, but a liability to punishment for violation of God's law (Grounds).

HUMANISM. A philosophy which recognizes the value and dignity of man and makes him the measure of all things, confident that man has the capacity to shape his life in the world. A type of naturalism.

HYPOTHESIS. A tentative explanation proposed for confirmation or disconfirmation taking the form, "If X, then Y" (Carnell).

IDEALISM. A philosophy teaching that knowledge of separate facts is not possible because the knower brings to the observation of any single fact a comprehensive interpretative system (Van Til).

IMMANENCE. A state of being present or dwelling within. In modern pantheism, God or the Absolute is completely within the world and identical with it. According to Deism, God is essentially absent from the world. According to theism, He is both immanent (in presence and activity) and transcendent (in essence) with respect to the world. Mysticism in its broadest sense assumes the mutual immanence of the human and the divine.

IMPLICIT. Capable of being understood from something else, though unexpressed: implied. Involved in the nature of something, though not disclosed.

INDUCTION. Reasoning from particular facts to general principles. The process by which one collects many particular cases, finds out by experiment what is common to all of them, and forms a general rule which is probably true; e.g., Every person I have observed has been a sinner, so it is highly probable that X is a sinner. See "deduction."

INFINITE. Without limits or bounds; subject to no external determination; not confined by time or space. See "finite."

INTUITION. Perception of truths without reasoning; immediate apprehension (seeing) of objects as real without inductive or deductive inferences.

LOGIC. The division of philosophy that examines the methods and principles used in distinguishing correct from incorrect reasoning; the formal laws of thought that apply in reasoning about any subject matter.

LOGICAL STARTING POINT. The highest principle which one introduces to give unity and order to his interpretation of reality. This is why it is the logical starting point: what one logically conceives as the over-all synthesizing element which unites the particulars. For materialists, it is matter; for idealists, it is idea or principle; for empiricists, it is experience, but, for Clark, Van Til, and Carnell, it is the triune God of the Bible.

METAPHYSICS. The division of philosophy which studies the nature of ultimate reality or the characteristics common to all reality (all).

MYSTICISM, CHRISTIAN. A philosophy maintaining that God is best known, not by reason, but by direct personal experience occasioned by worship and Bible reading (Barrett).

MYSTICISM, NON-CHRISTIAN. A philosophy maintaining that reality is best known by an experience (sometimes drug-induced) in which the self is absorbed into ultimate reality, time stops, and words lose their meaning.

MORAL RESPONSIBILITY. A view that accountability for right and wrong is not to individual tastes or to limited cultures, but to a transcultural Administrator of moral values (Carnell).

NATURALISM. A world-view that rejects the arguments for the existence of God and holds that the universe requires no supernatural cause but is self-explanatory. Nature, then, is deterministic, not fulfilling any purpose nor centered upon man. Only incidental to nature is the production of human life. Man's ethical values need no supernatural sanctions, and man faces neither life after death nor an eternal destiny.

NON-CONTRADICTION, LAW OF. A law of logic in this form emphasizing that, while consistency is not a guarantee of truth, contradiction is a sure sign of error. See "contradiction."

ONTOLOGICAL ARGUMENT. An a priori argument for the existence of God from the idea of God. God is defined as a self-existing or necessarily existing Being. Therefore God cannot not exist. His ontological Being is argued from what we mean by God. No evidence is necessary.

PARADOX. (1) An apparent contradiction to attract attention, but resolvable logically upon further thought (Carnell and others); (2) A logical contradiction for both God and man (mysticism); (3) A logical contradiction only for man (Kierkegaard).

PHENOMENA (plural of phenomenon). Objects of experience in space and time known through the senses rather than intuition or mere thought. Broadly, appearance or that which appears.

PHILOSOPHY. Love of wisdom. The study of the principles underlying all knowledge (epistemology) and all reality (metaphysics), morality (ethics), values (axiology), science (philosophy of science), history (philosophy of history), politics (political philosophy), etc.

PLURALISM. A metaphysical view that there are not one (monism) or two (dualism) but many ultimate substances or beings. Also a political view that the acceptable religious beliefs in a given country are not one or two but many.

PRAGMATISM. A view of knowing that tests the truth and value of ideas by their practical consequences. Pragmatists agree in accepting what works as meaningful and true, but do not agree on the definition of "works."

PRESUPPOSITION. A specific, unprovable assertion postulated to make experience meaningful (Clark, Van Til).

PROBABILITY. That state of coherence in which more evidences can be corralled for a given hypothesis than can be amassed against it (Carnell).

PROPOSITION. An assertion in the form, S (subject) is P (predicate). Four kinds are primary in traditional logic: (1) universal affirmative, "All S is P"; (2) universal negative, "No S is P"; (3) particular affirmative, "Some S is P"; and (4) particular negative, "Some S is not P." Propositional content is either affirmed or denied, true or false. That meaning is distinct from the sentences and statements conveying it.

RATIONALISM. (1) A theory of knowing asserting that knowledge is attained through the reason independent of sense perception, in opposition to empiricism. (2) More popularly, a view that all knowledge can be obtained through reason (in its broadest senses) independent of divine revelation, in opposition to the authority of sacred writings.

REASON. (1) The ability of the human mind to make judgments and draw conclusions from observed data or from intuited or revealed truths by means of logical principles; the intellect (as in "the role of reason"). (2) The ground—evidence or argument—upon which a given conclusion (truth-claim) is set forth, as in "give a reason for your hope."

SENSES. The powers of the body and brain to see, hear, feel, taste, smell, etc.

SENSE DATA. The immediate, unanalyzed presentations of redness, smoothness, loudness, etc., to the mind.

SENSE PERCEPTION. Intellectual awareness of the given data, an interpretation of it, and an assertion made on the basis of it.

SKEPTICISM. The view (theory of knowledge!) that no true knowledge is possible or that in a particular area, such as religion, knowledge of truth is impossible for man.

SUBJECTIVISM. The view in epistemology that all that is known is the knower's (subject's) thoughts and feelings; nothing is known about alleged "objects" in reality.

SYLLOGISM. A form of argument consisting of two propositions called premises from which is deduced a third proposition called a conclusion; e.g., All trees have roots. An aspen is a tree. Therefore, an aspen has roots. To be valid, this form of argument must follow a number of rules explained in most introductions to logic.

SYNOPTIC. Affording a general view of a whole, characterized by comprehensiveness or breadth of view. In Carnell, the more general starting point is common ground among all men on the basis of which to defend his distinctively Christian logical starting point—the triune God of the Bible.

SYSTEM. A regularly interacting and interdependent group of items forming a unified whole; an organized set of doctrines, ideas, or principles intended to explain the arrangement or working of a systematic whole.

SYSTEMATIC CONSISTENCY. The test of truth requiring a proposal to be logically consistent and in accord with all relevant facts.

SYSTEM OF APOLOGETICS. An organized set of consistent ideas urged in defense of a world view, such as Christianity. Here, of consistent ideas on such matters as: logical starting point, common ground, test for truth, role of reason, and basis of faith. See Summary of Apologetic Systems, chapter 11.

TABULA RASA. A smooth tablet (Latin). Used by Locke and other empiricists to describe the condition of the human mind by nature, prior to its reception of experiential data. Contrast "rationalism," according to which the mind is "programmed" by nature with certain logical categories of thought or innate ideas.

TELEOLOGICAL ARGUMENT. The world (inorganic as well as organic) is an ordered design. Therefore the cause of the world is an intelligent Designer (Buswell, Hackett).

TEST OF TRUTH. The decisive criterion by which to determine whether a proposed view is true or false; i.e., for a Christian, in correspondence with the mind of God or not.

THEISM. The world-view that asserts the reality of a personal infinite Creator, who is both immanent in His creation and transcendent to it. See "immanence."

TRANSCENDENT. Surpassing ordinary limits, excelling, superior; of God, as existing prior to, distinct from, and exalted over the space-time universe.

TRUTH. The quality of propositions which conform to reality or the quality of beings which realize in existence what ought to be (Carnell).

TRUTH-CLAIM. A view of reality proposed for acceptance and action.

UNIVOCAL. Meaning that is one, the same in at least one respect, as opposed to equivocal and analogical meanings; e.g., to say that man has a mind and that God has a mind is to imply at least one identical aspect in the mind of man and God.

UNIVOCAL MEANING. The view that language about God is not ambiguous or merely figurative, but also in some respects identical to its meaning for man.

VERIFIABLE. A truth-claim that can be tested and confirmed as true or disconfirmed as false by observable evidence, not definition.

WORLD VIEW. A systematic philosophy or insight into the movement and plan of the entire universe.

SUBJECT INDEX

*An asterisk (*) indicates a term that is
defined in the glossary.*

INDEX OF PERSONS

Pascal, 159
Paul 90, 163, 196-97, 243
Pieters, Albertus, 189
Pinnock, Clark, 301-4
Plato, 158, 178-79
Plotinus, 33
Pratt, J.B., 172

Quirinius, 90

Rahab, 265
Ramm, Bernard, 187-98, 327-31
Ramsey, Sir William, 31
Rauschenbusch, Walter, 276
Rushdoony, Rousas J., 144, 301
Russell, Bertrand, 40, 247

Sargon, 191
Sartre, Jean-Paul, 16. See *also*
  Existential in Subject Index.
Satan, 112, 129
Schaeffer, Francis, 296-301, 324
Schmidt, Paul F., 171
Schopenhauer, 51, 159
Sennacherib, 90, 191
Shaw, George Bernard, 62
Shishak, 90, 106
Sinclair, Robert, 165
Smith, Joseph, 34, 225. *See also*
  Mormonism in Subject Index

Socrates, 121, 158, 234, 256
Solomon, 90, 191
Stace, T. Walter, 165, 171
Strauss, 92

Tennant, F.R., 52-53, 57
Thompson, Samuel M., 20-22
Tillich, Paul, 22, 231
Treglown, G.L., 273
Trueblood, David Elton, 27, 183, 187,
  200, 205

Van Buren, Paul, 15. *See also* Logical
  Positivism.
Van Til, Cornelius, 37-38, 125-48,
  168, 176, 178-79, 203-4, 285-94,
  297-98, 301, 305

Warfield, Benjamin B., 26, 125, 140
Whitehead, 159
Wiley, H. Orton, 165
Wisdom, John, 35-36
Wolff, Christian, 157

Young, Warren J., 151-56, 168-73,
  177, 292, 314

Zoroaster, 62

SCRIPTURE INDEX

Old Testament

Genesis
2:15	273
8:22	190
14	89

Exodus
5:2	27
14:18, 31	28

Numbers
23:19	185

Deuteronomy
13:1-3	145
13:1-5	186
18:21-22	186
18:22	145

1 Samuel
15:29	185